Oracle8i from scratch

Dan Hotka

201 West 103rd Street,
Indianapolis, Indiana 46290

Oracle8i from scratch

International Standard Book Number: 0-7897-2369-7

Library of Congress Catalog Card Number: 00-100267

Printed in the United States of America

First Printing: October 2000

02 01 00 4 3 2 1

Associate Publisher
Tracy Dunkelberger

Acquisitions Editor
Michelle Newcomb

Development Editors
Laura Bulcher
Victoria Elzey

Managing Editor
Thomas F. Hayes

Project Editor
Tricia Sterling

Copy Editor
Megan Wade

Indexer
Chris Barrick

Proofreader
Jeanne Clark

Technical Editors
Karen Edge-Clere
Vanda Gillingham

Team Coordinator
Cindy Teeters

Media Developer
Michael Hunter

Interior Designer
Anne Jones

Cover Designer
Maureen McCarty

Production
Ayanna Lacey
Stacey DeRome

Overview

Contents

From the Series Editor

Welcome to *Jesse Liberty's Programming from scratch* series. I created this series because I believe that traditional primers do not meet the needs of every student. A typical introductory computer programming book teaches a series of skills in logical order and then, when you have mastered a topic, the book endeavors to show how the skills might be applied. This approach works very well for many people, but not for everyone.

I've taught programming to over 10,000 students: in small groups, large groups, and through the Internet. Many students have told me that they wish they could just sit down at the computer with an expert and work on a program together. Rather than being taught each skill step by step in a vacuum, they'd like to create a product and learn the necessary skills as they go.

From this idea was born the *Programming from scratch* series. In each of these books, an industry expert will guide you through the design and implementation of a complex program, starting from scratch and teaching you the necessary skills as you go.

You might want to make a *from scratch* book the first book you read on a subject, or you might prefer to read a more traditional primer first and then use one of these books as supplemental reading. Either approach can work; which is better depends on your personal learning style.

All of the *from scratch* series books share a common commitment to showing you the entire development process, from the initial concept through implementation. We do not assume that you know anything about programming: *from scratch* means from the very beginning, with no prior assumptions.

While I didn't write every book in the series, as Series Editor I have a powerful sense of personal responsibility for each one. I provide supporting material and a discussion group on my Web site (`www.libertyassociates.com`), and I encourage you to write to me at `jliberty@libertyassociates.com` if you have questions or concerns.

Thank you for considering this book.

Jesse Liberty

from scratch Series Editor

About the Author

Dan Hotka is a Director of Database Field Operations for Quest Software, Inc. He has more than 22 years of experience in the computer industry and more than 17 years of experience with Oracle products. He is an acknowledged Oracle expert with Oracle experience dating back to the Oracle V4.0 days. He has co-authored popular books such as *Oracle Unleashed*, *Oracle8 Server Unleashed*, *Oracle Development Unleashed* (all by Sams Publishing), and *Special Edition Using Oracle8/8i* (by Que Publishing); is a monthly contributing editor to *Oracle Professional*, a Pinnacle Publication; is frequently published in trade journals; and regularly speaks at Oracle conferences and user groups around the world. Dan can be reached at `dhotka@earthlink.net`.

Acknowledgments

This is my first solo-authored book and my first opportunity to thank those who have not only contributed to my work in this book but have made a positive difference in my career and life.

A special thanks goes out to my wife of 22 years, Gail Hackett, and my family. Her patience, love, and understanding have allowed me to take on opportunities such as writing and the travel that comes with my work. My family suffers the most with my line of work. I want to thank Elizabeth, Emily, and Thomas, my children, for giving me the foundation that continues to fuel my success.

I want to be sure to thank the people who help make my writing a success. First and foremost, a thank-you-very-much to Debbie Smith, who ensures my English is correct in all that I write. She is the polish on my writing endeavors. Tim Gorman has to be the most Oracle-knowledgeable person I know. His advice and wisdom have definitely enhanced almost every Oracle project I have undertaken. Other technical advice has been gleaned from Steve Blair, Gary Dodge, Swamy Kanathur, Robert Nightingale, Doug Tracy, and D. Scott Wheeler. Thank you for your technical assistance on this project and through the years.

Thanks to those editors who trusted me through the years to produce quality manuscript: Michelle Newcomb, Angela Koslowski, Heidi Frost, Andy McMillan, and Rosemarie Graham, as well as their staffs.

I want to thank Mike Swing, Dave Oldroyd, and Jaren Jones of the TruTek Company (`www.trutek.com`) for generating the illustrations for Chapters 9, 10, and 11. Their assistance was critical to completing this book in a timely manner. I want to thank those managers who have helped mold my career into the success that I continue to enjoy today: Karl Lenk (Sperry-Rand, Inc.), Gary Dodge (Oracle Corp.), Deb Jenson (Platinum Technology, Inc.), and Mike Coffman (Quest Software, Inc.).

Thank you to all the people listed below, who have made a positive difference in my life and career: Tom Villhauer, Bert Spencer, Bob Emly, Bob Kenward, Bradley Brown, Brian Hengen, Buff Emslie, Carol Thompson, Cathy (CW) Fountain, Cathy (CL) Langhurst, Chauncey Kupferschmidt, Cheryl McCarthy, Colin Blignault, Conny Vandeweyer, Craig Mullins, Dan Wulfman, Dave Brainard, David Wagner, Dee Pollock, Derek Ashmore, Don Bishop, Don Kerker, Dorothy Campbell, Doug Garn, Dwight Miller, Elsie Bishop, Gayln Underwood, Gniadeks, Greg Goodnow, Greg Slaymaker, Greg Spence, Haydn Pinnell, Heath Race, Heidi Yocki, Jackie Fry, Jane Hambright, Janet Jones, Jay Johnson, Jason Dean, Jeff Sheppard, Jerry Fox, Jerry Matza, Jerry Wegner, John Koszarek, Jon Styre, Juli Ackerman, Julie Nelson,

Karen Wicker, Kathie Danielson, Kathleen Morehouse, Kathy Metcalf, Kelsey Thompson, Kevin McGinnis, Kevin Schell, Larry Kleinmeyer, Laurie Nelson, Leyria Walters, Linda Litton, Lori Thomas, Lynette Kleinmeyer, Marita Welch, Martin N. Greenfield, Mary Kenyon, Melvin Morehouse, Michel Clerin, Michelle Campbell, Mike Curtis, Mike Hotz, Mike Metcalf, Michael R. Nelson, Mike Sanchez, Patricia Hemphill, Penny Loupakos, Peter Weenik, Randy Spiese, Richard Neimiec, Rick Born, Rick Magnuson, Robert Hotz, Robert Thompson, Robyn Cincinnati, Ron Danielson, Ron Hahn, Ron Innis, Ron Mattia, Ron Smith, Rudy Neimiec, Russ Greene, Sarah Hackett, Scott Bickel, Scott Kane, Sean Kennedy, Sean McGrath, Sheri Ballard, Shona Freese, Simone Abawat, Steve Black, Steve Jaschen, Steve Macklin, Tom Bickel, Troy Amyett, Valda-Jean Robison, Vinny Smith, Wass Pogerelov, Wayne Smith, and (add your name here ______________________________).

I also want to thank Ken Jacobs of Oracle Corporation and his staff for their support of my efforts to produce a current and accurate tutorial of the Oracle8i Database development environment.

And finally, thank you very much to my parents, Philip and Dorothy Hotka; my in-laws, Dean and Marian Hackett; my siblings, Mike Hotka and Janice Hotka; and to my grandmothers, Mamie and Gladys, who will always have a special place in my heart.

Tell Us What You Think!

As the reader of this book, *you* are our most important critic and commentator. We value your opinion and want to know what we're doing right, what we could do better, what areas you'd like to see us publish in, and any other words of wisdom you're willing to pass our way.

As an Associate Publisher for Que, I welcome your comments. You can fax, email, or write me directly to let me know what you did or didn't like about this book—as well as what we can do to make our books stronger.

Please note that I cannot help you with technical problems related to the topic of this book, and that due to the high volume of mail I receive, I might not be able to reply to every message.

When you write, please be sure to include this book's title and author as well as your name and phone or fax number. I will carefully review your comments and share them with the author and editors who worked on the book.

Fax: 317-581-4666

Email: `quetechnical@macmillanusa.com`

Mail: Associate Publisher, Programming
Que Publishing
201 West 103rd Street
Indianapolis, IN 46290 USA

Foreword

The Internet's Event Horizon

The *event horizon* is that area where you become close enough to a black hole to be pulled in by the gravity. The acceleration and ensuing pressure increase as you are pulled closer. A black hole has infinite gravity and not even light can escape. In 1784, John Michell developed his theory of a black hole just as the Industrial Revolution hit its stride. The Industrial Revolution brought business within the event horizon for the first time. Business accelerated and the pressure on people to change was enormous. Those who did not adapt went out of business. It was "I-Business or Out-of-Business." The I stood for industrialize. The key to success was education and adapting to change.

In 1905, Einstein's theory of relativity was released at a time when the speed at which life was changing was greatly increasing. In a span of just 30 years (1867–1903), the phonograph, gasoline car, electric lights, submarine, radioactivity, telephone, plane, and typewriter were all invented. Those living at this time were once again forced to become educated and to change. The key to business success was to use the technology created in this era.

The event horizon is once more upon us. Both the Internet and business are now being accelerated by the enormous gravity created by technology. Xerox, Apple, and Microsoft were the pre-cursors to this movement; Oracle, Cisco, and Sun are bringing it to fruition. The blue-collar educators and implementers who will complete this era are yet to be determined (perhaps Quest and TUSC will continue to lead the way). "E-Business or Out-of-Business" is what we hear from Oracle. If you are in information technology, you are now inside the event horizon, and you will not get out without adapting, changing, and educating yourself. Your business will fail if you do not succeed in utilizing technology for your business. Gold has once again been discovered in California—this time, it is in the heart of Silicon Valley. The route to get there is no longer a wagon train, but a point-and-click on the Internet. Gene Kranz, who safely brought home the Apollo 13 crew, showed us all how it is done. The solution is known as "adapt and overcome" or be consumed by the changes around you. Work the problem; don't make it worse by guessing. Educate yourself and put in the hours required to succeed. Build teams with character and you will succeed.

Dan Hotka, who has authored many books, once again puts the answers to adapting in your hands by providing you with the education necessary to prepare for this change. Read this book from cover to cover to learn how to design, monitor, and implement the solutions to your problems. Java is highlighted in this book because it is one of the keys to unlocking the power of the Internet for your business. I recommend that you expand your horizons by reading this book.

Late 1700s:	The Industrial Revolution Begins
Late 1800s:	The Electricity Revolution Begins
Late 1900s:	The Internet Revolution Begins
Year 2000:	You are here; make the most of it.

Rich Niemiec
President, IOUG-A
CEO, TUSC

Introduction

In this introduction

- *How This Book Is Organized*
- *Conventions Used in This Book*

This book is part of the *from scratch* series, which uses the philosophy of learning by working on a project. Most of the books that teach you database application development focus on teaching you a lot of syntax and programming techniques throughout the book. In such books, parts of a sample application are demonstrated to reinforce the skills. This book is different.

In this book, we go through the various phases of developing a Windows and then a Web-enabled database application using Oracle8i and various techniques in SQL*Plus, PL/SQL, Oracle Developer, and Java. We will look at the requirements, analysis, design, implementation, monitoring, tuning, and deployment of a Sales Tracking Application from scratch. This book is ideal as a meeting point for people from several streams of the IT industry:

- The power-user who needs to build a Windows- or Web-based application using Oracle8i
- IT professionals familiar with Oracle who want to update their development skills with the current Oracle8i features
- Developers who want to break into the relational world of Oracle8i

This book shows you the project development from scratch—without any assumptions of Oracle knowledge. A basic programming background in any 3GL would be helpful but not necessary because this book even contains complete tutorials on learning SQL and PL/SQL. This book will build a complete, functional application from the database design phase in which the basis for a high-performance system gets its start, through building a complete Windows-based application. You will enhance the application by building a complete, functional Web site using PL/SQL, Java, or WebDB. You also will learn how to tune SQL and back up the application in a variety of environments as we build upon the skills already learned.

This book is not intended to be an exhaustive repository of Oracle syntax or Web-building techniques. Neither will this book teach you all the nuts and bolts of the Java and PL/SQL languages. Numerous books are available for that purpose. What we do, however, want to focus on are things such as

- What features are available in Oracle8i?
- How do I build an Oracle8i application from scratch?
- What is Referential Integrity and how do I use it?
- How do I design a relational database application with performance in mind?
- How do I build Windows-based applications using Oracle8i and Oracle Developer?
- How do I build Web-based applications with WebDB, PL/SQL, or Java?
- How do I monitor the Oracle8i database as well as the Web environment?
- How do I tune the SQL within this application?
- How can I use PL/SQL or Java to create a Web site for my database applications?

These and other such questions will be answered by this book using a hands-on approach.

How This Book Is Organized

This book doesn't make assumptions about prior Oracle, Windows, or Web development background and therefore will give you the opportunity to learn what you need to know about Oracle8i and developing applications in the Oracle8i database environment. The main focus of the book is to understand the issues in such a project and how to use the various tools and capabilities of Oracle8i to resolve these issues. Unlike other books on programming languages, this book won't show you a very long code listing and try to explain it all at once. This is because the application development project is multitiered. We will see code sections used in the various tiers, such as database development, code to connect the browser to the database, and so on.

The chapters are organized as follows:

- Chapter 1, "Introduction to Oracle8i and the Auto Sales Tracking Application," discusses the base knowledge of what a relational database is and then discusses the various tools that will be used throughout the book. This chapter also introduces you to the Sales Tracking Application, the project that will be built as part of the learning process.

- Chapter 2, "Building the Sales Tracking Application Database," actually creates the database discussed in Chapter 1. You learn database design as it applies to application performance. This chapter also introduces you to good Oracle coding techniques.
- Chapter 3, "Building the Sales Tracking Application Forms and Reports," builds the Windows-based applications discussed in Chapter 1 using the Oracle Development tools. You also learn how to build character-mode reports using SQL*Plus.
- Chapter 4, "Basic Oracle8i Administration Tasks," teaches you the base knowledge needed to start and stop the database, allow additional users to use the Sales Tracking Application, and maintain the proper security for the database objects created in Chapter 2. You also learn the new Oracle8i tablespace options for data storage and how to implement and maintain data storage for the Sales Tracking Application.
- Chapter 5, "Monitoring the Sales Tracking Application," introduces you to more important knowledge about Oracle8i, including how to monitor and adjust the Oracle8i database environment as well as how to monitor the Sales Tracking Application.
- Chapter 6, "Tuning the Sales Tracking Application," introduces you to tuning the actual Sales Tracking Application SQL statements. You learn step by step what is involved and how to tune poorly performing SQL statements.
- Chapter 7, "Oracle8i Backup and Recovery," illustrates various backup and recovery methods available in the Oracle8i database environment. This chapter contains scripts to assist you in performing each of the different kinds of backup scenarios available.
- Chapter 8, "Understanding Oracle8i Index and Partitioning Features," introduces you to various Oracle8i indexing and partitioning features.
- Chapter 9, "Planning the Sales Tracking Web Site," introduces you to the Sales Tracking Web Site, the Oracle Web environment (including setup and administration), and advantages and disadvantages of the various methods available to build this Web site.
- Chapter 10, "Building the Web Site with PL/SQL," is where you learn how to build the Sales Tracking Web site discussed in Chapter 9 using Oracle8i PL/SQL Web extensions. You learn by first learning the necessary basic skills and then applying them to the Sales Tracking Web site.
- Chapter 11, "Building the Web Site with Java," introduces you to the Java VM and Java Development tools by first building simple servlet applications and then using these skills to again build the Sales Tracking Web site discussed in Chapter 9 using Java.

- Chapter 12, "Building Web-Based Forms with WebDB," introduces you to wizard-based Web development using Oracle's WebDB tool. You learn what WebDB is and how to create Web-based forms by building one of the Windows-based Sales Tracking forms using WebDB.

This book also contains some key appendixes:

- Appendix A, "Installation and Configuration of Oracle8i NT-Based Software," illustrates the installation of all the software used in this book.
- Appendix B, "Learning SQL—A Complete Tutorial," is exactly what the title indicates: a complete hands-on approach to learning SQL, the key ingredient to the Oracle8i database environment.
- Appendix C, "PL/SQL Basics," is a good hands-on introduction to PL/SQL, Oracle8i's procedural language.
- Appendix D, "Advanced SQL Queries," includes additional coding features deemed important to coding in the Oracle8i database environment but that were not used in other examples in this book.

Each chapter first looks at the issues and then shows you ways in which to resolve them. Also, we first identify the action that needs to be taken and then learn the skills to complete the task.

Conventions Used in This Book

Some of the unique features in this series include the following items.

Geek Speak—An icon in the margin indicates the use of a new term. New terms will appear in *italic*.

With a book of this type, a topic might be discussed in multiple places as a result of when and where we add functionality during application development. To help make this clear, we've included a Concept Web that provides a graphical representation of how all the programming concepts relate to one another. You'll find it on the inside front cover of this book.

Notes offer comments and asides about the topic at hand, as well as full explanations of certain concepts.

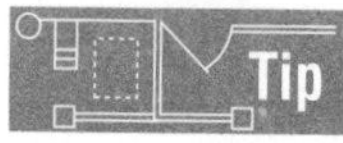

Tips provide great shortcuts and hints that enhance the current topic.

Warnings help you avoid problems, thus preventing you from making mistakes that will hinder your project.

In addition, you'll find various typographic conventions throughout this book:

- Commands, variables, and other code appear in text in a special `computer font`.
- In this book, I build on existing listings as we examine code further. When I add new sections to existing code, you'll spot it in **`bold computer font`**.
- Commands and such that you type appear in **boldface type**.
- Code continuation characters (➥) indicate lines of code that are continuous, but that had to be broken to fit on the book page. Whenever you see a code continuation character, you should type those lines as all one.
- Placeholders in syntax descriptions appear in an *`italic computer font`* typeface. This indicates that you will replace the placeholder with the actual file name, parameter, or other element that it represents.

This book is a powerful learning-by-using tool that gives you the skills you need to build your Oracle8i-based application. The organization of the chapters takes you from the beginning of the design phase and quickly gets you into actual application development. This book is enhanced by the numerous appendixes that will assist those who might need assistance with Oracle8i installation issues as well as assistance to those readers who might not be proficient with SQL and PL/SQL. Building an application "from scratch" is the best learning tool available from a book.

Chapter 1

In this chapter

- *Oracle—A Relational Database*
- *Oracle8/8i Features*
- *Oracle's Implementation of SQL*
- *Introduction to Oracle Tools*
- *Introduction to the Auto Sales Tracking Application*

Introduction to Oracle8i and the Auto Sales Tracking Application

Oracle—A Relational Database

Relational databases are simply a way of accessing and merging data together where the end user does not need to know how the data will be extracted by the computer. A relational database differs from other kinds of data retrieval methods in that the end user needs to have only an understanding of the data, not an understanding of how to retrieve the data. Other data retrieval methods include hierarchical and network database systems. *Hierarchical* data retrieval systems such as ISAM and VSAM are traditionally accessed via *COBOL* programs in a *mainframe* environment. *Network* data retrieval systems such as DMSII (Burroughs), IMS, and IDMS (IBM Mainframe Systems) also are traditionally accessed with a COBOL program utilizing a programmer or a team of programmers who have the knowledge and understanding of the arrangement of the data. The advantage of these COBOL-based data storage systems is that the access time is traditionally very fast compared to that of relational databases. The huge disadvantage is the complex process for accessing particular data for particular needs. The access to data is very specific and does not lend itself well to today's data warehouse and ad-hoc accesses.

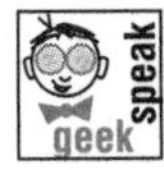

Mainframe computers—Typically computer environments such as IBM System 390.

COBOL—Common Business Oriented Language. Popular for years in the mainframe-computing environment, this programming language handles the transfer of information between terminals and data storage, creates reports from data storage, and manipulates data in the data storage.

COBOL programming is not for novices. A simple program can consist of hundreds of lines of code.

What Is a Database?

A hierarchical system stores its data by a *key* value. The data is then stored in the order of this key and can be accessed only by this key. Figure 1.1 depicts how a department and an employee database might be stored in an ISAM hierarchical storage system, or ISAM *files*. Accessing data in ISAM files is very quick, but the data can be accessed only via its key value. This kind of storage mechanism is very handy for online systems in which the data is always accessed via a known number such as a Social Security number or by last name. Selecting data between ISAM files is handled by the COBOL program by reading the department file first and then reading the employee file, searching for the particular field. Access can be very fast if the department information is accessed via the employee file. Selecting the data for all employees of department 10 could be a lengthy process, though, as can selecting employees who report to a certain manager. Selecting employees by their EmployeeID number, however, is a very quick process. In addition, no relationship exists between the department file and the employee file.

Figure 1.1

Hierarchical file configuration.

Department ISAM File
DepartmentID (key field)
Department Name Department Location

Employee ISAM File
EmployeeID (key field)
Name Address City State Zip Salary Manager Department

A network system also stores its data by a key value, but dissimilar data types can be separated into separate storage areas and be reassembled via an access path. For example, in Figure 1.2, accessing data through the department table first would be the only access to the employee data. This storage mechanism is more flexible because files with single record data, such as departments within a company, easily can be related to all the employees who belong to that department. Once again, access to the data is very quick, but the way in which the data is accessed is always fixed. Selecting data for all the employees of department 10 could be a quick process; however, selecting all the employees who report to a certain manager could be a very slow process. Note the location of the *crow's foot*, which indicates there are employee records associated with each department record. In a network database environment, these employee records can be retrieved only by first reading the department record.

Figure 1.2

Network file configuration.

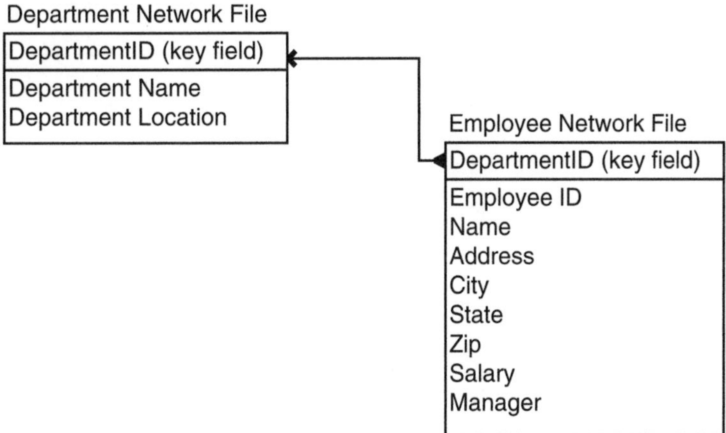

Crow's foot—This data modeling term indicates that a one-to-many relationship exists from this object or file to the one to which it points.

The relational database supports a single, logical structure called a *relation*, which is a two-dimensional data structure commonly called a *table* in the database. *Attributes*, or *columns*, contain information about the structure. In Figure 1.3, the table named EMPLOYEE contains attributes such as employee name, salary, manager, and so on. The actual data values of a table are called *tuples* or *rows*. A relationship can exist between two or more tables that have no data at all.

Attributes can be grouped with other attributes based on their relationship with one another and become a *composite key* or even a composite primary key. A *primary key* is an attribute or group of attributes (composite key) that uniquely identifies a row in a table. Oracle will automatically create a unique index on a primary key. A table can have only one primary key, and when using referential integrity, every table will have one defined. Because primary key values are used as identifiers, they must contain a data item; that is, they cannot be null.

Composite key—One or more columns, placed at the beginning of the table in the order of importance, and in which the group becomes the key value.

You can have additional attributes in a relation with values you define as unique to the relation. Unlike primary keys, *unique* keys can contain null values. In practice, unique keys are used to prevent duplication in the table rather than to identify rows.

Figure 1.3

Components of the EMPLOYEE table.

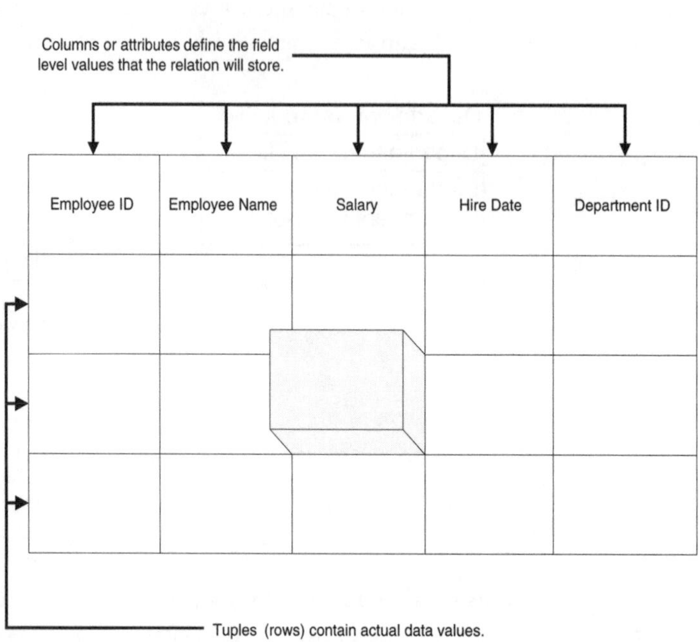
Relation (table)
Columns or attributes define the field level values that the relation will store.
Employee ID
Employee Name
Salary
Hire Date
Department ID
Tuples (rows) contain actual data values.

Consider a relation that contains the attribute United States Social Security number (SSN). In some rows, this attribute might be null because not every person has an SSN; however, for a row that contains a non-null value for the SSN attribute, the value must be unique to the relation.

Selecting data from two tables involves a column attribute common to both tables. Figure 1.4 shows the relationship between two tables, which can be maintained by the relational database. The *primary* table or *parent* table can have one or more related rows in another table or *child* table. This automatic maintenance and definition is called *referential integrity.* Referential integrity rules dictate that foreign key values in one relation reference the primary key values in another relation.

geek speak

Referential integrity—SQL code that enforces the relationship between two or more tables, based on primary and foreign keys. This makes the programmer's life easy in our example of employees and departments. With referential integrity defined, the programmer does not need to make sure the department exists in the department table when adding new employees. The Oracle database will check and enforce these rules when defined.

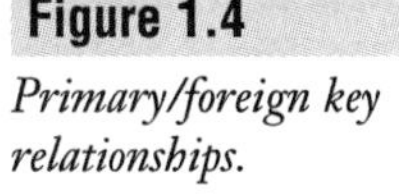

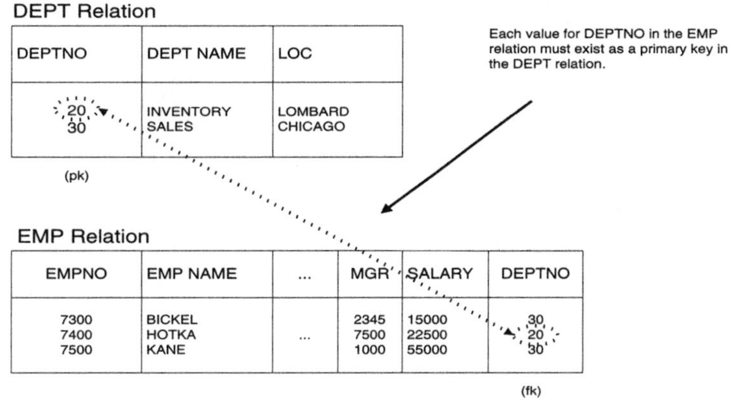

Figure 1.4

Primary/foreign key relationships.

Many tools can take advantage of primary/foreign key relationships and referential integrity rules. You will learn how to use these tools throughout this book. In addition, this book will make references to the DEPT and EMP sample tables that install with the Oracle database because these tables are perfect for learning the SQL syntax; they are used in the examples of Appendix B, "Learning SQL—A Complete Tutorial"; Appendix C, "PL/SQL Basics"; and Appendix D, "Advanced SQL Queries."

A relational system stores its data in individual groupings of data called *tables.* The advantages of tables include being easy to create, easy to add to or change, and easily related to other tables to present the desired results. The end user simply needs to understand his or her data, not how to access the data (refer to Figure 1.3). Selecting all the employees of department 10 is as easy as selecting all the employees who report to a certain manager. The user would have the knowledge of the data stored by department and employee and could select data based on any of the columns, not just certain key fields. Selecting data from two or more tables involves a column type (or attribute) that is common to both (or all) tables. You would not relate the Employee Name with the Department ID; however, you could relate the Department IDs from each table together.

What Is SQL?

The relational database uses an industry-standard language called *Structured Query Language* (known as *SQL*, which is pronounced "sequel"). Dr. E. F. Codd is considered the father of relational databases because of his research in this area. The language Structured English Query Language (SEQUEL) was developed by IBM Corporation, Inc., based on Dr. Codd's work. SEQUEL later became SQL (still pronounced "sequel"). Oracle Corp. (then Relational Software, Inc.) developed the first commercial relational database using the newly developed SQL language. SQL was adapted in the mid 1980s as the accepted *RDBMS* standard language.

RDBMS—Relational Database Management System.

This SQL language easily enables all types of users, including application programmers, database administrators, managers, and end users, to access data. Finally, a *relational database management system* is the software that manages a relational database. These systems come in several varieties and are available from many different software vendors ranging from single-user desktop systems to full-featured, global, enterprise-wide systems.

The purpose of SQL is to provide an interface to a relational database such as Oracle by using all SQL statements as instructions to the database. In this way, SQL differs from general-purpose programming languages such as C and BASIC. SQL processes data as groups of records (result set) rather than as individual records (as in COBOL and other procedural programming languages).

SQL provides automatic navigation to the data by using statements that are complex and powerful individually, and that therefore stand alone. Flow-control statements were not part of SQL originally, but they are found in the recently accepted optional part of SQL, ISO/IEC 9075-5: 1996. Flow-control statements are commonly known as *persistent stored modules* (PSM), and Oracle's PL/SQL extension to SQL is similar to PSM.

Essentially, SQL enables you to work with data at the logical level. You need to be concerned with the implementation details only when you want to manipulate the data. For example, to retrieve a set of rows from a table, you define a condition used to filter the rows. All rows satisfying the condition are retrieved in a single step and can be passed as a unit to the user, to another SQL statement, or to an application. You need not deal with the rows one by one, nor do you have to worry about how they are physically stored or retrieved. All SQL statements use the *optimizer*, a part of Oracle that determines the most efficient means of accessing the specified data. In addition, Oracle provides techniques you can use to make the optimizer perform its job better.

SQL provides a consistent language to control the whole relational database environment. It is used to select data from the tables; manipulate data (inserts, updates, and deletes) within the tables; create, secure, and drop objects; protect the data and structures (backup and recovery); and share data with other relational database environments.

All major relational database management systems support SQL, so the skills you learn in this book can be used with non-Oracle relational database tools.

The academic theory underlying the relational database is somewhat complex, but using and building applications is rather easy. The three basic components of a relational database are the relational data structures (tables and indexes), the rules that govern the organization of the data structures (constraints), and the creation and manipulation operations that can be performed on the data structures (inserts, updates, and deletes).

Figure 1.5 shows the complexity of traditional programming languages versus the relative ease of using SQL to produce the same results.

Figure 1.5

SQL programming versus traditional programming.

Traditional Procedural Coding Method (pseudo code)

```
raise_date_cutoff := get_delta_date
(get_sysdate(), -6,"month") open/read_write
employee_file
whole not EOF
        read employee_record
        if employee_record(20:2) =: target_department
        then    last_raise := convert_date(employee_rec (43:7))
                if last_raise > raise_date_cutoff
                then    salary := decimal_unpack(employee_rec(31:4))
                        salary := salary * 1.06
                        emplyee_rec(31:4) := decimal_pack(salary)
                        rewrite employee
                end if
        end if
end while
close employee file
```

Nonprocedural Coding Method Using SQL

```
update employee
        set salary = salary * 1.06
        where deptno = :target_department
        and last_raise > add_months(sysdate, -6)
```

Oracle8/8i Features

The Oracle8 family of database products introduced new features such as partitioned tables and indexes (the ability to break each table and index the table into pieces by a key value and locate it across many disk drives). Oracle8 also contains enhancements to previous versions of Oracle, such as additional backup and recovery features, enhancements to the SQL*Net environment (Net8 and Connection Manager), enhanced replication features (automatically copying data to other Oracle databases), additional parallel features (the ability to have several computer processes working on parts of the same SQL statement), enhanced standby database technology (a backup strategy introduced in Oracle7), deferred constraints (enhancements to the rules governing data relationships between tables), enhancements to PL/SQL (Oracle's procedural language), better LOB (long objects such as pictures or video streams) management, and reverse-key indexes (new tuning features). Oracle8 also introduced Java and SQLJ into the Oracle database environment. Java is one of today's most popular programming languages. Developers can now code procedures, functions, and triggers using pure Java, as you will learn by example in Chapter 11, "Building the Web Site with Java."

Oracle8 can be called an *object-oriented* database because it enables you to define objects and object types. For example, you can define data fields such as address, city, state, and zip code as an object and repeatedly use it (see Listing 1.1). Oracle8 supports the use of *nested* tables, which are tables within tables. Nested tables are similar to the network database previously described in this chapter in that their rows are easily associated with the parent table. However, they differ from the network database in that they can still be accessed as standalone tables. Oracle8 also supports *varrays*, an object type that is similar to a nested table in functionality but is actually part of the row within a table.

Listing 1.1—Creating and Using an Object Type

```
SQL*Plus: Release 8.1.5.0.0 - Production on Fri Dec 10 10:35:37 1999
Copyright 1999 Oracle Corporation. All rights reserved.
Connected to:
Oracle8 Release 8.1.5.0.0 - Production
PL/SQL Release 8.1.5.0.0 - Production

SQL> CREATE TYPE addr AS OBJECT (
  2       address           varchar2(30),
  3       city              varchar2(20),
  4       state             varchar2(2),
  5       zip_code          varchar2(10)
  6       );

Type Created.

SQL> CREATE TABLE obj_type_test (
  2                             Name       varchar2(30),
  3                             Addr       addr
  4                             );

Table Created.

SQL> INSERT INTO obj_type_test VALUES
➥2  ('Tom', addr('123 Main Street','Any Place','IA','11111');

1 Row Inserted.

SQL> SELECT name, addr.city
  2  FROM obj_type_test;

NAME                           ADDR.CITY
------------------------------ -------------------
Tom                            Any Place


SQL>
```

Many terms are associated with *object-oriented databases* or object-oriented programming languages (such as C++ and Java). An *object* consists of attributes (character, number, date, and so on) and information (data). *Tables* and *indexes* are types of objects, and a *class* is a way of grouping related items together. An example of a class is an Oracle view that combines two or more tables together, providing either a subset or a superset of the combined columns of each table. *Encapsulation* means that access to the data occurs only when the rules are followed. An Oracle8 example of this would be the referential constraints that govern the relationship of data between objects. *Extensibility* is the ability to create new objects without affecting other objects, which Listing 1.1 describes. *Inheritance* means that a change in one related object type is reflected in all the objects that use the object type. In Listing 1.1, a change in the length of the state field would automatically be implemented in all objects that use the `address_type` object. Currently, however, the Oracle8 database does not implement this level of inheritance. *Polymorphism* means that the same object can be given information in different contexts and will react according to the context of the input. A good example of this in an Oracle8 environment that can be visualized using the `DATE` data type. Notice in Figure 1.6 that the contents of a date field are displayed and the contents of the same field are manipulated by addition. Notice that the field behaves differently based on its point of context, either standalone or adapting to the addition, even though no other functions were called.

Figure 1.6

Polymorphism with a `DATE` *object.*

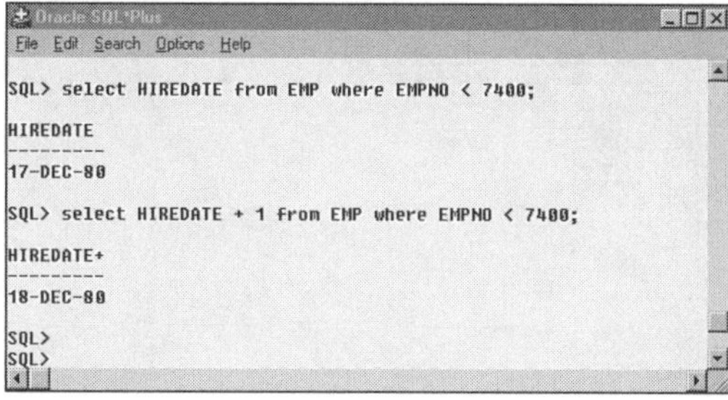

Object-oriented database—A database that can store the data, information about the data, and methods for accessing the data. Oracle has implemented most of the object-oriented features in Oracle8i.

Oracle8i supports the index-organized tables. An *index-organized* table has all the performance features of a standard index on a table, but all the data is stored within the index. Index-organized tables are used exactly like tables but with the performance gains of using an index.

Oracle *WebDB* is an integrated development and monitoring tool for Web-based applications within the Oracle8i Server environment. It enables developers to easily build and deploy Web-based applications, with its only software requirement being a Web browser. We will cover the WebDB in depth in Chapter 12, "Building Web-Based Forms with WebDB."

The Oracle *Internet File System* (iFS) is a combination of a relational database and a file system. It is a Java application that utilizes the Oracle8i Java environment and appears to end users and applications as just another file system (similar to the `c:\` drive on your PC). In addition, iFS gives access to any file or data stored in the database and enables Web browsers to display its contents as normal Web pages. iFS is an easier way of storing various types of files inside the database.

Oracle's Implementation of SQL

SQL is a set of commands that all programs and users must use to communicate with the Oracle database (see Figure 1.7). SQL is a nonprocedural language in that it processes whole sets of records at a time rather than single records at a time. Oracle uses its optimizer to determine the best method of accessing the data. It has two optimizers: the original rule-based optimizer that makes its decisions based on 19 rules (which include using indexes if they exist, the order of items in the `where` clause, and so on), and the cost-based optimizer that makes its decisions based on statistics gathered by Oracle's `ANALYZE` command.

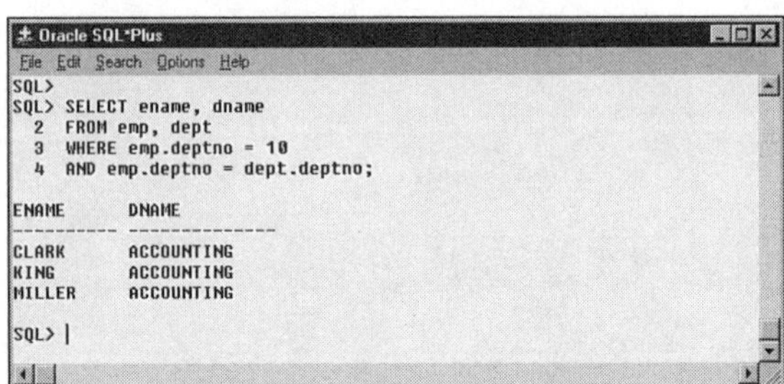

Figure 1.7

Using SQL to communicate with relational databases.

SQL provides commands for almost any task, including

- Querying data
- Inserting, updating, truncating, and deleting rows in a table (data manipulation language or DML)
- Controlling the access to the database and its objects
- Creating, altering, and dropping objects (data definition language or DDL)
- Administrative tasks such as database startup/shutdown, backup, and recovery.

The basic SQL syntax is comprised of the following commands. (Details of these commands will be covered in various chapters in this book.) `SELECT` is used to retrieve information from tables, whereas `UPDATE` makes changes to existing data in tables and indexes. `INSERT` adds data to tables and indexes, but `DELETE`, on the other hand, removes data from tables and indexes. `CREATE` is used to create almost any object, and `ALTER` makes changes to object definitions and database settings. In addition, to remove objects from the database, you can use the `DROP` command. `COMMIT` saves the current pending changes to the database, whereas `ROLLBACK` removes any uncommitted changes. Finally, you can use `GRANT` and `REVOKE` for privilege maintenance on the objects.

Other SQL commands perform specific tasks. `TRUNCATE` quickly removes all the data from a table, `RENAME` enables objects to be renamed, and `AUDIT` is used to track who is doing what to the database. Another command, `EXPLAIN PLAN`, is used to view the choices the Oracle optimizer is making for any SQL statement. In addition, `ANALYZE` is used to collect statistics (such as sort order, number of rows, size of rows, and so on) for the Oracle cost-based optimizer. You can use `SET TRANSACTION` to identify a unit of work, which is useful if there will be several SQL statements that will comprise a unit of work. This transaction mode enables all the SQL statements to be committed or rolled back as one unit of work. Roles are a way of grouping user privileges together and easily assigning these roles to users who must perform similar tasks.

If you aren't already familiar with the SQL language, Appendix B covers the basics. The better you understand the SQL language, the better you will understand relational databases.

Introduction to Oracle Tools

This book covers the Oracle tools necessary to produce a working Windows and Web-based application. It also covers several monitoring and tuning tools used to aid in the maintenance, performance tuning, and problem solving of both the Sales Tracking application environment and the Oracle8i environment.

Oracle development tools have been in the Oracle product set since the version 4 days when forms were called Fast Forms—the equivalent of today's wizard that walks the user through building a base form. The reporting tool was a version of today's SQL*Plus, then called UFI or user-friendly interface. The base reporting tool was called RPT and had some interesting undocumented features. This RPT language was the procedural language of Oracle at the time. In time, though, Oracle v5 brought serious enhancements to the forms and reports-based tools. The forms tool was renamed SQL*Forms v2.0 and a new report writer was added, SQL*ReportWriter v1.0. This version of forms greatly enhanced the programming and capabilities of the online forms, and through the years, this package of development tools was enhanced with the addition of a menu package and a graphics development package. Eventually, Oracle v7 brought some major changes to the database as well as to these tools. The tool set was renamed Developer/2000 and was much more Windows-based than the previous character-mode development and screens.

The power of the Oracle application-development environment is that these tools are supported on all environments that the database itself supports. This means that the developer can develop and test an application in a PC environment and deploy it on large UNIX or even mainframe computers. This portability of development has been a strength of Oracle since Oracle v4.1.

This book works with Developer v6.0, the latest version of Oracle's application development tools. This environment includes Project Builder, Form Builder, Report Builder, Graphics Builder, Translation Builder, Schema Builder, and Query Builder. This book concentrates on the forms and reports aspects of this tool.

Oracle Developer 6.0 (Forms, Reports, and Graphics)

The Project Builder component is where developers keep all the pieces of the application, such as the various forms, report *source code*, and intermediate code. Project Builder enables developers to *compile* either a single program or all the programs in the project. It's a convenient tool that can organize all the parts of a particular application-development effort that is using Developer v6.0. Figure 1.8 shows the Project Builder main screen. Note the icons down the left side of the screen, which bring up the Form Builder, Report Builder, Graphics Builder, Procedure Builder, and Query Builder tools.

Machine language—Computers only understand a series of 0s and 1s, which is called machine language. Electronic devices such as a computer understand a pulse of electricity (a 1) or the lack of a pulse of electricity (a 0). These 1s and 0s are grouped together to create instructions or commands for the computer to follow. Individually, though, each 0 or 1 is known as a *bit*. In PCs and UNIX, it takes 6 bits to represent a single text character. Imagine the difficulty of programming computers using only a string of 0s and 1s!

First-generation language—Another term for machine code. The computer understands only a series of 1s and 0s, which makes for very difficult coding. The second-generation languages are languages such as easy-coder and assembler that are more English-like but are formatted similarly to the instructions the machine is expecting. They are much easier to code in than 1s and 0s but not very English-like either. Third-generation languages such as COBOL have made programming much easier. Compilers are then used to read this code (source sode) and translate it either into the assembly code (p-code per se) or directly into machine language. A runtime interpreter is needed to read the p-code (pseudo code), translating it into machine code that the computer can understand. Sometimes the interpreter reads the source code and translates it into machine language, but it's more efficient for the interpreter to translate the p-code. The p-code is very portable across various types of computers, and the runtime interpreter is specific to each type of computer.

Compiler—A name for the previously mentioned interpreter that converts the program source code into either p-code or machine language.

Figure 1.8

Oracle Project Builder is used to coordinate all the parts of an application.

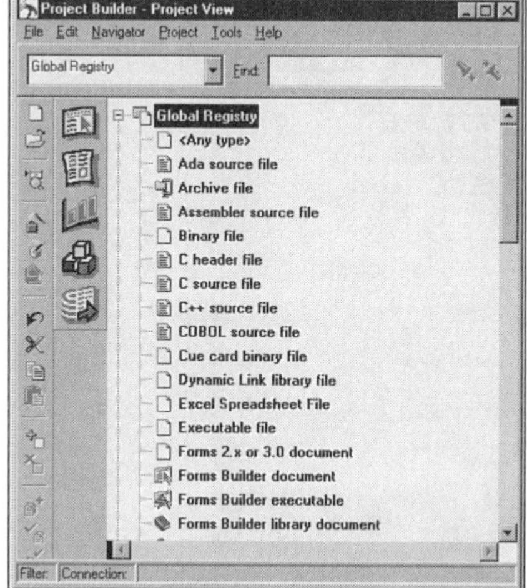

Oracle Developer is based on common elements that are used throughout the tool. After you learn how to use the functionality of one tool, you will understand how to use it throughout the Developer environment.

Oracle Developer contains an Object Navigator that provides a hierarchical structure of all application objects. The Object Navigator provides you with two views: the Ownership view (see Figure 1.9) or the Visual view (see Figure 1.10). The Ownership view displays the objects according to the block representing rows from a table. The Visual view, on the other hand, displays objects according to how they appear on the output screen.

Form Builder is used to build and maintain form-based applications. Programming in Oracle Developer is much different from third-generation languages in which the programmer used a text editor and physically wrote the program source code. Applications are built with Oracle Developer by creating onscreen objects that represent the data elements that will be retrieved from the database, visual aspects, program navigation, and so on (see Figure 1.11). Selected activities or events are coded in triggers (or program units) that are used whenever the event occurs. *Events* are similar to screen navigation, for example, entering a field or exiting a field. A common event to code upon exiting a field would be the data-editing criteria to ensure what was entered in this particular field onscreen was the correct information. This event could be as simple as enforcing a particular date format or ensuring that this data element appears in another table (used as a reference table).

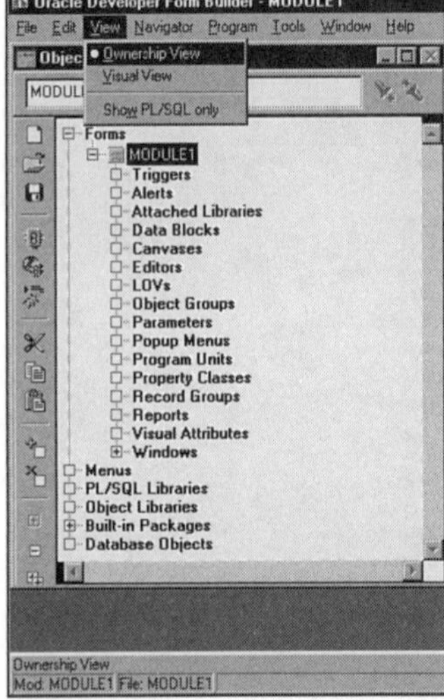

Figure 1.9

Oracle Object Navigator Ownership view displays the developed items in navigator form.

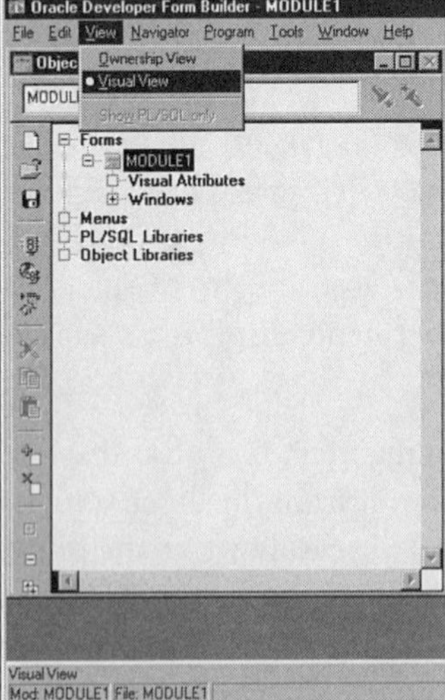

Figure 1.10

Oracle Object Navigator Visual view displays the development in a WYSIWYG format.

Figure 1.11

The Form Builder screen.

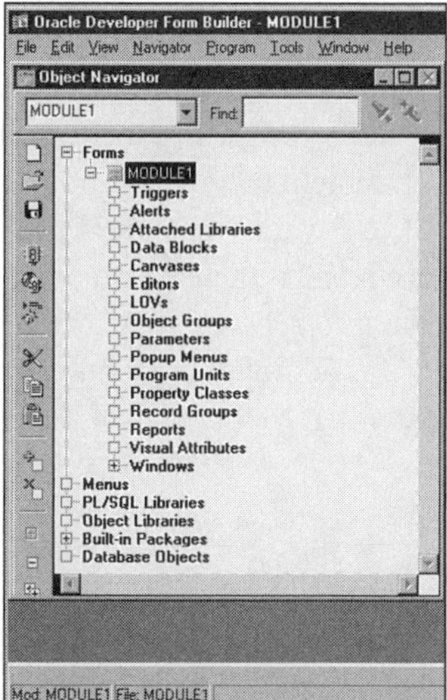

WYSIWYG—What You See Is What You Get.

Report Builder is a wizard-based tool used to create a variety of reports from data in the database (see Figure 1.12). This tool also has a WYSIWYG layout editor and procedural constructs for data formatting, calculating summary information, and so on. This tool also can be used to perform database maintenance, but these tasks are better performed by PL/SQL.

Graphics Builder is used to generate a variety of charts based on data from the database.

Figure 1.12

The Report Builder screen.

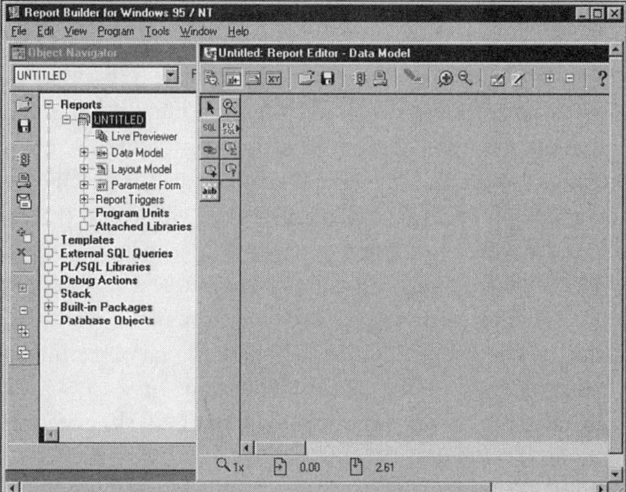

SQL*Plus

SQL*Plus (pronounced "sequel plus") is an interactive character-mode tool for the Oracle8i RDBMS environment. It has a variety of functions in the Oracle environment, including processing SQL statements one at a time or interactively with end users. SQL*Plus can initiate PL/SQL for the procedural processing of SQL statements as well as list and print query results. Its powerful character-mode reporting capabilities can format query results into reports. In addition, it also acts as the character-mode or script processor for administrative functions, and has the capability to accept input from operating system files or SQL scripts.

> SQL scripts can contain SQL*Plus report-formatting commands as well as SQL or PL/SQL code. Scripts are commonly used for any repetitive process. SQL*Plus can accept these scripts from the command prompt, and these scripts can also be scheduled to run at predetermined times.

SQL*Plus originated from the beginning of the Oracle RDBMS days as a tool called User Friendly Interface, or UFI (pronounced "U-fee"). UFI was used primarily to administer the Oracle database prior to Oracle4. Early administrative tasks included adding users and managing the tablespaces. Oracle5 introduced many enhancements as well as new names for many of the tools, including SQL*Plus for UFI. Some enhancements have been added to SQL*Plus through the years; however, most of the formatting commands and the process for creating reports are as easy today as they were with the UFI product. Enhancements have included additions to several of the command capabilities, additional ways of starting SQL*Plus, and a changed role for SQL*Plus through the major releases of the Oracle RDBMS kernel. Before Oracle6, for example, using UFI or SQL*Plus was the only way to administer the Oracle database. With Oracle6 came a new tool called SQL*DBA that took over many of the database's administrative responsibilities and had both a graphical mode and a character mode. In Oracle6, additional administrative tasks were added, such as database startup/shutdown and backup/recovery responsibilities. The character mode was still able to run scripts from an operating system command prompt, though. Then came Oracle7 and 8, which provided a new interface called Enterprise Manager that replaced SQL*DBA as a database management tool. And it was at this time that the character-mode version of SQL*DBA was renamed Server Manager. However, future releases of Oracle will not have the Server Manager product. Oracle8i has given these character-mode administrative functions back to SQL*Plus, which also exists in the world of client/server and is available with all the major graphical interfaces.

Chapter 3, "Building the Sales Tracking Application Forms and Reports," concentrates on learning SQL and SQL*Plus formatting commands. You will learn how to use SQL*Plus to format output into a variety of reports and be introduced to methods of using SQL*Plus to create dynamic, data-driven SQL*Plus programs and operating system–specific command-language programs.

SQL*Loader

Today, Oracle databases are ever-increasing in complexity and size. Gigabyte-sized databases are common, and data warehouses are often reaching the terabyte-sized range. With the growth of these databases, the need to populate them with external data quickly and efficiently is of paramount importance. To handle this challenge, Oracle provides a tool called SQL*Loader to load data from external data files into an Oracle database.

SQL*Loader has many functions that include the following capabilities:

- Data can be loaded from multiple input data files of differing file types.
- Input records can be of fixed and variable lengths.
- Multiple tables can be loaded in the same run. It can also logically load selected records into each respective table.
- SQL functions can be used against input data before loading into tables.
- Multiple physical records can be combined into a single logical record. Likewise, SQL can take a single physical record and load it as multiple logical records.

SQL*Loader can be invoked by typing in **`sqlload`**, **`sqlldr`**, or **`sqlldr80`** at the command line. The exact command might differ depending on your operating system. Refer to your Oracle operating system–specific manual for the exact syntax. Please note that all listings and server responses in this chapter might differ from your results based on the operating system you are using. The `sqlldr` command accepts numerous command-line parameters. Invoking SQL*Loader without any parameters displays help information on all the valid parameters (see Listing 1.2).

Listing 1.2—SQL*Loader Help Information

```
Invoking SQL*Loader without parameters:
$ sqlldr

SQL*Loader: Release 8.1.5.0.0 - Production on Sun Jan 2 15:18:10 2000

 Copyright 1999 Oracle Corporation.  All rights reserved.
```

Listing 1.2—continued

```
Usage: SQLLOAD keyword=value [,keyword=value,...]

Valid Keywords:

    userid -- ORACLE username/password
   control -- Control file name
       log -- Log file name
       bad -- Bad file name
      data -- Data file name
   discard -- Discard file name
discardmax -- Number of discards to allow          (Default all)
      skip -- Number of logical records to skip    (Default 0)
      load -- Number of logical records to load    (Default all)
    errors -- Number of errors to allow            (Default 50)
      rows -- Number of rows in bind array
               (Default: Conventional path 64, Direct path all)
  bindsize -- Size of conventional path bind array in bytes  (Default 65536)
    silent -- Suppress messages during run
    direct -- use direct path                      (Default FALSE)
   parfile -- parameter file: name of file that contains parameter specs
  parallel -- do parallel load                     (Default FALSE)
      file -- File to allocate extents from
skip_unusable_indexes -- disallow/allow unusable indexes or index partitions
skip_index_maintenance -- do not maintain indexes, mark affected indexes
➥as unusable
commit_discontinued -- commit loaded rows when load is discontinued
readsize -- Size of Read buffer                    (Default 65535)

PLEASE NOTE: Command-line parameters may be specified either by
position or by keywords.  An example of the former case is 'sqlload
scott/tiger foo'; an example of the latter is 'sqlload control=foo
userid=scott/tiger'.  One may specify parameters by position before
but not after parameters specified by keywords.  For example,
'sqlload scott/tiger control=foo logfile=log' is allowed, but
'sqlload scott/tiger control=foo log' is not, even though the
position of the parameter 'log' is correct.
```

Net8—Oracle's Networking Protocol

Net8 (called SQL*Net in Oracle7 and before) is the basis of the Oracle client/server technology. Net8 enables the end user to transparently work with Oracle8/8i on any computer in about any environment without having to program or specifically handle any of the network or connectivity issues. Net8 simplifies Oracle programming because programs (such as Oracle Forms and SQL*Plus) can be developed and tested on one computer environment and run in a totally different computer environment without any modifications. In the client/server environment, Net8 enables programs to reside and execute on inexpensive PC computers and access data on larger and faster computers (see Figure 1.13). Net8 also can handle thousands of users accessing an Oracle8i environment with the connection manager and multithreaded technology component installed (see Figure 1.14).

1

Figure 1.13

The Net8 client/server environment.

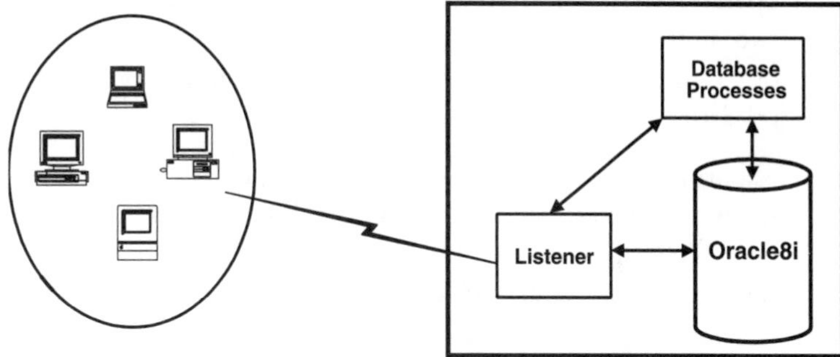

Figure 1.14

The Net8 client/server environment using a multithreaded server.

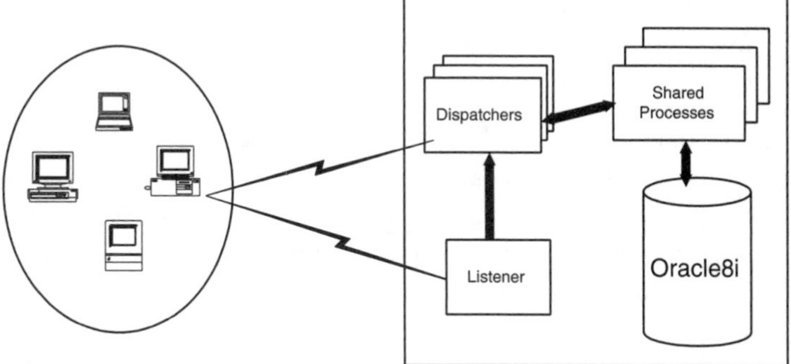

An in-depth study of Net8 is beyond the scope of this book. Net8 is a flexible networking protocol that can handle various *networking topologies*, enabling it to communicate between the users and the Oracle8i database no matter what the network in place is. Net8 hides the complexities of the network from the programmer and the end user, simplifying the programming of Oracle applications, making Oracle applications very portable, and so on.

Network topologies—Names given to various network technologies such as the common TCP/IP (the Internet makes big use of this type of network), IPX/SPX (Novell's protocol), and various IBM protocols such as LU6.2 and SNA.

The Export and Import Utilities

Export and Import are two character-mode utilities supplied by Oracle Corporation as early as Oracle4. The utilities perform the functions their names imply: *Export* creates operating system files of data from Oracle tables, and *Import* reads these operating system files, creates the tables, and loads the data back into the tables. The two utilities are used together primarily to back up and restore data, move data to other Oracle databases, and migrate data from earlier releases of Oracle to newer releases.

Export and Import can perform many important tasks in the Oracle8i environment. Export can be used to store data in archives, removing rows that are not being used but which can easily be added back in with Import if necessary. Export and Import can play an important backup and recovery role, which will be discussed in detail in Chapter 7, "Oracle8i Backup and Recovery." Export and Import also can be used to create test environments; they have the capability to capture all of a particular user's tables, indexes, and data and re-create them in another Oracle instance. In addition, they play an important role in database tuning by eliminating certain kinds of fragmentation. Oracle fragmentation and other tuning issues will be covered in detail in Chapter 5, "Monitoring the Sales Tracking Application."

The operation of the Import and Export utilities is quite straightforward. Export writes the DDL (table definitions, index definitions, privileges, and so on) as well as the data itself. Many options are available to both Export and Import, such as just capturing the DDL information and not the data. Export saves this information to named operating system files. The operating system files that Export creates are known as *dump* files which are in an Oracle proprietary format and are useful only to the Import utility. These dump files can be given specific names (operating system–dependent) or allowed to default to the preassigned name of `EXPDAT.DMP`.

Listing 1.3 shows the various parameters available for Export, and Listing 1.4 shows the various parameters available for Import.

Export creates files that only Import can read and process. Be careful when using Export and Import to move data between different versions of Oracle because older releases of Import will not necessarily read operating system files created by newer versions of Export.

Listing 1.3—SQL*Export Help Information

```
Invoking SQL*Export:
$ exp help=y

Export: Release 8.1.5.0.0 - Production on Sun Jan 2 15:22:28 2000

 Copyright 1999 Oracle Corporation.  All rights reserved.



You can let Export prompt you for parameters by entering the EXP
command followed by your username/password:

     Example: EXP SCOTT/TIGER

Or, you can control how Export runs by entering the EXP command followed
by various arguments. To specify parameters, you use keywords:

     Format:  EXP KEYWORD=value or KEYWORD=(value1,value2,...,valueN)
     Example: EXP SCOTT/TIGER GRANTS=Y TABLES=(EMP,DEPT,MGR)
               or TABLES=(T1:P1,T1:P2), if T1 is partitioned table

USERID must be the first parameter on the command line.

Keyword  Description (Default)        Keyword      Description (Default)
--------------------------------------------------------------------------
USERID   username/password            FULL         export entire file (N)
BUFFER   size of data buffer          OWNER        list of owner usernames
FILE     output files (EXPDAT.DMP)    TABLES       list of table names
COMPRESS import into one extent (Y)   RECORDLENGTH length of IO record
GRANTS   export grants (Y)            INCTYPE      incremental export type
INDEXES  export indexes (Y)           RECORD       track incr. export (Y)
ROWS     export data rows (Y)         PARFILE      parameter filename
CONSTRAINTS export constraints (Y)    CONSISTENT   cross-table consistency
LOG      log file of screen output    STATISTICS   analyze objects (ESTIMATE)
DIRECT   direct path (N)              TRIGGERS     export triggers (Y)
FEEDBACK display progress every x rows (0)
FILESIZE maximum size of each dump file
QUERY    select clause used to export a subset of a table

The following keywords only apply to transportable tablespaces
TRANSPORT_TABLESPACE export transportable tablespace metadata (N)
TABLESPACES list of tablespaces to transport

Export terminated successfully without warnings.
```

Listing 1.4—SQL*Import Help Information

```
Invoking SQL*Import:
$ imp help=y

Import: Release 8.1.5.0.0 - Production on Sun Jan 2 15:22:53 2000

 Copyright 1999 Oracle Corporation.  All rights reserved.



You can let Import prompt you for parameters by entering the IMP
command followed by your username/password:

     Example: IMP SCOTT/TIGER

Or, you can control how Import runs by entering the IMP command followed
by various arguments. To specify parameters, you use keywords:

     Format:  IMP KEYWORD=value or KEYWORD=(value1,value2,...,valueN)
     Example: IMP SCOTT/TIGER IGNORE=Y TABLES=(EMP,DEPT) FULL=N
               or TABLES=(T1:P1,T1:P2), if T1 is partitioned table

USERID must be the first parameter on the command line.

Keyword  Description (Default)       Keyword      Description (Default)
------------------------------------------------------------------------
USERID   username/password           FULL         import entire file (N)
BUFFER   size of data buffer         FROMUSER     list of owner usernames
FILE     input files (EXPDAT.DMP)    TOUSER       list of usernames
SHOW     just list file contents (N) TABLES       list of table names
IGNORE   ignore create errors (N)    RECORDLENGTH length of IO record
GRANTS   import grants (Y)           INCTYPE      incremental import type
INDEXES  import indexes (Y)          COMMIT       commit array insert (N)
ROWS     import data rows (Y)        PARFILE      parameter filename
LOG      log file of screen output   CONSTRAINTS  import constraints (Y)
DESTROY  overwrite tablespace data file (N)
INDEXFILE write table/index info to specified file
SKIP_UNUSABLE_INDEXES  skip maintenance of unusable indexes (N)
ANALYZE  execute ANALYZE statements in dump file (Y)
FEEDBACK display progress every x rows(0)
TOID_NOVALIDATE  skip validation of specified type ids
FILESIZE maximum size of each dump file
RECALCULATE_STATISTICS recalculate statistics (N)

The following keywords only apply to transportable tablespaces
TRANSPORT_TABLESPACE import transportable tablespace metadata (N)
TABLESPACES tablespaces to be transported into database
DATAFILES datafiles to be transported into database
TTS_OWNERS users that own data in the transportable tablespace set

Import terminated successfully without warnings.
```

Introduction to the Auto Sales Tracking Application

The Auto Sales Tracking Application is based on a hypothetical car dealership that repairs used cars and then resells these cars to the public. The sale price of the completed car is based on the original cost of the car plus all the time and repairs. This application tracks all the information necessary: the location from which the car came, the location from which the parts came, to whom the car was sold, plus all the costs associated with each individual car.

I have used a naming convention here so that the relational objects associated with this application can be easily identified when looking at any data dictionary view such as DBA_TABLES, or even TAB. Because this is a Sales Tracking Application, I chose ST to depict the initial prefix to every table, index, or object (tables, indexes, triggers, and so on) that is part of this application. I also like to use part of the table as a prefix to each column name. This helps the programmer or end user when working with the SQL language by having a column name that directly refers to one table or another. You will notice that I have prefixed all the application objects with `ST_`. All the column attributes have part or all of the table name in them, such as the ST_INVENTORY table, and all the entities begin with INV_. Your data center might have its own standards, so consult your database administrator if you need assistance in the naming of application objects or programs.

The Sales Tracking Database Layout

The Sales Tracking database consists of 11 relational tables, 3 sequence generators, and 5 database triggers (see Figure 1.15). Three major tables that track the inventory (used automobiles in this case) support the application: ST_INVENTORY, ST_PARTS, and ST_BILL_TIME. In addition, three minor tables are related to the major tables: ST_VENDOR, ST_CUSTOMER, and ST_STAFF. Finally, five reference tables contain consistent data used to ensure that valid data is being stored in the five major and minor tables as well as give descriptions to this same data when displaying information on a screen or in a report. These reference tables are ST_DEPARTMENTS, ST_JOB_CODE, ST_MODEL, ST_MAKE, and ST_TYPE.

A *crow's foot* depicts that there is a *many* relationship between the object to which this is pointing and the object at the other end. Let's look at ST_CUSTOMER and ST_INVENTORY. The ST_CUSTOMER table has just one record per record in the ST_INVENTORY table—which is a *one-to-one* relationship. This makes sense to the application because only one person will be purchasing each individual car. The ST_PARTS table has a *many-to-one* relationship to the ST_INVENTORY table because many parts (ST_PARTS) can exist for each car (ST_INVENTORY) being processed.

Figure 1.15

Select the FROM tab to show the Sales Tracking objects.

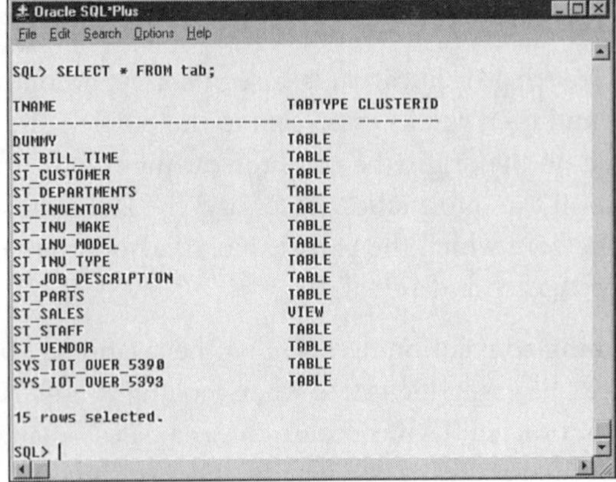

```
SQL> SELECT * FROM tab;

TNAME                          TABTYPE CLUSTERID
------------------------------ ------- ---------
DUMMY                          TABLE
ST_BILL_TIME                   TABLE
ST_CUSTOMER                    TABLE
ST_DEPARTMENTS                 TABLE
ST_INVENTORY                   TABLE
ST_INV_MAKE                    TABLE
ST_INV_MODEL                   TABLE
ST_INV_TYPE                    TABLE
ST_JOB_DESCRIPTION             TABLE
ST_PARTS                       TABLE
ST_SALES                       VIEW
ST_STAFF                       TABLE
ST_VENDOR                      TABLE
SYS_IOT_OVER_5390              TABLE
SYS_IOT_OVER_5393              TABLE

15 rows selected.

SQL>
```

The Entity Relationship Diagram (ERD) in Figure 1.16 shows the major and minor tables of the Sales Tracking Application. The central table, the ST_INVENTORY table, is the central repository for the main business focus, which is the inventory of the automobiles that have been purchased, that are in various stages of repair, that are ready for sale, or that have been sold. The two other major tables are the ST_PARTS and ST_BILL_TIME tables. These tables are used in conjunction with ST_INVENTORY to provide useful information such as what the car originally cost, the total cost of repairing the car, and the profit/loss of each automobile sold. Notice the many-to-one relationship between ST_PARTS and ST_INVENTORY. This indicates that one or more parts can be associated with each car in the ST_INVENTORY table. A part can be a fender, a tire, or a complete motor. Likewise with ST_BILL_TIME, one or more mechanics can work on each car, especially through several stages of repairs—for example, a welder, who might fix any physical damage; a mechanic, who might install a new motor or transmission; and a painter, who might repaint the car.

Notice that ST_INVENTORY and ST_PARTS share a table used for reference, the ST_VENDOR table. This table contains information about who is supplying the dealership with both cars and parts. A salvage yard, for example, could be supplying repairable cars as well as fenders and motors.

The ST_INVENTORY table has three supporting reference tables (look up/editing) associated with it that are not shown in Figure 1.16. These tables are ST_TYPE, which is the type of automobile such as an SUV or sedan; the ST_MAKE, which is the name of the car such as Intrepid, Camry, or Corolla; and the ST_MODEL, which is the model of the car such as 4-door, hatchback, or automatic. Each of these tables will be used by the forms programs to ensure only valid information is entered into the ST_INVENTORY table.

Figure 1.16

Entity Relationship Diagram (ERD) of the Sales Tracking Application database objects.

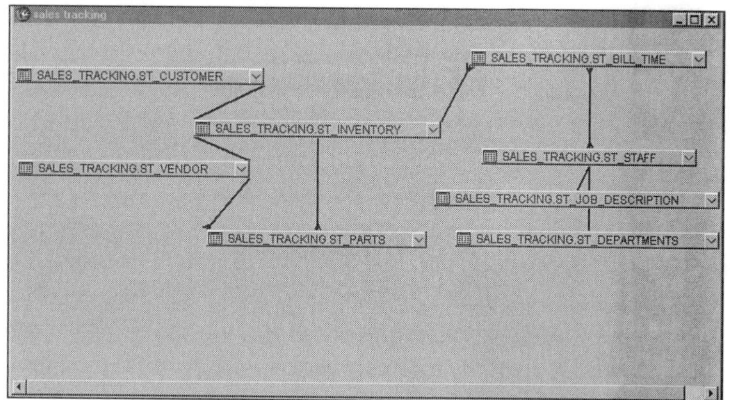

The ST_CUSTOMER table records the automobiles' buyers. The one-to-one relationship indicates that only one record in the ST_INVENTORY is associated with a single record in the ST_CUSTOMER table. For simplicity's sake, this application will make the assumption that only one person can purchase a single automobile from this dealership.

The ST_BILL_TIME table has a many-to-one relationship to the ST_INVENTORY table. Several staff members could be involved in the various stages of preparation of a single automobile for final sale. The ST_BILL_TIME and ST_STAFF tables have a many-to-many relationship in that staff members could work on more than one automobile, even in a single day.

The ST_STAFF table is supported by ST_DEPARTMENTS and ST_JOB_DESCRIPTION. Each staff member is associated with a different department, such as collision repair, mechanic, detailing (cleanup), painting, sales, or management. This information could be useful to see how much time each department spends on a car. The ST_JOB_DESCRIPTION table is a reference table to ST_STAFF (note the one-to-one relationship), ensuring the correct job code is assigned to each staff member recorded in ST_STAFF. ST_DEPARTMENTS is another reference table to ST_STAFF (note the one-to-one relationship) that ensures the correct department code is assigned to each staff member recorded in ST_STAFF.

Entity—In relational terms, another name for fields or columns in a table.

The ST_INVENTORY table contains the necessary entities or columns to store a unique identifier for each automobile—the ST_INV entity (see Figure 1.17). This field is associated with one of the Oracle sequence generators, ST_INV_SEQ, which is used to ensure that a unique number is associated with each automobile, no matter how many people might enter cars into the ST_INVENTORY table. This field also is the primary key, enabling referential integrity constraints to be established and enforcing the relationships between the tables (refer to Figure 1.16). INV_PURCHASE_VENDOR_ID and INV_SALE_CUSTOMER_ID are foreign keys, or fields that have relationships to other tables as well. In addition, these fields are related to ST_VENDOR and ST_CUSTOMER, respectively. The referential integrity rule ensures that a valid record exists in ST_VENDOR and ST_CUSTOMER before the ST_INV record is recorded (or *committed*, in relational terms) to the database. INV_MODEL, INV_TYPE, and INV_MAKE are enforced by the ST_MAIN program used to maintain the ST_INV table. The remainder of the fields are used to store pertinent information that relates to a particular car.

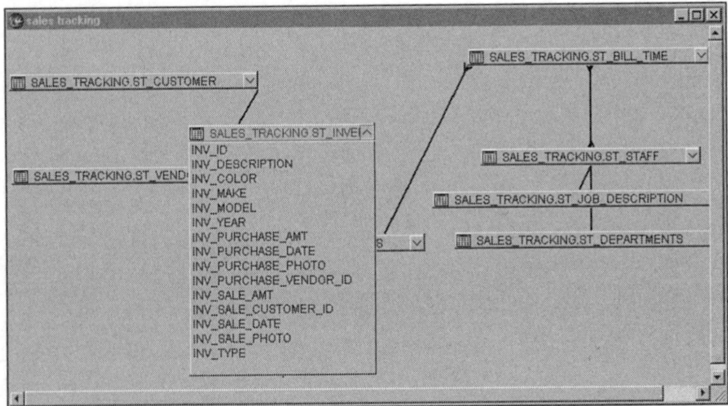

Figure 1.17

Sales Tracking Application ERD diagram focusing on the ST_INVENTORY entities.

The ST_PARTS table, shown in Figure 1.18, contains the information necessary to track parts purchased for the cars in ST_INVENTORY—for example, the price of the part, the date it was purchased, a brief description, and two foreign keys. The first foreign key, PARTS_INV_ID, is related to ST_INVENTORY INV_ID to ensure that all parts acquired are associated with a particular automobile. The second foreign key, PARTS_VENDOR_ID, is associated with the ST_VENDORS table to ensure that all parts purchased can be traced back to their origin.

The ST_STAFF table contains all the information about the members of the staff, including address, picture, hire and termination dates, as well as various rates (see Figure 1.19). The STAFF_BILLING_RATE field is used when calculating the total cost of work done on a particular vehicle. The STAFF_HOURLY_RATE, on the other hand, is used in the calculation of profitability of each vehicle. Two foreign keys exist: STAFF_DEPT_ID, which is used to look up particular department info in ST_DEPARTMENTS, and STAFF_JOB_ID, which is used to look up job descriptions for staff members.

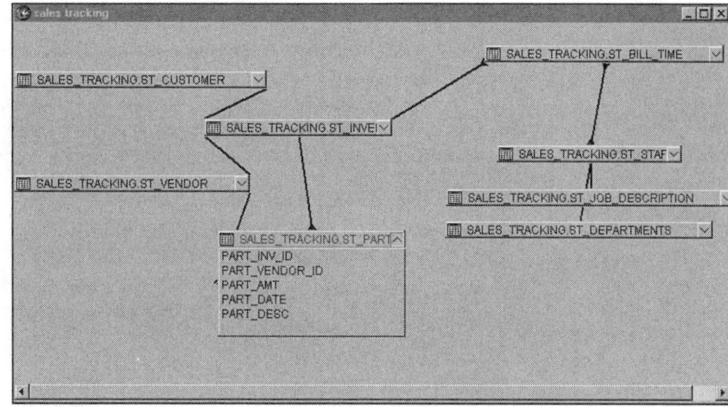

Figure 1.18

Sales Tracking Application ERD diagram focusing on the ST_PARTS entities.

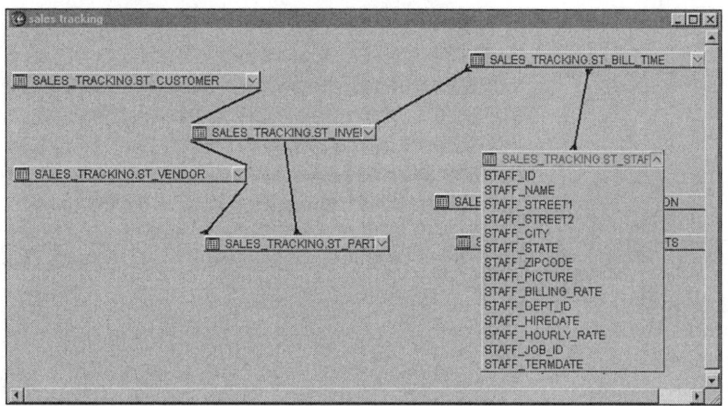

Figure 1.19

Sales Tracking Application ERD diagram focusing on the ST_STAFF entities.

The ST_BILL_TIME table, as you can see in Figure 1.20, tracks the amount of time each employee spends on each automobile. Two foreign keys exist on this table as well. The BT_INV_ID is related to the inventory table so that records that do not have a valid INVENTORY_ID in the ST_INVENTORY table are not added to ST_BILL_TIME. Similarly, the ST_BILL_TIME table can't have records that do not relate to a staff member, so the foreign key BT_STAFF_ID must exist in the ST_STAFF table. Notice the only two other fields are the date on which the work was performed and the time (in hours) of that effort. The amount of the effort is calculated with the rate fields in the ST_STAFF table. It would be redundant to record this information again in this table.

The four remaining tables are primarily used for reference data (see Figure 1.21). This application has two kinds of vendors: the vendor where the automobile itself was originally purchased and vendors that supply various parts for the repair of the automobiles. Both kinds of vendors are stored in the ST_VENDOR table. The ST_CUSTOMER table, on the other hand, is used to track the people who purchased the automobiles. ST_JOB_DESCRIPTIONS and ST_DEPARTMENTS are both reference tables to the ST_STAFF table. Each of these tables has a primary key of the first column in each table, and a primary key/foreign key relationship to other tables (refer to Figure 1.16).

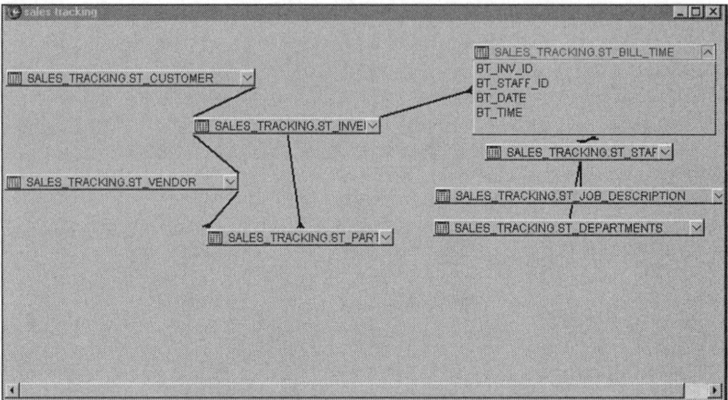

Figure 1.20

Sales Tracking Application ERD diagram focusing on the ST_BILL_TIME entities.

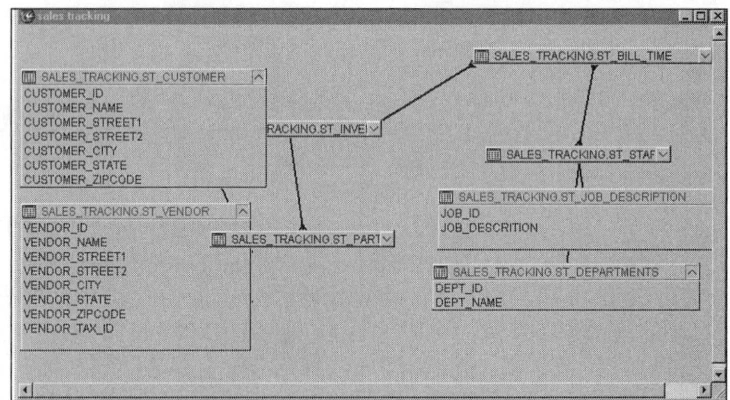

Figure 1.21

Sales Tracking Application ERD diagram focusing on the four reference tables.

Four fields do not appear in this list: INV_INSERT_USER, INV_INSERT_DATE, INV_UPDATE_USER, and INV_UPDATE_DATE. These same fields appear in all the major and minor tables of this application (ST_PARTS, ST_VENDOR, ST_BILL_TIME, ST_STAFF, and so on). Plus, these four fields track which user inserted the record into the table and which user was the last to update the table. This information could be useful if differing information appears in the fields and you need to determine whether it was entered erroneously and who you should contact. Maintaining these fields is done automatically by database triggers, or by some code that executes each time a record is inserted or updated in these tables (see Figure 1.22).

Figure 1.22

ST_INVENTORY's database trigger.

Untitled - Notepad

File Edit Search Help

```
CREATE TRIGGER st_inventory_trg BEFORE INSERT OR UPDATE ON st_inventory
        FOR EACH ROW
        BEGIN
                IF :old.inv_insert_user IS NULL THEN
                        :new.inv_insert_user := USER;
                        :new.inv_insert_date := SYSDATE;
                        :new.inv_update_user := NULL;
                        :new.inv_update_date := NULL;
                ELSE
                        :new.inv_insert_user := :old.inv_insert_user;
                        :new.inv_insert_date := :old.inv_insert_user;
                        :new.inv_update_user := USER;
                        :new.inv_update_date := SYSDATE;
                END IF;
        END;
```

The Sales Tracking Programs

This book walks you through the creation of an integrated application. I will teach you how to build screen-based GUI programs called *forms*. We will use Oracle Developer v6.0 to build these screens. Also, you will learn two methods for developing reports: using Oracle Developer v6.0 for GUI-based reports and using SQL*Plus for character-mode–based reports.

Form—Typically refers to any screen-based data entry or data retrieval screen on a computer. Reports can be displayed and printed.

GUI versus character mode—GUI stands for graphical user interface. Windows and Motif (UNIX) are just two computer environments that support GUI. Programs developed for GUI must conform to rules for these environments governing mouse movements, mouse clicks in certain screen positions, size and placement of screens and fields, and so on. Character mode, on the other hand, is based strictly on positions on a screen or report. A report typically has either 80 or 132 columns in which to place data or characters of information.

The Sales Tracking Application consists of nine screen-based programs that add or maintain the data in the eleven database tables. Each of these programs has an *icon* that starts the program. ST_INVENTORY is the main program used to enter and track important information as it relates to a particular vehicle. Figure 1.23 shows the main entry screen. Each of these tabs represents a different part of the process of a vehicle. The final tab shows the profitability of the vehicle, enabling the salesperson to see how much the firm has invested in this particular vehicle (see Figure 1.24).

Icon—A term given to a small picture or graphical representation of a task. The icon is typically associated with a button or an object on a GUI screen that can be clicked with the mouse to run the underlying program or perform the assigned computer task. You will learn in this book how to set up these icons for the Sales Tracking Application.

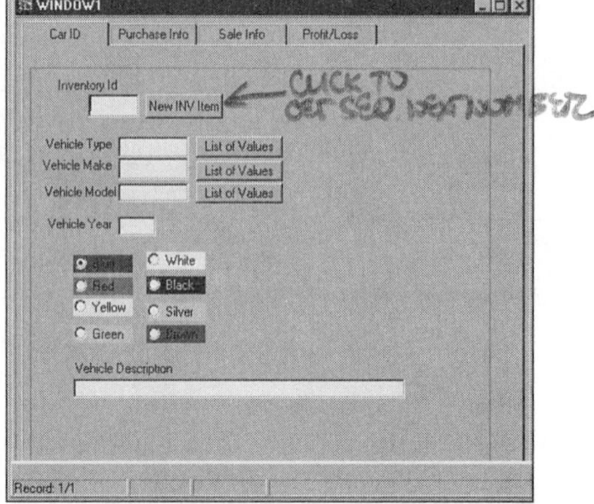

Figure 1.23
Sales Tracking Application ST_INVENTORY program.

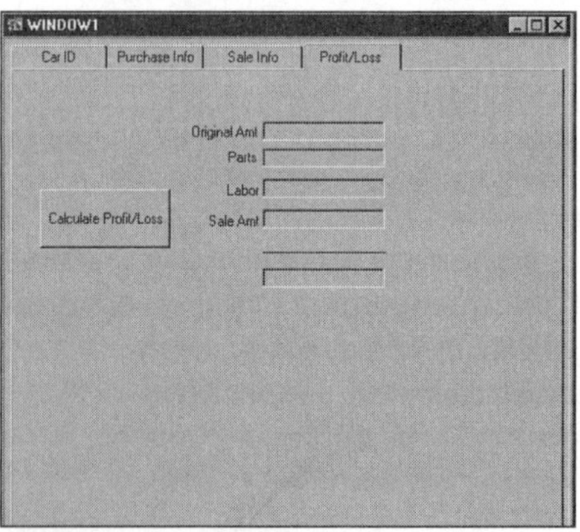

Figure 1.24
ST_INVENTORY Profit/Loss tab.

Figure 1.25 shows the Windows-based icons for the Sales Tracking Application. They appear in order of importance, with the main programs at the top, the reporting programs next, and the application-maintenance programs at the bottom. The main application programs are the ST_INVENTORY, ST_PARTS, and ST_BILL_TIME programs. These programs are accessed by the icons Inventory, Parts, and Time Clock.

Figure 1.25

Sales tracking icons.

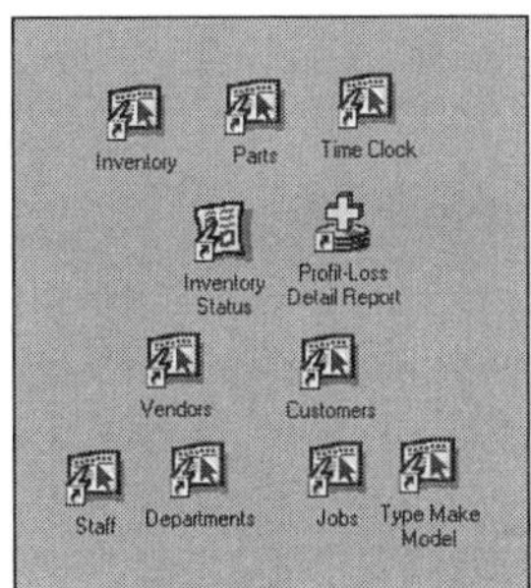

Notice icons also exist for the two reports (Inventory Status and Profit/Loss Detail); for Vendor and Customer entry and maintenance; and for Staff, Departments, Jobs, and Type/Make/Model entry and maintenance. Each of these entry programs relates directly to one of the relational table objects, as their names would imply. The icon depicts the type of program assigned to it: the Oracle Forms-based icon is used for the Oracle Developer forms-based programs; the Oracle Reports icon is used for the Oracle Developer reports-based programs; and the SQL*Plus icon is used for the SQL*Plus-based reports.

Reports are needed to display data from the underlying relational tables in a meaningful manner. We will use one GUI-based report and one character-mode–based report. There is no reason why they cannot be all be either GUI or character based, but for learning purposes, we will create both kinds. Typically, character-mode printers are much less expensive (dot-matrix printers) than printers that can handle images, such as laser printers. Figure 1.26 shows the Oracle Developer–based report, and Figure 1.27 shows the character-mode SQL*Plus–based report.

Figure 1.26

The Sales Tracking Application Profit/Loss report generated with Oracle Developer.

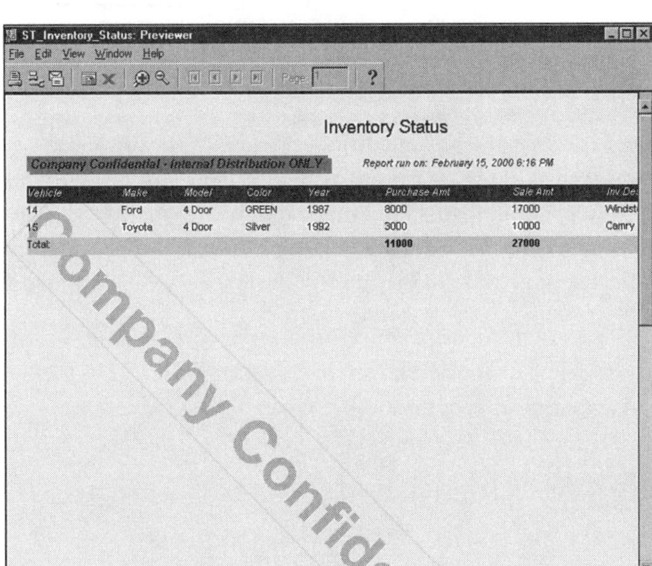

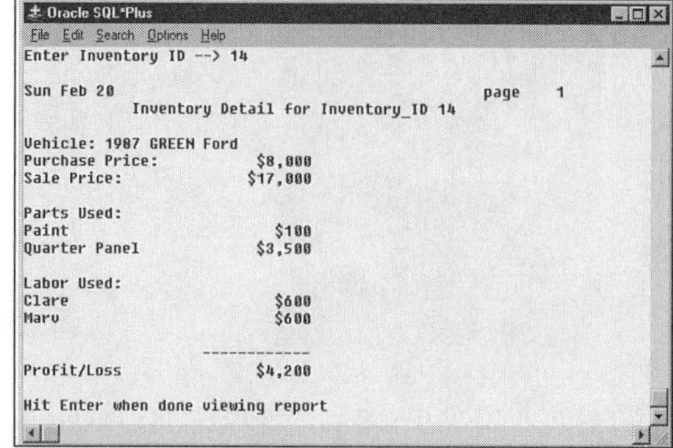

Figure 1.27

*Sales Tracking Application Profit/Loss Detail report generated with character-mode SQL*Plus.*

Several database administrative and tuning tasks are associated with any computer-based application, such as adding or deleting (when employment is terminated) users who have access to the system, starting up and shutting down the database, adding more disk space for the relational tables, monitoring how busy the computer is, monitoring how well the database is performing, and so on.

The first item, Oracle Enterprise Manager, is the main administrative tool that comes with the Oracle8 and 8i software (see Figure 1.28). Quest Software has an easy-to-use tool, Instance Monitor, which helps identify and explain various issues in the Oracle8i database environment (see Figure 1.29). Quest SQL Navigator, however, is used throughout this book to develop the server-side PL/SQL triggers, procedures, and functions (see Figure 1.30). This product has many features intended to assist the developer with the development and debugging of the Oracle PL/SQL code. You also will learn how to use Quest SQLab Xpert, a popular tool used to tune SQL statements (see Figure 1.31). Software availability and trial keys for the Oracle and Quest software can be found in Appendix A, "Installation and Configuration of Oracle8i NT-Based Software."

Oracle Enterprise Manager from Oracle Corporation is the tool you should use to start and stop the Oracle8i environment; add, modify, and delete users; add space to the Oracle8i tablespaces; and make quick changes to the Sales Tracking tables, such as adding a column to a table, adding indexes, or dropping indexes. You will learn how to use this tool in Chapter 4, "Basic Oracle8i Administration Tasks."

Many tools are available for Oracle8i to perform a variety of functions, including monitoring and SQL tuning. I will reference and use the Quest Software tools in this book because I am familiar with them and find them easy to install and learn.

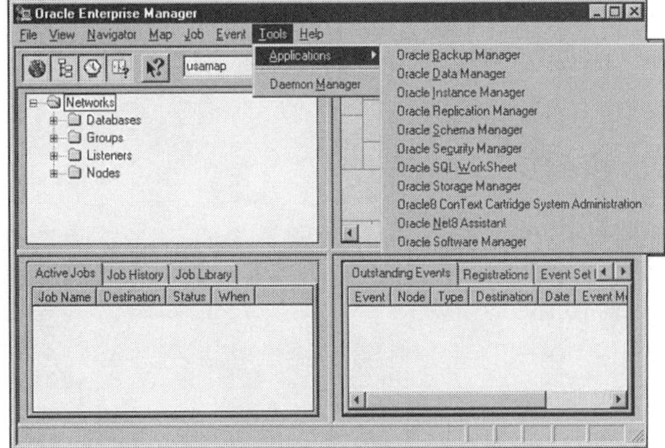

Figure 1.28

Oracle Enterprise Manager administrative tool.

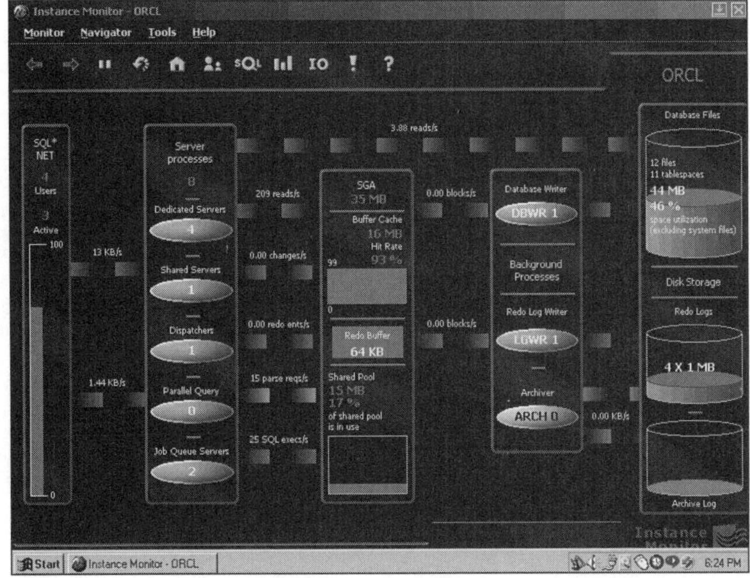

Figure 1.29

Quest Instance Monitor, an Oracle8i monitor/ diagnostics tool.

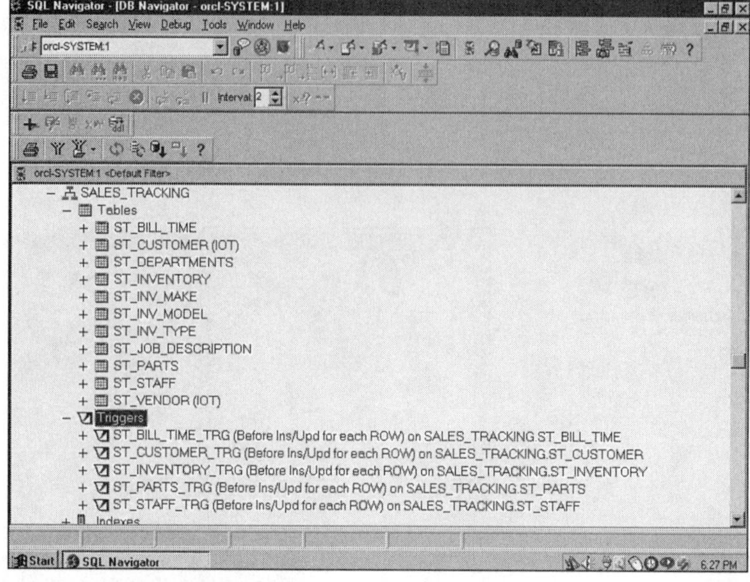

Figure 1.30

Quest SQL Navigator, an Oracle8i PL/SQL development/debugging tool.

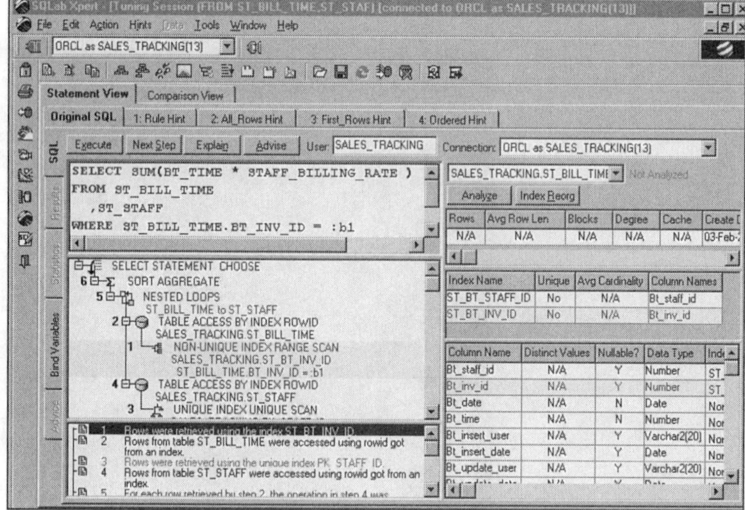

Figure 1.31

Quest SQLab Xpert, an Oracle8i SQL tuning tool.

Summary

This chapter laid the groundwork for the remaining chapters of this book. For anyone new to the Oracle database environment, the appendixes contain an excellent SQL tutorial and a PL/SQL basics primer. While the rest of this book is a complete guide for building Windows- and Web-based applications in the Oracle8i database, this chapter discussed the various Oracle tools and utilities that you will use. You learned about the Oracle8i database and the database object relationships, as well as the programs that uses these objects.

Next Steps

The objective of this book is to teach you, step by step, how to use Oracle8i to create a complete application from beginning to end.

In the upcoming chapters, you will learn the following:

- How to create GUI forms-based programs
- How to create GUI and character-mode reports
- How to use SQL and SQL*Plus
- What is necessary to administer Oracle8i
- How to monitor and tune the Sales Tracking Application
- How to build Oracle PL/SQL and implement it in the Sales Tracking Application
- How to build Java and implement it in the Sales Tracking Application

Chapter 2

In this chapter

- *Relational Schema Design and Database Construction*
- *Building the Sample Application Database*

Building the Sales Tracking Application Database

This chapter builds the Sales Tracking Application, starting with the database objects. You will learn how to design a relational application, load data into it, and then build the forms and reports that will manipulate and report on the data.

Relational Schema Design and Database Construction

The section "The Sales Tracking Database Layout" in Chapter 1, "Introduction to Oracle8i and the Auto Sales Tracking Application," discussed the various database objects we'll be using and their roles in the Sales Tracking Application. Figure 2.1 shows the Entity Relationship Diagram (ERD) charting all the Sales Tracking database objects and their relationships to one another.

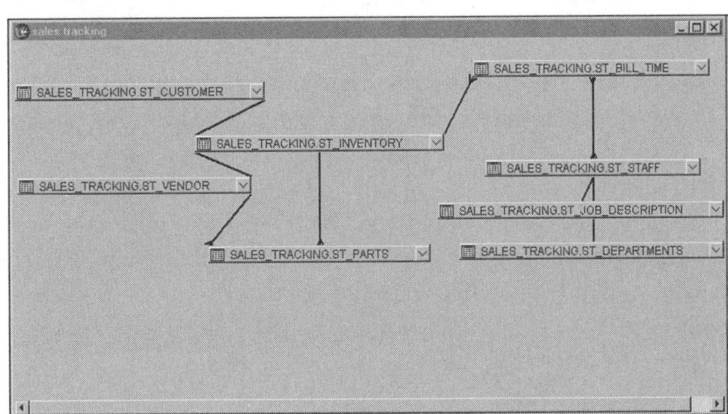

Figure 2.1

Entity Relationship Diagram (ERD) of the Sales Tracking Application database objects.

An Overview of Tables and Indexes

The ST_INVENTORY table is the main table of our application. This table tracks the vehicles, including their initial cost, their sales cost, where they were purchased, and to whom they were sold. The INV_ID is identified as a primary key, so Oracle8i will build an index on this column to ensure that its values are always unique and to provide fast access to the data. Two foreign keys also are on the INV_VENDOR_ID and INV_CUSTOMER_ID to guarantee that the related VENDOR_ID and CUSTOMER_ID exist in the ST_VENDOR and the ST_CUSTOMER tables prior to any INVENTORY activity. The business rule that applies here is that one cannot purchase a vehicle from a vendor who is not in the Sales Tracking Application, nor can one sell a vehicle to a customer who is not in the Sales Tracking Application. The ST_INVENTORY table also has three reference tables, used by the ST_INVENTORY application to assist the *data entry operator* in filling in columns with valid data: INV_TYPE, INV_MAKE, and INV_MODEL. These three tables are used to load ST_INVENTORY columns with data or to verify that valid information is entered.

Data entry operator—Can be most anyone who is working with the application and entering data into the application. This data entry is usually done via a screen-based form. The term comes from the days of punched cards when these folks were known as key punch operators.

- When vehicles require repairs, the software will need to track associated labor costs and required parts costs to correctly arrive at a cost of each vehicle. This information will help determine a sale price for the vehicle to ensure that a profit is made on each vehicle. The ST_PARTS table is used to track parts used on the vehicles. The business rule that applies here is that parts must be associated with an individual vehicle, so a foreign key constraint links this table to the ST_INVENTORY table. Another business rule that applies to ST_PARTS is that the parts must be purchased from a valid vendor in the ST_VENDOR table, so a foreign key constraint also links this table to the ST_VENDOR table.

- The other table used to track the total cost of a vehicle is the ST_BILL_TIME table, which is used to track labor costs associated with each vehicle. The two business rules that govern this table are that time must be recorded against valid inventory items and that the person doing the work must be a valid staff member. A foreign key exists between this table and the inventory table to ensure that valid vehicles are being worked on. The ST_STAFF table contains information about the employee, including a picture, billing rate, hourly rate, and contact information. In our example, the billing rate and hourly rate will be the same. A foreign key links the ST_BILL_TIME table with the ST_STAFF table to ensure that only valid employees are performing the work on the vehicles.

- The ST_STAFF table has two reference-type tables: ST_DEPARTMENTS and ST_JOB_DESCRIPTIONS. The business rules that apply here are that each employee must be associated with a valid department and that each employee must be associated with a valid job description. Foreign key constraints exist between ST_STAFF and ST_DEPARTMENTS/ST_JOB_DESCRIPTIONS to ensure that each employee contains a correct department and job description.

The ST_STAFF department/job description will be handled with foreign key constraints to ensure proper data in the ST_STAFF fields. This concept differs from that of the ST_INVENTORY model/make/type in which the Oracle Form-based application performs the integrity check. The first reason for this difference is that we want to introduce you to a variety of ways of performing similar tasks. The second reason is that the data in the model/make/type might be subject to ad hoc entries, whereas the fields of ST_STAFF are not.

Building the Sample Application Database

Appendix A, "Installation and Configuration of Oracle8i NT-Based Software," has the Oracle8i architecture. This appendix discusses the relationship of physical computer files being created and assigned to Oracle8i tablespaces. Chapter 4, "Basic Oracle8i Administration Tasks," illustrates how to create these tablespaces and assign a computer file to them.

The tablespaces of an Oracle database are similar to the folders or directories found on a PC in that they are storage areas for information. These tablespaces, folders, and directories are designed to help locate information, sometimes on different parts of the computer. For example, the `bin` folder on a computer is typically used to store programs. Folders or directories such as `data` are used for information files. The Oracle tablespace is similar in that different database objects such as tables and indexes can be assigned to various tablespaces for both convenience (such as enabling the users and administrators to relate a tablespace name easily with a particular application or parts of an application) and performance.

Tablespace Layout

Chapter 5, "Monitoring the Sales Tracking Application," will utilize the tablespace arrangement built in this chapter to adequately separate the Sales Tracking database objects by their disk-related activity. Figure 2.2 shows all the tablespaces assigned to the ORCL Oracle8i database. Notice all the tablespaces that begin with an ST_ belong to the Sales Tracking Application and were created with the script in Listing 2.1.

Figure 2.2

Tablespaces assigned to the Oracle8i database ORCL.

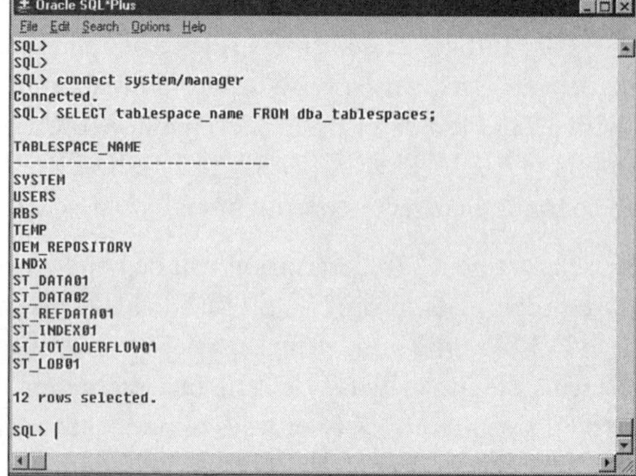
Oracle SQL*Plus
File Edit Search Options Help
SQL>
SQL>
SQL> connect system/manager
Connected.
SQL> SELECT tablespace_name FROM dba_tablespaces;
TABLESPACE_NAME
SYSTEM
USERS
RBS
TEMP
OEM_REPOSITORY
INDX
ST_DATA01
ST_DATA02
ST_REFDATA01
ST_INDEX01
ST_IOT_OVERFLOW01
ST_LOB01
12 rows selected.
SQL>

Note

Each tablespace has its own computer file or files, and these files are not shared by other tablespaces. This method of creating files on the computer system is a great way to physically separate database objects. On larger computer systems with many disk drives, these tablespace files would be created on separate physical disks. My single-disk-drive Windows NT 4.0 system will still create multiple tablespaces. This technique greatly aids the administrator who must move this application from a smaller computer to a larger one. The database administrator only has to adjust the file names on the DATAFILE lines in Listing 2.1 to accommodate most any computer system.

Listing 2.1—Installing the Sales Tracking Database

```
rem
rem    Sales Tracking Application Oracle8i Initial Database Setup
rem        Oracle8i From Scratch
rem            by Dan Hotka
rem         Que Publications March 2000
rem         All Rights Reserved
rem
spool INSTALL_sales_tracking_database.log

DROP TABLESPACE st_data01          INCLUDING CONTENTS CASCADE CONSTRAINTS;
DROP TABLESPACE st_data02          INCLUDING CONTENTS CASCADE CONSTRAINTS;
DROP TABLESPACE st_index01         INCLUDING CONTENTS CASCADE CONSTRAINTS;
DROP TABLESPACE st_refdata01       INCLUDING CONTENTS CASCADE CONSTRAINTS;
DROP TABLESPACE st_iot_overflow01  INCLUDING CONTENTS CASCADE CONSTRAINTS;
DROP TABLESPACE st_lob01           INCLUDING CONTENTS CASCADE CONSTRAINTS;

CREATE TABLESPACE st_data01
    DATAFILE 'd:\Oracle\Oradata\ORCL\st_data01.dbf' SIZE 10M REUSE
    DEFAULT STORAGE (INITIAL 10K
```

```
            NEXT 10K
            MINEXTENTS 5
            MAXEXTENTS 100
            )
    ONLINE;

CREATE TABLESPACE st_data02
    DATAFILE 'd:\Oracle\Oradata\ORCL\st_data02.dbf' SIZE 10M REUSE
    DEFAULT STORAGE (INITIAL 5K
            NEXT 5K
            MINEXTENTS 5
            MAXEXTENTS 100
            )
    ONLINE;

CREATE TABLESPACE st_refdata01
    DATAFILE 'd:\Oracle\Oradata\ORCL\st_refdata01.dbf' SIZE 1M REUSE
    DEFAULT STORAGE (INITIAL 1K
            NEXT 1K
            MINEXTENTS 1
            MAXEXTENTS 100
            )
    ONLINE;

CREATE TABLESPACE st_index01
    DATAFILE 'd:\Oracle\Oradata\ORCL\st_index01.dbf' SIZE 5M REUSE
    DEFAULT STORAGE (INITIAL 5K
            NEXT 5K
            MINEXTENTS 5
            MAXEXTENTS 100
            )
    ONLINE;

CREATE TABLESPACE st_iot_overflow01
    DATAFILE 'd:\Oracle\Oradata\ORCL\st_iot_overflow01.dbf' SIZE 10M REUSE
    DEFAULT STORAGE (INITIAL 5K
            NEXT 5K
            MINEXTENTS 5
            MAXEXTENTS 100
            )
    ONLINE;

CREATE TABLESPACE st_lob01
    DATAFILE 'd:\Oracle\Oradata\ORCL\st_lob01.dbf' SIZE 10M REUSE
    DEFAULT STORAGE (INITIAL 10K
            NEXT 10K
            MINEXTENTS 1
            MAXEXTENTS 100
            )
    ONLINE;
```

Listing 2.1—continued

```
CREATE USER sales_tracking
    IDENTIFIED BY sales_tracking
    DEFAULT TABLESPACE st_data01
    TEMPORARY TABLESPACE temp;

GRANT CONNECT, DBA TO sales_tracking;

spool off
exit
```

Listing 2.1 is designed to be run from SQL*Plus, and the SYSTEM password must be used. My Windows NT system has one physical hard drive with four logical partitions: `C:`, `D:`, `E:`, and `G:`. The Oracle8i ORCL database is installed on the `D:` partition, as shown in Figure 2.3. Notice that the file path in the DATAFILE lines in Listing 2.1 corresponds to the directory path of the Oracle8i ORCL installation on the `D:` partition.

The two major Oracle user accounts are SYS and SYSTEM. SYS is the owner of the Oracle Data Dictionary Objects, and great care must be taken when using this account because it is allowed to do almost anything in the Oracle database environment. The SYSTEM account is the main DBA account, which has the capability to do all the administrative tasks (in this case, add tablespaces). Listing 2.1 must be run by the SYSTEM account or by an account with the DBA role assigned. More information on Oracle accounts and the SYSTEM account can be found in Appendix B, "Learning SQL—A Complete Tutorial."

Be sure you adjust the operating system directory path to that of your own computer prior to running this script.

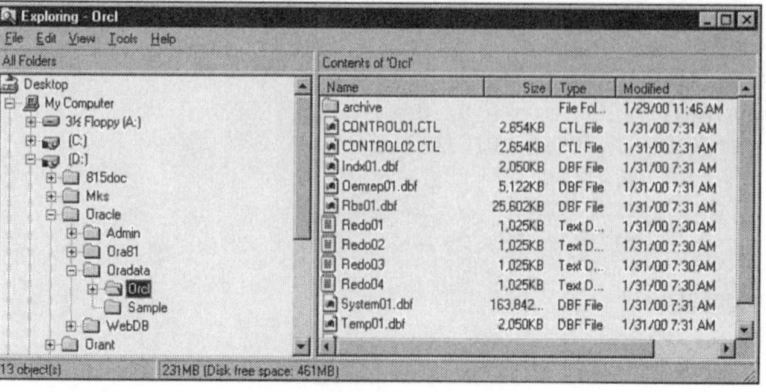

Figure 2.3

The Oracle8i ORCL database file directory.

> **Warning**
>
> Notice the `DROP TABLESPACE` commands at the beginning of Listing 2.1. This script should be used only for initial installation on a computer.

Each tablespace has its own assigned default storage parameters. These parameters will become the default for any object being created in this tablespace that does not have its own storage clause. It is more efficient for Oracle8i if all the *extents* (or units of storage) are the same size. This will be discussed more in detail in Chapter 5.

This script also creates the Sales Tracking DBA account. All the objects will be created by a single user called `sales_tracking`. This benefits administration, backup, and recovery—topics that will be covered in detail in Chapter 4 and Chapter 7, "Oracle8i Backup and Recovery."

The following command-line syntax is used to run this script (Listing 2.1) against the Oracle8i ORCL database:

```
sqlplus system/manager@ORCL @INSTALL_Sales_Tracking_Database.sql
```

Figure 2.4 shows the newly created tablespaces, and Figure 2.5 shows the Windows NT physical files that are assigned to the tablespaces in Figure 2.4.

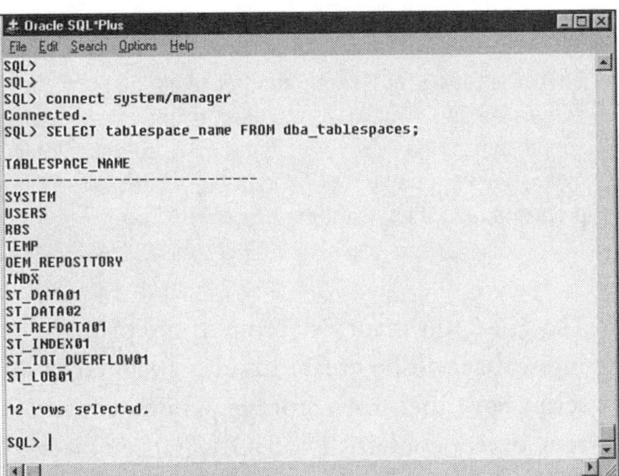
Oracle SQL*Plus
File Edit Search Options Help
SQL>
SQL>
SQL> connect system/manager
Connected.
SQL> SELECT tablespace_name FROM dba_tablespaces;
TABLESPACE_NAME

SYSTEM
USERS
RBS
TEMP
OEM_REPOSITORY
INDX
ST_DATA01
ST_DATA02
ST_REFDATA01
ST_INDEX01
ST_IOT_OVERFLOW01
ST_LOB01
12 rows selected.
SQL>

Figure 2.4

The Oracle8i ORCL tablespaces.

Creating the Database (Tables, Indexes, and Constraints)

The Sales Tracking database objects have many relationships. Many times, these relationships or constraints cannot be created until all the objects or tables first have been created. Oracle8i does not allow a constraint or relationship to be created on an object that does not exist. Listing 2.2 is only a partial listing of the `INSTALL_sales_tracking_database_objects.sql` file. (Listings in this book are available for download at the companion Web site for this book.) This script is also intended to be run only once per computer system. Listing 2.2 begins with creating a log file to capture the status of each `DROP` and `CREATE` statement of the script. Notice the `DROP` commands used to clean up any database objects and prevent `Object already exists` errors in the event that this script must be run more than once on a particular computer system.

Figure 2.5

Windows NT physical files assigned to the Oracle8i ORCL tablespaces.

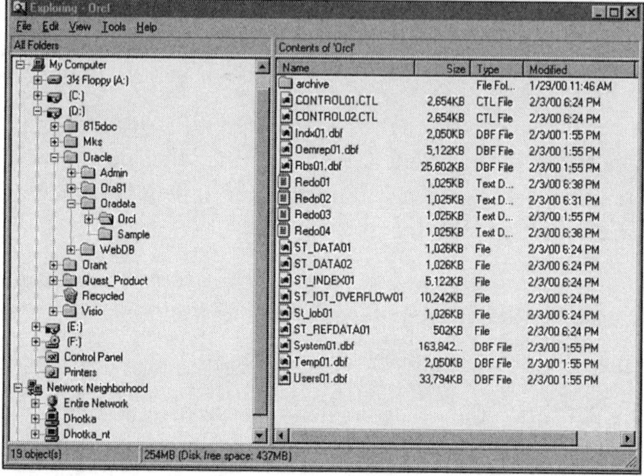

The SQL*Plus `spool` command in Listing 2.2 shows a way to capture all the completed and error messages that might have been displayed. These longer scripts more than fill a computer screen, so using a log file to capture all the messages is not only a good idea but a necessity to see whether there were any problems, and if so, what the problem was.

In the `CREATE TABLE st_inventory` statement, the primary key constraint is defined *in line* and the index that will be created is also assigned to its own tablespace. All the objects in this script have their own storage parameters and tablespace assignments. This `st_inventory` object contains two LOBs (large objects, such as pictures, video, sound files, and so on), both of which are pictures and will be stored in the tablespace `ST_LOB01` as noted by the syntax in the storage clause. The `st_inv_seq` sequence is then created and used by the ST_INVENTORY form to always create a unique number for the primary key ST_INV_ID. The next object to be created is the ST_VENDOR table. Notice the *out of line* constraint in the `ALTER TABLE` command near the end of Listing 2.2. The foreign key constraint, which ensures that any VENDOR_ID being inserted in the ST_INVENTORY table first exists in the ST_VENDOR table, can't be created until after the ST_VENDOR table is created (review the entire listing in Appendix C, "PL/SQL Basics").

The Sales Tracking objects can be created in SQL*Plus as we discuss in Appendix B or by using tools such as SQL Navigator. However, I find it convenient to use `INSTALL_xxx.sql` files in this method to ensure that all objects are initially created in the correct order and without error.

2

In line constraint—One that is defined where the field to which it applies is defined. An *out of line* constraint is one that is added with separate syntax at a later time.

In Listing 2.2, the INV_ID column in the ST_INVENTORY table has an in line constraint—the primary key constraint is defined at the same time as the INV_ID column. The last command in Listing 2.2 is an out of line constraint in which the `ALTER TABLE` syntax adds a foreign key constraint.

Listing 2.2—Installing Sales Tracking Database Objects (Partial Listing)

```
rem
rem    Sales Tracking Application Oracle8i Objects
rem        Oracle8i From Scratch
rem            by Dan Hotka
rem         Que Publications March 2000
rem         All Rights Reserved
rem
spool INSTALL_sales_tracking_objects.log

DROP TABLE st_inventory     CASCADE CONSTRAINTS;
DROP SEQUENCE st_inv_seq;
DROP OBJECT address_field;
DROP TABLE st_parts         CASCADE CONSTRAINTS;
DROP TABLE st_inv_type         CASCADE CONSTRAINTS;
.
.
.
DROP TRIGGER st_bill_time_trg;

CREATE TABLE st_inventory
    (inv_id                 NUMBER(6)     CONSTRAINT pk_inv_id PRIMARY KEY
                                          USING INDEX TABLESPACE st_index01,
    inv_type                VARCHAR2(10),
    inv_make                VARCHAR2(10),
    inv_model               VARCHAR2(10),
    inv_color               VARCHAR(10),
    inv_year                NUMBER(4),
    inv_purchase_vendor_id  NUMBER(6),
    inv_purchase_amt        NUMBER(9,2)    NOT NULL,
    inv_purchase_date       DATE           NOT NULL,
    inv_purchase_photo      BLOB,
    inv_sale_customer_id    NUMBER(6),
    inv_sale_amt            NUMBER(9,2),
```

Listing 2.2—continued

```
    inv_sale_date          DATE,
    inv_sale_photo         BLOB,
    inv_description        VARCHAR2(20),
    inv_insert_user        VARCHAR2(20),
    inv_insert_date        DATE,
    inv_update_user        VARCHAR2(20),
    inv_update_date        DATE)
    TABLESPACE st_data01
    PCTFREE  30
    PCTUSED  50
    STORAGE (INITIAL 10K
            NEXT 10K
            MINEXTENTS 5
            MAXEXTENTS 10)
    LOB (inv_purchase_photo, inv_sale_photo) STORE AS
            (TABLESPACE st_lob01
            STORAGE (INITIAL 10K
                    NEXT 10K
                    MINEXTENTS 5
                    MAXEXTENTS 100)
            CHUNK 500
            NOCACHE
            NOLOGGING);


CREATE SEQUENCE st_inv_seq
        START WITH 1
        INCREMENT BY 1
        CACHE 10;

.
.
.


CREATE TABLE st_vendor
        (vendor_id          NUMBER(6)        PRIMARY KEY,
        vendor_name         VARCHAR2(30)     NOT NULL,
.
.
.
.

ALTER TABLE st_inventory    ADD CONSTRAINT fk_inv_purchase_vendor_id FOREIGN KEY
        (inv_purchase_vendor_id)
                            REFERENCES sales_tracking.st_vendor(vendor_id);
.
.
.
.
/
```

```
spool off
exit
```

Use the following `sqlplus` syntax to run Listing 2.2:

```
sqlplus sales_tracking/sales_tracking@ORCL @INSTALL_sales_tracking_objects.sql
```


Creating Database Triggers

Notice the last four fields of the ST_INVENTORY table (INV_INSERT_USER, INV_INSERT_DATE, INV_UPDATE_USER, and INV_UPDATE_DATE). These are fields that will track who inserted the record into the table and who made the last change to the table. SYSDATE will be used for each of the date fields, which are important for applications that contain data critical to the needs of the business. This is a method of tracking who did what and when to the database. If erroneous data appears in the tables, the database administrator has an idea of where to begin to look for problems in programs or to determine who you should contact to track down any data entry issues.

A database *trigger* is a piece of PL/SQL code run by the Oracle8i database based on certain types of DML activity on any table for which the trigger is created. Listing 2.3 illustrates a database trigger that will execute before an insert or update to the ST_INVENTORY table, assigning the correct values to the four audit fields. A database trigger is useful in this instance to ensure that these fields are maintained, no matter what program was used to perform the DML, such as Oracle Forms, SQL*Plus, or a third-party program.

Notice the `new.` and `old.` prefixes on the fields. In database triggers, the prior value and the new value of any field are accessible with these two prefixes. The use of these prefixes to reset any of the values ensures that these fields accurately reflect the users' activity.

Listing 2.3—Sales Tracking Database Triggers (Partial Listing)

```
rem
rem    Sales Tracking Application Oracle8i Objects
rem        Oracle8i From Scratch
rem            by Dan Hotka
rem         Que Publications March 2000
rem         All Rights Reserved
rem
spool INSTALL_sales_tracking_objects.log

.
.
.

CREATE TABLE st_inventory
       (.
```

Listing 2.3—continued

```
   .
   .
   .
   .

CREATE TRIGGER st_inventory_trg BEFORE INSERT OR UPDATE ON st_inventory
        FOR EACH ROW
        BEGIN
               IF :old.inv_insert_user IS NULL THEN
                      :new.inv_insert_user := USER;
                      :new.inv_insert_date := SYSDATE;
                      :new.inv_update_user := NULL;
                      :new.inv_update_date := NULL;
               ELSE
                      :new.inv_insert_user := :old.inv_insert_user;
                      :new.inv_insert_date := :old.inv_insert_date;
                      :new.inv_update_user := USER;
                      :new.inv_update_date := SYSDATE;
               END IF;
        END;
/

   .
   .
   .
/

spool off
exit
```

Summary

This chapter built the Sales Tracking database. The next chapter will build the Sales Tracking Application based on the objects created in this chapter. This chapter also talked about the importance of a good database design. The importance of this design will be highlighted again in Chapter 5. Also, you learned several techniques for preparing application installation scripts and methods of tracking changes to records in the database.

Next Steps

In the next chapter, we'll get to the task at hand and build our Sales Tracking Application. It consists of 11 forms-based programs, which we'll construct. We'll also configure two reports using the Oracle Developer and SQL*Plus reporting techniques.

In this chapter

- *Building the Sales Tracking Forms*
- *Sales Tracking Application Icon Setup*

Chapter 3

Building the Sales Tracking Application Forms and Reports

Building the Sales Tracking Forms

Our Sales Tracking Application consists of 11 forms-based programs. The next section will begin with a simple form, describing in detail the terms associated with Oracle Developer and illustrating common techniques for building forms-based applications. Each forms-based program built draws up the knowledge gained with the previous program. In this chapter, we also will build two reports: one with Oracle Developer and one using SQL*Plus reporting techniques.

Oracle Developer for Forms

The program units within Oracle Form Builder are called *modules*. Four kinds of modules exist: form modules, menu modules, object library modules, and PL/SQL library modules. This section will concentrate on the form modules. You will learn how to build various types of forms, share code between programs, and discover the power of Oracle Forms.

The first application or program you will build is the ST_VENDOR application. This is a rather simple forms-based application based on a single database object: ST_VENDOR. Begin by starting the Form Builder program by double-clicking on its icon or by selecting Start, Oracle Developer 6.0, Form Builder. This will start the Where to Start Wizard (see Figure 3.1). Four main options are available: Use the Data Block Wizard, Build a new form manually, Open an existing form, and Build a form based on a template. In addition, two learning selections are available:

Run the Quick Tour (concepts) and Explore the Cue Cards (tasks). These two learning sections make excellent review.

Figure 3.1

The Form Builder Where to Start Wizard.

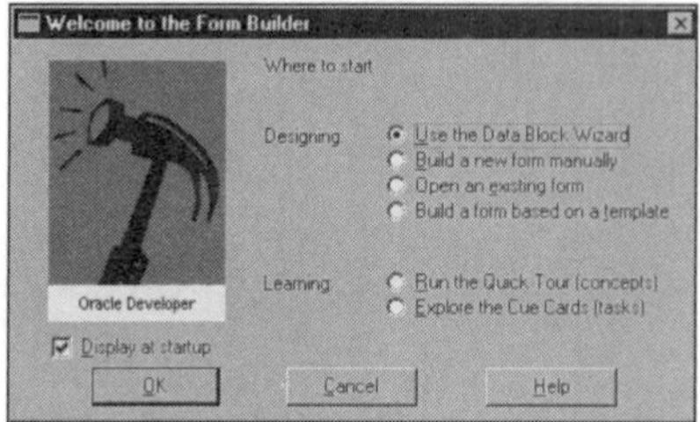

Radio group—The selections on this wizard. Notice that single-clicking on each option places a black dot in that option and removes the black dot from the previously selected item. This is similar to car radios, where only one button can be pressed at a time, making the selection.

Select the Use the Data Block Wizard option. This brings up the Welcome to the Data Block Wizard screen. Click Next and the next screen displays the first choice (see Figure 3.2). Forms can be based on tables, views, or stored procedures. This section will build applications that are always based on tables or views. Make sure the radio button next to Table or View is selected and click the Next button.

Figure 3.2

Tables, views, or stored procedure options.

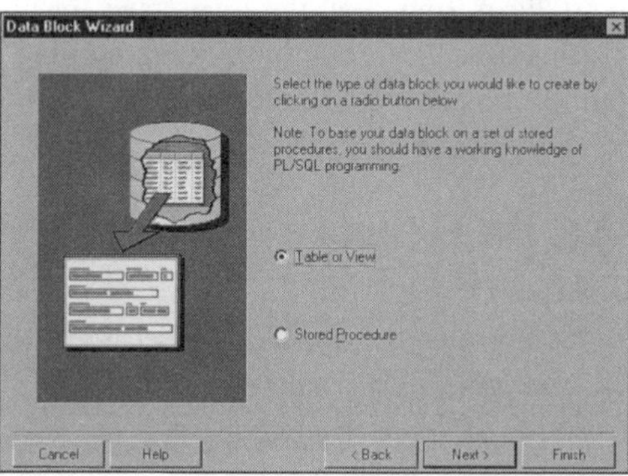

The next screen asks for the table or view on which to base the application. Click the Browse button (see Figure 3.3). This will cause Form Builder to access the database. Figure 3.4 shows one way of logging in to the database. Another method is to select Connect from the File at the top of the Form Builder menu bar (upper-left corner of the screen). The example database uses the user ID `sales_tracking`, and the password is the same: `sales_tracking`. The database is `ORCL`, as per the installation we performed in Chapter 2, "Building the Sales Tracking Application Database." After you're successfully logged in, a selection box will appear with all the tables and views available to this particular login (see Figure 3.5). The `sales_tracking` user ID was used to build all these objects.

Our application uses the `sales_tracking` user ID (the password is the same) and the `ORCL` database name (tnsnames entry) as selected during the database installation back in Chapter 2. Your installation might have required a different user ID and password and even a different database name.

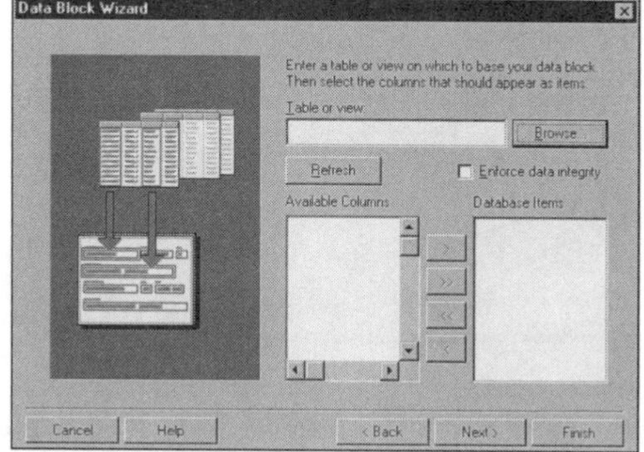

Figure 3.3

Data Block Wizard—table or view entry.

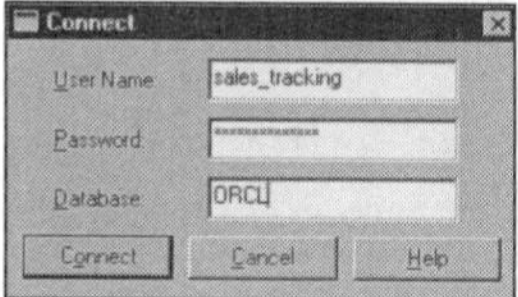

Figure 3.4

Data Block Wizard—connect to database.

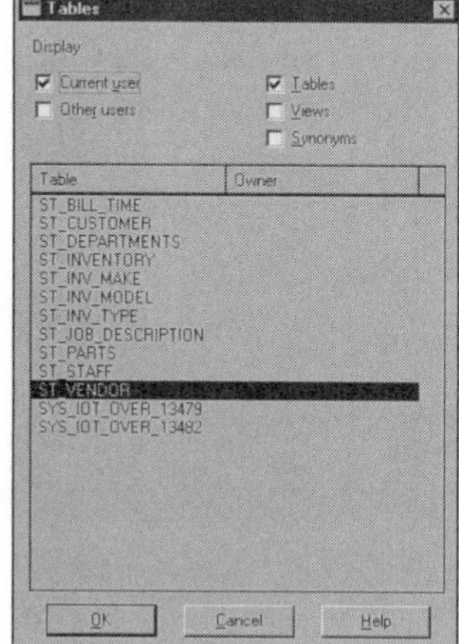

Figure 3.5

Data Block Wizard—table/view selection.

Select ST_VENDOR from this list. All the ST_VENDOR columns to which the user has access are now displayed in the lower-left pane. You can select each column you want to have in the form individually by clicking the column (to highlight it) and then the > button, or you can select all the columns by clicking the >> button (see Figure 3.6). Sometimes it is easier to select all the columns and then deselect the few that are not desired by clicking to highlight them and clicking the < button. The << button will deselect all the columns.

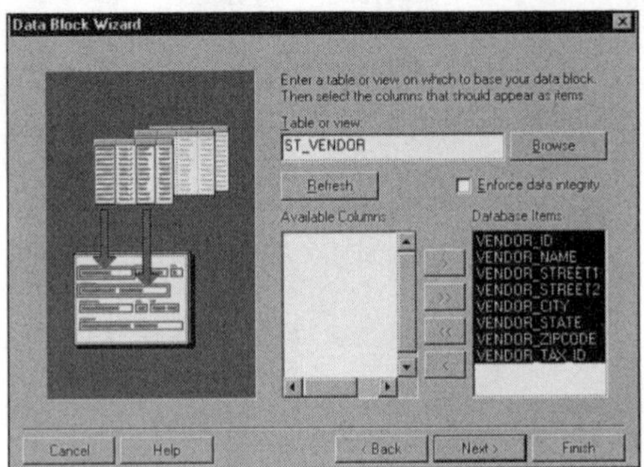

Figure 3.6

Data Block Wizard—column selection.

Click the >> button to select all the columns and then click Next. The final screen in the Data Block Wizard will appear. Select the default option Create the data block, call the Layout Wizard, and then click Finish. When the Welcome to the Layout Wizard screen appears, click Next. Figure 3.7 shows some options on the next screen: Content, Stacked, Vertical Toolbar, Horizontal Toolbar, and Tab. A *canvas* is the visual part of the application. A *content canvas* is the canvas that appears when the application first starts up. Each form must have a content canvas. A *stacked canvas*, on the other hand, has the capability to overlay or appear on top of other canvases to hide information or to show parts of information when other information is being accessed. A *toolbar* automatically appears in all forms, and, finally, *tab* canvases, like stacked canvases, automatically overlay one another. Tab canvases differ in that a tab remains visible along the top of the canvas, and when clicked, brings the associated tab canvas to the top. You will learn how to use both the content canvases and tab canvases in this section.

Select Content in the second box, leaving (New Canvas) as the only option in the first box. Then, click Next. Figure 3.8 shows the Layout Wizard Data Block layout screen. Only one block has been selected from the Data Block Wizard; select this and select all the columns in the same manner as you learned in the Data Block Wizard, and then click Next.

Figure 3.7

The Layout Wizard canvas selection.

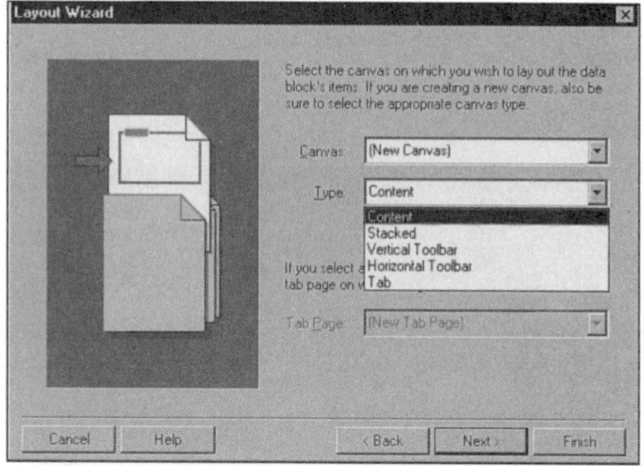

Figure 3.8

Layout Wizard Data Block/Column selection.

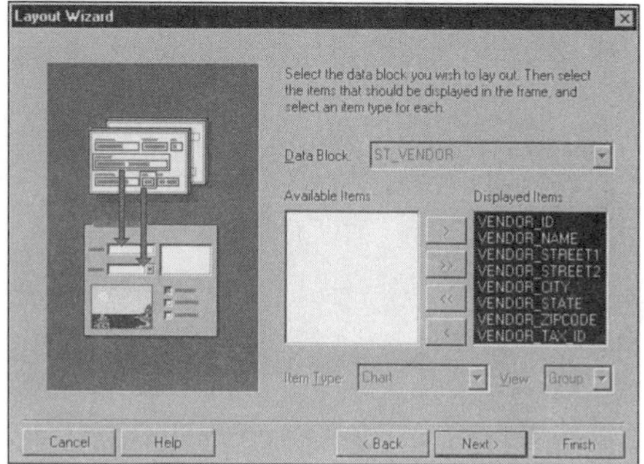

The next screen is illustrated in Figure 3.9. This Layout Wizard screen is a convenient place to change the prompts that will appear onscreen and the size of the fields onscreen. Several ways are available to make these kinds of changes; for now, accept the defaults on this screen and click the Next button.

The next screen is where you can make the selection of a form (single row per screen) or tabular (multiple rows per screen) layout. A *frame* is directly related to a block, and of course, the block has a direct reference to a table or view. Keep in mind that more than one frame can exist per canvas. Our ST_VENDOR application will display only one record at a time, so be sure the Form radio button is selected and click Next.

The next screen gives the frame a name (see Figure 3.10). No set standard for names exists, but using some kind of naming convention that includes what the form relates to is advisable. A naming convention will make the objects easier to find and relate to their function in the Object Navigator of Form Builder. Use a similar naming convention for the blocks as well. Type a name in the Frame Title and let the other fields default to one record displayed and no other selections made. Click the Next button.

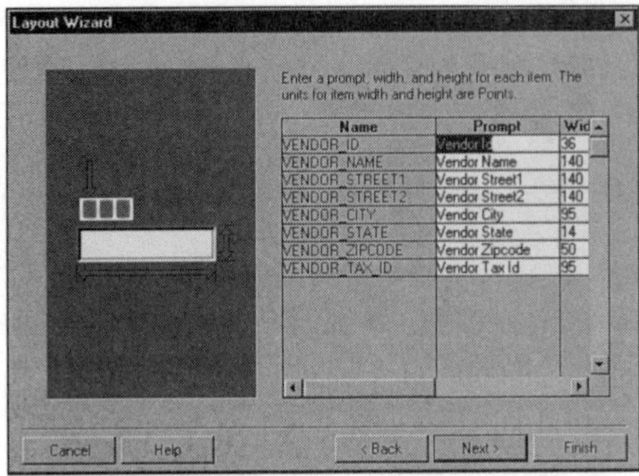

Figure 3.9

Layout Wizard prompt and field size screen.

I display only one record on a forms-based application and as many as 15 records on tabular-type forms. I also always use a scrollbar on the tabular-type forms.

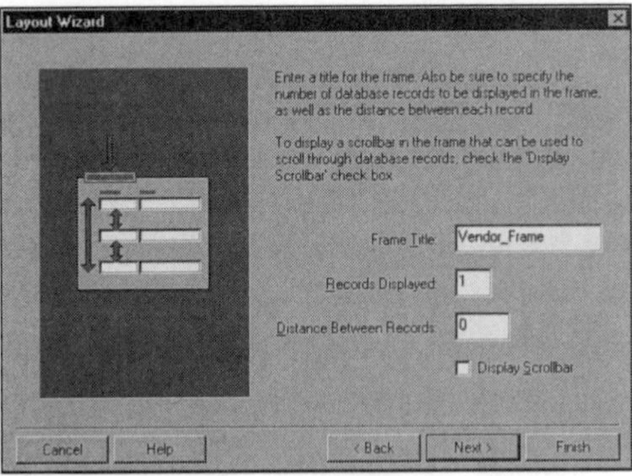

Figure 3.10

Layout Wizard form name and record count selection.

This will complete the Layout Wizard. Click the Finish button and the Object Navigator will appear, as well as the canvas layout (see Figure 3.11).

Figure 3.11

Object Navigator and Canvas Layout windows.

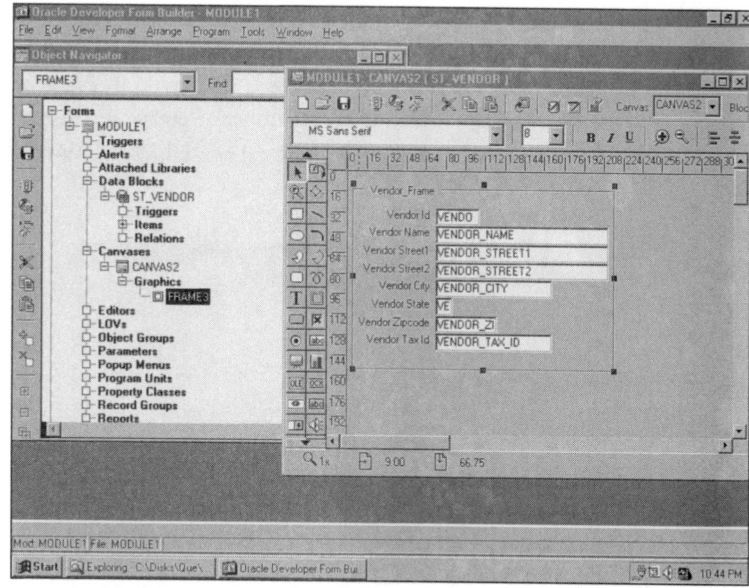

The fields and labels can be easily moved around onscreen by first single-clicking the item to be moved and then clicking and holding down (this will pick up the object) while moving the mouse and moving the object to the place desired on the canvas. Labels can be double-clicked to highlight them, enabling the text within to be changed. These fields can easily be moved by single-clicking and then clicking and holding to move to a new location as well. Make sure you notice the Object Navigator. You can now see the data block, the name you gave the data block, the canvas, the name you gave the canvas, and the frame with the name you gave the frame. Canvases are the physical screen layout, and all the triggers and the data block area control data access.

All the Oracle manuals are available by clicking the Help button at the right end of the toolbar. Figure 3.12 shows the main help screen. Each of these manuals is accessed by double-clicking the desired selection. Each manual has a hyperlinked index, which means that any item can be instantly referenced in the index by simply clicking the phrase or term.

Just about every item, canvas, block, frame, and so on has a *property palette* that contains all the information about the particular item. This palette can be accessed with a variety of methods. You can either double-click the item or canvas or double-click the item, block, or canvas in the Object Navigator. In addition, you can right-click these same items and then select Property Palette from the pop-up menu. Notice that the items are now displayed in the Object Navigator. This was easily accomplished by clicking the + next to the Items entry in the Object Navigator under the data blocks (see Figure 3.13). You should notice that as you click items on the canvas, the associated item automatically highlights in the Object Navigator. The ST_VENDOR Block Property Palette is displayed in Figures 3.13 and 3.14. Review all the items available in the Block Property Palette. For instance, you can see that the block name can be changed, the database tables being referenced are named, and so on.

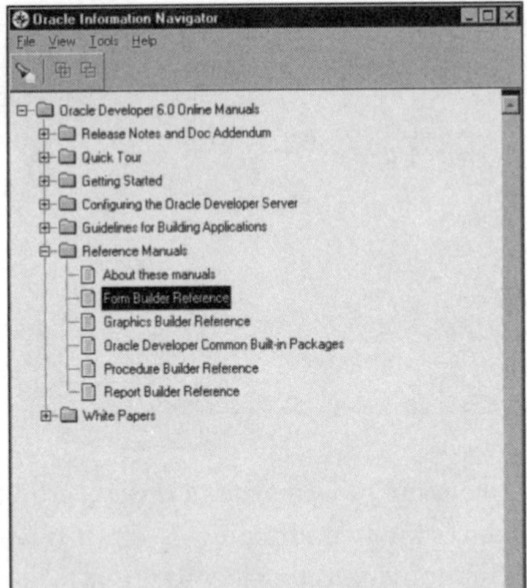

Figure 3.12

Oracle online help manuals.

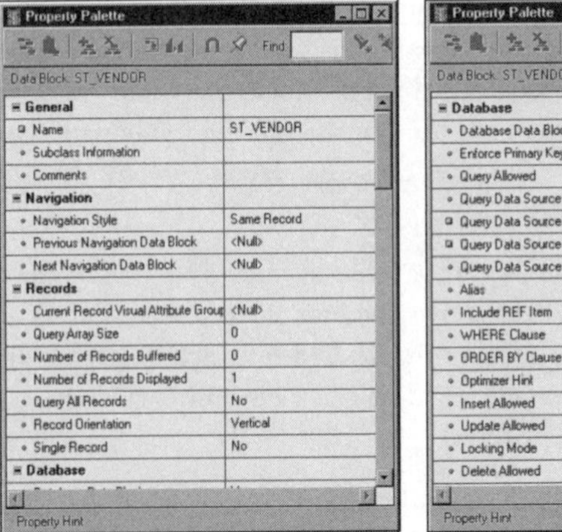

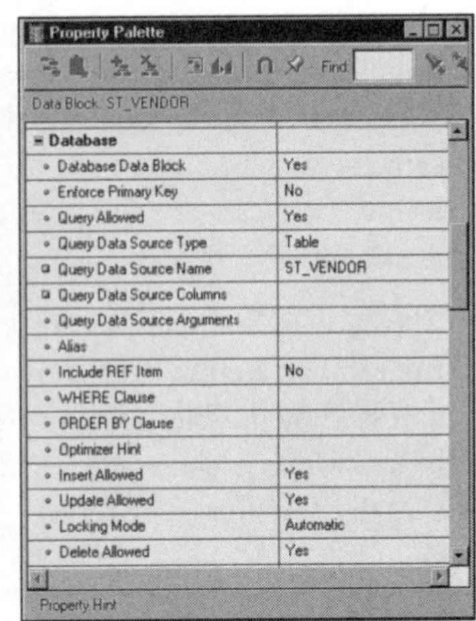

Figure 3.13

The Data Block Property Palette.

Many of the forms features are controlled by the Item Property Palette. This palette controls all the aspects of each item, including its visual attributes, how text is entered, and whether the field is even enterable, as well as its associated help text and its list-of-values (LOVs). Take a moment to look at the Item Property Palette.

It is important to understand most of the options on this palette to be able to better control how the form appears and interacts with users. For instance, the General area gives the item a specific name, typically the same name the item receives if assigned to a database field. The next item is the item type. This item could be a picture, sound, radio button, or text item. Later, we will see how to control the attributes of the text items (such as numbers, dates, and so on). The Functional area of the Item Property Palette controls how the computer cursor will work when in the field. This area also controls how the text will be entered, if the cursor is to be automatically moved to the next enterable field upon completely filling the field (Auto Skip), and whether the data will be displayed in the field (Conceal Data). Next, take a look at the Navigation and Data parts of the Item Property Palette. The important field in the Navigation part is Keyboard Navigable, which indicates whether the computer cursor is allowed to enter this field. The Data part of the palette controls the type of item; notice that this item is a number field with a maximum enterable length of seven positions. The Initial Value is useful to display any default values, whereas the Required Field is useful to ensure that all NOT NULL defined fields are entered.

The Data Block Wizard picks up the type, length, and required field information from the database table. Copy Item From (Item Property Palette) is useful in multi-tab– or multi-canvas–type applications so that users need to input data only once for use throughout the application. The Synchronize With Item will push this value to other items in the same form application. Important fields in the database part of the Item Property Palette include whether this item is assigned to a database table/column (Database Item) and the name of that database column if the answer is yes (Column Name). Other fields in this area help control how this particular item will interact with the Oracle8i database—namely, whether it can be queried, updated, and so on. You also should take a look at the List of Values (LOV), Editor, and Physical parts of the Item Property Palette. The List of Values part indicates whether an LOV is assigned to this particular item. This is simply a pointer to the actual LOV. (LOVs are covered in detail later in this section.) The Physical part of this Item Property Palette indicates with which canvas (Canvas) this item is associated and whether it is displayed (Visible). The other item of interest in the Physical section of the palette is the scrollbar setting. Remember, for our form, we asked that the scrollbar not be displayed from the Layout Wizard.

Other items of interest in the Item Property Palette are physical attributes of the item, such as its font, colors, and so on. You also have the option of configuring the same type of attributes for the prompt. The Hint and Display Hint Automatically attributes are the highlights of the Help part of this property palette. Any hint text defined will appear at the bottom of the form, and it will appear automatically when the field is entered if the Display Hint Automatically is set to Yes.

List of values—A forms feature that opens up an additional window with data from another database table so the user can easily make entry selections from this list.

When you look at the Data Block Property Palette on your system, you'll see that it has just a few key areas of interest. Most of these areas were already set up during the Data Block Wizard, and little reason should exist to make changes. When you open the Item Property Palette, it displays the General, Navigation, and Records settings. The General area contains the block name, and the Navigation area controls the relationship of this block to other blocks that might be defined in the application. This application has only the single block that references the ST_VENDOR table, so the previous and next blocks are automatically set to null. The Database part of the palette shows that this data block is assigned to a database table, the name of that table, and any default forms behaviors that are desired for this application.

The highlights of the Frame Property Palette are the physical attributes, such as the Color section that controls the foreground, background, edges, fill patterns, and so on. Figure 3.14 displays this part of the Frame Property Palette and shows where the frame itself (Edge Pattern) is set to transparent. This removes the box that appears around the items by default.

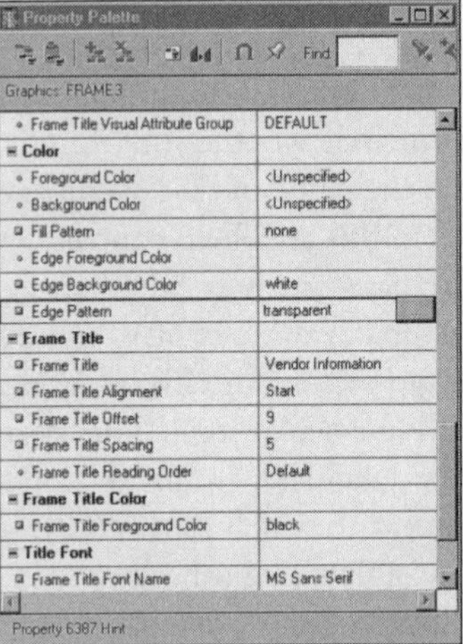

Figure 3.14

The Frame section of the Item Property Palette.

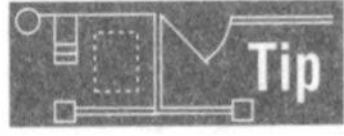

It is a good idea to save your work from time to time. I recommend creating a directory and keeping all the application programs together in the same directory or folder. Save your form as ST_VENDOR in the folder named Sales_Tracking_Pgms. When the form is saved, this name then replaces the default MODULE1 name with the new name of the form.

Figure 3.15 displays the frame after rearranging the items and prompts and making the Edge Pattern transparent. To make navigation between the fields flow nicely when using the Tab key, the items in the Object Navigator (left side of Figure 3.15) should be in the same order as they appear on the Canvas layout (right side of the figure). This is easily accomplished by clicking the item to be moved in the Object Navigator, clicking and holding, and then moving the mouse up or down; as the item moves, a line will appear between the other items. Release the button when the line is between the items, placing the moved item in the correct sequence with the items on the canvas.

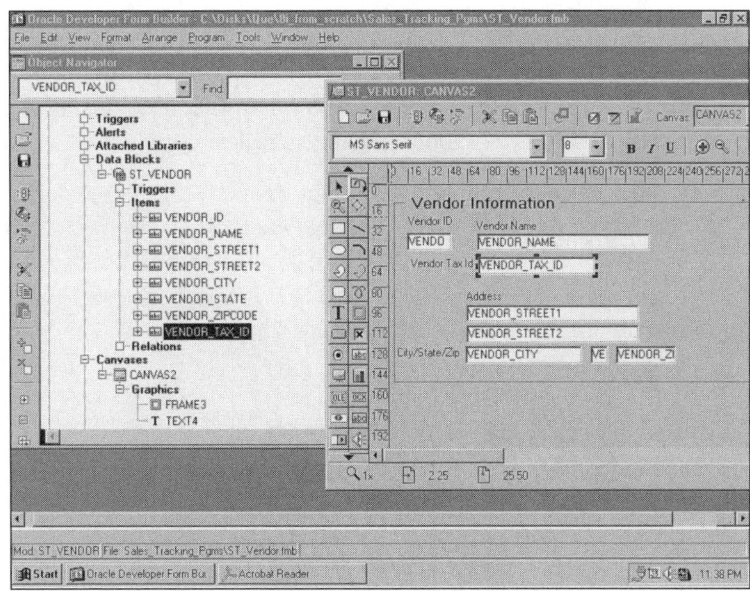

Figure 3.15

Canvas layout of the ST_VENDOR form.

The ST_VENDOR database table has an associated sequence—ST_VENDOR_SEQ—that is used to ensure a unique VENDOR_ID (which happens to be a primary key). A sequence is used so that no matter how many users are entering vendor information with this form, a unique vendor identification will always be generated. Several *triggers* are associated with a form-level data block, and many more types of triggers can be used to control keystrokes, change the functionality of pre-assigned forms keys, and so on. The desired function is to retrieve and display the next available sequence number in the VENDOR_ID item prior to the record being inserted into the database. This functionality is implemented with a block-level Pre-Insert trigger. This trigger will run the assigned PL/SQL code just prior to inserting the record in the database. When you right-click the data block ST_VENDOR, a pop-up menu appears and you can select the PL/SQL editor.

Trigger—Some code that executes on an event, such as a keystroke or before or after a record is inserted, updated, or deleted. The Forms Development Guide (from the Help menu) lists all the types of triggers supported in Oracle Developer V6.0. (Appendix C, "PL/SQL Basics," covers how to create and use PL/SQL.)

The PL/SQL Editor immediately prompts you for the type of trigger desired (see Figure 3.16; this is actually an LOV!). Select PRE-INSERT, which causes a PL/SQL editing window to appear (see Figure 3.17). Click the Compile button when you're finished entering the code. If any errors occur, a box will appear at the bottom of this window with the line number and problem discovered. However, if no problems exist, the `Compiled Successfully` message will appear in the lower-right part of the screen. Notice the `:ST_VENDOR.VENDOR_ID` in the `INTO` clause. The `:` tells Oracle Forms that this is an item within the form. `ST_VENDOR` is the name of the data block, and `VENDOR_ID` is the name of the item. Notice that this SQL statement is referring to the form item and not the database item.

Compiling—A computer term that refers to the conversion of the source code (PL/SQL code in this example) to code that the computer will understand. Oracle Forms are *run-time interpreted*, which means that all the PL/SQL and forms code (from the palettes, and so on) will be converted into some intermediate code, which is then interpreted into instructions the computer will understand by the Oracle Forms Runtime program.

Figure 3.16

Selecting the trigger type.

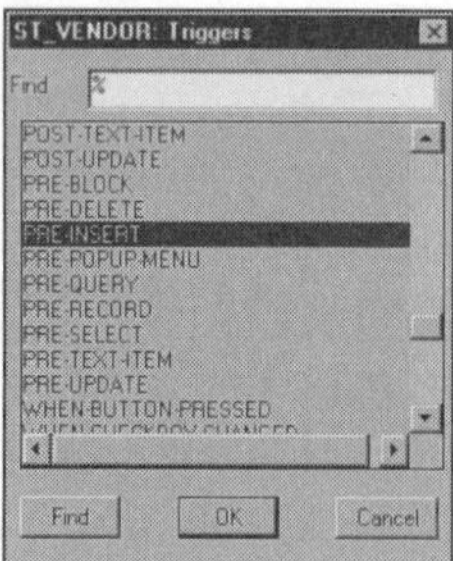

Save your work by selecting File, Save from the upper-left menu bar. Click the traffic light on the Canvas window. This compiles the form and starts the Forms Runtime environment (runs the newly developed form).

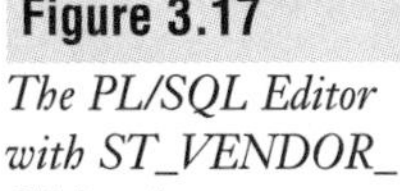

Figure 3.17

The PL/SQL Editor with ST_VENDOR_SEQ code.

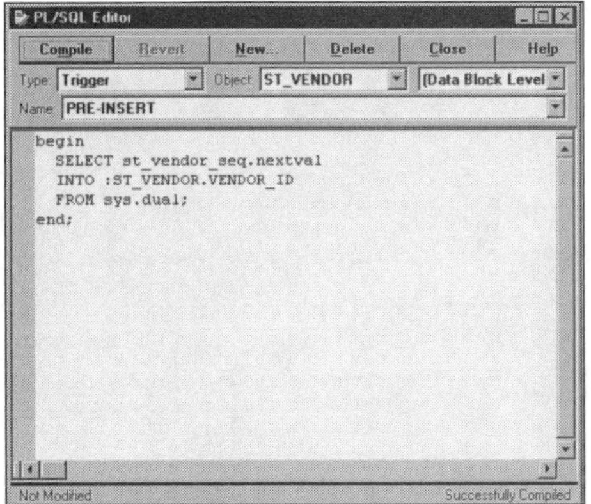

Note

When a form is saved, it is given a file suffix of .fmb, which stands for forms binary file. When a form is compiled, a file is generated with the same name as the save but with a suffix of .fmx. This .fmx file is what the Oracle Developer Forms Runtime program reads and converts to instructions the computer understands. These .fmb and .fmx files are portable across various types of hardware platforms, which makes the Oracle application very portable in the computing environment. Oracle Developer Forms Runtime is coded specifically for these various environments, not the .fmb and .fmx files.

Figure 3.18 shows the newly developed ST_VENDOR form application and puts the cursor in the first enterable field: Vendor ID. The first issue you will discover is that the Vendor ID is a primary key field to the underlying database table ST_VENDOR, so the Layout Wizard made this a mandatory entered field. However, the behavior we want is to enter the other fields and have this field filled in for us from the sequence generator when we click the Save button (the disk icon button on the toolbar). Click the Exit button (the open door on the toolbar) and access the VENDOR_ID Item Property Palette (see Figure 3.19). Find the Required field in the Data section of this palette and change it to No. Because we really do not need to enter this field first, move the item to be the last item in the Item list in the Object Navigator. The field will still appear first onscreen, but the Vendor Name field will now be the field the computer cursor will stop at first. When you return to Runtime by clicking the traffic light, you can enter data, beginning with the Vendor Name field (see Figure 3.20). Notice that the Vendor ID automatically fills in when the Save button is clicked.

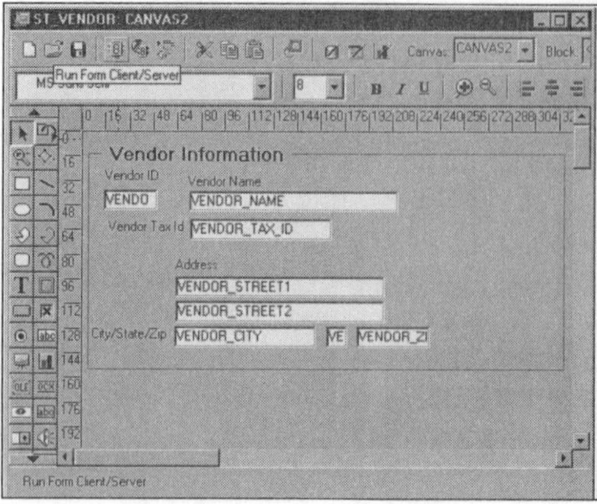

Figure 3.18

Running the ST_Vendor form.

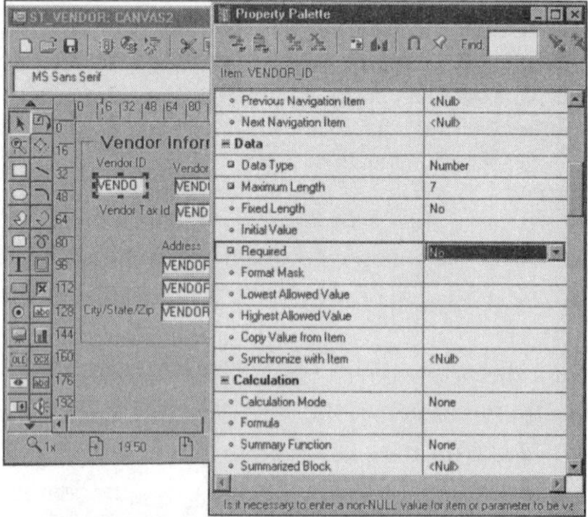

Figure 3.19

The VENDOR_ID Property Palette.

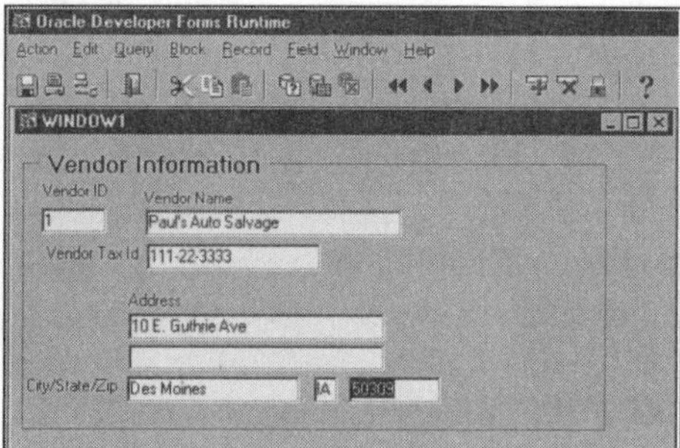

Figure 3.20

ST_Vendor Runtime with data.

Oracle Forms has many features that do not have to be programmed or set up in the Object Navigator. For example, Oracle Forms can enter data, change data, delete data, and query data without having to add any code in the Object Navigator to perform these tasks. The buttons on the toolbar are quite useful as well (see Figure 3.21). Starting from left to right: The disk button is the Save or Commit Records button. The next one to the right is the Print button, and the button next to it is the Printer Setup button. The open-door button is the Forms Exit button. Then you see the Cut, Copy, and Paste buttons (starting with the scissors). The next three buttons are the Query Mode buttons. The first in the trio is Enter Query Mode, the middle one is Execute Query, and the rightmost button of the three is Exit Query Mode. The << button navigates the form to the previous block; the < button positions the cursor at the previous record. The > button is the Next Record button (this button and the Previous Record button are very useful with tabular-type displays where multiple records are displayed onscreen), and the >> button navigates the form to the next block. The + button inserts a record, and the X button deletes a record. The padlock button places an Oracle lock on the record the cursor is in (not allowing others to make changes to this row), and the ? button is the Forms Help button.

Query Mode is a powerful feature. When in Query Mode, one or more fields can be filled in to search for records. Notice in Figure 3.21 that the pattern searching learned in Appendix B, "Learning SQL—A Complete Tutorial," works in Query Mode as well. When the Enter Query button is clicked, only the Execute Query and Exit Query buttons are highlighted. Figure 3.22 shows the results of the query. If no fields were filled in during the Query Mode, Oracle Forms begins returning all the rows from the assigned database table. The < and > buttons are useful for scrolling through the returned rows.

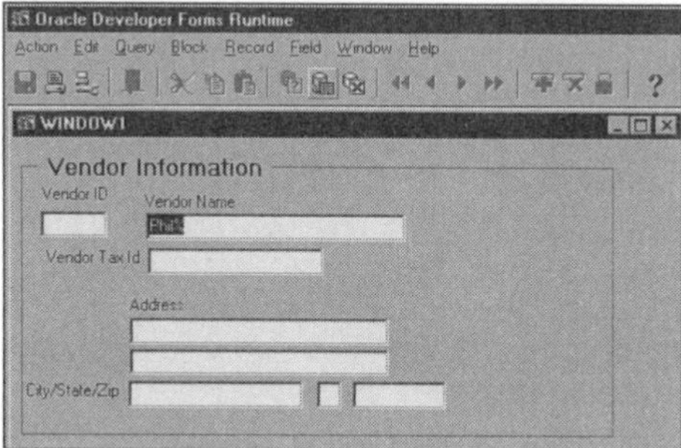

Figure 3.21

Oracle Forms query mode.

Another toolbar exists to the left of the Object Navigator. This toolbar has many of the options in the File menu as well as some useful runtime buttons (see Figure 3.23). The top button on this toolbar, which looks like a white page of paper, is the New Module button. Click this and `MODULE2` appears in Object Navigator, as you see in Figure 3.23. The folder button is the Open Existing Form button, and the disk button is the Save button. The next three buttons deal with the Forms Runtime: the traffic light runs the form in Windows Mode, the traffic light with the globe behind it runs the form in a Web browser (Web Mode), and the button under that one (a yellow bug) is the Forms Runtime in Debug Mode. Next are the Cut-Copy-Paste buttons. After those three is a button with a + and white box, which creates a new item in the Object Navigator (the item is based on where the cursor is in the Object Navigator). The next button, -, deletes the item that is currently highlighted. The +, -, and ++ in boxes (the last three buttons) simulate entering or exiting items in the Object Navigator that have a + or X next to them. If an Object Navigator item has a + next to it, more levels of items exist that can be displayed.

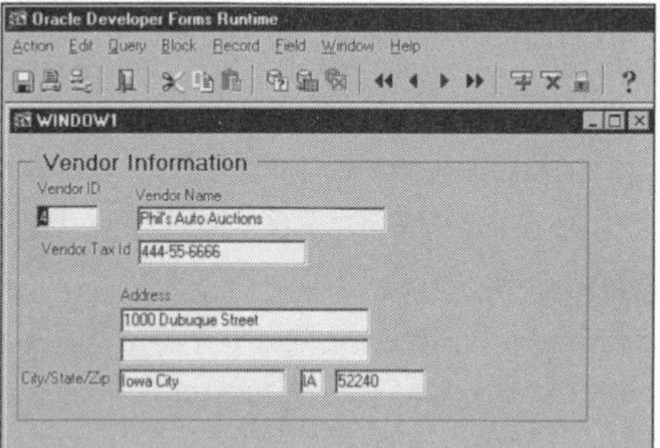

Figure 3.22
Results of the query mode.

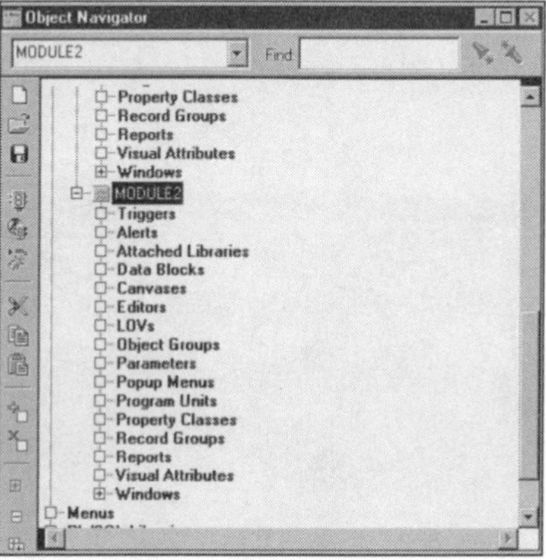

Figure 3.23
New module in Object Navigator.

To start the Data Block Wizard, select Data Block Wizard from the Tools menu. Notice that `MODULE2` is highlighted in the Object Navigator. This is how Form Builder knows to which form to add a data block. Build a block for the database table ST_CUSTOMER using the same options you learned when creating the ST_VENDOR form.

Scroll up in the Object Navigator (or Open the ST_VENDOR form if it is closed) and access the PRE_INSERT trigger we created in ST_VENDOR. Click the Copy button on the toolbar, scroll down to MODULE2, and click the Paste button. This should copy the trigger from the previous form to this new form. Double-click the new trigger and change it so that this trigger accesses the customer sequence and CUSTOMER_ID items instead of the vendor sequence and the VENDOR_ID item (see Figure 3.24). Save this new form as ST_CUSTOMER and try it out.

Figure 3.24

Editing the PL/SQL trigger from ST_VENDOR.

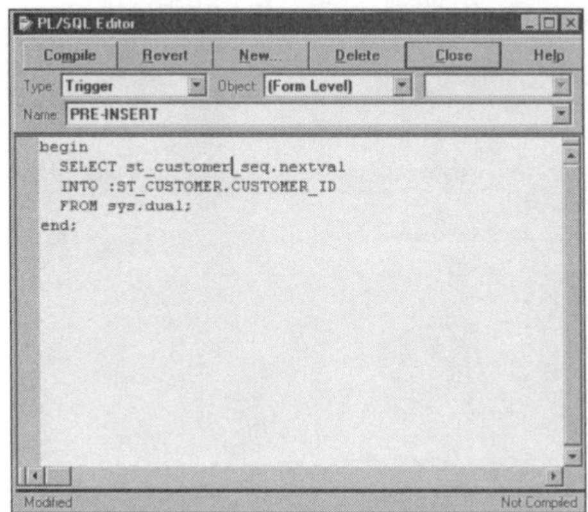

Let's build a tabular-type form. First, we need to create a new module in the Object Navigator and start the Data Block Wizard. The database table will be ST_DEPARTMENTS (see Figure 3.25). On the screen that follows, be sure to select the Tabular Style radio button this time. Figure 3.26 shows how to configure the number of rows displayed as well as how to select a scrollbar that will provide easy access to additional records not displayed when in Query Mode. Figure 3.27 shows what the default canvas layout looks like. Save this module as ST_DEPARTMENTS.

Figure 3.25

The Data Block Wizard for ST_DEPARTMENTS.

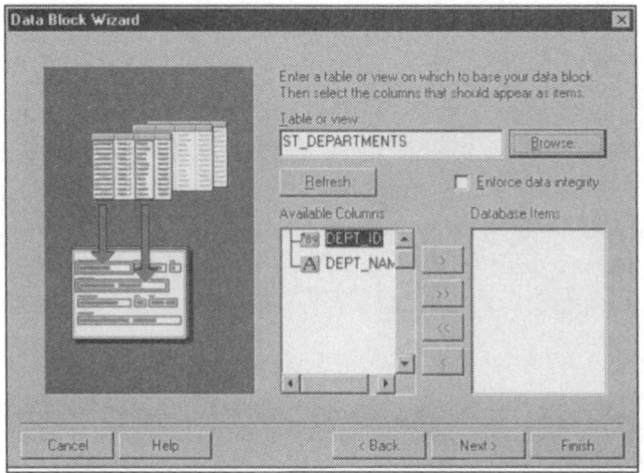

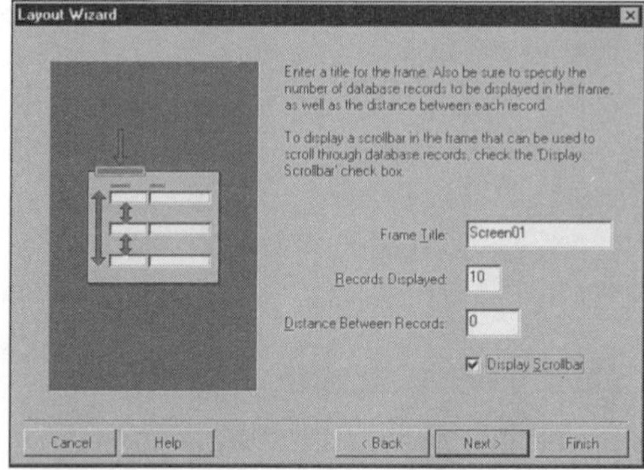

Figure 3.26

Layout Wizard rows displayed.

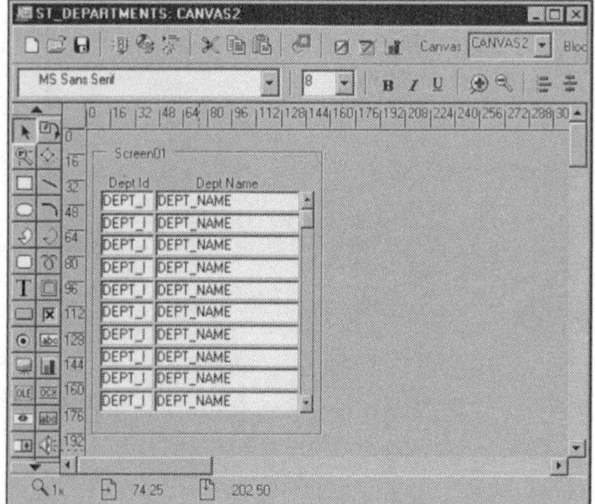

Figure 3.27

Module ST_DEPARTMENTS canvas layout.

Be sure you create the PRE-INSERT trigger for the database sequence. Your Runtime screen with data should look similar to the left screen in Figure 3.28. The ST_JOBS application has the same features as ST_DEPARTMENTS; we now need to build this form, as well as access the ST_JOB_DESCRIPTIONS database table. The completed form should look similar to the right screen in Figure 3.28.

The Que companion Web site for this book at `www.quepublishing.com` contains all the examples, installation scripts, and data illustrated in this book. Appendix A, "Installation and Configuration of Oracle8i NT-Based Software," contains the instructions necessary to retrieve the book examples and the software products used throughout this book.

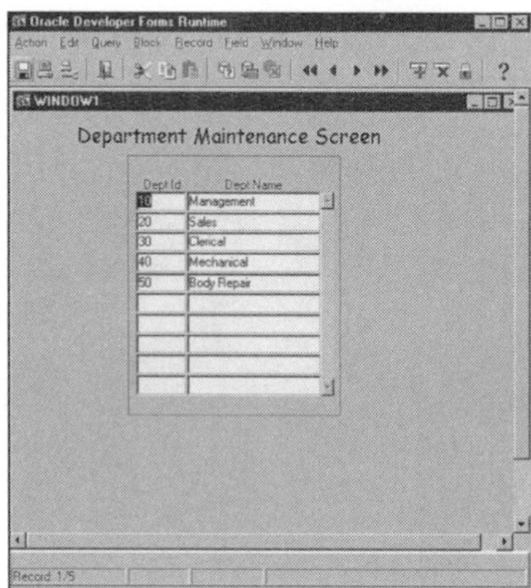

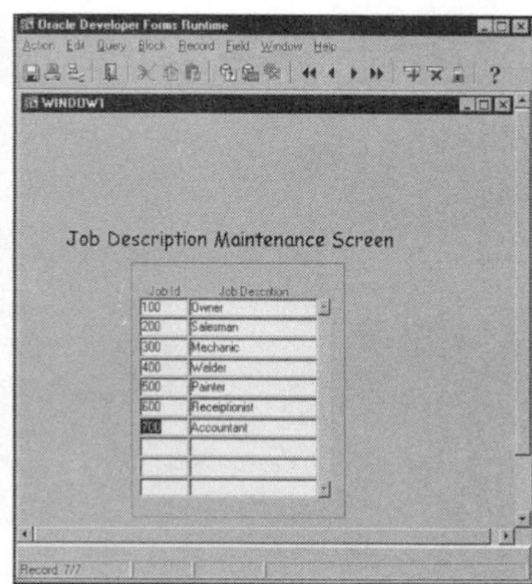

Figure 3.28

ST_DEPARTMENTS and ST_JOB_DESCRIPTIONS runtime with entered data.

The next application uses a tab-type canvas style. This application, ST_TYPE_MAKE_MODEL, will be a table-maintenance application that is used just to maintain the records in the following three tables: ST_INV_TYPE, ST_INV_MAKE, and ST_INV_MODEL. These tables will become LOVs in our final forms-based application example. This application could easily be three separate forms-type programs because each of the tabs will be unrelated to any of the other tabs. This is probably not the best use of a tab-type application, but it works as an example.

Now, let's create a new module in the Object Navigator and run the Data Block Wizard for database table ST_INV_TPYE. In the Layout Wizard, select Tab type canvas in the second window. This will create a default canvas display similar to the one shown in Figure 3.29. Start the Data Block Wizard again for ST_INV_MAKE (see Figure 3.30). Because another table is being added to the same form, the Data Block Wizard is smart enough to know that a relationship might be necessary between this block and the ST_INV_TYPE block just added. However, for this application, no such relationship exists, so you can leave the fields blank.

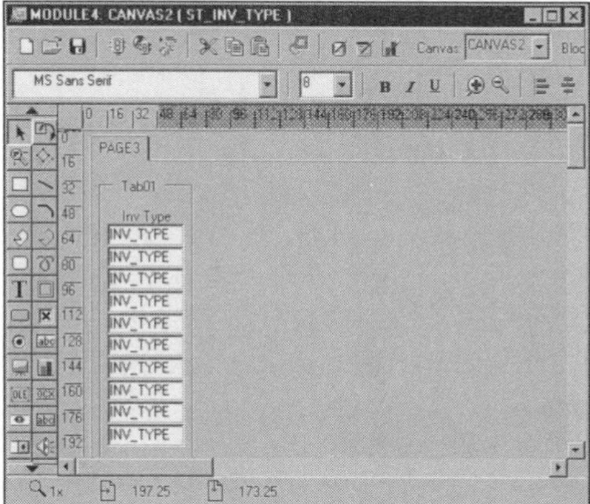

Figure 3.29

Canvas layout ST_INV_TYPE tab.

Figure 3.30

The Data Block Wizard for ST_INV_MAKE.

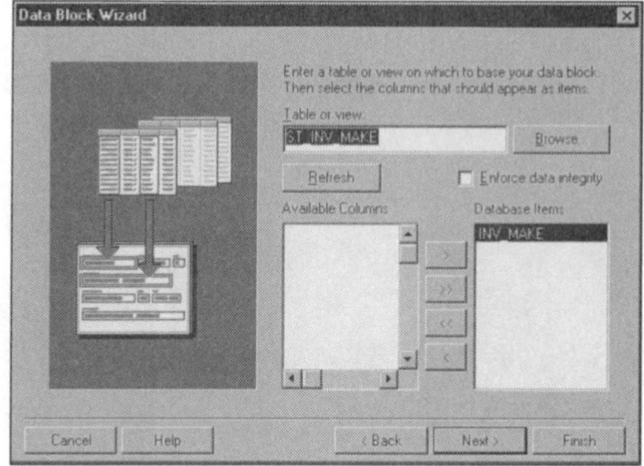

Once again, the Layout Wizard is smart enough to see that we are building a tab-type application and appropriately takes the correct defaults (see Figure 3.31). Figure 3.32 shows what the canvas now looks like with the two tabs on the canvas. No sequences are involved with these three database tables. Following the process just outlined for the ST_INV_MODEL table, change the tab headings in the property palette or on the canvas, which should cause your application to look similar to Figure 3.33.

Figure 3.31

The Data Block Wizard screen to create relationships.

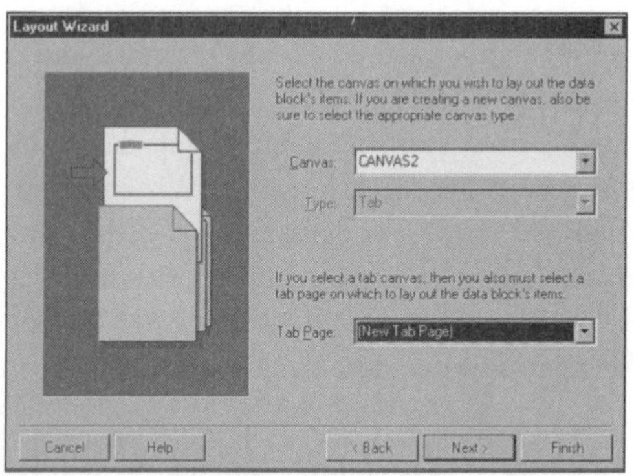

Our ST_STAFF application will build on the forms-style application you have already learned. It will introduce how to set up the LOVs on a particular screen item. To get started, let's create a new module and go through the Data Block Wizard (for the ST_STAFF database object) and Layout Wizard (forms-based, single-row-displayed style). Save this new application with the name ST_STAFF. Your newly created form should look similar to Figure 3.34. As you can see in Figure 3.34, you can add an LOV when you select the LOV Wizard from the Tools item on the top menu bar.

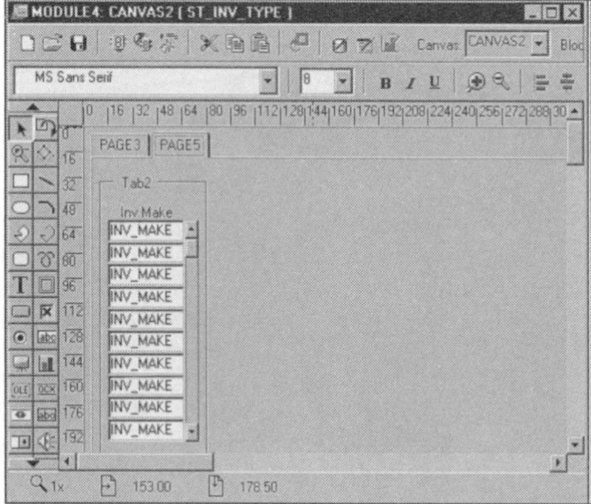

Figure 3.32

Layout Wizard with new canvas tab.

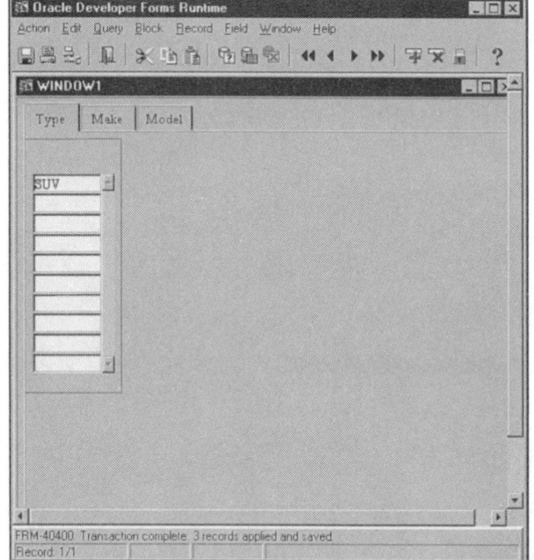

Figure 3.33

ST_TYPE_MAKE_MODEL runtime with entered data.

When you work with the LOV Wizard, ensure that the radio button New Record Group Based on a Query is selected and click Next. This accesses the Query Builder, prompting you to select a table from a list (see Figure 3.35). Click the Include button, and a check box of items to display will appear (see Figure 3.36). Click both items for this application and then click OK. Figure 3.37 shows how the LOV Wizard is filled in with the newly built query.

Figure 3.34

LOV Wizard access on ST_STAFF application.

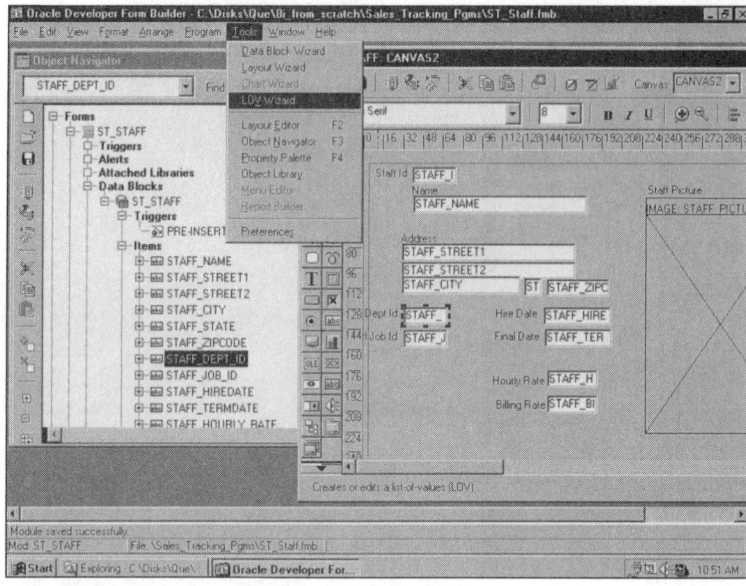

Figure 3.35

Select a database table.

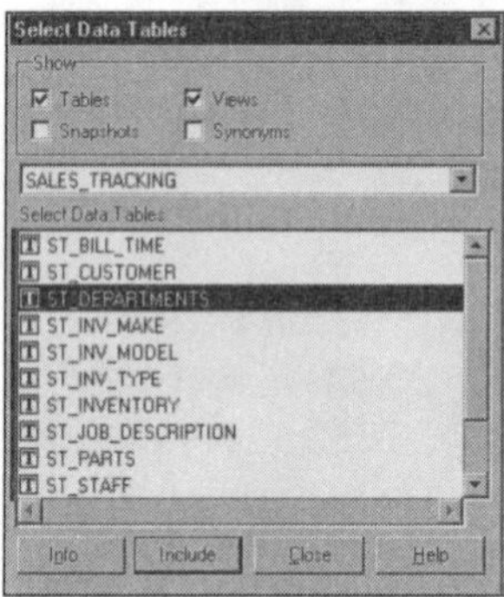

Figure 3.36

The Select Display Items pop-up menu.

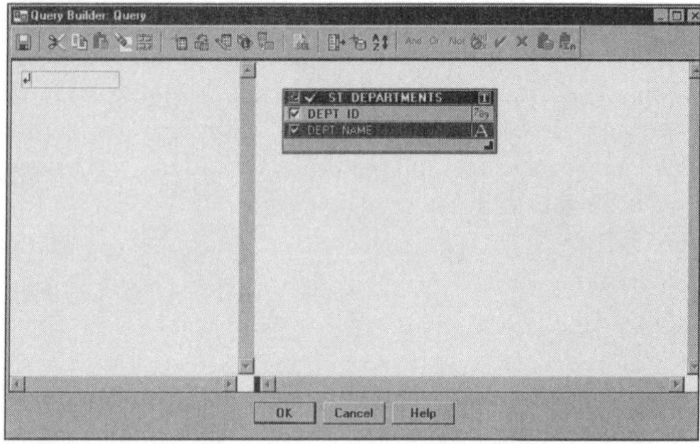

Figure 3.37

The LOV Wizard with a newly built query.

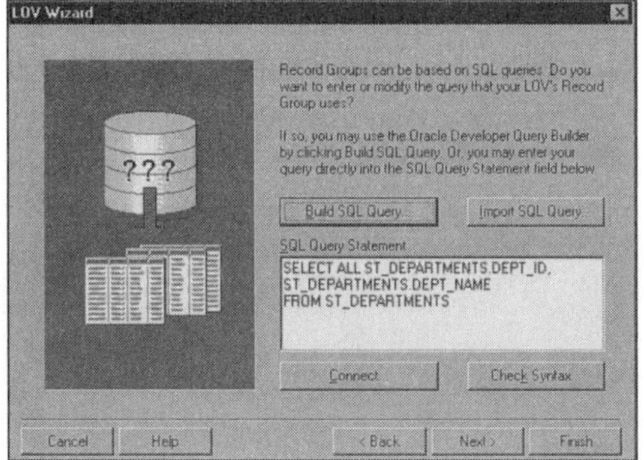

As you can see in Figure 3.38, you should select the items for display in the LOV from the assigned query that we just built. Select both columns by clicking the >> button. This will bring up the LOV Wizard Column Properties screen (see Figure 3.39). Be sure you click Look up return item because doing so generates the Items and Parameters box. This selection shows which field from the database table assigned to the LOV will be passed back to the assigned application item. Select the ST_STAFF.STAFF_DEPT_ID item from this list and click the Next button. This brings up an LOV Wizard screen where you choose how many database rows to display in the LOV (see Figure 3.40). Enter 20 and click Refresh record group data before displaying LOV. This feature reruns the query to ensure the most current values appear onscreen from the LOV. Finally, click Next.

Figure 3.38

LOV Wizard display columns.

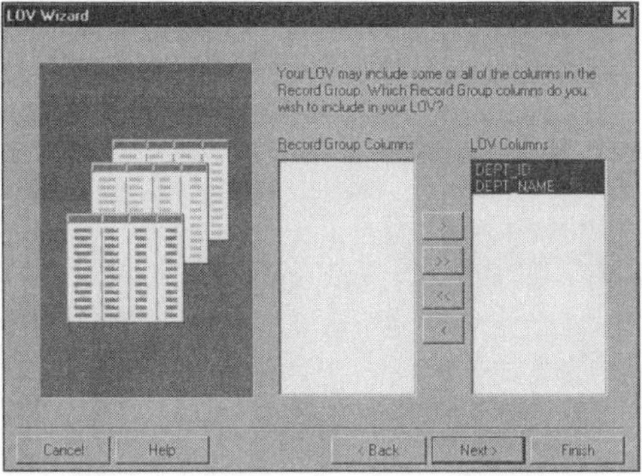

Figure 3.41 shows the last LOV Wizard screen, which will enable you to select a screen item for the return value you selected in Figure 3.39. Select the STAFF_DEPT_ID item from the list with either the > or >> button. Click Next or Finish because the only screen left is the final LOV Wizard screen. Figure 3.42 shows how the new LOV appears in the ST_STAFF_ID Property Palette. To access the LOV

from the Oracle Forms Runtime of ST_STAFF, select Display List from the Runtime Edit menu. Figure 3.41 shows what the LOV looks like.

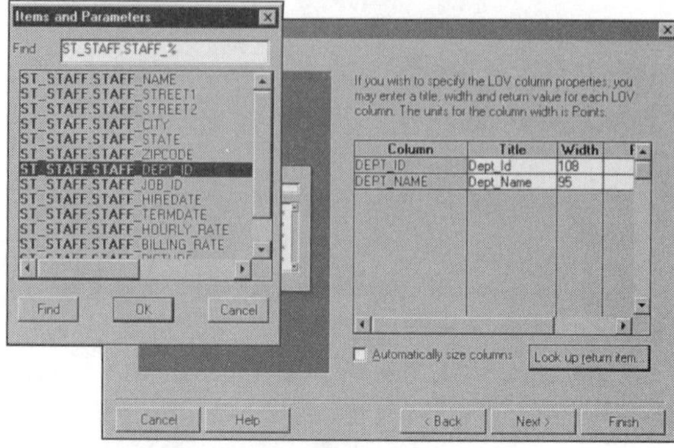

Figure 3.39

LOV Wizard return items.

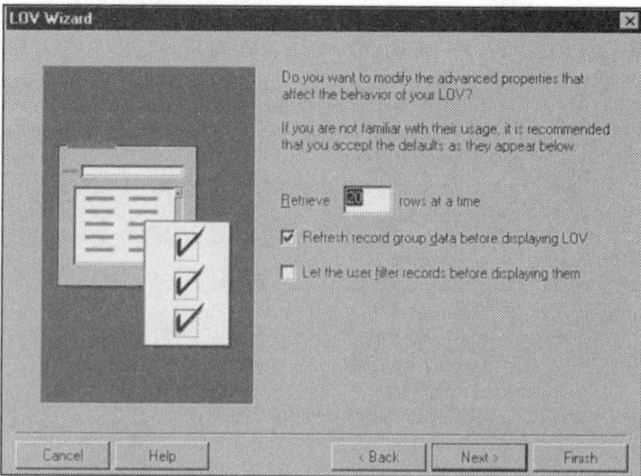

Figure 3.40

LOV Wizard for rows to display.

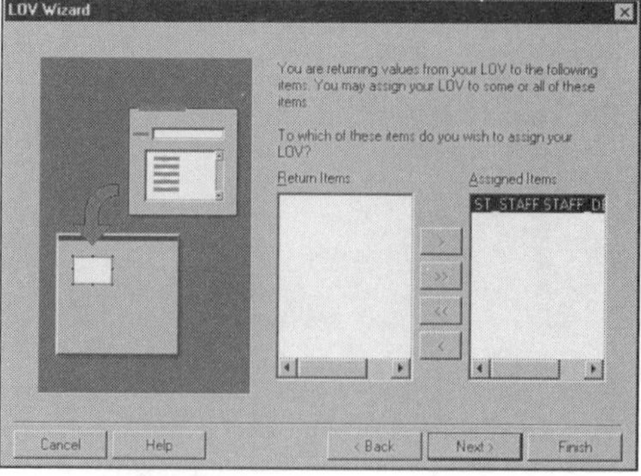

Figure 3.41

LOV Wizard returned value screen item assignment.

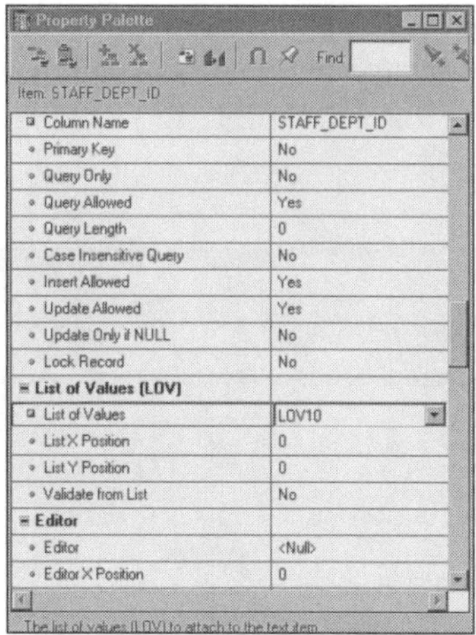

Figure 3.42

STAFF_ID Property Palette showing LOV assignment.

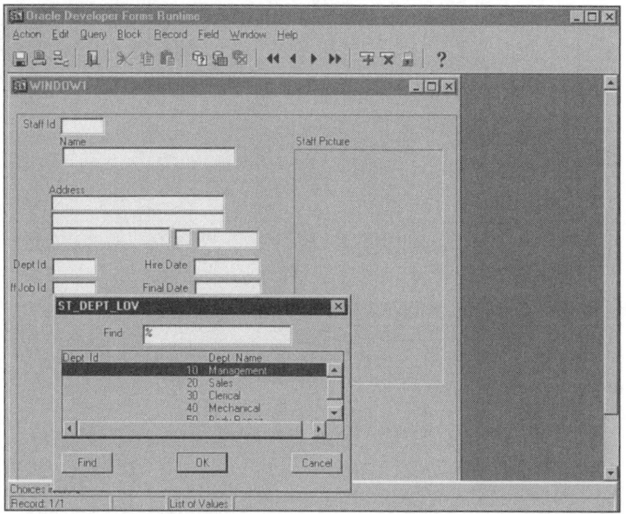

Figure 3.43

LOV in the forms run-time of ST_STAFF.

It is much more convenient for the person using the application to activate the LOV when a button is assigned to access the LOV. The presence of this button indicates to the user that more information is available for this field by clicking the button. The Button tool is the rectangular item just under the T (Text Item) on the left toolbar on the canvas layout screen (see Figure 3.44). This button item is automatically assigned a name. In addition, it is always recommended that you change the name of these buttons to reflect the nature of the buttons. Right-click the new button item in the Object Navigator and add a WHEN-MOUSE_CLICK trigger. The only contents of this trigger is to call the LIST_VALUES key built-in (see Figure 3.45). A built-in function is also available that replicates any key or menu item function in the Forms environment. This particular function runs when the WHEN-MOUSE-CLICK trigger fires and has the same functionality as calling the LOV from the menu bar. Figure 3.45 also shows the ST_DEPT_LOV being displayed after the button is clicked.

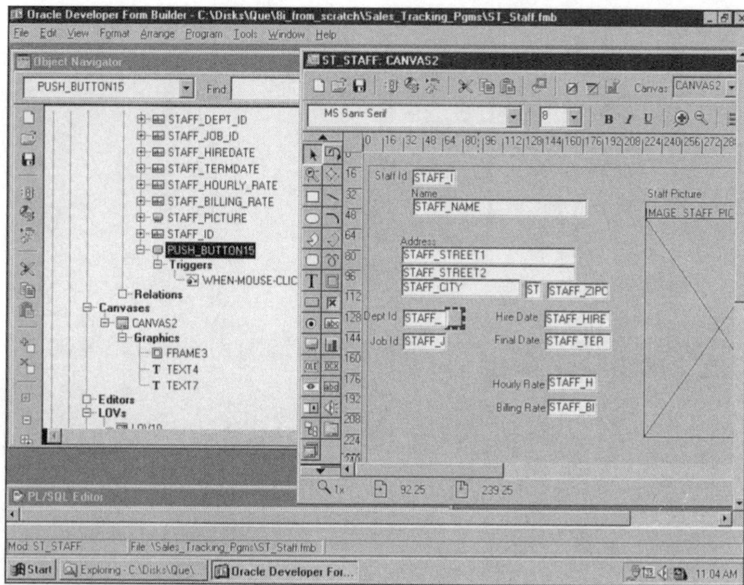

Figure 3.44

Adding a push button for the LOV.

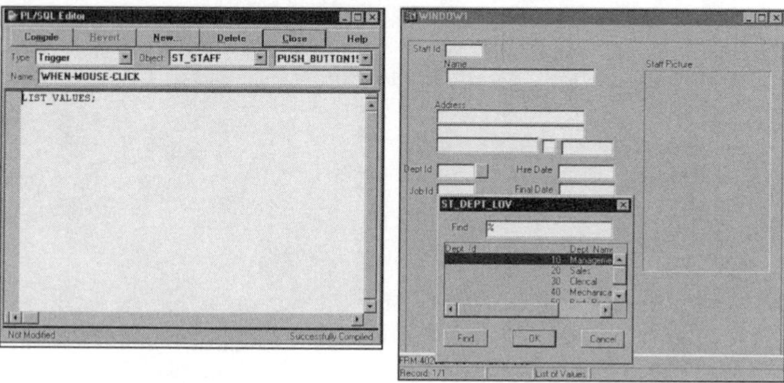

Figure 3.45

Continuing the process of adding a push button for the LOV.

In most cases, it is desirable to edit or verify that the data entered into a particular field is valid data. The Item Property Palette is a useful place to ensure that if a field is to contain a number, only numbers can be entered. This again is the default behavior of Forms Runtime, which verifies that information entered into a field matches the assigned attributes of that field. When the data in a field can be checked for particular content (all uppercase, containing a certain range of numbers or dates, and so on) or to ensure that it's a valid entry in a database table, a PL/SQL trigger must be coded to check for the particular attributes or existence of a row. The WHEN-VALIDATE-ITEM trigger, if defined, runs when the cursor attempts to leave the forms item to which the trigger is assigned. Figure 3.46 shows how to add this trigger, accessing it by right-clicking STAFF_DEPT_ID and selecting the Smart Triggers menu item. The Smart Triggers menu item contains the commonly used triggers for the particular part of the Object Navigator being accessed. For example, a different list of Smart Triggers will be at the block and form levels of a form. Figure 3.47 shows the PL/SQL and SQL code necessary to check to see whether the STAFF_DEPT_ID item exists in the ST_DEPARTMENTS table. Notice several of the PL/SQL techniques that are discussed in Appendix C at work here, such as the variable naming convention, the `%TYPE`, and so on. The RAISE Form-Trigger-Failure returns a failure to the form from this trigger, thus displaying the message in the `EXCEPTIONS` clause. Notice in Figure 3.47 that an invalid entry of 5000 was entered and indeed the message that was coded in the trigger is the message that appears at the bottom of the screen. The cursor will not be able to move from this field until a valid entry is made.

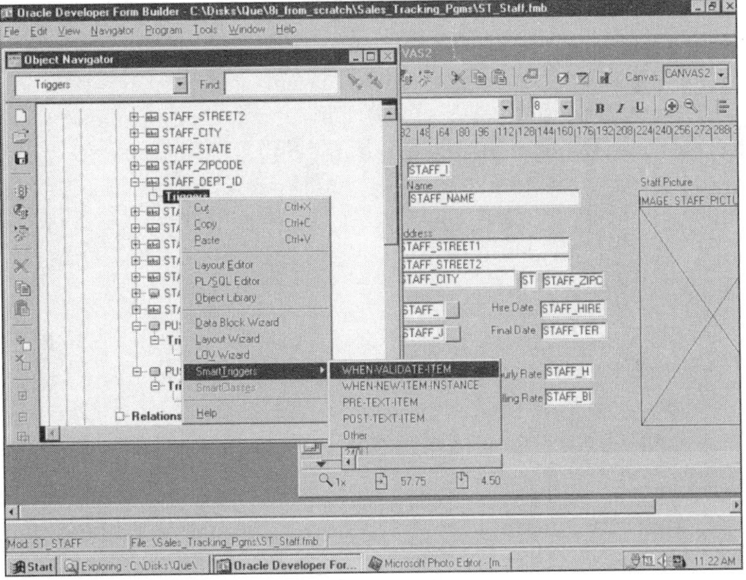

Figure 3.46

Adding the WHEN-VALIDATE-ITEM trigger.

Add a button for the Job ID item to access the LOV for that item. Also add a WHEN-VALIDATE-ITEM trigger to verify the contents of the Job ID item with that of the ST_JOB_DESCRIPTION database table.

Figure 3.47

The WHEN-VALIDATE-ITEM trigger code.

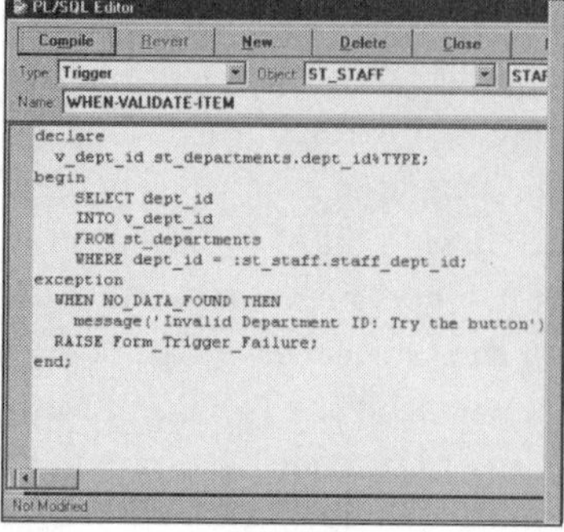

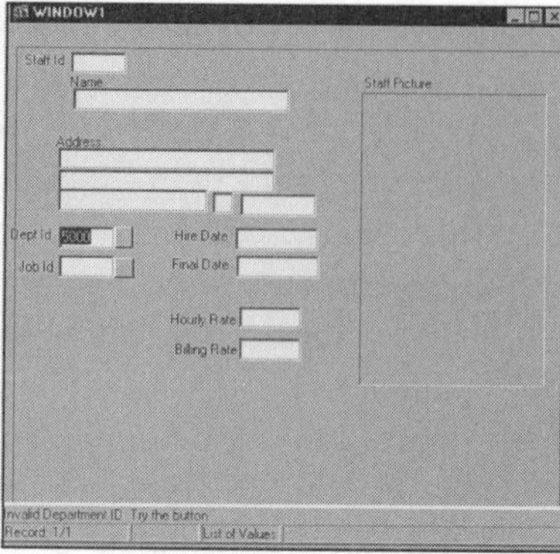

As we enter a new area of development in our project, you'll see that the ST_STAFF application makes reference to a picture field. This was defined at the database level as a binary long object (BLOB). The property palette for this particular item contains options to the various types of BLOBs, such as video, sound streams, and so on. To store a picture in the database, we will use the Windows cut/paste edit features to accomplish putting the picture in the application. Access the picture via a Windows program such as Paintbrush or Microsoft Photo Editor (see Figure 3.48). Two methods of copying this picture are available: You can either click Edit on the top menu bar and select Copy, or some programs will allow a right-click to access the Edit menu (and then select Copy). This copies the image into a work area in the Windows operating system. In the ST_STAFF application, click the picture object one time (the gray box under Staff Picture in Figure 3.49), click Edit on the top menu bar, and then click Paste. The picture from the Windows program should now appear in the Staff Picture box (see Figure 3.50). Click the Save button to commit this record to the database.

Build the ST_BILL_TIME application based on the ST_BILL_TIME table; do not display the four audit fields (INSERT_USER, INSERT_DATE, and so on). Display ten records on the canvas with a scrollbar on the right. Be sure to save your work with Save As from the File menu and name the form ST_BILL_TIME.

Sometimes displayed items are not associated with a block, such as totals. In addition, sometimes it's convenient to add buttons to help the application user with tasks such as adding up a column of numbers just entered and saving records to the database. It is good design to limit the mouse movements within an application.

As you have learned, all form items are associated with a block. And blocks so far have always been associated with a database table. However, a *control* block is a form block that is not based on a database table. This control block is where total fields are placed and is a convenient place for buttons, hidden fields (often used to hold variables), or any item that is not to be associated with a data block.

Figure 3.48

Access the picture via a Windows application.

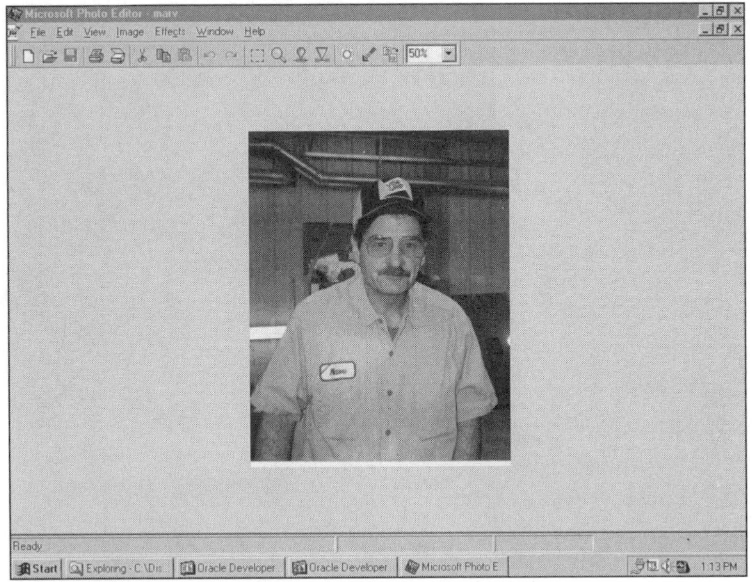

Figure 3.49

Paste the picture into the ST_STAFF picture item.

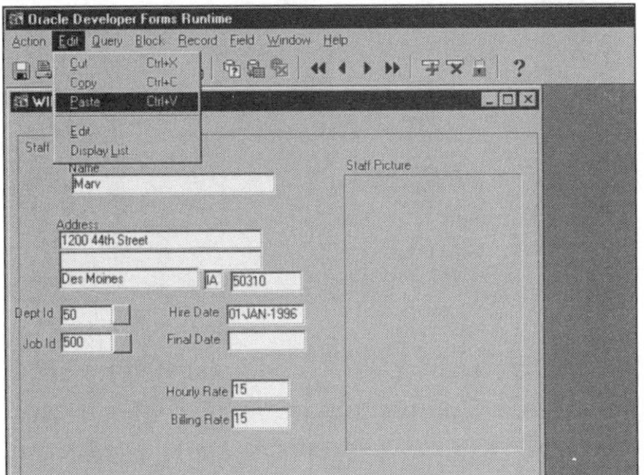

Add a new block to the ST_BILL_TIME application by first clicking the Data Blocks label in the Object Navigator and then clicking the green + on the toolbar along the left side of the Object Navigator. This will bring up a New Data Block box (see Figure 3.51). Check the Build a new data block manually radio button and click OK. Access the New Blocks Property Palette by double-clicking the block item (or right-click the block item and select Property Palette with a click) and then name the block Control Block, ensuring the Database Data Block item under Database is set to No.

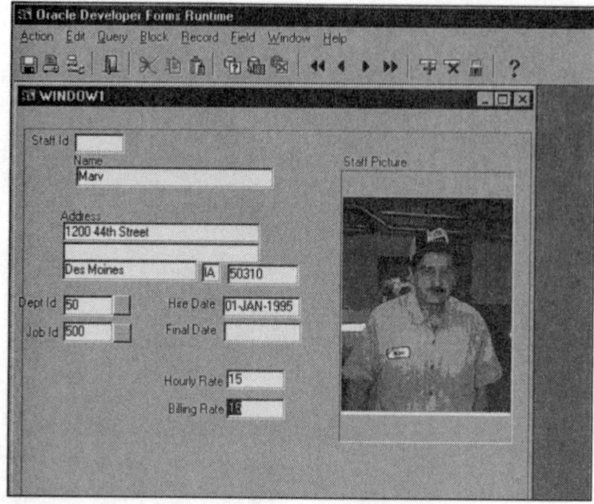

Figure 3.50

ST_STAFF data with the picture object.

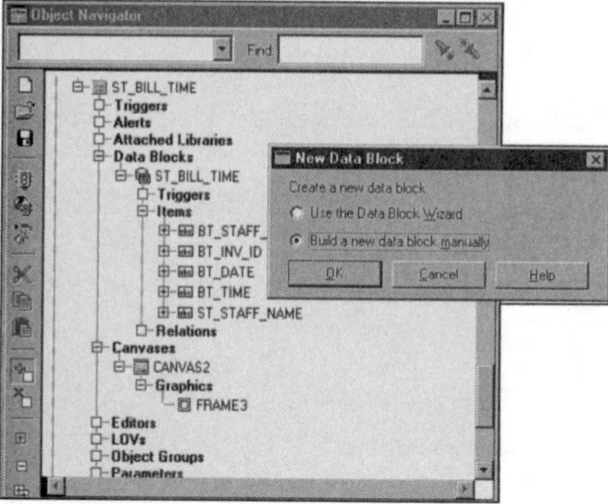

Figure 3.51

Adding a control block.

Blocks assigned to a database table have the inherited functionality of Insert, Update, Delete, and Query Mode features. Anything that happens to a control block must be specifically set up. The requirement for ST_BILL_TIME is to provide an easy method for the user to ensure the time entered adds up to 40. An item will need to be added to the control block to hold this calculation, as well as a button added for the user to click when this calculation is to occur. It would also be nice to add a Save Records button so the user does not have to move the mouse from the bottom of the form to the top of the form just to save the work performed.

Click the control block in the Object Navigator and then click the Text Item tool (T in the canvas tool palette) and create the text item exactly under the BT_TIME column of the tabular database item (see Figure 3.52). Clicking the control block first will ensure that the new text item gets created in the control block. Use the Button tool to add two buttons, as illustrated in Figure 3.53.

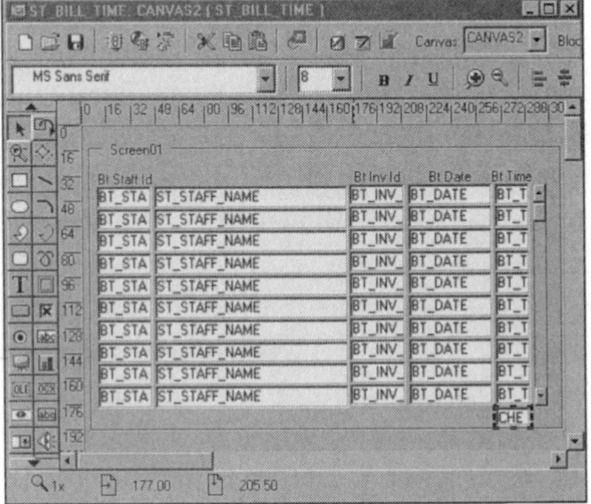

Figure 3.52

Adding a text item to the control block.

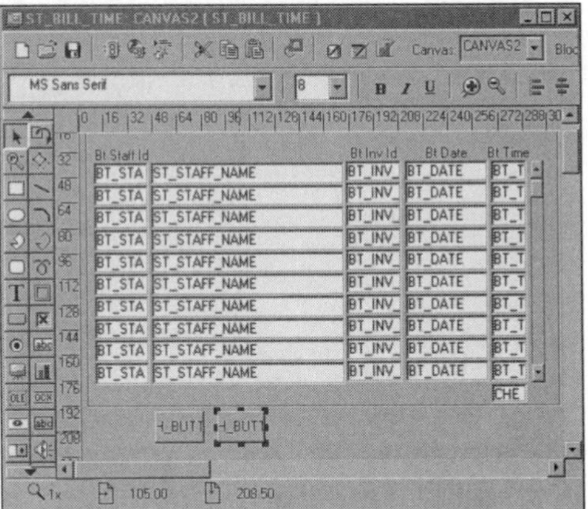

Figure 3.53

Add two additional buttons to the control block.

The desired behavior in this example is to access each row of the ST_BILL_TIME data block, add the contents to a field on the control block named CHECK_TIME, and perform this task repeatedly for each row that appears onscreen. This can be accomplished with a series of PRE and POST item triggers on the ST_BILL_TIME item, or this task can be accomplished by clicking a button and having a trigger loop through the records and perform the calculations. This method is more accurate and dependable because of adding records and deleting records. This method will add only those records that are currently being displayed.

Built-in sub-programs exist for all the keystrokes available in Forms (see the built-ins overview in the online help). You might want to review all the built-ins available for use within the Forms development environment.

The logic to perform the field additions is illustrated in Figure 3.54. This logic will be assigned to a WHEN-BUTTON-PRESSED trigger to the first button on the Control Panel. Change the label on this button to Check Time. Notice the use of built-ins: GO_BLOCK, FIRST_RECORD, and NEXT_RECORD. GO_BLOCK goes to the named block as if you were using the >> and << keys. The FIRST_RECORD built-in positions the cursor at the first record of the block. Finally, NEXT_RECORD in the loop is similar to clicking the > key. The `:system.last_record` gets set when the last record of the form has been accessed. The logic now resides all in a single PL/SQL trigger and is easy to follow. The property palette in Figure 3.54 illustrates the CHECK_TIME item on the CONTROL_BLOCK. Also notice in the figure the Data section where Data Type is set to a number and the Maximum Length is set to 4.

Figure 3.54

Adding up the BT_TIME field.

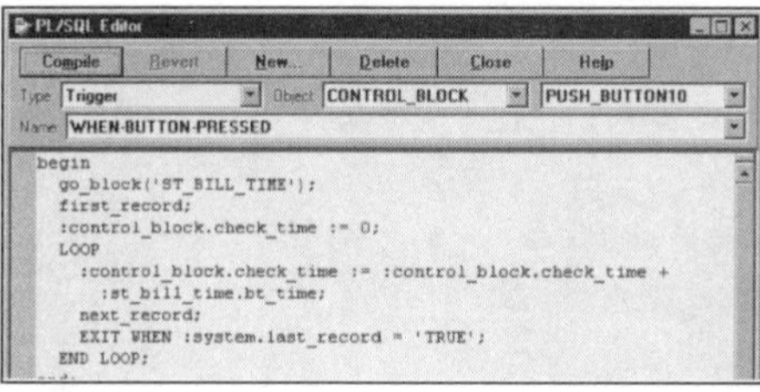

Numerous ways exist to populate display items with information from blocks, default dates or entries, and so on. Figure 3.55 is a version of the WHEN-VALIDATE-ITEM seen previously in Figure 3.47. Notice the difference. Instead of just checking that the displayed item is in a database table, Figure 3.55 populates the ST_STAFF_NAME item when the ST_STAFF_ID is being validated; otherwise, an error message is returned. Figure 3.56 is a way of populating a field with the default date. Notice that the PRE-TEXT-ITEM trigger will fire before the cursor is placed in the field. This puts the default date into the field but enables the application user to change the date if so desired.

Figure 3.57 illustrates all the work performed on the ST_BILL_TIME application. The staff member's name automatically fills in, as well as the current date. Notice that the Time does not add correctly; 45 would be the correct answer. To restart the ST_BILL_TIME application in Forms Debug Mode, click Program from the menu, choose Run From, and click Debug. This mode enables you to see what variables are set to, as well as watch the trigger activity (see Figure 3.58).

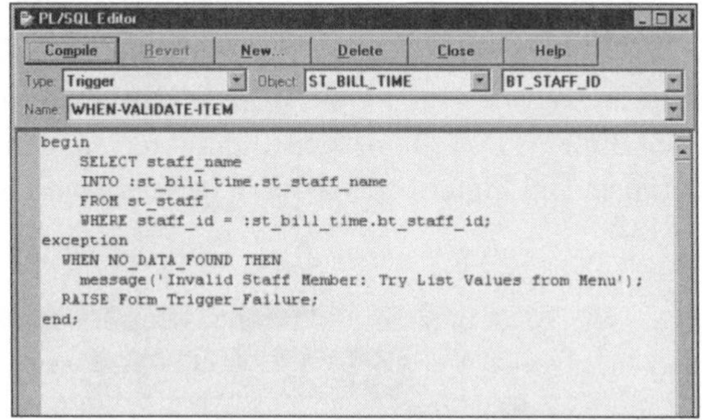

Figure 3.55

BT_STAFF_ID item WHEN-VALIDATE-ITEM trigger.

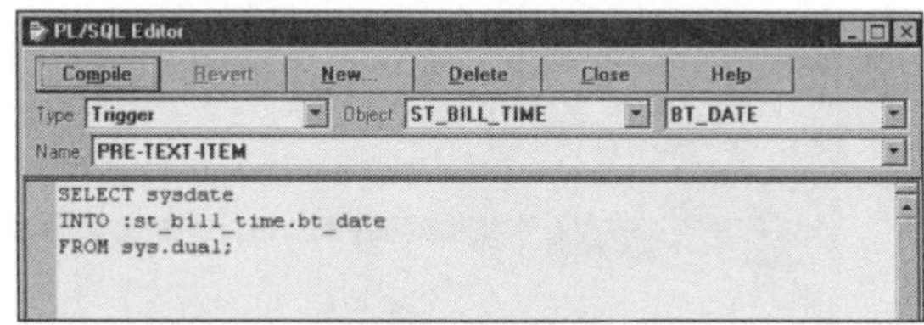

Figure 3.56

BT_DATE item PRE-TEXT-ITEM trigger.

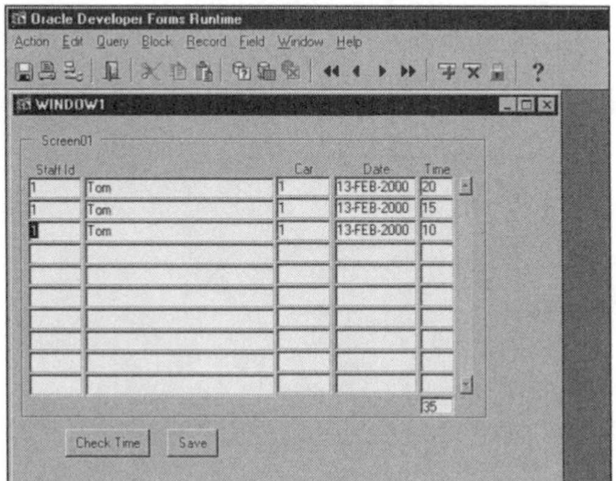

Figure 3.57

ST_BILL_TIME application with an addition error.

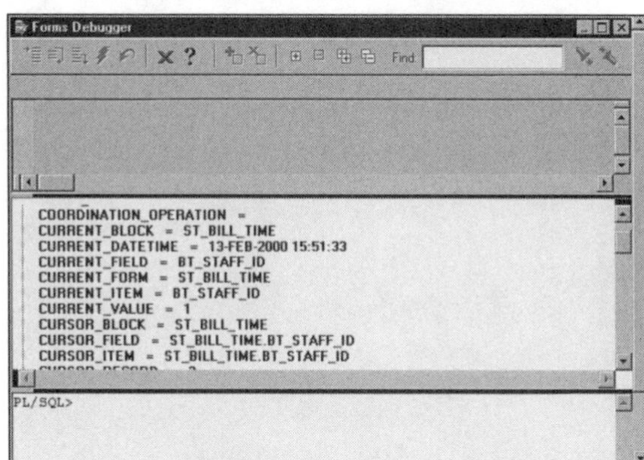

Figure 3.58

Debug Mode information.

Notice the code inside the loop in Figure 3.59. The CHECK_TIME field is accumulated at the beginning of the loop, the next record is incremented, and—if this happens to be the last record—the loop is exited. The last record displayed never got added into the CHECK_TIME item. The highlighted code in Figure 3.59 shows how to fix the trigger, and Figure 3.60 shows a perfectly working ST_BILL_TIME application.

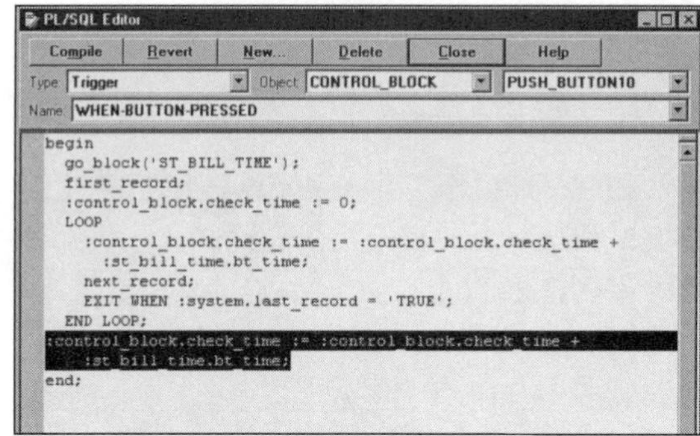

Figure 3.59

Editing the WHEN-BUTTON-PRESSED trigger.

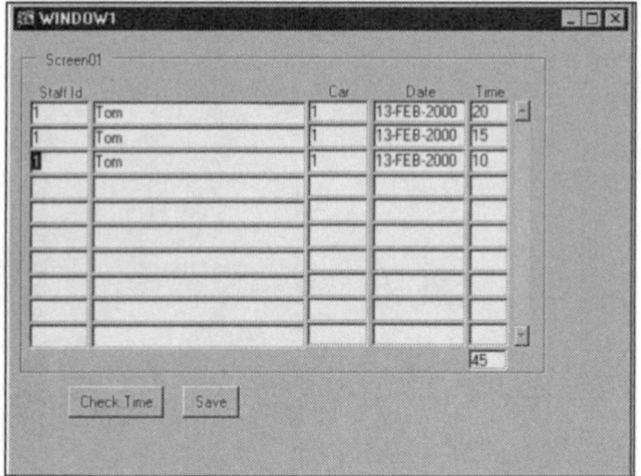

Figure 3.60

ST_BILL_TIME application working correctly.

So far we have discussed how to create all the supporting applications to the main ST_INVENTORY application. Figures 3.61–3.64 illustrate the four tabs of the ST_INVENTORY application. This tab-type application is still based on a single block but has related information grouped together on each tab page. Figure 3.61 utilizes radio buttons for the automobile color, whereas Figure 3.64 uses a database function to calculate the final profit/loss total.

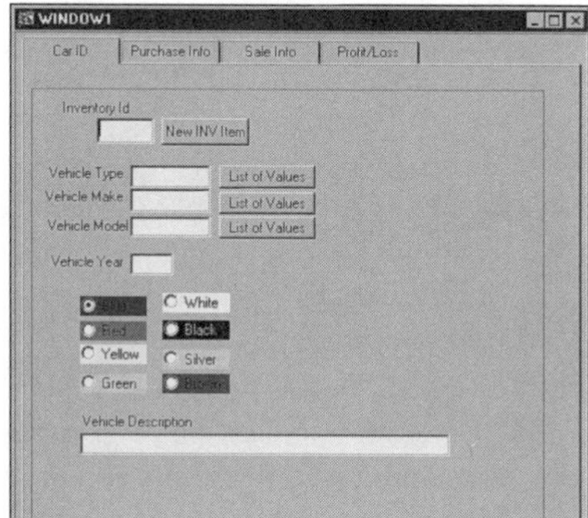

Figure 3.61

ST_INVENTORY application Car ID tab.

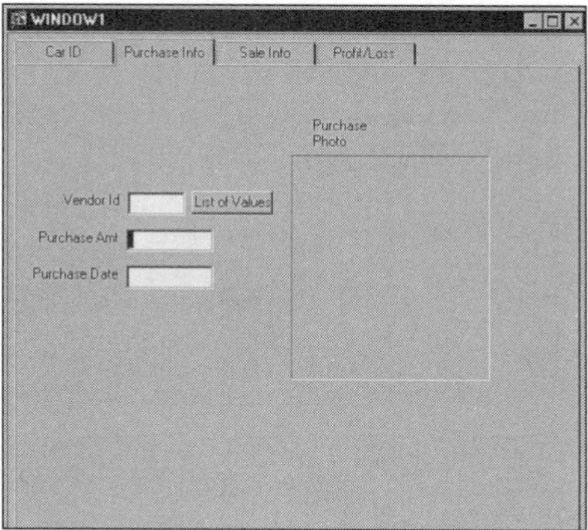

Figure 3.62

ST_INVENTORY application Purchase Info tab.

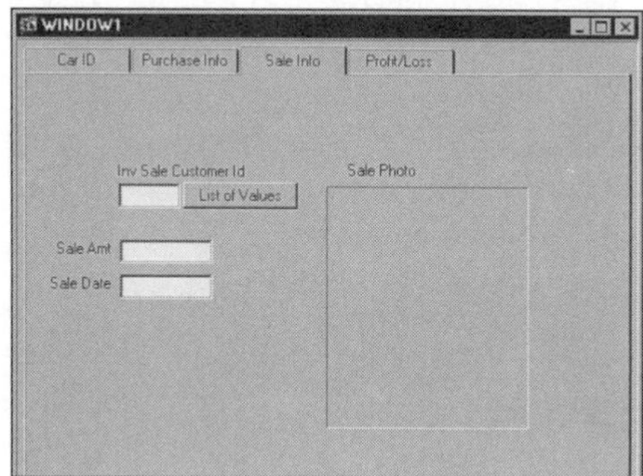

Figure 3.63

ST_INVENTORY application Sale Info tab.

3

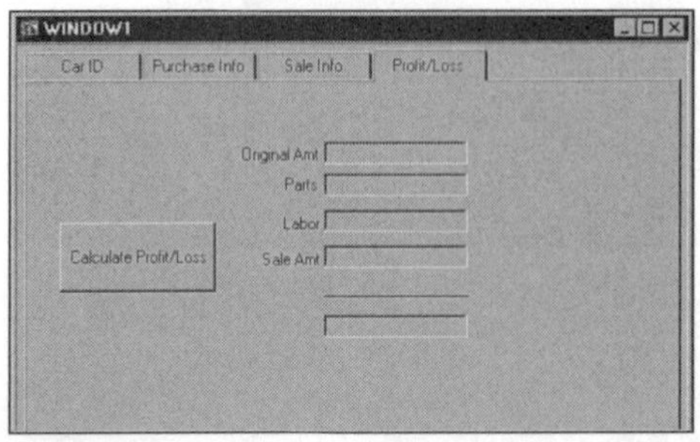

Figure 3.64
ST_INVENTORY application Profit/Loss tab.

Begin building the ST_INVENTORY application by creating a tab canvas and placing all the ST_INVENTORY fields on this first tab, except for the four maintenance fields (INV_INSERT_USER, INV_INSERT_DATE, and so on). Use the Layout Wizard to create the other three tabs, but do not assign any fields to them in the Layout Wizard. You can highlight several items at a time by holding down the Shift key while clicking items. Use the Edit and Cut menu items on the top toolbar to remove the items from the first tab canvas and move them to the other canvases. Add the New INV Item button; its WHEN-BUTTON-PRESSED trigger should receive the next sequence number from the ST_INV_SEQUENCE generator. Add LOVs to the following: INV_TYPE (Vehicle Type), INV_MAKE (Vehicle Make), INV_MODEL (Vehicle Model), INV_PURCHASE_VENDOR_ID (Vendor ID, Purchase Info tab), and INV_SALE_CUSTOMER_ID (Inv Sale Customer ID, Sale Info tab).

Figure 3.65 shows how to change the INV_COLOR item from a text item to a radio group (Item Type on the property palette). Notice the Initial Value on this same property palette. Be sure the INV_COLOR item is highlighted in the Object Navigator so that the radio buttons will be created and assigned to this item. On the tab canvas, add eight radio buttons using the radio button on the canvas tool palette, and use Tools, Align Objects (from the top menu bar) to align the radio buttons with one another (see Figure 3.66). Use the Item Property Palette for each radio button to change its name and label to the color, to change its default value to the color, and to change its background color to be the color it is representing.

Figure 3.64 could easily be a control block because none of these fields are derived from the database. The Original Amt and Sale Amt are copied or synchronized with other items from this same form (INV_PURCHASE_AMT item and INV_SALE_AMT). This is accomplished by placing the fields with which to synchronize these in the Synchronize with Item window. Then, on each item's property palette, you must name the block item from which to perform the copying. Figure 3.67 illustrates the Calculate Profit/Loss WHEN-BUTTON-PRESSED trigger. Two SQL queries exist to populate the parts cost and the labor cost items; notice the use of the `SUM` SQL function. The total easily could have been derived with a simple calculation statement (this calculation is commented out in the trigger), but the `ST_CALC_PROFIT` function will be used instead. This will show how to incorporate a function into a form. Using PL/SQL functions and procedures enables the reuse of code. For example, the `ST_CALC_PROFIT` function could be used in reports as well. Notice how the PL_TOTAL item is populated with the return value from the function. Also notice that the function calls for an input variable, INVENTORY_ID, and that the INV_ID from the first tab is passed to the function.

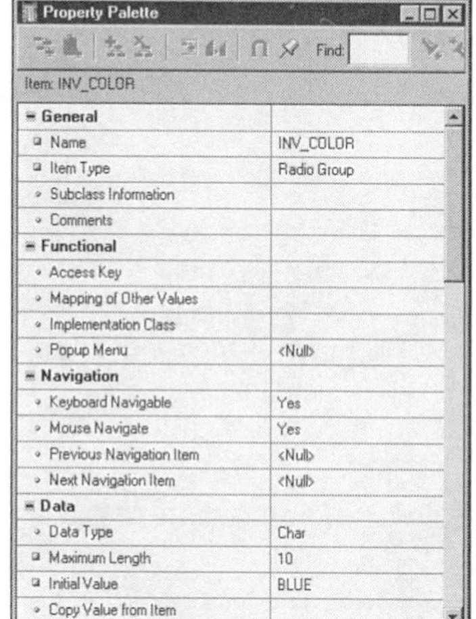

Figure 3.65

INV_COLOR item radio group property palette.

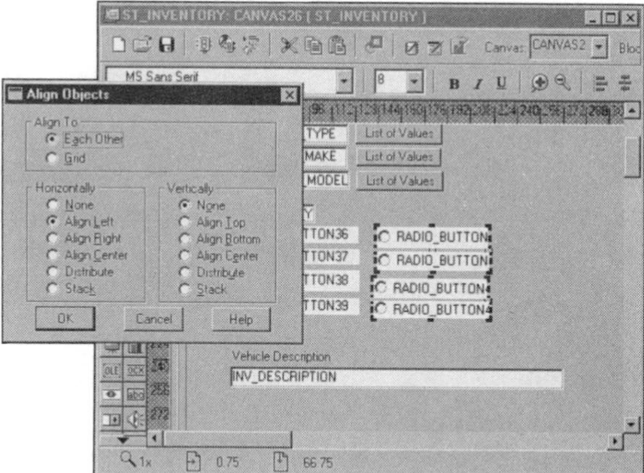

Figure 3.66

Canvas item alignment tool.

Figure 3.67

The Calculate Profit/Loss button's WHEN-BUTTON-PRESSED trigger.

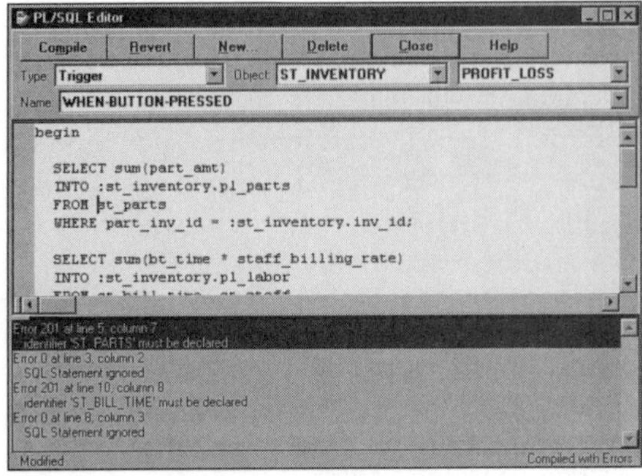

If you are getting questionable errors from the PL/SQL Editor, such as the PL/SQL Editor thinking a table name in the `From` clause of a SQL statement should be a variable name, the cause of the problem is that you are not connected to the database. Click File, Connect (see Figure 3.68) and connect to the database.

Figure 3.68

PL/SQL Editor with Connect box.

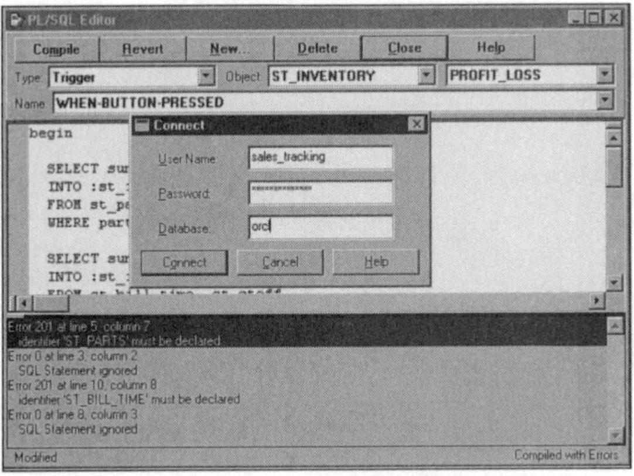

Listing 3.1 illustrates the ST_CALC_FUNCTION that was built using the Quest SQL Navigator tool as shown in Appendix C. Notice that the `part_amt` calculation (under the comment `-- add in parts --`) uses a cursor loop and the `labor_amt` (under the comment `-- add in labor costs --`). No real reason exists that the `part_amt` could not have been calculated with a similar SQL statement using the `SUM` function. This function, as well as using the function at all, aids in the learning process by illustrating as many topics as possible. A function always returns a value: Notice how this is accomplished, especially in the Exceptions part of the function.

Listing 3.1—ST_CALC_PROFIT Function

```
CREATE OR REPLACE
Function ST_CALC_PROFIT
  ( v_inv_id IN NUMBER)
  RETURN  NUMBER IS PROFIT_LOSS NUMBER(8,2);
--
-- MODIFICATION HISTORY
-- Person      Date    Comments
-- ---------   ------  ------------------------------------------
-- Hotka       2/13/00 Used to calculate profit or loss from INV_ID
--
   v_purchase_amt   st_inventory.inv_purchase_amt%TYPE;
   v_labor_amt      NUMBER(8,2);
   v_sale_amt       st_inventory.inv_sale_amt%TYPE;
   CURSOR c_inv_parts IS
        SELECT part_amt
        FROM st_parts
        WHERE part_inv_id = v_inv_id;

BEGIN
-- get purchase amount --
    PROFIT_LOSS := 0;
    SELECT inv_purchase_amt
    INTO v_purchase_amt
    FROM st_inventory
    WHERE inv_id = v_inv_id;

    PROFIT_LOSS := v_purchase_amt;
-- add in parts --

    FOR c_inv_parts_record IN c_inv_parts LOOP
        PROFIT_LOSS := PROFIT_LOSS + c_inv_parts_record.part_amt;
    END LOOP;

-- add in labor costs --

    SELECT sum(bt_time * staff_billing_rate)
    INTO v_labor_amt
    FROM st_bill_time, st_staff
    WHERE st_bill_time.bt_inv_id = v_inv_id
    AND st_bill_time.bt_staff_id = st_staff.staff_id;

    PROFIT_LOSS := PROFIT_LOSS + v_labor_amt;

-- make result negative --

    PROFIT_LOSS := PROFIT_LOSS * -1;

-- add in sold amount (if sold) --

    SELECT NVL(inv_sale_amt,0)
    INTO v_sale_amt
```

Listing 3.1—continued

```
    FROM st_inventory
    WHERE inv_id = v_inv_id;

    PROFIT_LOSS := PROFIT_LOSS + v_sale_amt;

    RETURN PROFIT_LOSS ;
EXCEPTION
    WHEN TOO_MANY_ROWS THEN
        return(0);
    WHEN NO_DATA_FOUND THEN
        return(PROFIT_LOSS);
    WHEN others THEN
        return(PROFIT_LOSS);
END; -- Function ST_CALC_PROFIT
/
```

Oracle Developer for Reports

Reports are easy to create using the Oracle Developer Report Builder. Figure 3.69 shows the first selection box, which is very similar to that of the Form Builder. Run the Quick Tour and Explore the Cue Cards are an excellent way to become familiar with the terminology and capabilities of Oracle Reports.

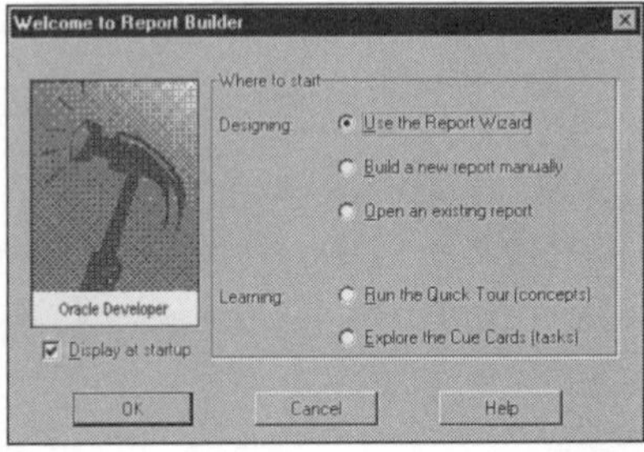

Figure 3.69

The Welcome to Report Builder window.

Selecting the Use the Report Wizard radio button opens the Report Builder Object Navigator (which is quite similar to the Form Builder Object Navigator), as shown in Figure 3.70.

The Report Wizard supports eight different report styles, as illustrated in Figure 3.71. The Tabular report is the typical style with rows and columns, whereas Form-like can print a row of data per page. This style is useful in the Sales Tracking Application to build a sales receipt or a sales document that includes the picture of the vehicle. Mailing Labels are useful for quickly assembling addresses from the database into the correct format (for example, thirty labels per page, three labels in a row, with ten rows per page). Form Letter, on the other hand, incorporates data from a table (such as name, amount, and so on) and embeds this information around text in the form of a letter. A form letter is generated for each row returned from the associated SQL query. Group Left and Group Above are useful for situations in which rows will appear on the report. Finally, a Matrix report is a summation-type report in which two related types of data are totaled together in the form of a graph. A relationship in our Sales Tracking Application would be sales by month by types of vehicles.

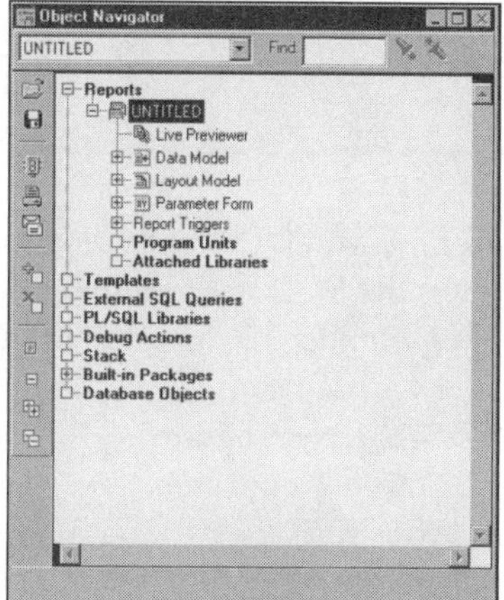

Figure 3.70

The Report Builder Object Navigator window.

Enter the title Inventory Status, ensuring that the Tabular radio button is selected, and click Next. Select the default SQL statement on the Type tab and click Next (see Figure 3.72).

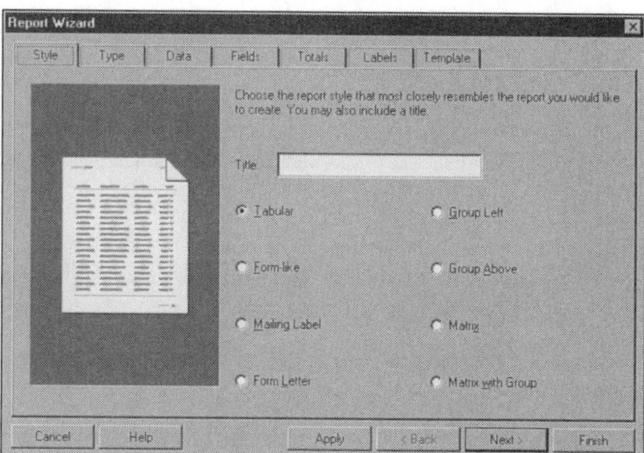

Figure 3.71

Report Builder Report Wizard Style tab.

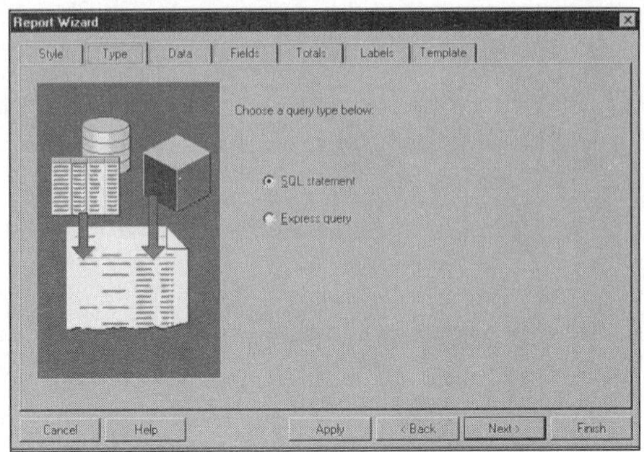

Figure 3.72

Report Builder Report Wizard Type tab.

The Report Wizard Data tab prompts you for a connection to the database (see Figure 3.73). Figure 3.74 illustrates the SQL statement used for this report. Notice that you could have used the Query Builder (as discussed in the previous section) to build the query, or you could have accessed a previously built SQL statement stored on the computer's file system. Click the Next button.

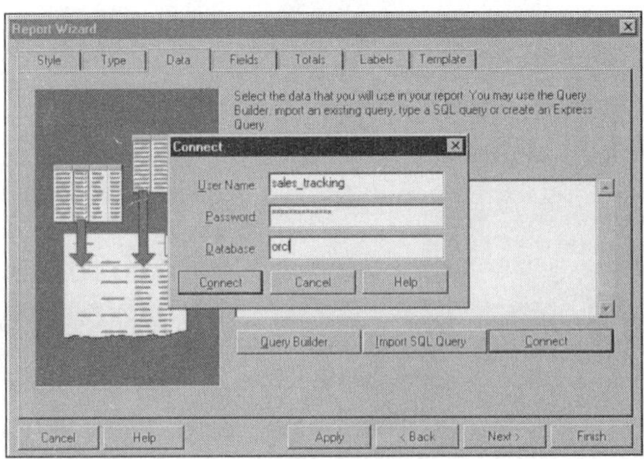

Figure 3.73

Report Builder Report Wizard Data tab with a database connection.

Click the >> button to select all the fields from the Data tab for display in the report (see Figure 3.75). The Totals tab shows how to select fields for report totals (see Figure 3.76). Select the INV_PURCHASE_AMT and the INV_SALE_AMT fields for totals. Notice that the INV_SALE_AMT has a null value assignment. Also, remember that the INV_PURCHASE_AMT is a mandatory field, whereas the INV_SALE_AMT is not. Therefore, that field could contain a null, making it unsuitable for display. Calculations without the `NVL` clause set the column to 0 if null. Finally, click the Next button when you are finished selecting fields for totals.

Figure 3.74

Report Builder Report Wizard Data tab with a SQL statement.

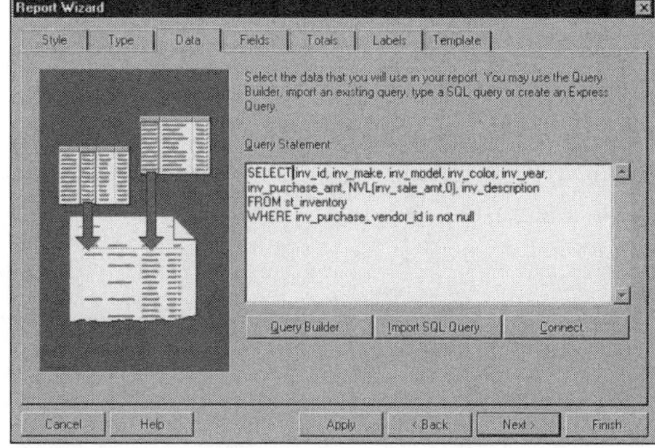

Figure 3.75

Report Builder Report Wizard Fields tab.

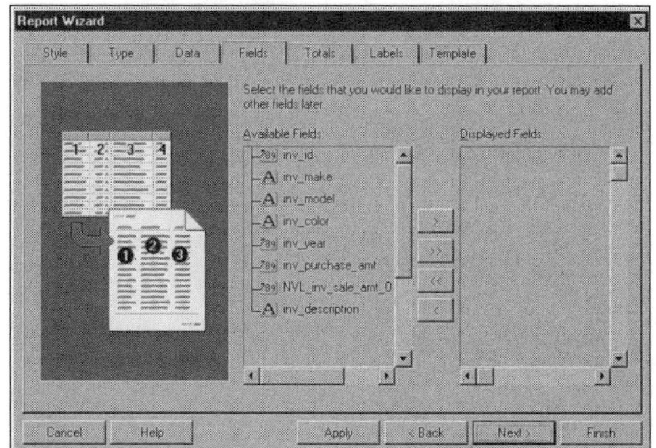

Figure 3.76

Report Builder Report Wizard Totals tab.

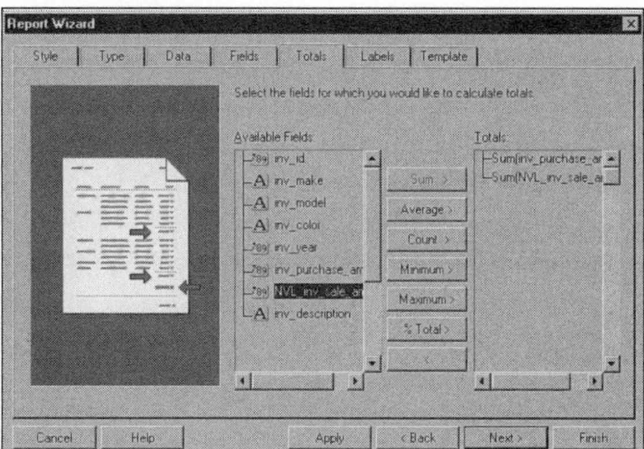

3

The Labels tab, as shown in Figure 3.77, enables you to easily change the column labels as they will appear on the report. This is also accomplished from the report layout (similar to the canvas layout of the Form Builder). Make any desired changes in the labels displayed and then click Next. The Template tab displays some default report templates. The Report Builder Online Documentation covers how to build these templates. Select the Confidential Background for this report, as you see in Figure 3.78, and click Finish.

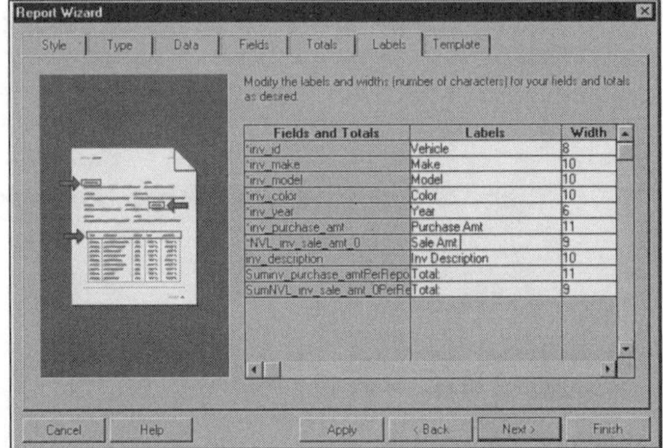

Figure 3.77

Report Builder Report Wizard Labels tab.

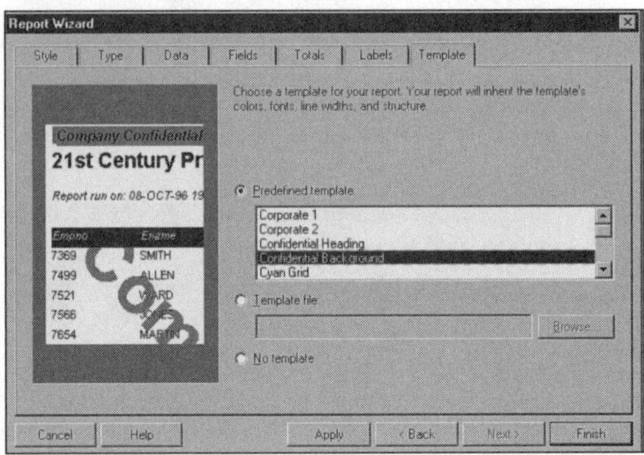

Figure 3.78

Report Builder Report Wizard Template tab.

Figure 3.79 shows what the newly developed ST_INVENTORY_STATUS report looks like.

Notice the relationships between items in the Object Navigator and items on the Live Previewer (see Figure 3.80).

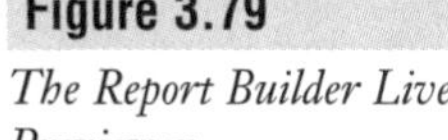

Figure 3.79

The Report Builder Live Previewer.

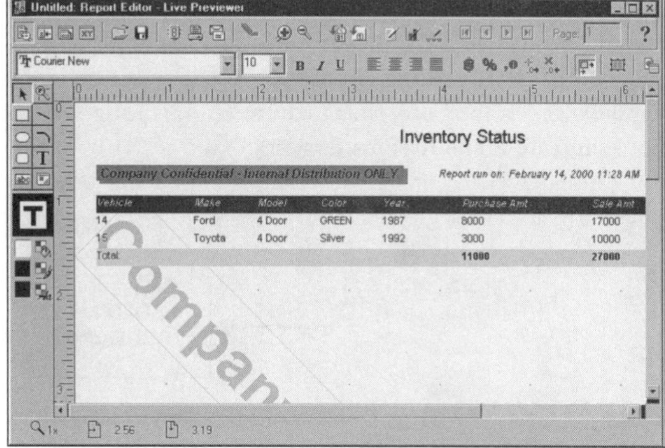

Figure 3.80

Object Navigator with the Live Previewer.

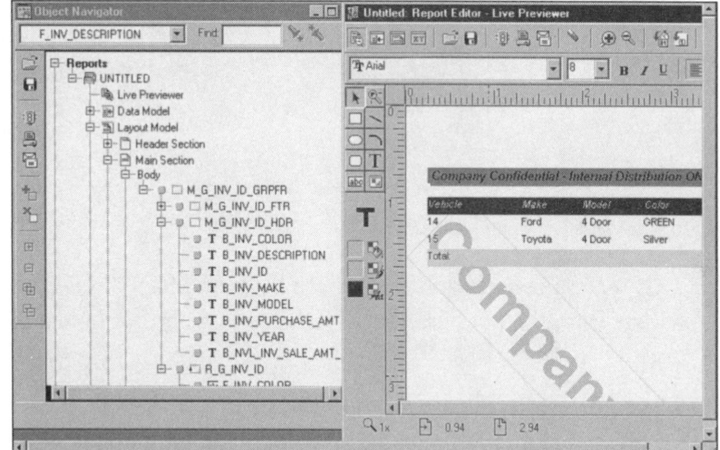

Oracle SQL*Plus for Reports

In Appendix B, you learn how to use SQL*Plus to submit SQL statements to Oracle8i for execution and a result set. We have also discussed how to manipulate SQL statements in the SQL*Plus SQL buffer. Oracle8i also has a SQL buffer where *all* SQL statements are submitted for execution. The Oracle8i SQL buffer accepts only ANSI standard SQL statements, or just SQL—not any of the SQL*Plus buffer commands or formatting commands. Figure 3.81 shows how SQL*Plus and Oracle8i relate together. SQL*Plus (and any other program working with Oracle8i) submits its SQL statements to Oracle8i for processing via Net8. Oracle8i puts this SQL statement in the SQL buffer for execution, where it is parsed (syntax checking), prepared (a plan on how Oracle8i will get the data, possibly using indexes), and executed. Then rows are returned back through Net8 to SQL*Plus. SQL*Plus then applies any of its formatting commands to the result set and displays the results on the end user's terminal or writes them to an operating system file (depending on the options given in the SQL*Plus session).

Figure 3.81

*SQL*Plus and Oracle8i SQL statement processing.*

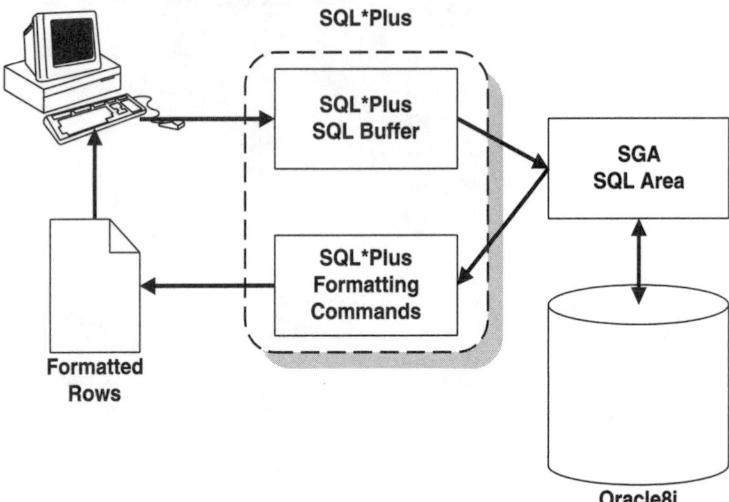

This section teaches you how to use SQL and SQL*Plus commands to format the output from the queries. The SQL*Plus SQL buffer holds only one command at a time.

The SQL*Plus `COLUMN` command (illustrated with SQL Help in Figure 3.82) is useful for giving columns a meaningful format, applying dollar signs ($) and commas to numeric fields, and providing a better column title. Figure 3.83 shows how to apply this technique to a SQL query. The `COLUMN FORMAT` command correctly sizes the fields and applies the numeric mask. Also notice the heading fields and the fact that the ENAME column contains a vertical bar (|). Whenever any special character or space appears in the title, it must be enclosed with single quotes. The single vertical bar tells SQL*Plus to put each line of the heading on a separate line.

The SQL language offers an *alias*, which is the ability to give columns more complete names or give a calculated field a name. Figure 3.84 shows how an alias is used in a SQL query. Aliases have many uses. Here they provide a better heading to the SQL statement. Aliases are also useful for giving calculated columns better headings and true names. Figure 3.84 also shows how you can use an alias to give a column a name and then use the SQL*Plus `COLUMN` command to give some further definition to the output. Notice that the `COLUMN FORMAT` command and the alias name are the same.

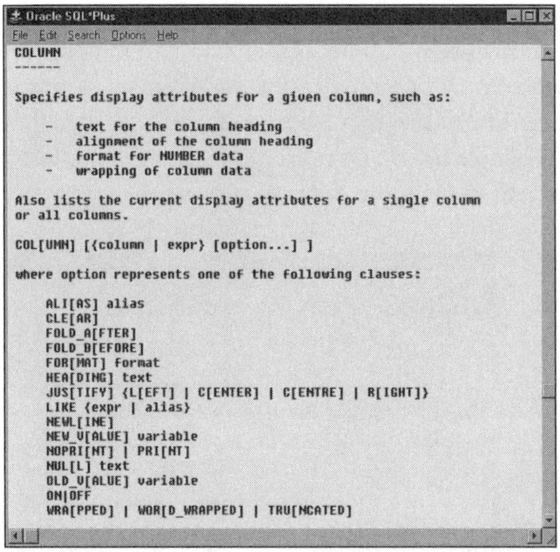

Figure 3.82

*SQL*Plus column help text.*

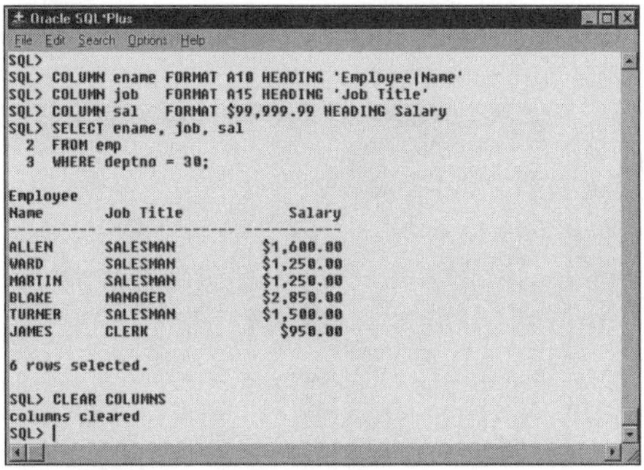

```
COLUMN
------

Specifies display attributes for a given column, such as:

     -   text for the column heading
     -   alignment of the column heading
     -   format for NUMBER data
     -   wrapping of column data

Also lists the current display attributes for a single column
or all columns.

COL[UMN] [{column | expr} [option...] ]

where option represents one of the following clauses:

     ALI[AS] alias
     CLE[AR]
     FOLD_A[FTER]
     FOLD_B[EFORE]
     FOR[MAT] format
     HEA[DING] text
     JUS[TIFY] {L[EFT] | C[ENTER] | C[ENTRE] | R[IGHT]}
     LIKE {expr | alias}
     NEWL[INE]
     NEW_V[ALUE] variable
     NOPRI[NT] | PRI[NT]
     NUL[L] text
     OLD_V[ALUE] variable
     ON|OFF
     WRA[PPED] | WOR[D_WRAPPED] | TRU[NCATED]
```

Figure 3.83

*SQL*Plus column formatting.*

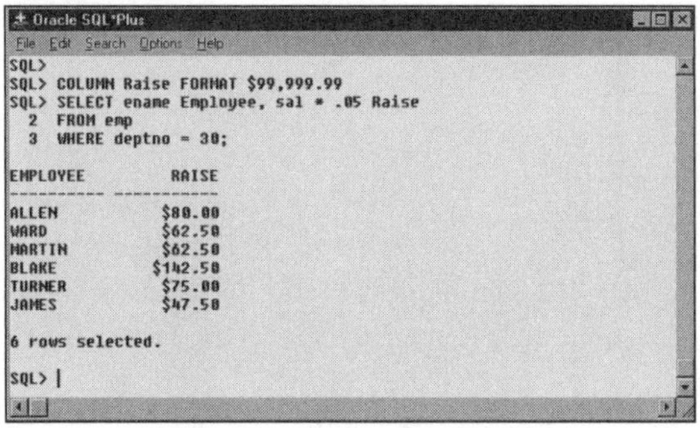

```
SQL>
SQL> COLUMN ename FORMAT A10 HEADING 'Employee|Name'
SQL> COLUMN job   FORMAT A15 HEADING 'Job Title'
SQL> COLUMN sal   FORMAT $99,999.99 HEADING Salary
SQL> SELECT ename, job, sal
  2  FROM emp
  3  WHERE deptno = 30;

Employee
Name       Job Title            Salary
---------- --------------- -----------
ALLEN      SALESMAN          $1,600.00
WARD       SALESMAN          $1,250.00
MARTIN     SALESMAN          $1,250.00
BLAKE      MANAGER           $2,850.00
TURNER     SALESMAN          $1,500.00
JAMES      CLERK               $950.00

6 rows selected.

SQL> CLEAR COLUMNS
columns cleared
SQL> |
```

Figure 3.84

Using an alias with column formatting.

```
SQL>
SQL> COLUMN Raise FORMAT $99,999.99
SQL> SELECT ename Employee, sal * .05 Raise
  2  FROM emp
  3  WHERE deptno = 30;

EMPLOYEE         RAISE
---------- -----------
ALLEN           $80.00
WARD            $62.50
MARTIN          $62.50
BLAKE          $142.50
TURNER          $75.00
JAMES           $47.50

6 rows selected.

SQL> |
```

SQL statement output also can be ordered together by using the BREAK command (see Figure 3.85). This SQL*Plus command, used in conjunction with the ORDER BY clause, suppresses values on the break column, giving a master/detail appearance, as seen in Figure 3.86. Notice that BREAK and ORDER BY contain the same columns. BREAK also can handle breaks on more than one column, but ORDER BY will need the same columns and in the same order to provide the correct results.

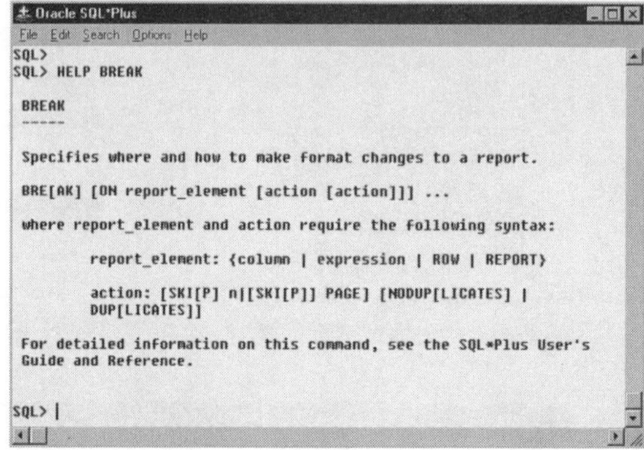

Figure 3.85

*SQL*Plus BREAK command syntax.*

```
SQL>
SQL> BREAK ON deptno SKIP 2
SQL> SELECT deptno, ename, sal
  2  FROM emp
  3  ORDER BY deptno;

   DEPTNO ENAME            SAL
--------- ---------- ---------
       10 CLARK           2450
          KING            5000
          MILLER          1300


       20 SMITH            800
          ADAMS           1100
          FORD            3000
          SCOTT           3000
          JONES           2975


       30 ALLEN           1600
          BLAKE           2850
          MARTIN          1250
          JAMES            950
          TURNER          1500
          WARD            1250


14 rows selected.

SQL> |
```

Figure 3.86

*Using the SQL*Plus BREAK command.*

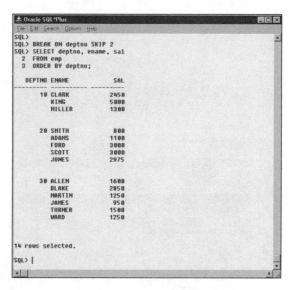

The SQL*Plus COMPUTE command is useful for creating subtotals and grand totals with the BREAK command. Figure 3.87 shows the syntax for the COMPUTE command, and Figure 3.88 shows the COMPUTE command in use with the BREAK command. The example has two separate COMPUTE commands: one for the DEPTNO breaks and one for the break on report, which causes the final total to appear.

Figure 3.87

*SQL*Plus* COMPUTE *command syntax.*

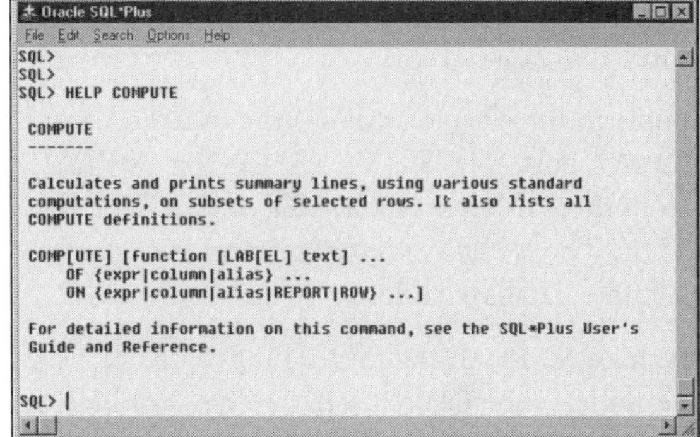

```
SQL>
SQL>
SQL> HELP COMPUTE

 COMPUTE
 -------

 Calculates and prints summary lines, using various standard
 computations, on subsets of selected rows. It also lists all
 COMPUTE definitions.

 COMP[UTE] [function [LAB[EL] text] ...
     OF {expr|column|alias} ...
     ON {expr|column|alias|REPORT|ROW} ...]

 For detailed information on this command, see the SQL*Plus User's
 Guide and Reference.

SQL> |
```

Figure 3.88

*Using the SQL*Plus* BREAK *and* COMPUTE *commands.*

```
SQL> BREAK ON deptno SKIP 1 ON report SKIP 2
SQL> COMPUTE SUM OF sal ON deptno
SQL> COMPUTE SUM OF sal ON report
SQL> L
  1  SELECT deptno, ename, sal
  2  FROM emp
  3  WHERE deptno < 30
  4* ORDER BY deptno
SQL> /

   DEPTNO ENAME            SAL
--------- ---------- ---------
       10 CLARK           2450
          KING            5000
          MILLER          1300
*********            ---------
sum                       8750

       20 SMITH            800
          ADAMS           1100
          FORD            3000
          SCOTT           3000
          JONES           2975
*********            ---------
sum                      10875

                     ---------
sum                      19625


8 rows selected.

SQL> |
```

The COMPUTE command can do more than simply add fields (which is accomplished with the SUM option). Other COMPUTE options include the following:

AVG	Average value of non-null values
COUNT	Number of non-null values
MAX	Highest value
MIN	Lowest value
NUMBER	Number of rows
STD	Standard deviation
VAR	Variance

Appendix D, "Advanced SQL Queries," contains additional ways of using SQL*Plus to format reports.

The final example in this chapter will use the `UNION` operator to create a master/detail type report. The ST_INVENTORY_DETAIL report will contain information from three different tables: ST_INVENTORY, ST_PARTS, and ST_BILL_TIME. The `UNION` operator will enable a report to easily contain the output from these three database tables.

Listing 3.2 creates a Master/Detail SQL*Plus report by using the SQL `UNION` command. In this example, nine distinct separate types of lines are to be printed: the Vehicle Type line (line 24), a line of dashes before the final total (line 60), the Purchase Price (line 28), the Sale Price (line 32), the Parts header (line 39), the Parts detail line (line 42), the Labor Used header line (line 49), the labor detail line (line 52), and the total line (63). In addition, a few blank lines will be included (lines 36, 46, and 57). Thirteen separate queries are used, which have their output merged and sorted together by the SQL `JOIN` statement (see lines 24, 28, 32, 36, 39, 42, 46, 49, 52, 57, 60, 63, and 66). When using `JOIN` to merge the output of two or more queries, the output result set *must* have the same number of columns and column types. The headings are turned off (line 17) because regular SQL*Plus column headings are not desired for this type of report. The first column of each query has an alias column name of DUMMY. This DUMMY column is used to sort the order of the six types of lines (denoted by each of the thirteen queries). The DUMMY column's only role is to maintain the order of the output lines, so the `NOPRINT` option is specified in line 21. The final `ORDER BY` (line 68) actually merges the result set lines to form the report in Listing 3.2. Notice the use of the `TO_CHAR` function to ensure that the output from this query is indeed character mode for the `UNION` operator. Also notice that each of the queries returns two columns: DUMMY and a character string. Each SQL query builds one output line. The SQL queries on ST_PARTS and ST_BILL_TIME might return zero or more rows. The DUMMY column will maintain the order of the output lines.

The final section of this chapter discusses setting up icons for the Sales Tracking Application. Figure 3.89 shows the output report from Listing 3.2.

Listing 3.2—`ST_INVENTORY_DETAIL.SQL`

```
1:  rem
2:  rem    ST_Inventory_Detail.SQL - Demonstrates how to create a Master/Detail
3:  rem                    report using the UNION operator. This technique is
4:  rem                    useful whenever records/text from different tables
5:  rem                    need to appear in the same report.
6:  rem
7:  rem       Oracle8i From Scratch
8:  rem          by Dan Hotka
```

```
rem         Que Publications March 2000
rem         All Rights Reserved
rem
ACCEPT INV_ID PROMPT 'Enter Inventory ID --> '
SET FEEDBACK OFF
SET VERIFY OFF
SET LINESIZE 60
SET PAGESIZE 24
SET HEADING OFF

TTITLE 'Inventory Detail for Inventory_ID &INV_ID'

COLUMN DUMMY NOPRINT

SPOOL ST_Inventory_Detail.OUT
SELECT 1 DUMMY, 'Vehicle: ' || inv_year
➥|| ' ' || inv_color || ' ' || inv_make
FROM st_inventory
WHERE inv_id = &INV_ID
UNION
SELECT 2 DUMMY, 'Purchase Price:         '
➥|| TO_CHAR(inv_purchase_amt,'$999,999')
FROM st_inventory
WHERE inv_id = &INV_ID
UNION
SELECT 3 DUMMY, 'Sale Price:             '
➥|| TO_CHAR(NVL(inv_sale_amt,0),'$999,999')
FROM st_inventory
WHERE inv_id = &INV_ID
UNION
SELECT 4 DUMMY, ' '
FROM dual
UNION
SELECT 5 DUMMY, 'Parts Used:  '
FROM dual
UNION
SELECT 6 DUMMY, RPAD(part_desc,20) || '    ' || TO_CHAR(part_amt,'$999,999')
FROM st_parts
WHERE part_inv_id = &INV_ID
UNION
SELECT 7 DUMMY, ' '
FROM dual
UNION
SELECT 8 DUMMY, 'Labor Used: '
FROM dual
UNION
SELECT 9 DUMMY , RPAD(staff_name,10) || '              ' || TO_CHAR(bt_time
➥*staff_billing_rate,'$999,999')
FROM st_bill_time, st_staff
WHERE st_bill_time.bt_inv_id = &INV_ID
AND st_bill_time.bt_staff_id = st_staff.staff_id
UNION
SELECT 10 DUMMY, '   '
```

Listing 3.2—continued

```
FROM dual
UNION
SELECT 11 DUMMY, '                          ------------'
FROM dual
UNION
SELECT 12 DUMMY, 'Profit/Loss                '
    ||  TO_CHAR(st_calc_profit(&INV_ID),'$999,999')
FROM dual
UNION
SELECT 13 DUMMY, '   '
FROM dual
ORDER BY 1,2
/
SPOOL OFF

ACCEPT anything PROMPT 'Hit Enter when done viewing report'
EXIT
```

Figure 3.89

*SQL*Plus Report ST_INVENTORY_DETAIL.*

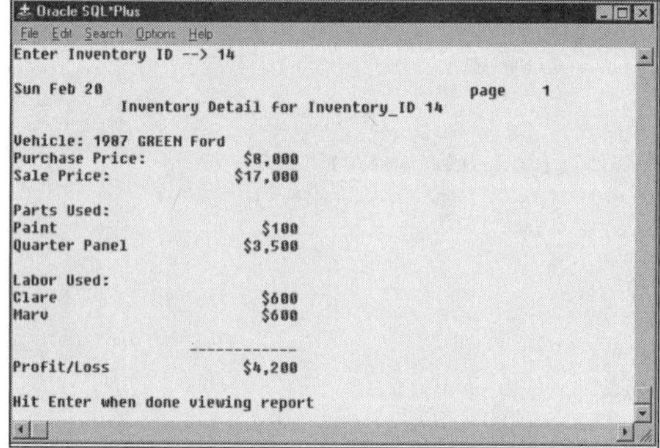

Sales Tracking Application Icon Setup

It is relatively easy to set up icons for the new applications we created. In addition, it is easier to copy an existing icon and change its properties than to set up one from scratch. Figure 3.90 shows the icons that were configured for the Sales Tracking Application. Each of these icons was copied from existing icons by right-clicking the desired icon and selecting Create Shortcut. You can right-click the newly created icon and then use the Rename option to give the new icon a descriptive name. Right-click the same icon again and select Properties from the menu. Click the center Shortcut tab, where you will see the actual program name in the Target field. For Oracle Forms, add the full operating system path and name of the `.fmx` program to be run when this icon is selected after this program name. For Oracle Reports, enter the full path of the `.RDF` file. In SQL*Plus scripts, add the same information that you would use in a DOS command window. After the program name, enter **`userid/ passwd@<tnsnames> @<full path & SQL*Plus script>.SQL`**. The ST_INVENTORY_DETAIL report has a target line that looks similar to this:

```
C:\ORANT\BIN\PLUS80W.EXE sales_tracking/sales_tracking@orcl
➥@c:\disks\que\8i_from_scratch\sales_tracking_pgms\
➥st_inventory_detail.sql
```

The ST_INVENTORY_DETAIL report target line should be typed as all one line. The ➥ symbols are to help the line fit within the character requirements of this page.

3

Figure 3.90 shows the Oracle Reports icon setup, and Figure 3.91 shows the shortcut properties.

Figure 3.90

Sales Tracking Application icons.

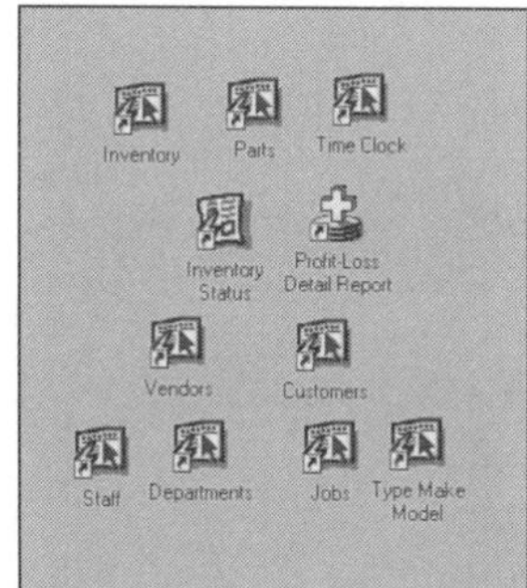

Figure 3.91

ST_INVENTORY_STATUS report icon property page.

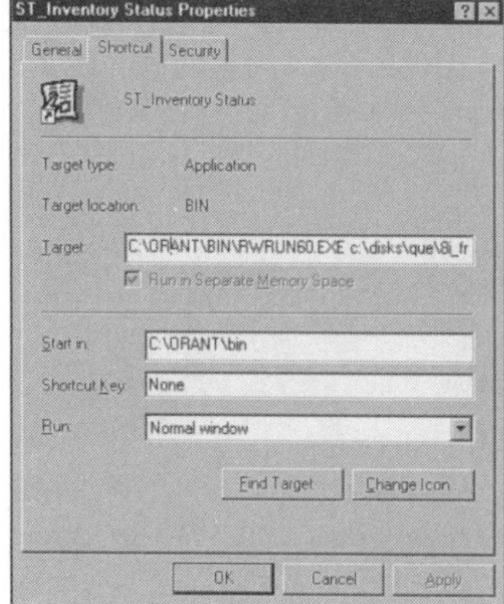

Summary

This chapter introduced Oracle Developer, where you learned to build various forms with varying levels of complexity. You learned how to format and change the physical screen attributes as well as add specific coding functionality using PL/SQL. You also learned how to create reports using two different Oracle tools: Oracle Reports and SQL*Plus.

Next Steps

In the next chapter, we'll talk about the skills needed to start, stop, and perform the basic administration (such as adding users and adding space to the database) required by almost any application in the Oracle8i database.

Chapter 4

In this chapter

- *Database Startup/Shutdown*
- *Adding Users*
- *Grants, Privileges, and Roles*
- *Owner/Location Transparency—Synonyms*
- *Basic Tablespace Maintenance*
- *Oracle8i Tablespace Options*

Basic Oracle8i Administration Tasks

The focus of this chapter is on the basic Oracle administrative tasks necessary to start and stop Oracle processes, assign users, and ensure that adequate space is available for the data of the Sales Tracking Application.

Various tools are available that can perform these tasks. This chapter will show you how to perform each task using SQL*Plus, the Oracle Enterprise Manager (OEM), and Oracle WebDB.

SQL*Plus is Oracle's longtime interactive query tool. Prior versions of Oracle divided the character-mode administrative functions into separate tools, such as the Server Manager and SQL*DBA in Oracle v6 and early versions of v.7. Prior to Oracle v6, SQL*Plus was the primary administrative and reporting tool. Oracle8i introduces SQL*Plus back into the role of character-mode administration. This chapter will highlight these administrative features; other parts of the book feature the reporting features of SQL*Plus.

Server Manager is present in the 8.1.5 release; it may not be enhanced, and there is no guarantee that future releases of Oracle will even contain the Server Manager tool.

Oracle Enterprise Manager (OEM) is a collection of *GUI-based* tools designed to help the database administrator with the day-to-day administration tasks. These tools are included with the Oracle software and can be installed when the Oracle *RDBMS* is installed, depending on the type of installation chosen—default or custom—and the products chosen from the software asset manager screen of the install utility. The Oracle Enterprise Manager runs in the Microsoft Windows environment. These tools can be accessed from a central console (see Figure 4.1) or individually from either the console or the Start menu.

Figure 4.1

Oracle Enterprise Manager console.

GUI—An acronym for graphical user interface. Microsoft Corporation provides Windows as its GUI to the computer; most UNIX operating systems provides Motif as a GUI to the computer.

RDBMS—An acronym for Relational Database Management System.

Oracle WebDB is a Web publishing tool that can be used by end users, developers, and database administrators (DBAs) to create Web sites and database objects, and to perform administrative tasks from any Web browser. This chapter concentrates on the administrative features of WebDB (see Figure 4.2).

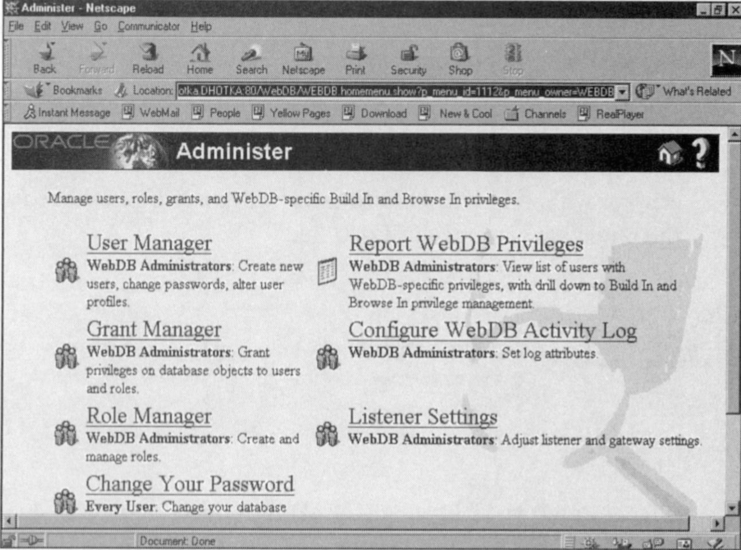

Figure 4.2

Oracle WebDB Administer panel.

Oracle8i supports two administrative privileges that have the proper authority to perform most, if not all, administrative tasks. These privileges are SYSDBA and SYSOPER, and Oracle user accounts must have them to perform special database tasks such as startup, shutdown, backup, and recovery.

Oracle8i still has the famous INTERNAL user account, but it might be phased out in future releases of Oracle. The functionality has been complemented by the SYSDBA and SYSOPER accounts on sites that implement this type of security at the operating system level.

Database Startup/Shutdown

Database startup reads the `INIT.ORA` parameter file (usually found in the `ORACLE_HOME\database` directory). (Listing 4.1 is a sample `INIT.ORA` configuration file.) STARTUO (no options) reads the `INIT.ORA` parameter file (found in the `ORACLE_HOME\database` directory), builds the SGA, and starts the Oracle background processes.

The `INIT.ORA` file can be explicitly referred to in the `pfile` parameter during a startup of the database as follows:

```
startup pfile=<full operating-system file path and name>
```

This command directs the `STARTUP` command to use a specific `INIT.ORA` parameter file. Some shops regularly use two different `INIT.ORA` parameter files: one tuned for daytime, online data entry/query mode and one tuned for night batch processing.

The `STARTUP` command has several options. During database recovery, the database must be closed (not available to users) until the recovery process is complete. When the `STARTUP MOUNT` command is issued, the instance is started, the control file is read, and the database is mounted. The database is not yet open for users to log in, however. After tasks performed in the database mounted mode are complete, the `ALTER DATABASE OPEN` command can be executed, making the database available to users.

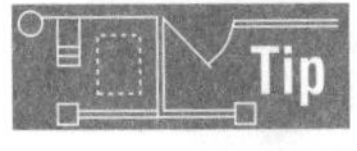

You should perform a shutdown and a startup after performing tasks in Startup Mount Mode.

The `STARTUP NOMOUNT` command can be used to re-create control files in the event that they become damaged or lost and also can be employed in the creation of a new database.

The STARTUP FORCE command is useful when problems are preventing the database from performing a normal startup. This command essentially performs a shutdown and then a startup.

The SHUTDOWN command has several options. The standard shutdown, referred to as a *shutdown normal*, waits for all users to log off the database. This is the best way to shut down the database. The SHUTDOWN IMMEDIATE command, on the other hand, logs off users from the database, allowing their current SQL statement to finish processing and rolling back any other open transactions. The SHUTDOWN TRANSACTIONAL command waits for the current transaction to complete and then logs the user off. Conversely, the SHUTDOWN ABORT command is the fastest way to stop the Oracle environment. This option logs off all the users and cancels transactions. Choosing this option requires Oracle to perform an instance recovery (roll back any uncommitted transactions and so on) just as if the computer had suddenly lost its power.

To start up the Oracle8i database environment from SQL*Plus, use the following commands:

```
O/S Prompt>sqlplus /nolog

SQL> connect scott/tiger as SYSDBA

SQL> startup
```

The OEM Instance Manager (see Figure 4.3) can be used to start and stop the database and access the parameters of the INIT.ORA parameter file.

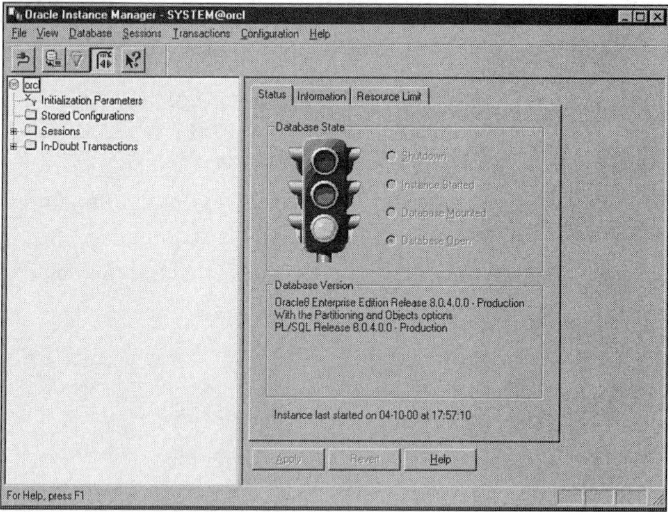

Figure 4.3

OEM Instance Manager.

What Is the Initialization File (INIT.ORA)?

Oracle determines the sizes of the various SGA components from parameters in the INIT.ORA file. This file by default is named init<Oracle SID>.ora and is located by default in the ORACLE_HOME\database directory. Upon a database startup, the parameter pfile= can be specified to refer to point to the INIT.ORA file, which resides in a location other than the default location or has a different name than the default name. The STARTUP command references this INIT.ORA file.

Listing 4.1 illustrates a sample INIT.ORA parameter file. A default INIT.ORA file is created with the initial installation of the Oracle software. The next section of this chapter discusses the various components of this file as well as possible changes for your application environment.

Listing 4.1—Sample INIT.ORA Parameter File

```
##############################################################################
# Example INIT.ORA file
#
# This file is provided by Oracle Corporation to help you customize
# your RDBMS installation for your site.  Important system parameters
# are discussed, and example settings given.
#

db_name = oracle
db_files = 20
control_files = (C:\ORANT\DATABASE\ctl1orcl.ora, C:\ORANT\DATABASE\ctl2orcl.ora)


db_file_multiblock_read_count =  8 # INITIAL
# db_file_multiblock_read_count = 8                                   # SMALL
# db_file_multiblock_read_count = 16                                  # MEDIUM
# db_file_multiblock_read_count = 32                                  # LARGE

db_block_buffers =  200                               # INITIAL
# db_block_buffers = 200                                              # SMALL
# db_block_buffers = 550                                              # MEDIUM
# db_block_buffers = 3200                                             # LARGE

shared_pool_size =  6500000                             # INITIAL
# shared_pool_size = 3500000                                          # SMALL
# shared_pool_size = 6000000                                          # MEDIUM
# shared_pool_size = 9000000                                          # LARGE

log_checkpoint_interval = 10000

processes =  50                                           # INITIAL
# processes = 50                                                      # SMALL
# processes = 100                                                     # MEDIUM
# processes = 200                                                     # LARGE
```

Listing 4.1—continued

```
dml_locks =  100                                        # INITIAL
# dml_locks = 100                                                    # SMALL
# dml_locks = 200                                                    # MEDIUM
# dml_locks = 500                                                    # LARGE

log_buffer =  8192                                      # INITIAL
# log_buffer = 8192                                                  # SMALL
# log_buffer = 32768                                                 # MEDIUM
# log_buffer = 163840                                                # LARGE

sequence_cache_entries =  10              # INITIAL
# sequence_cache_entries = 10                                        # SMALL
# sequence_cache_entries = 30                                        # MEDIUM
# sequence_cache_entries = 100                                       # LARGE

sequence_cache_hash_buckets =  10     # INITIAL
# sequence_cache_hash_buckets = 10                                   # SMALL
# sequence_cache_hash_buckets = 23                                   # MEDIUM
# sequence_cache_hash_buckets = 89                                   # LARGE

# audit_trail = true          # if you want auditing
# timed_statistics = true     # if you want timed statistics
max_dump_file_size = 10240    # limit trace file size to 5 Meg each

# log_archive_start = true    # if you want automatic archiving

# define directories to store trace and alert files
background_dump_dest=%RDBMS%\trace
user_dump_dest=%RDBMS%\trace

db_block_size = 2048

snapshot_refresh_processes = 1

remote_login_passwordfile = shared

text_enable = true
```

The value of the BACKGROUND_DUMP_DEST parameter specifies the location of the directory location in which the `alert.log` and any Oracle trace files are created.

Alert log—File maintained by Oracle. This file records changes made to the database. A typical `alert.log` file contains information as to when the Oracle database was started and stopped, and any major problems that Oracle might have encountered during operation.

Oracle Trace files can be turned on at the user session or by individual Oracle programs to capture SQL and statistics from the session or originating program. The TKPROF utility is used to interpret these files into meaningful information.

Oracle checkpoint—Associated with log archiving. The checkpoint places a "mark" in the log files when information in the various Oracle buffer pools is physically written to the hard disks.

Control file—Contains information about the particular instance of an Oracle database at a particular time. A time stamp appears on each of the Oracle data files, backup information, and so on. Oracle will not mount the database without a valid control file. You can have many copies of the control files. In addition, we recommend that you have three or more copies on separate disks so that, if one of the control files is damaged or lost, you will still be able to bring up your database.

Table 4.1 lists the more common parameters and their values.

4

Table 4.1 Common Parameters and Their Values

Parameter	*Value*
`CHECKPOINT_PROCESS`	Is set to true or false depending on whether checkpointing is desired.
`CONTROL_FILES`	Lists the Oracle-maintained control files.
`DB_BLOCK_BUFFERS`	Specifies the size of the buffer cache in the System Global Area (SGA).
`DB_BLOCK_SIZE`	Specifies the size of the database blocks. It is used in the `create database sql` statement.
`DB_FILES`	Determines how many operating system files (including the control files, all tablespace files, and so on) Oracle can have access to at any one time.
`DB_FILE_MULTI_BLOCK_READ_COUNT`	Specifies how many blocks will be read with each read request. The value of `DB_FILE_MULTI_BLOCK_READ_COUNT` multiplied by `DB_BLOCK_SIZE` should be equal to 64KB.
`HASH_JOIN_ENABLE`	Defaults to `true`, enabling memory hash joins (discussed in Chapter 6, "Tuning the Sales Tracking Application").
`HASH_AREA_SIZE`	Defaults to twice the `SORT_AREA_SIZE`.
`HASH_MULTI_BLOCK_IO_COUNT`	Defaults to `DB_FILE_MULTI_BLOCK_READ_COUNT`.
`LARGE_POOL_SIZE`	Defaults to `0` and can be specified in kilobytes (KB) or megabytes (MB).
`LARGE_POOL_MIN_ALLOC`	Is the minimum size of the large pool.
`LOG_ARCHIVE_BUFFERS` and `LOG_ARCHIVE_BUFFER_SIZE`	Associated with the writing of online redo logs to archive logs. These parameters might need to be increased if you are archiving directly onto tape devices, and monitoring the redo log buffers shows that the Oracle background processes are waiting on archive log buffers to become available.

Table 4.1 continued

Parameter	Value
LOG_ARCHIVE_DEST	Specifies the location of the archive logs if log archive mode is enabled.
LOG_ARCHIVE_FORMAT	Determines the naming convention used for the archive logs created.
LOG_ARCHIVE_START	Enables or disables the log archive mode.
LOG_BUFFER	Determines the size of the redo log buffer in the SGA.
LOG_CHECKPOINT_INTERVAL	Determines the frequency of checkpointing. LOG_CHECKPOINT_INTERVAL is set to the number of redo buffer blocks processed before taking a checkpoint.
MAX_ROLLBACK_SEGMENTS	Specifies the maximum number of rollback segments that can be kept available for user processes.
OPTIMIZER_GOAL	Is used by the cost-based optimizer and can globally force an application's default behavior by specifying FIRST_ROWS or ALL_ROWS.
OPTIMIZER_MODE	Defaults to COST and uses the cost-based optimizer, if collected statistics exist. Changing this parameter to RULE causes the rule-based optimizer to be used, unless SQL hints are specified. If CHOOSE is specified and any of the objects involved have statistics, Oracle uses the cost-based optimizer.
ROLLBACK_SEGMENTS	Identifies rollback segments by name, assigning them to the Oracle environment.
SHARED_POOL_SIZE	Is the size of the shared pool in the SGA.
SHARED_POOL_RESERVED_SIZE	Is used for packages.
SHARED_POOL_RESERVED_MIN_ALLOC	Is the minimum memory allotment.
SORT_AREA_SIZE	Is the size of the sort area in the SGA.
SQL_TRACE	Is used to collect tuning statistics from the Oracle environment. By default, it is false.
TIMED_STATISTICS	Is used by some Oracle processes to collect timing statistics. It is off by default.

The optimizer is covered in detail in Chapter 6.

Adding Users

User accounts give users access to the database, supply permission to perform required tasks, and track who is doing what. Figure 4.4 illustrates how to add a user with SQL*Plus. Figure 4.5 illustrates how to add a user with the OEM Security Manager tool, and Figure 4.6 illustrates how to add a user with WebDB.

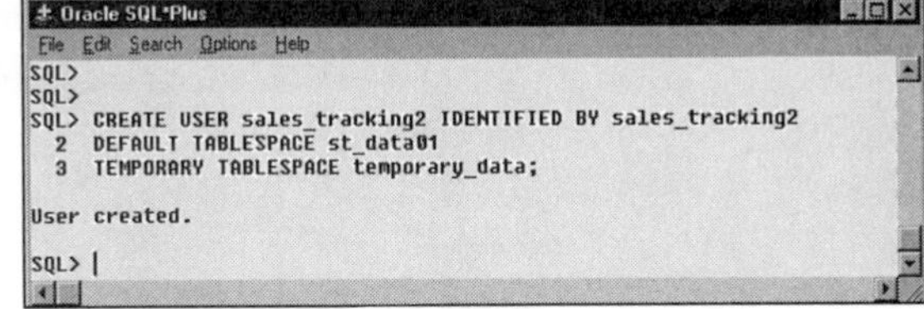

Figure 4.4

*Adding a user with SQL*Plus.*

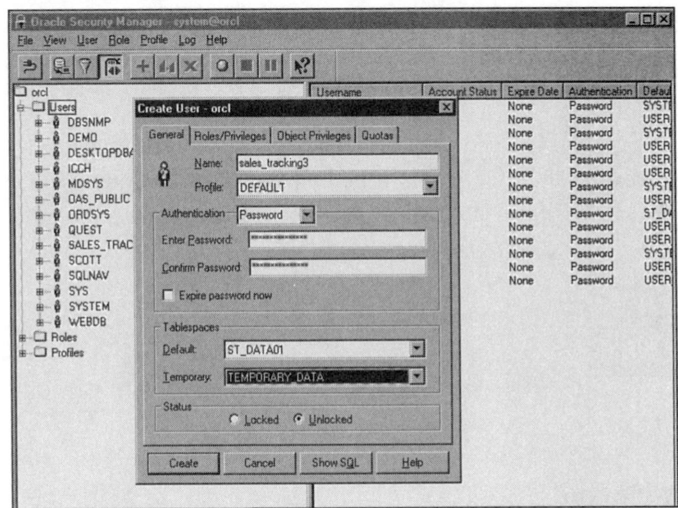

Figure 4.5

Adding a user with OEM Security Manager.

When adding users, you assign an initial password and assign a default tablespace and a temporary tablespace. The Oracle authentication is quite extensive, in regards to password expiration, format of the password, and so on. Consult the Oracle8i documentation if this is a requirement at your site. The *default* tablespace is where any objects the user creates will reside if the user does not specify an explicit tablespace name. The *temporary* tablespace is the default tablespace the user will be assigned when using SQL statements that require a sort temporary space due to regular SQL processing. Note that each example assigns a password and defines the default tablespaces.

Figure 4.6

Adding a user with WebDB.

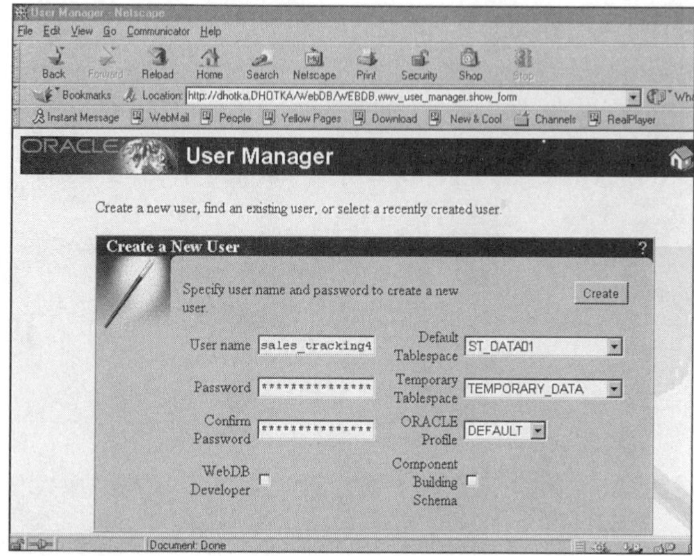

With SQL*Plus, the password is assigned with the keywords `IDENTIFIED BY`. Prior to creating the user, it might be helpful to run the query via SQL*Plus. Use `SELECT tablespace_name FROM dba_tablespaces` to visualize the tablespaces. The GUI and Web interfaces of OEM and WebDB easily list the available tablespaces.

The user account used to create other users must have the DBA role or the `CREATE USER` privilege.

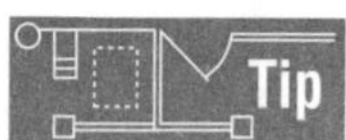

You should create a user account with the DBA role from the SYSTEM user account. This new user account then becomes the owner of the application, creating all the objects as well as the other users.

Grants, Privileges, and Roles

The Oracle8i database is a secure database allowing only the users with permission to access the database and its various components. This next section describes how grants, privileges, and roles are used to ensure that users have the correct permissions and controls to perform their tasks but not any more tasks than necessary.

Grants

The GRANT command is used to give users specific privileges and roles, whereas the REVOKE command is used to take away privileges and roles from users.

One special user account has no connect privileges but has access to all user-created objects. This account is called PUBLIC. When privileges are granted to PUBLIC, all users of the database have the permission being granted. Figure 4.7 shows several GRANT commands.

Figure 4.7

*Granting privileges with SQL*Plus.*

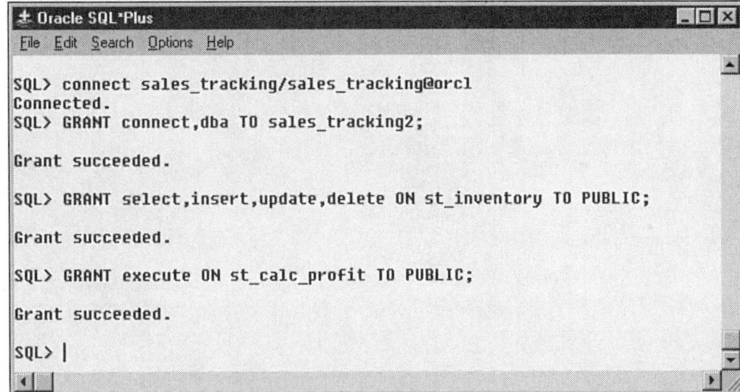

Oracle SQL*Plus
File Edit Search Options Help
SQL> connect sales_tracking/sales_tracking@orcl
Connected.
SQL> GRANT connect,dba TO sales_tracking2;
Grant succeeded.
SQL> GRANT select,insert,update,delete ON st_inventory TO PUBLIC;
Grant succeeded.
SQL> GRANT execute ON st_calc_profit TO PUBLIC;
Grant succeeded.
SQL> |

A user can share his roles and privileges with other users if he was given the WITH GRANT OPTION when his privileges were originally granted.

Privileges

Several privileges are available in an Oracle database. The basic privilege is CONNECT. Without the CONNECT privilege, users are unable to log on to the Oracle database. You might not want to drop users because they might have several tables, objects, and so on that are still required by the business. Revoking their CONNECT privilege prevents them from logging on to the Oracle database.

Privileges fall into three major categories: Select and DML (data manipulation language) privileges (SELECT, INSERT, UPDATE, and DELETE), DDL (data definition language) privileges (CREATE, DROP, and ALTER objects), and DBA privileges (database STARTUP, SHUTDOWN, RECOVERY ISSUES, and so on).

The SQL language is broken into three parts based on the nature of the SQL statement. The Select category simply retrieves data from the database. DML (Data Manipulation Language) is used to make changes to the data in the tables. DDL (Data Definition Language) is used to create objects such as tables and indexes.

Select and DML privileges can be granted to users and roles on objects owned by another user, thus enabling these objects to be viewed or manipulated depending on the privileges granted by the owner. The common privileges are `SELECT`, `UPDATE`, `INSERT`, and `DELETE`. Figure 4.8 shows how to view all the available privileges with OEM Security Manager.

Figure 4.8

Available privileges.

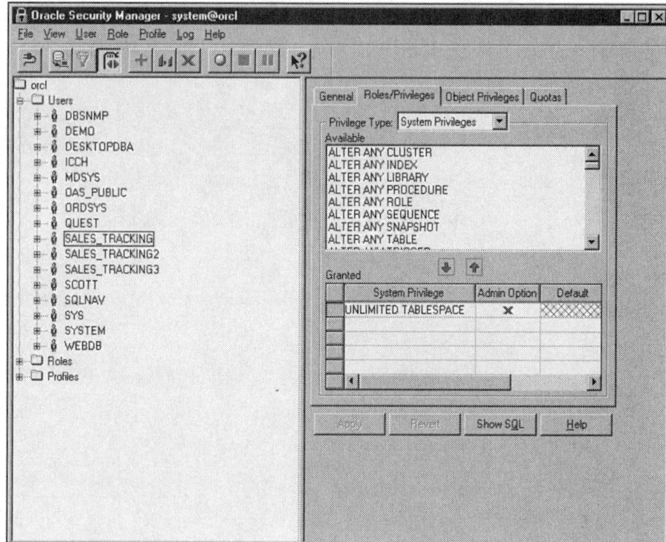

DDL privileges are granted to specific users, enabling them to create, drop, or change objects. The common privileges are `CREATE`, `DROP`, `ALTER`, and `EXECUTE`.

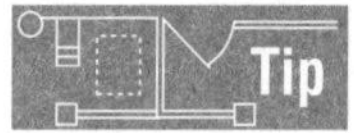

A user can share her roles and privileges with others if she was given the `WITH GRANT OPTION` (or `WITH ADMIN OPTION`) when her privileges were originally granted.

Roles

Roles are a way of grouping various privileges together and giving them a name. Roles enable simplification of security administration because group roles are granted and revoked to users just as individual privileges are. When a new object is added, the new object privileges can be added to the role instead of to individual existing users. Users granted the role privilege will have the new privileges on their next successful logon to the database. For example, for the Sales Tracking Application, a role called Clerk_Users gives all users the `SELECT`, `INSERT`, and `UPDATE` privileges to the core tables (ST_INVENTORY, ST_BILL_TIME, and so on). The Mngr_Users role can have the same privileges as Clerk_Users. In addition, Mngr_Users can have `DELETE` privileges on these objects, as well as `INSERT`, `UPDATE`, and `DELETE` privileges on the reference tables (ST_DEPARTMENTS, ST_STAFF, and so on).

A series of default roles also is supplied with Oracle8i. The standard roles are CONNECT, RESOURCE, and DBA. CONNECT enables users to connect to the database, and RESOURCE enables users to create and change (DDL privileges) objects. Finally, DBA enables users to perform all the previously mentioned tasks as well as many administrative tasks, such as database startup, shutdown, adding space, backup and recovery, and so on. Figure 4.9 shows how to view and grant roles with OEM Security Manager.

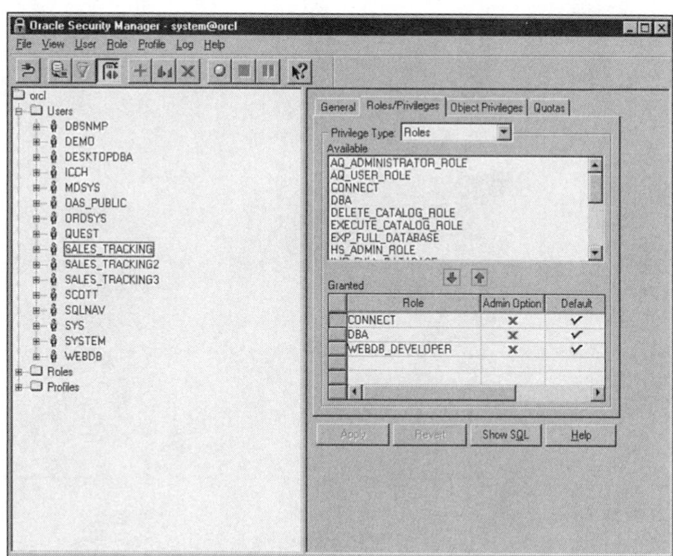

Figure 4.9

Role management with OEM Security Manager.

New roles easily can be created using SQL*Plus, OEM Security Manager, or WebDB.

Owner/Location Transparency—Synonyms

Synonyms give an object another name. They can be used to create shortcut names and to reference an object name that is not owned by a user, without the user having to include the name of the owner with the object.

Figure 4.10 illustrates how this concept works. Notice that user SCOTT attempts to extract some information from the ST_INVENTORY table, owned by SALES_TRACKING. The request is immediately denied because SCOTT either did not qualify ST_INVENTORY with the owner's name or did not have `SELECT` privileges to that object.

SALES_TRACKING grants the appropriate privileges required, such as `SELECT`, `UPDATE`, `INSERT`, and `DELETE`, on the object and creates a public synonym for ST_INVENTORY. When the public synonym is created, the full name of the table, including the owner of the object, is given. This allows other users or applications to access the ST_INVENTORY object as if it were their own. This concept is known as *owner transparency*.

Figure 4.10

Synonyms and the Sales Tracking Application.

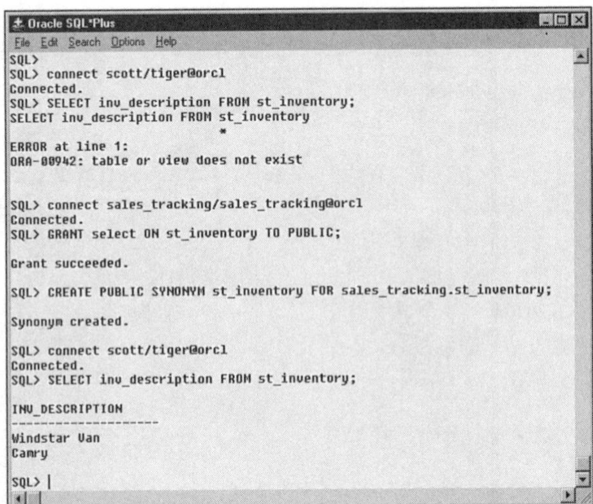

Synonyms are useful when using database links to access objects in other Oracle databases on other instances. By using synonyms, objects can be moved between owners and between instances of Oracle without having to change a single line of code in any SQL statement. This concept is known as *location transparency*.

Basic Tablespace Maintenance

The Oracle *tablespace* is a logical storage area. Physical disk files are added to the tablespace level and its size is limited by the amount of available disk space. In addition, the SYSTEM tablespace is the home of the Oracle data dictionary. The TEMP tablespace, on the other hand, is typically used for sorts, merge/joins, and so on. Database administrators and developers have control over how the space within the tablespace is allocated and shared. Figure 4.11 illustrates the relationship between tablespaces and physical operating system–level files. Performance can be enhanced by assigning the physical files to various tablespaces on physically different disk drives.

Figure 4.11

Oracle8i and Sales Tracking (partial) tablespace layout.

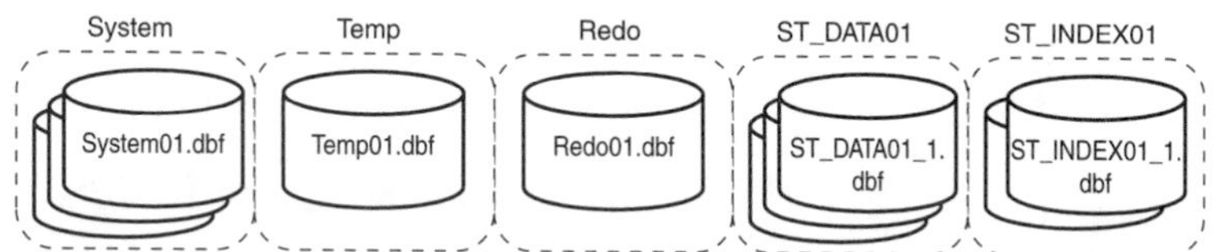

4

The Database administrator must ensure that adequate space is available in the tablespaces for the data being added to the objects assigned to the tablespaces. Figure 4.12 shows how SQL Navigator can be used to monitor the amount of free space in the Oracle8i tablespaces.

Figure 4.12

Monitoring tablespace free space with SQL Navigator.

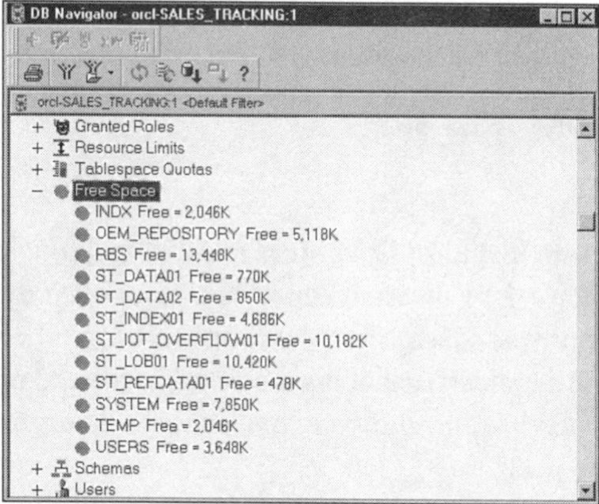

Oracle8 supports the READ-ONLY tablespace. READ-ONLY tablespaces are more efficient than traditional full-access tablespaces: No updates can occur, so the read consistency and recovery mechanisms need not apply to this type of tablespace. This feature is useful for tablespaces targeted for CD-ROM devices.

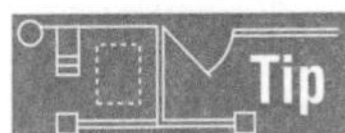

Prior to running the `READ-ONLY` command, run the SQL statement `select count(*) from...` against each table in the READ-ONLY tablespace. This will reset the check block level transaction status remaining from any recent updates, and performance should be improved.

Adding a Tablespace

Adding a tablespace requires the DBA role or the specific privilege `CREATE TABLESPACE`. Figure 4.13 shows the basic syntax for creating a tablespace. The name for the tablespace must be unique for the instance and have an assigned unique file name. The `SIZE` option on the file command can be specified in either KB (thousands of bytes) or MB (megabytes).

Figure 4.13

*Adding a tablespace with SQL*Plus.*

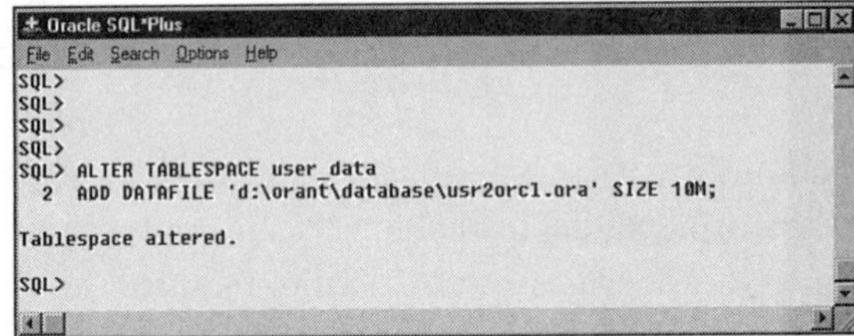

Establish and use a naming pattern for the files associated with the tablespace. This will ease administrative tasks that references these files, such as hot backups and database restores.

Using a GUI interface, such as OEM Storage Manager, to add tablespaces makes this task simple. Figure 4.14 illustrates how easy it is to see the total size of the tablespaces, the amount of free space, and—by simply clicking the tablespace—the physical files assigned to the tablespace. This makes not only the operating system directory path easy to examine and copy but also visualizes the naming pattern of the tablespace file name itself.

Figure 4.15 illustrates how easily a tablespace can be created using OEM Storage Manager.

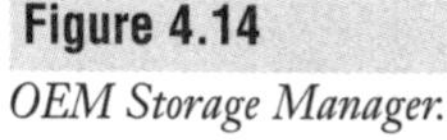

Figure 4.14

OEM Storage Manager.

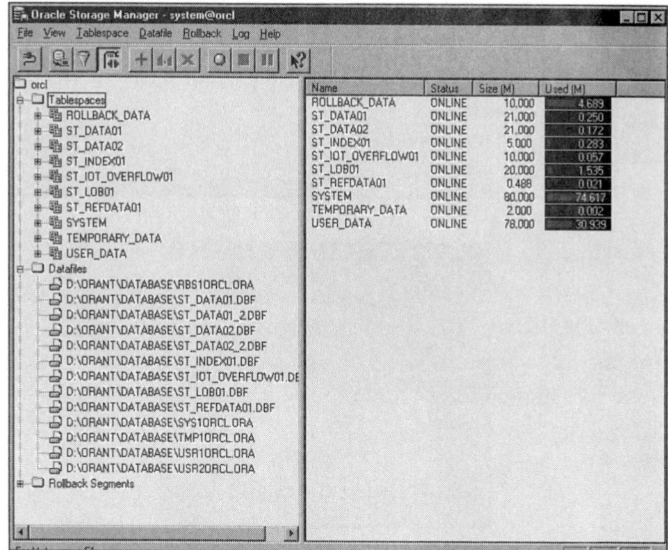

Figure 4.15

Adding a tablespace with OEM Storage Manager.

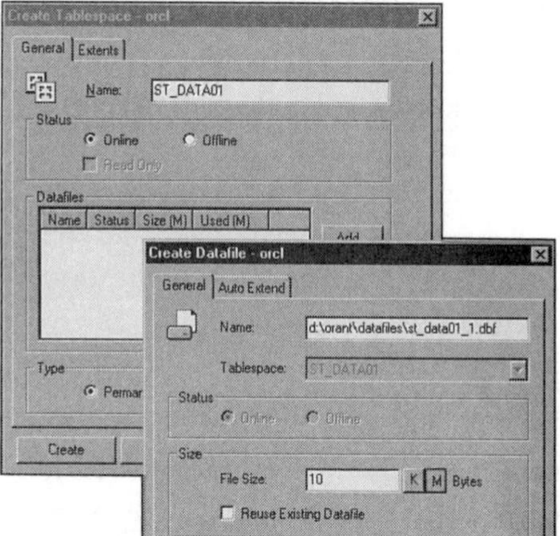

Adding Space to Tablespaces

As data is added to the table objects, adding more storage space to the tablespace will be necessary. Figure 4.16 illustrates the syntax necessary to add a file using SQL*Plus, and Figure 4.17 shows how to add an additional file using OEM Storage Manager.

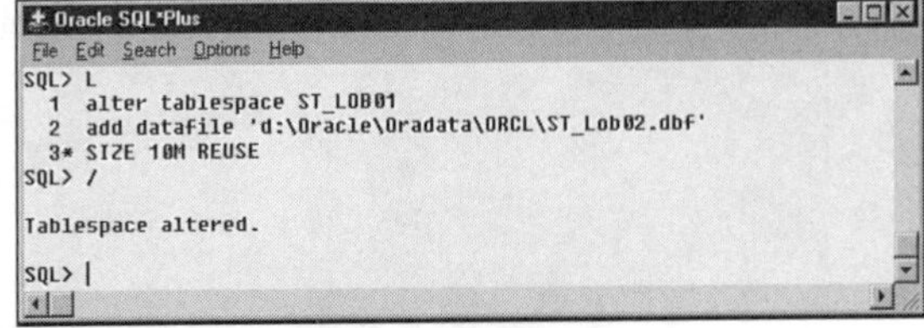

Figure 4.16

*Adding a data file to a tablespace with SQL*Plus.*

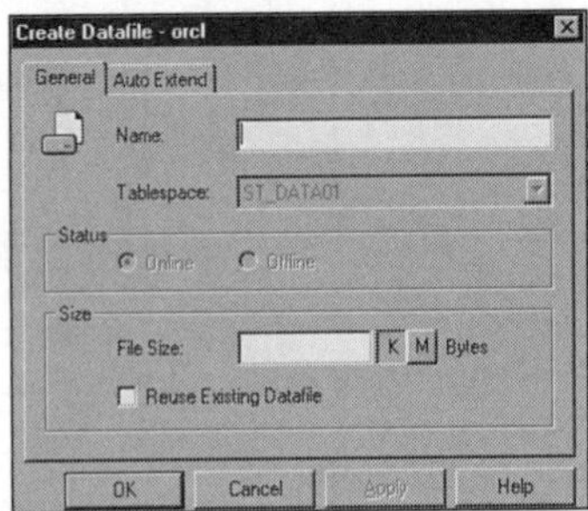

Figure 4.17

Adding a data file to a tablespace with OEM Storage Manager.

Oracle8i Tablespace Options

Oracle8i offers two new tablespace options: the locally managed tablespace and the transportable tablespace. The standard tablespace option (the one that we have been discussing) is the *dictionary-managed* tablespace because it stores information on the free tablespace and uses extents in the Oracle data dictionary. The traditional dictionary-managed tablespace tracks the allocated and free extents in tables within the data dictionary. Object extent size based on application needs is flexible and is assigned either by default storage parameters at the tablespace level or by storage parameters at the object level. These object-level storage parameters override default storage parameters defined at the tablespace level.

Locally managed tablespaces use a bitmap in each data file to keep track of the extent availability. Locally managed tablespaces also use the same extent size throughout the tablespace so there is no need for Oracle to search for the correct extent size when additional extents are being added to the objects. Because all the extents are the same size, this tablespace tracks and uses any free space very effectively. Listing 4.2 creates a locally managed tablespace within SQL*Plus.

Listing 4.2—Locally Managed Tablespace Syntax

```
CREATE TABLESPACE <tablespace name>
EXTENT MANAGEMENT LOCAL;
```

LTMS has two types of extents: uniform size and autoallocate. *Autoallocate* creates extent sizes based on the size of the data file. The minimum autoallocate extent size is 64KB. When an object fills the current extent, Oracle8i looks in each of the extent bitmaps associated with the data files assigned to the tablespace for enough adjacent free data blocks to fill the extent requirements.

The UNIFORM SIZE clause enables you to have some input on the extent size and uses this uniform size for all extents in the tablespace.

> If the UNIFORM SIZE clause is left off the CREATE TABLESPACE command, Oracle8i will default to AUTOALLOCATE.

Locally managed tablespaces are useful for read-only tablespaces (for CD-ROM distribution and so on) and temporary tablespaces.

The *transportable* tablespace option enables you to move a tablespace from one database to another Oracle8i database. This option can be useful in the sharing of data with other offices via CD-ROM technology. Any data can be loaded and indexed, and then the tablespace can be moved to other Oracle8i databases.

The steps necessary to transport a tablespace from one database to another are as follows:

1. Put the tablespace in read-only mode with the syntax ALTER <tablespace name> READ ONLY (this is used to prevent any changes to the tablespace).
2. Use the Oracle Export facility to capture the dictionary information by using the option TRANSPORT TABLESPACE=Y TABLESPACE=<tablespace name>.
3. Copy the tablespace data files and the export file to the other computer, magnetic tape, or CD-ROM.
4. Use the Oracle Import facility to import the export file from step 2 using these options: TRANSPORT TABLESPACE=Y DATAFILES=(<source database full-path file name>, ...).
5. Put the existing and new tablespace back in read/write mode (if desired) with the syntax ALTER <tablespace name> READ WRITE.

Some restrictions apply to the transportable tablespaces:

- They only work with Oracle8.1 or higher.
- The computer type and operating system version levels must be the same. All databases involved must have the same block size and character set.
- Index-organized tables are not supported.
- Object-oriented extensions are not supported.
- Anything owned by the SYS user account cannot be transported.

Summary

This chapter covered the basic administrative tasks necessary to maintain both the Oracle8i database as well as the users and applications that will use this same Oracle8i database.

The next chapter, "Monitoring the Sales Tracking Application," builds on the skills learned here by discussing the memory structures being created from the parameters in the `INIT.ORA` file, building on the tablespace concepts learned in this chapter, and illustrating how to control how the data is stored within the tablespaces.

Chapter 5

In this chapter

- *Oracle System Global Area*
- *Understanding the INIT.ORA Parameters*
- *Using Tablespaces for Table and Index Placement on Disk Storage*
- *Monitoring Oracle8i and the Sales Tracking Application*
- *Understanding Database Fragmentation*

Monitoring the Sales Tracking Application

This chapter focuses on how the various parts of Oracle8i work together. Oracle8i requires regular monitoring for quick diagnosis of issues that impact performance.

This chapter discusses how the Oracle8i System Global Area (SGA) works, its importance, how to size it correctly, and how to monitor it for performance issues. Storage management, that is, storage clause options, can cause performance issues such as inefficient storage of data. Such a situation is known as *data fragmentation*. This chapter also discusses how Oracle8i becomes fragmented and what you can do to solve and even prevent fragmentation.

Oracle System Global Area

The System Global Area (SGA) is Oracle's workspace. The SGA is created, based on parameters in the INIT.ORA file, when the Oracle8i database is started. The SGA contains all the memory components used by Oracle8i. Many of these components have a direct impact on the performance of the applications accessing the database. Because applications differ greatly, the SGA allows flexibility in the size and usage of the various parts (see Figure 5.1).

The SGA contains many different memory structures. It contains the buffer cache and its components, the shared pool and its components, the large pool, the log buffer, and the sort area.

Figure 5.1

The Oracle8i System Global Area.

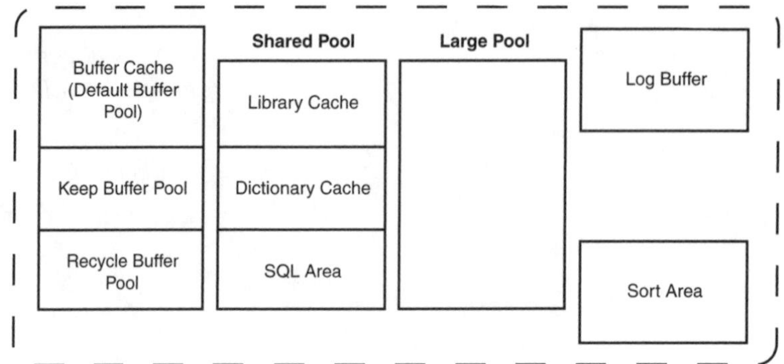

Buffer Cache

The *buffer cache* is a work area for database blocks from disk. Oracle8i checks whether the required data block is in this buffer cache before performing a disk read to retrieve it. The buffer cache *hit ratio* is a comparison between the number of times a data block was requested and the number of times that data block was already in the SGA. This buffer cache hit ratio is the main way of determining how well the buffer cache is using data. This ratio can vary according to the type of application using the database. The recommended buffer cache hit ratio is greater than 90%. Listing 5.1 illustrates a buffer cache hit ratio SQL statement.

Listing 5.1—Tablespace Files Report

```
select round((( sum(decode(name,'db block gets',value))
           +  sum(decode(name,'consistent gets',value)))
            -  sum(decode(name,'physical reads',value))) /
              (sum(decode(name,'db block gets',value))
            +  sum(decode(name,'consistent gets',value))) * 100)
               "Buffer Cache Hit Ratio"
from v$sysstat
```

The size of the buffer cache is determined by the INIT.ORA parameter `DB_BLOCK_BUFFERS`.

To find the optimal size of the buffer cache, do the following: Increase the INIT.ORA parameter `DB_BLOCK_BUFFERS` until the buffer cache hit ratio is minimally affected by increasing this `DB_BLOCK_BUFFERS` parameter. Then, decrease the `DB_BLOCK_BUFFERS` until the buffer cache hit ratio begins to be adversely affected. This will be the optimal size of the buffer cache.

This process might take several days of monitoring the buffer cache hit ratio and adjusting the INIT.ORA parameter `DB_BLOCK_BUFFERS`.

The buffer cache handles all input/output (I/O) requests from all SQL statements. The size of the buffer cache is determined by the `DB_BLOCK_BUFFERS` parameter. When this cache fills with data blocks, Oracle8i uses a least recently used (LRU) algorithm to determine which blocks have not been accessed and should be cycled out of the buffer cache. Depending on the application, I/O to the temporary tablespace (such as a merge/join operation discussed later in this chapter) or long-running queries that are selecting many rows could be prematurely cycling out data blocks from smaller reference type tables (such as ST_STAFF, ST_MODEL, and so on). This behavior might adversely affect the buffer cache hit ratio.

I/O—Stands for input/output and typically refers to reads and writes from physical hard disk drives.

5

Oracle8 introduced a method of subdividing the buffer cache into three areas to better manage the various individual needs of the object. The subdivisions are known as the keep buffer pool, recycle buffer pool, and default (or just buffer cache) buffer pool. The *keep* buffer pool is designed to help keep objects in the buffer cache; the *recycle* buffer pool is for those infrequently used objects; and the *default* buffer pool is for everything else.

Data blocks of smaller reference-type tables and indexes with few, if any, updates that are frequently accessed by an application should be assigned to the keep buffer pool. Data blocks with inserts that won't be reused in the near future should be quickly cycled out of the buffer cache to make room for other Data Manipulation Language–type (DML-type) SQL statements. In addition, blocks that are newly created but seldom reused can be cycled out of memory more frequently. Both of these should be assigned to the recycle buffer pool. Enabling reference tables or frequently read indexes to remain in memory and not be cycled out would be beneficial because of read/redo/sort activity in the buffer pool. All these situations are reasons to configure the new buffer pools of Oracle8.

The buffer cache uses the value of the parameter DB_BLOCK_BUFFERS specified in the INIT.ORA configuration file. The keep and recycle buffer pools are subsets of the buffer cache. The INIT.ORA parameters BUFFER_POOL_KEEP and the BUFFER_POOL_RECYCLE buffer, and LRU_LATCHES are subtracted from the total value of the DB_BLOCK_BUFFERS parameter and from the total value of the DB_BLOCK_LRU_LATCHES parameter. In Listing 5.2, notice that more LRUs are assigned to the recycle buffer pool. This is because extra I/O is assigned to this pool, so the need for LRUs is greatest. With tables and indexes that are not changing much (if at all) and that are assigned to the keep buffer pool, this pool will experience little contention for LRUs and will therefore need fewer of them. Notice that in the example illustrated by Listing 5.2, the default buffer pool will have 6,000 data blocks assigned to it, with a total of 3 LRU *latches*.

Latch—A type of internal Oracle lock. A latch tells other processes that this particular resource (in this case, a buffer cache block) is currently being used by another resource.

The number of buffers cannot be less than 50 times the number of LRUs. If the number of buffers is less than 50 times the number of LRUs, Oracle adjusts the number of buffers up to this ratio.

Listing 5.2—Buffer Pool Configuration INIT.ORA Parameters

```
DB_BLOCK_BUFFERS=10000
DB_BLOCK_LRU_LATCHES=10
BUFFER_POOL_KEEP=(BUFFERS:1500, LRU_LATCHES:1)
BUFFER_POOL_RECYCLE=(BUFFERS:2500, LRU_LATCHES:6)
```

Contention describes a situation in which one process is waiting for a latch or a resource to become free because another process is using the resource. Sometimes contention is unavoidable, and sometimes areas exist in which the amount of contention can be monitored and corrected. Whenever contention exists, a user of an Oracle-based application is waiting.

If contention exists for these LRU latches, processes are waiting for latches to become available. Listing 5.3 is a useful SQL statement that can detect LRU latch contention. Listing 5.4 lists the name of the buffer pool with the LRU contention. If contention is discovered, make the appropriate adjustments in the INIT.ORA parameters in Listing 5.2, which will allocate more of these LRU latches to the buffer pool with the contention.

Listing 5.3—Discovering LRU Contention

```
SELECT child# "Child Number", sleeps / gets "LRU Latch Ratio"
FROM v$latch_children
WHERE name = 'cache buffers lru chain';
```

Listing 5.4—The Buffer Pool with the LRU Contention

```
SELECT name "Buffer Pool"
FROM v$buffer_pool_statistics
WHERE lo_setid <= <Child Number from Listing 5.3>
AND hi_setid >= <Child Number from Listing 5.3>
```

Two ways are available to assign objects to these buffer pools. The `ALTER TABLE <table name> STORAGE (BUFFER_POOL <[KEEP|RECYCLE|DEFAULT]>` command is useful for changing the assignments of existing objects. For example, to assign the existing table ST_DEPARTMENTS to the keep buffer pool, use this syntax: `ALTER TABLE ST_DEPARTMENTS STORAGE(BUFFER_POOL keep);`. Listing 5.5 shows how to include the buffer pool assignment in the `CREATE TABLE` syntax.

Listing 5.5—Buffer Pool Assignment Sales Tracking Example

```
CREATE TABLE st_inv_type
    (inv_type         VARCHAR(10))
    TABLESPACE st_refdata01
    CACHE
    PCTFREE 1
    PCTUSED    90
    STORAGE (INITIAL 1K
        NEXT 1K
        MINEXTENTS 1
        MAXEXTENTS 100);
```

Listing 5.6 shows some possible buffer pool assignments for the various objects of the Sales Tracking database. Any indexes on any of these table objects should be assigned to the same buffer pool. The keep pool assignments are the reference tables or tables that probably will not change much over time. The recycle pool assignments are those table objects that primarily contain inserts and other DML-type statements (table objects that are rather dynamic—that is, always changing in size). The `ST_INVENTORY` object is assigned to the default buffer pool because of the LOBs (INV_SALES_PHOTO is a blob, or binary long object—a picture in this example) that will be typically retrieved and because it does not necessarily fit well in the keep or recycle buffer pools.

Listing 5.6—Sales Tracking Buffer Pool Recommendations

```
ST_INVENTORY               DEFAULT Buffer Pool
ST_PARTS                RECYCLE Buffer Pool
ST_INV_TYPE                  KEEP Buffer Pool
ST_INV_MAKE                KEEP Buffer Pool
ST_INV_MODEL             KEEP Buffer Pool
ST_VENDOR                KEEP Buffer Pool
ST_CUSTOMER                KEEP Buffer Pool
ST_STAFF                 KEEP Buffer Pool
ST_BILL_TIME               RECYCLE Buffer Pool
ST_DEPARTMENTS             KEEP Buffer Pool
ST_JOB_DESCRIPTION             KEEP Buffer Pool
```

The SQL script in Listing 5.7 is useful for finding candidates for the keep buffer pool.

The SQL script in Listing 5.7 retrieves data from an X$ table. X$ tables are owned by SYS, so this SQL script will have to be run from the SYS user account. Do not run any DML statements using the SYS account. The SYS account owns the Oracle8i data dictionary, so any changes—accidental or otherwise—can cause severe damage to the Oracle8i environment.

Listing 5.7—SQL Script to Find Additional Keep Buffer Pool Candidates

```
column owner format a10 heading Owner
column object_name format a20 heading 'Object Name'
column object_type format a20 heading Type
column obj format 999999 heading 'Object ID'
column count(file#) format 999999 heading 'Memory Blocks'
SELECT owner, object_name, object_type, obj, count(file#)
FROM x$bh, dba_objects
WHERE x$bh.obj = dba_objects.object_id
GROUP BY owner, object_name, object_type, obj
order by count(file#) DESC
/
```

Sizing the various buffer pools to adequately accommodate the object assignments is important. For example, if the keep buffer pool is not large enough to hold all the assigned tables, it cannot achieve its intended effect of not having to read from disk. To evaluate buffer pool sizing, use the ANALYZE command to collect statistics for the Oracle8i cost-based optimizer. (The optimizer will be discussed in Chapter 6, "Tuning the Sales Tracking Application.") One of the statistics gathered by the ANALYZE command is the number of blocks currently used by the object.

Use the ANALYZE TABLE <table name> COMPUTE STATISTICS (or ANALYZE INDEX ...) command to collect all the statistics. This is necessary to get an accurate count of the blocks used by the object. To find out more about the ANALYZE command, use the SQL*Plus Help command (see Figure 5.2).

You must make the keep buffer pool large enough to hold all the assigned blocks. The buffer cache hit ratio for the keep buffer pool should be 100%. You should also make the recycle buffer pool 1/4 the size of the total blocks of the assigned objects. Do not worry about the buffer cache hit ratio of this buffer pool. Finally, you must adjust the default buffer pool (as previously described) so that this buffer pool's hit ratio is more than 90%. The SQL statement in Figure 5.3 can be used to get an accurate size of the objects for buffer cache sizing. The SQL statement in Listing 5.8 can be used to monitor the buffer cache hit ratios of the 3 buffer pools.

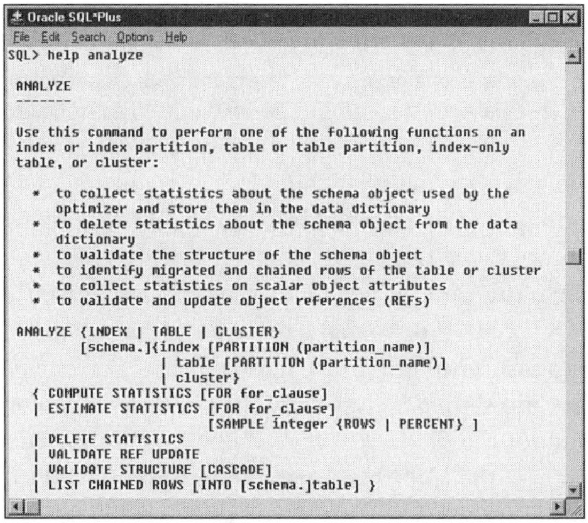

Figure 5.2

*SQL*Plus help on the* ANALYZE *command.*

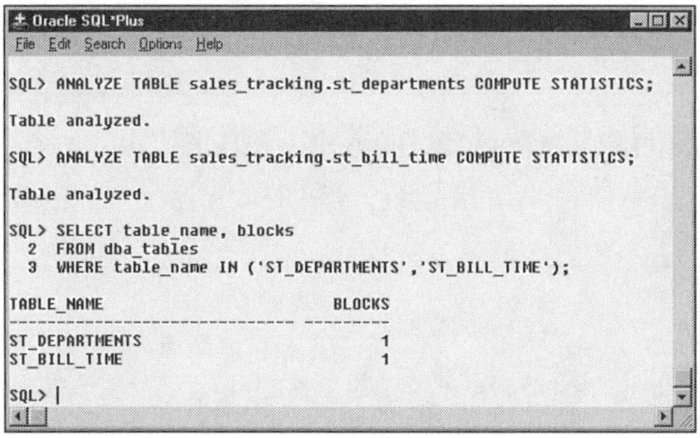

```
Oracle SQL*Plus
File Edit Search Options Help
SQL> help analyze

 ANALYZE
 -------

 Use this command to perform one of the following functions on an
 index or index partition, table or table partition, index-only
 table, or cluster:

   *  to collect statistics about the schema object used by the
      optimizer and store them in the data dictionary
   *  to delete statistics about the schema object from the data
      dictionary
   *  to validate the structure of the schema object
   *  to identify migrated and chained rows of the table or cluster
   *  to collect statistics on scalar object attributes
   *  to validate and update object references (REFs)

 ANALYZE {INDEX | TABLE | CLUSTER}
         [schema.]{index [PARTITION (partition_name)]
                  | table [PARTITION (partition_name)]
                  | cluster}
   { COMPUTE STATISTICS [FOR for_clause]
   | ESTIMATE STATISTICS [FOR for_clause]
                  [SAMPLE integer {ROWS | PERCENT} ]
   | DELETE STATISTICS
   | VALIDATE REF UPDATE
   | VALIDATE STRUCTURE [CASCADE]
   | LIST CHAINED ROWS [INTO [schema.]table] }
```

Figure 5.3

Block count for Analyzed Sales Tracking Objects.

```
Oracle SQL*Plus
File Edit Search Options Help

SQL> ANALYZE TABLE sales_tracking.st_departments COMPUTE STATISTICS;

Table analyzed.

SQL> ANALYZE TABLE sales_tracking.st_bill_time COMPUTE STATISTICS;

Table analyzed.

SQL> SELECT table_name, blocks
  2  FROM dba_tables
  3  WHERE table_name IN ('ST_DEPARTMENTS','ST_BILL_TIME');

TABLE_NAME                         BLOCKS
------------------------------ ----------
ST_DEPARTMENTS                          1
ST_BILL_TIME                            1

SQL> |
```

Listing 5.8—Multiple Buffer Pool Hit Ratio SQL Script

```
SELECT name "Buffer", (physical_reads /
    (db_block_gets + consistent_gets)) -1 "Hit Ratio"
FROM v$buffer_pool
```

Other SGA Structures: Library Cache, Dictionary Cache, and Large Pool

The *shared pool* consists of two buffer areas: the library cache and the dictionary cache. The SQL area contains the SQL statements and PL/SQL associated with the statistics in the library and dictionary caches. The SQL area contains only uniquely coded SQL statements, which are stored in memory in the SQL area when they are first executed so identical SQL statements are processed a bit more quickly.

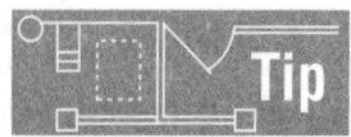

The more similar the SQL statements, the better the SQL area is used. Oracle tests for uniqueness by the text of the SQL statement, so using all caps or all lowercase will help, as well as not hard-coding variables that change frequently.

The shared pool size is determined by the INIT.ORA parameter SHARED_POOL_SIZE. The library cache ratio calculation in Listing 5.9 should be below 1%. The two ways to help this library cache hit ratio are to increase the INIT.ORA parameter SHARED_POOL_SIZE or to make more SQL statements identical by using substitution variables instead of using text/numeric strings in the `where` clause. The dictionary cache hit ratio should be less than 10%. The SQL statement in Listing 5.10 can be used to monitor the dictionary cache. The only tuning option for the dictionary cache is to increase the INIT.ORA parameter SHARED_POOL_SIZE.

Listing 5.9—Library Cache Hit Ratio SQL Script

```
Select (sum(reloads) / sum(pins))* 100 "Library Cache Hit Ratio"
from v$librarycache
```

Listing 5.10—Multiple Buffer Pool Hit Ratio SQL Script

```
select (sum(getmisses) / sum(gets) ) * 100 "Dictionary Cache Hit Ratio"
from v$rowcache
```

If increasing SHARED_POOL_SIZE has no effect on either of these cache hit ratios, the problem is that the SQL statements are different.

The *large pool* is primarily used by the Oracle *multithreaded server* and Oracle Recovery Manager. The large pool is defined by setting the LARGE_POOL_SIZE and LARGE_POOL_MIN_ALLOC parameters in the INIT.ORA file.

The Sales Tracking Application does not use a large pool. Unless the multithreaded server is defined, this memory allocation can be better used in the buffer cache.

Multithreaded server—Works in conjunction with the SQL*Net processes to better use memory on computer systems with large numbers of users.

Oracle *redo logs* enable the Oracle database to recover from a hardware problem and provide users with a read-consistent view of the database for the duration of their particular SQL statement. The redo log buffer can be monitored with the `redo-log-waits` SQL statement in Listing 5.11 or by right-clicking Redo Log Writer and selecting Wait Activity in the Spotlight for Oracle. If Redo Log Waits is not 0, users are waiting for log buffers to become available for their SQL statement. Increase the INIT.ORA LOG_BUFFER parameter and continue to adjust it until 0 redo log waits exist.

Listing 5.11—Redo Log Contention SQL Script

```
select value "Redo Log Waits" from v$sysstat
where name = 'redo log space requests'
```

The *sort area* is used when SQL statements contain the `order by` or `group by` syntax, such as the calculation used to arrive at the Profit/Loss figures in ST_INVENTORY. The calculation in Listing 5.12 illustrates the number of disk sorts performed. Tune this area much like the buffer cache—increase the INIT.ORA SORT_AREA_SIZE parameter until the result of the disk sorts calculation decreases. Then, reduce the INIT.ORA SORT_AREA_SIZE parameter until the disk sorts increase.

Listing 5.12—Disk Sort Identification SQL Script

```
select value "Disk Sorts" from v$sysstat
where name = 'sorts(disk)'
```

Understanding the INIT.ORA Parameters

The `init<Oracle SID>.ora` file is the configuration file Oracle uses to create the SGA and start up the database. Listing 5.13 is from the Oracle8i (version 8.1.5) installation (covered in Chapter 2, "Building the Sales Tracking Application Database") for the Sales Tracking Application. This file has many parts, but some are not used. Any line that begins with a `#` is ignored by the startup routine. (The `#` symbol represents a comment.) Notice that the `Log Archiving` parameter lines are commented out but are present, so that archiving can be easily enabled, if desired. The parameter `Timed Statistics` should be uncommented and set to `true`. This will allow many types of tuning measurements to be enabled.

Log archive mode—Enables the redo logs to be saved as archive log files. These files play an important role in some backup and recovery scenarios, discussed in detail in Chapter 7, "Oracle8i Backup and Recovery."

Listing 5.13—Oracle8i INIT.ORA Parameter File

```
##############################################################################
# Example INIT.ORA file
#
# This file is provided by Oracle Corporation to help you customize
# your RDBMS installation for your site. Important system parameters
# are discussed, and example settings given.
#
# Some parameter settings are generic to any size installation.
# For parameters that require different values in different size
# installations, three scenarios have been provided: SMALL, MEDIUM,
# and LARGE. Any parameter that needs to be tuned according to
# installation size will have three settings, each one commented
# according to installation size.
#
# Use the following table to approximate the SGA size needed for the
# three scenarios provided in this file:
#
#                      -------Installation/Database Size------
#                       SMALL           MEDIUM           LARGE
#  Block         2K     4500K            6800K          17000K
#  Size          4K     5500K            8800K          21000K
#
##############################################################################

db_name = ORCL

instance_name = ORCL

service_names = ORCL

db_files = 1024  # INITIAL

control_files = ("D:\Oracle\oradata\ORCL\control01.ctl",
                 "D:\Oracle\oradata\ORCL\control02.ctl")

db_file_multiblock_read_count = 8

db_block_buffers = 8192

shared_pool_size = 15728640

java_pool_size = 20971520

log_checkpoint_interval = 10000
log_checkpoint_timeout = 1800

processes = 59

log_buffer = 32768
```

```
#audit_trail = true  # if you want auditing
timed_statistics = true  # if you want timed statistics
max_dump_file_size = 10240  # limit trace file size to 5M each

# Uncommenting the line below will cause automatic archiving if archiving has
# been enabled using ALTER DATABASE ARCHIVELOG.
# log_archive_start = true
# log_archive_dest_1 = "location=D:\Oracle\oradata\ORCL\archive"
# log_archive_format = "%%ORCL%%T%TS%S.ARC"

# If using private rollback segments, place lines of the following
# form in each of your instance-specific init.ora files:
# rollback_segments = (r01, r02, r03, r04)

# If using public rollback segments, define how many
# rollback segments each instance will pick up, using the formula
#   # of rollback segments = transactions / transactions_per_rollback_segment
# In this example each instance will grab 40/5 = 8
# transactions = 40
# transactions_per_rollback_segment = 5

# Global Naming -- enforce that a dblink has same name as the db it connects to
global_names = true


# oracle_trace_enable = true

oracle_trace_collection_name = ""
# define directories to store trace and alert files
background_dump_dest = D:\Oracle\admin\ORCL\bdump
user_dump_dest = D:\Oracle\admin\ORCL\udump

db_block_size = 2048

remote_login_passwordfile = exclusive

os_authent_prefix = ""

# The following parameters are needed for the Advanced Replication Option
job_queue_processes = 2
job_queue_interval = 10
open_links = 4

distributed_transactions = 500
mts_dispatchers = "(PROTOCOL=TCP)(PRE=oracle.aurora.server.SGiopServer)"

mts_servers = 1
compatible = 8.1.0
```

The rest of this section provides a list of the more important INIT.ORA parameters and a brief description of what each option controls and what its initial setting should be:

- **BACKGROUND_DUMP_DEST**—Specifies the location of the directory in which the alert.log and any trace files will be created.
- **CHECKPOINT_PROCESS**—Is set to `true` or `false` depending on whether checkpointing is desired.
- **CONTROL_FILES**—Lists the Oracle-maintained control files. I recommend having at least three, each on a separate disk drive.
- **DB_BLOCK_BUFFERS**—Specifies the size of the buffer cache in the SGA.
- **DB_BLOCK_SIZE**—Specifies the size of the database blocks. This parameter is used in the `CREATE DATABASE` SQL statement.
- **DB_FILES**—Determines how many operating system files Oracle can have access to at any one time. The online redo logs are part of this number. In addition, this parameter does cause SGA space to be used.
- **DB_FILE_MULTI_BLOCK_READ_COUNT**—Specifies the number of blocks that will be read with each read request. This value times the value for the DB_BLOCK_SIZE parameter should equal 64KB.
- **HASH_JOIN_ENABLE**—Defaults to true, enabling memory hash joins (discussed in Chapter 6).
- **HASH_AREA_SIZE**—Defaults to twice the value of the SORT_AREA_SIZE parameter.
- **HASH_MULTI_BLOCK_IO_COUNT**—Defaults to the value of the DB_FILE_MULTI_BLOCK_READ_COUNT parameter.
- **LARGE_POOL_SIZE**—Defaults to 0 and can be specified in kilobytes (KB) or megabytes (MB).
- **LARGE_POOL_MIN_ALLOC**—Specifies the minimum size of the large pool.
- **LOG_ARCHIVE_BUFFERS and LOG_ARCHIVE_BUFFER_SIZE**—Associated with writing the online redo logs to the archive logs. These parameters might need to be increased only if archiving directly to tape devices and if the redo log buffers are waiting on archive log buffers.
- **LOG_ARCHIVE_DEST**—Specifies the location of the archive logs if log archive mode is enabled.
- **LOG_ARCHIVE_FORMAT**—Determines the naming convention used for the archive logs created.

- **LOG_ARCHIVE_START**—Is associated with automatic archiving when the database is started.
- **LOG_BUFFER**—Determines the size of the redo log buffer in the SGA.
- **LOG_CHECKPOINT_INTERVAL**—Is used to determine the frequency of checkpointing. This number is set to the number of redo buffer blocks processed before taking a checkpoint.
- **MAX_ROLLBACK_SEGMENTS**—Identifies the maximum number of rollback segments that can be kept available for user processes.
- **OPTIMIZER_GOAL**—Is used by the cost-based optimizer and can globally force an application's default behavior by specifying FIRST_ROWS or ALL_ROWS.
- **OPTIMIZER_MODE**—Defaults to `COST` and will use the cost-based optimizer if collected statistics exist. Setting OPTIMIZER_MODE to `RULE` will use the rule-based optimizer unless SQL hints are specified. If `CHOOSE` is specified and any of the objects involved have statistics, Oracle will use the cost-based optimizer.
- **ROLLBACK_SEGMENTS**—Specifies the rollback segments by name, which are placed online when the database is started.
- **SHARED_POOL_SIZE**—Is the size of the shared pool in the SGA.
- **SHARED_POOL_RESERVED_SIZE**—Is used for packages.
- **SHARED_POOL_RESERVED_MIN_ALLOC**—Specifies the minimum memory allotment.
- **SORT_AREA_SIZE**—Specifies the size of the sort area in the SGA.
- **SQL_TRACE**—Is used to collect tuning statistics from the Oracle environment. It is set to `false` by default.
- **TIMED_STATISTICS**—Is used by some v$ table statistics that are relative to clock time. Make sure this line is uncommented and set to `true`.

5

Using Tablespaces for Table and Index Placement on Disk Storage

Balancing the hard disk read and write (I/O) activity across many *physical disk drives* will probably provide the single biggest improvement on SQL statement response time. After this I/O activity has been balanced, true SQL issues, such as missing indexes or poor SQL coding techniques, can be addressed.

Physical disk drives—Actual separate hard disks, not a single hard disk that has been partitioned into C:\, D:\, and so on on Windows NT or logical partitions on UNIX. The idea here is to minimize the physical movement of the disk drive head. A single physical drive's head would have to shuffle over the drive surface to retrieve Oracle data blocks belonging to various tables being referenced in the same SQL statement.

Many methods are available for distributing this I/O activity. Oracle8 supports *object partitioning*, in which you can simply put a partitioned object in a single table or index having its data stored in different tablespaces. These various tablespaces have physical files on separate physical disk drives. Partitioning is covered in detail in Chapter 8, "Understanding Oracle8i Index and Partitioning Features." Another method is to rely on *RAID* technology to spread the data across many hard drives. RAID works on the theory of placing small pieces of a physical file randomly across many disk drives; the computer looks at the RAID device as a single disk drive. RAID hardware and software handle the spreading and retrieving of data.

RAID (redundant array of inexpensive disks)—A device that holds many small disk drives but which the computer will view as a single disk drive. The software on the RAID device handles striping and other features of RAID.

Figure 5.4 shows the tablespace for the Sales Tracking Application. The physical files assigned to these tablespaces should reside on separate physical hard drives. From an Oracle8i point of view, the underlying file structure is irrelevant. This tablespace structure would help the database administrator (DBA) move the Sales Tracking Application from a smaller computer to a larger computer or from a single hard disk to multiple hard disks. The underlying tablespace files can be redefined and the data easily exported and imported as long as the tablespace names do not change.

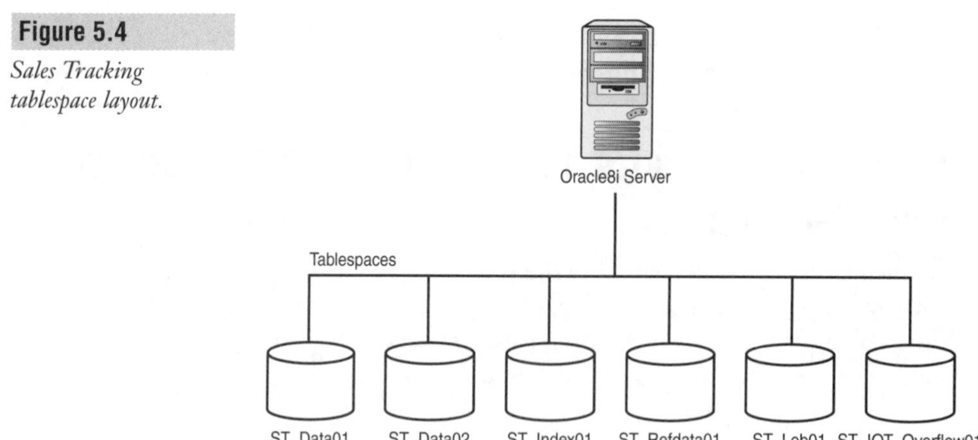

Figure 5.4

Sales Tracking tablespace layout.

The optimal hard disk configuration for the Sales Tracking Application is to have the NT (or UNIX) operating system reside on one hard disk (along with any other applications, such as word processing, user directories, and so on). This same hard disk could also be the home of the Oracle8i software. Each of the Sales Tracking tablespaces listed in Figure 5.4 would have its own hard disk. The data files belonging to the SYSTEM, TEMPORARY, and ROLLBACK tablespaces should be on separate hard disks, as well. In addition, if the Sales Tracking Application has a high volume of DML-type SQL (for example, a large auto repair business is using the Sales Tracking software), the online redo logs should be on yet another separate hard disk. Depending on application needs, you should have enough separate hard disks to evenly balance the I/O.

Experience has shown that the best performance gains come from physically separating related objects on to separate disk drives. Such objects include tables and their associated indexes and tables being routinely joined with other tables.

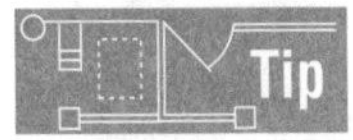

RAID level 5 is useful for those read-type applications that require a high degree of availability.

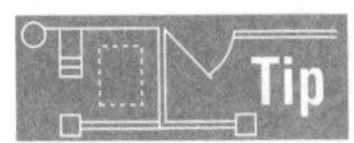

RAID technology is not recommended for the SYSTEM, TEMPORARY, or ROLLBACK tablespaces unless a need exists for a fault-tolerant computing environment at the expense of performance.

Hard disk activity easily can be monitored with Quest Spotlight for Oracle (see Figure 5.5; on the toolbar, select I/O, I/O by Datafile) and Quest SQLab Xpert (see Figure 5.6; on the menu, select Tools bar, I/O Bottleneck Resolution). Listing 5.14 produces similar information to that of Quest SQLab Xpert. Hard disk activity on UNIX can be monitored with the `sar -d` or `iostat -d` command. Either of these commands will report on read/write activity to all system disk drives. The Spotlight for Oracle is useful for visualizing the balance of I/O between the tablespaces. This information helps SQLab Xpert obtain the exact statistics from the I/O Bottleneck Resolution screen, which in turn enables you to see the actual SQL statements creating the activity. Position the pointer on the tablespace or data file in this window and right-click. Then, click the Show SQL button to see the SQL statements that are accessing this data file or tablespace.

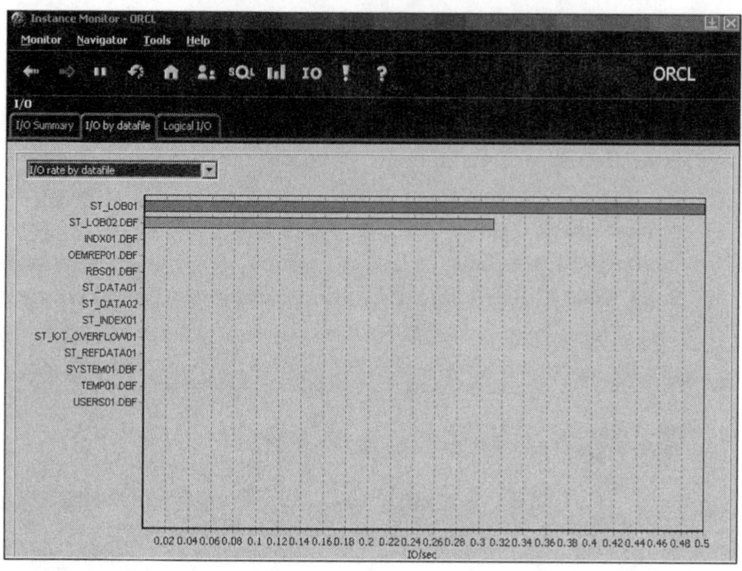

Figure 5.5

Spotlight for Oracle illustrating database file activity.

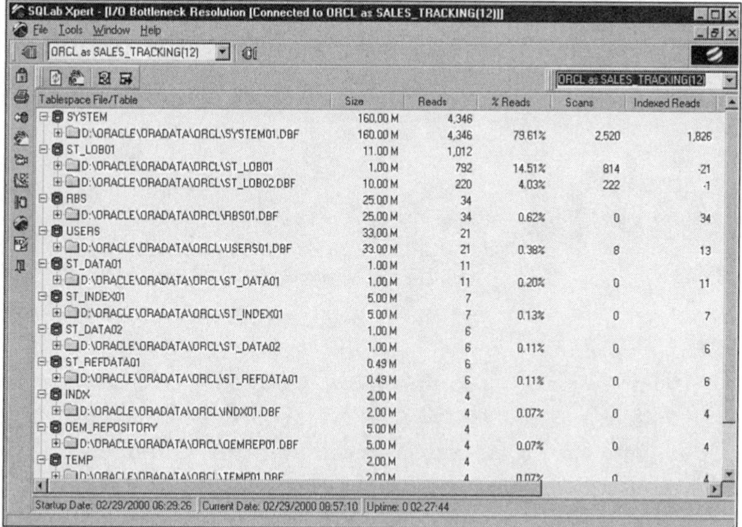

Figure 5.6

SQLab Xpert showing database file statistics.

Listing 5.14—Disk I/O Activity SQL Script

```
select b.name "File Name", a.phyrds "Physical Reads",
       a.phywrts "Physical Writes"
from v$filestat a, v$datafile
where a.file# = b.file#
```

Review the `from` and `where` clauses of these SQL statements. These SQL statements easily can be copied to the SQL tuning area of SQLab Xpert by right-clicking the

SQL statement as pictured in Figure 5.7. Figure 5.8 illustrates the SQLab Xpert SQL tuning area. SQL tuning is covered in depth in Chapter 6. This information shows which parts of the SQL statement are using indexes, and so on to see which objects should be moved to better balance the hard disk I/O activity. Try to keep the indexes on separate hard disks from their associated tables. Referential integrity can make the object distribution easy by placing the parent table, child tables, and primary/foreign key indexes all on separate hard disks if possible.

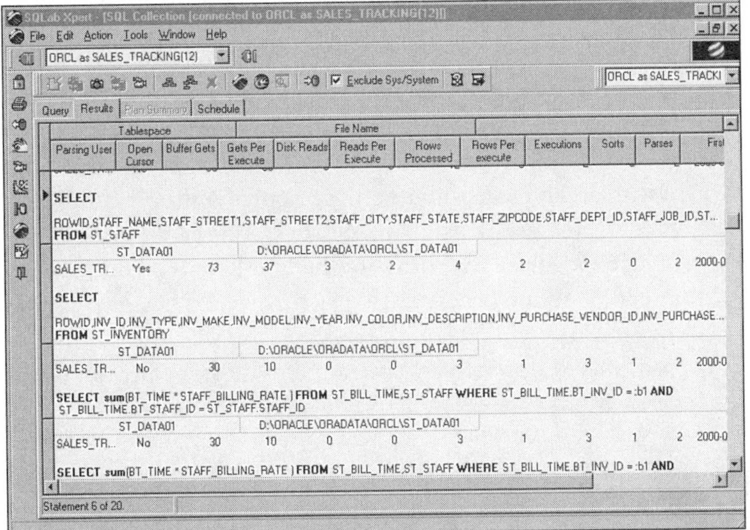

Figure 5.7

SQLab Xpert showing SQL activity at the Oracle8i data file level.

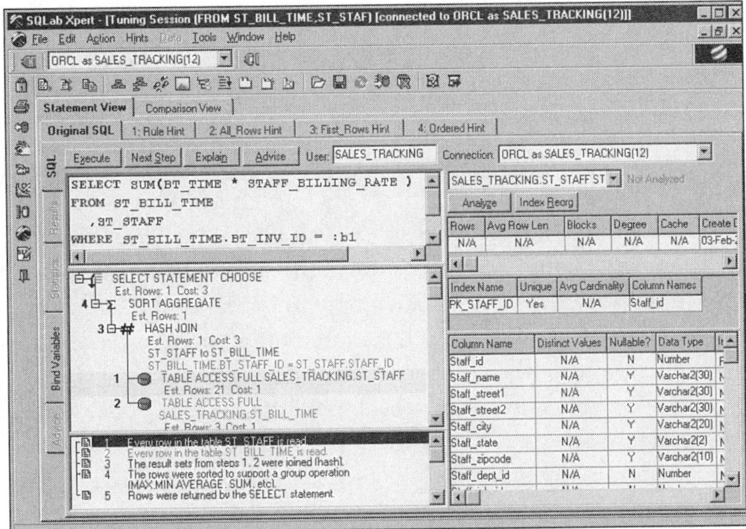

Figure 5.8

SQLab Xpert SQL tuning window showing explain plan, table, and index statistics.

5

Monitoring Oracle8i and the Sales Tracking Application

When performance issues exist in the database—usually noticed by users because of slow response time—determining the cause is important. Is it due to poorly performing SQL statements? Is it some kind of locking contention? Is it some kind of resource contention? We have discussed how to use Spotlight for Oracle to monitor for resource contention earlier in this chapter. Figure 5.9 is accessed either by right-clicking the Users area on the left side of Spotlight for Oracle or by clicking the 2 people icon (to the right of the house, or home icon). Notice that you can quickly identify a particular user. Unless something has turned red in the Spotlight for Oracle screen, looking up the SQL the user is currently running is usually a good place to begin searching for the performance problem. Notice all the information available: the logged-in user, the resource utilization (the pie chart on the right), computer statistics, database statistics, and the program the user is currently using. Notice the lower-left corner of the Spotlight for Oracle screen—an explain plan easily can be seen by clicking either of these two buttons. The left button is Spotlight for Oracle's explain plan; the right button with the globe starts SQLab/Xpert and loads this SQL statement into a tuning session. Explain plans are covered in depth in Chapter 6.

The icons under the toolbar access many of the various monitoring events in Spotlight for Oracle. The house icon, or home, places the main SGA display onscreen. All these monitoring events are also available under the Navigator menu item, as well as by clicking many of the items on the home or SGA screen.

The Spotlight for Oracle's main screen provides a good representation of the Oracle SGA. The Activity Summary tab (accessible from the Navigator on the menu bar or by clicking the three vertical bars just left of I/O) on the Activity screen is a good place to see the general health of an Oracle instance. Figure 5.10 illustrates the Activity Summary screen. Notice the six strip charts that will give the current and near-current status of many important areas in the Oracle environment, such as Physical I/O, Logical I/O, resource contention (lower-left chart), the miss rate of the library cache (the number of times SQL had to be reloaded into this area), and a visual of the number of sessions and their rate of activity (upper-right chart). Notice the tabs along the top of this screen that enable you to see details of the information from this screen.

Figure 5.9

Spotlight for Oracle top SQL sessions.

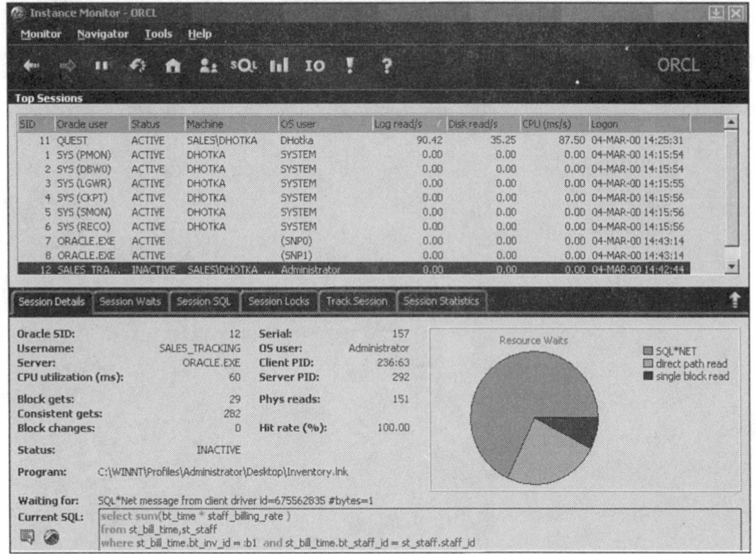

Figure 5.10

Spotlight for Oracle Activity Summary.

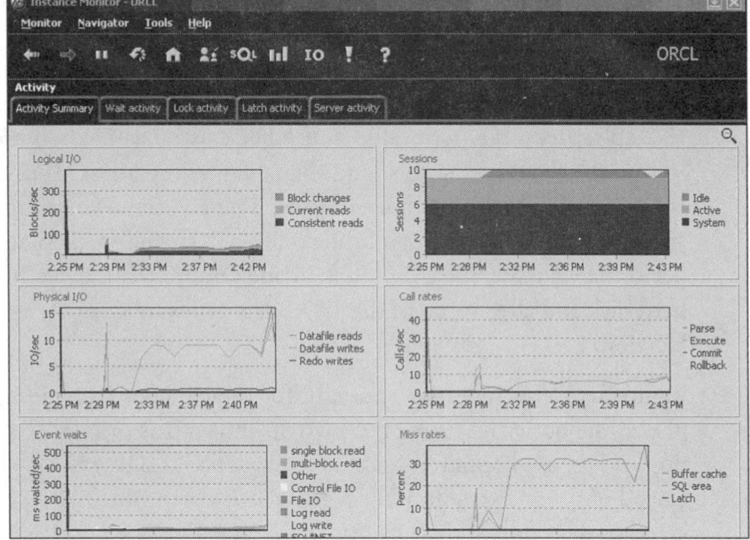

The I/O screen monitors the flow of data to and from the various parts of the SGA. This screen can be accessed by clicking the IO icon.

The important chart on the logical I/O screen is the rollback segment logical I/O in the lower left (see Figure 5.11). Any time any wait activity exists—that is, someone is waiting for a rollback segment to become available—it indicates that enough rollback segments do not exist for the application using the database.

5

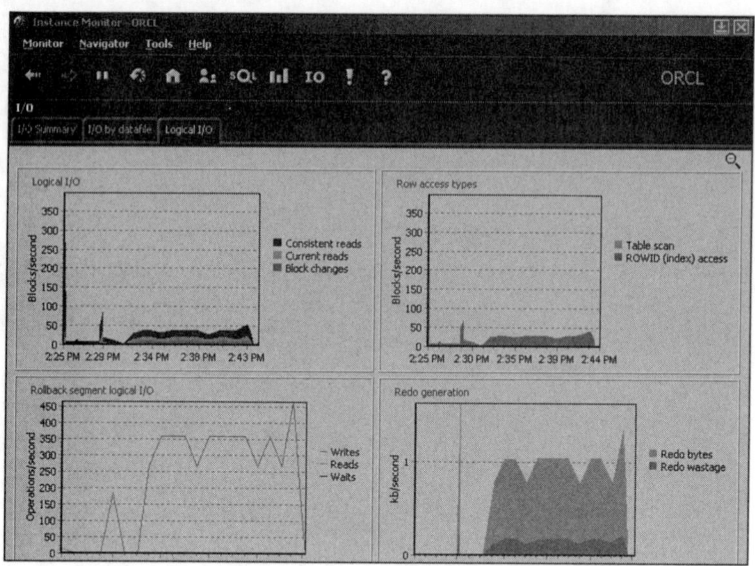

Figure 5.11

Spotlight on Oracle Logical I/O Summary.

The I/O Summary illustrated in Figure 5.12 is similar to the I/O by Data File discussed in Figure 5.7, except this information is from a tablespace point of view rather than the actual tablespace data file point of view as illustrated in Figure 5.7. This screen is useful in monitoring general Oracle I/O rates and the balance of I/O across the tablespaces. If a noticeable imbalance existed, you could use the I/O by Data File to find the SQL statements (and the tables being accessed) to determine a better distribution of the table or index objects. The I/O rate is high on the ST_LOB01 tablespace because we have put all the pictures in the one tablespace. If this becomes a performance issue, the solution is to add another tablespace for LOBs on a different hard disk and alter some of the LOB data types to store their contents in the new location.

Figure 5.13 illustrates the Spotlight for Oracle home screen. If this were a color photo, the buffer hit cache ratio would show up as orange. This is an alarm condition. It is caused because the buffer hit cache ratio was below 90% for a specified period of time. Two solutions to this particular problem are possible: You can increase the value of the DB_BLOCK_BUFFERS (tune it as per earlier discussions in this chapter) or you can implement the keep, recycle, and default buffer pools (also discussed earlier in this chapter).

Figure 5.12

Spotlight for Oracle I/O Summary.

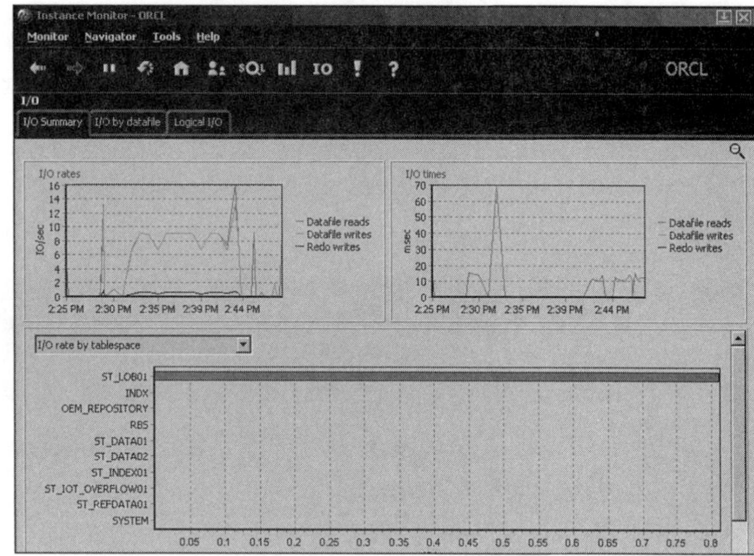

More information on the alarms is available by clicking the ! icon. Right-clicking these alarms brings up very specific help text about the alarm clicked.

Figure 5.13

Spotlight for Oracle home screen with buffer hit cache ratio alarm raised.

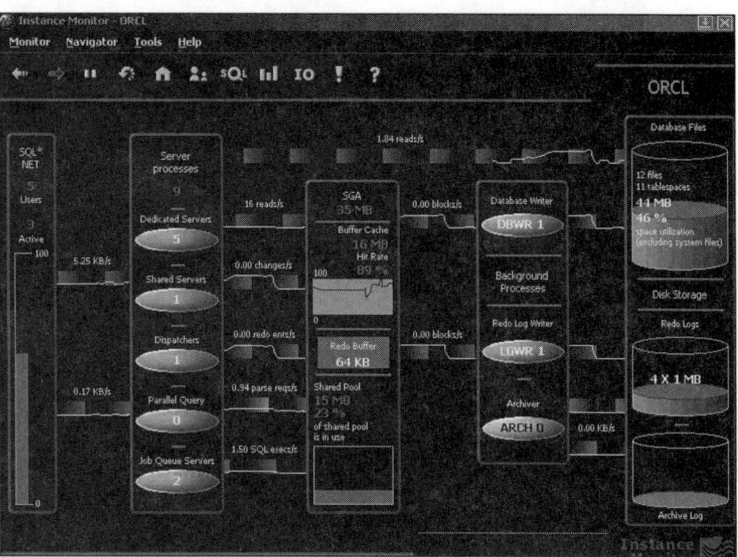

The final example in this section illustrates contention between two SQL statements, a locking issue in which two SQL statements want to update the same rows (see Figure 5.14). This screen shows the exact locking situation, the user who has it, and the user who wants it. Notice all the diagnostic information is also available, such as the application running the SQL statement, the users, I/O statistics, and the SQL statements. From here, you can right-click the offending session and kill or end the session.

Figure 5.14

Spotlight for Oracle Lock Activity screen.

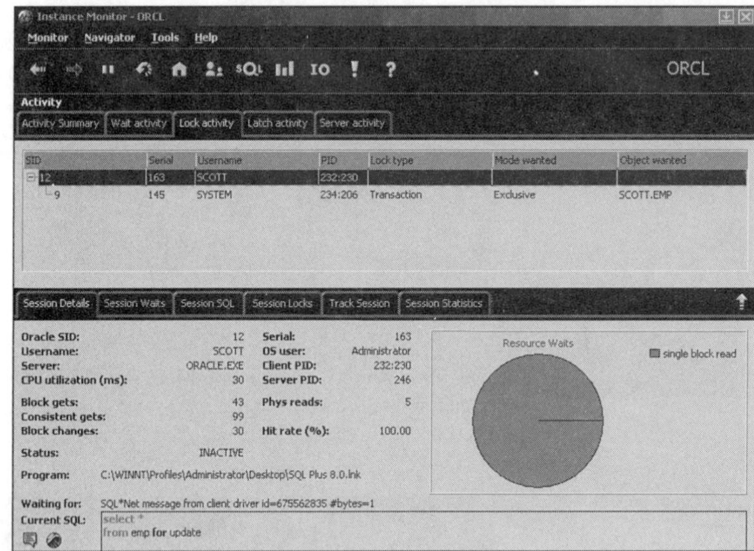

Understanding Database Fragmentation

Many kinds of database fragmentation exist; some kinds can be good, but most kinds of fragmentation can cause serious performance issues. Database fragmentation is a problem that grows over time, and the performance implications also grow over time. We will discuss the various kinds of fragmentation that have an adverse effect on Oracle-based applications, how to identify when fragmentation is occurring, how to correct the problems after they're discovered, and most importantly, what causes the fragmentation. This will enable you to design the database correctly to prevent the fragmentation from occurring in the first place.

What Is Database Fragmentation?

Fragmentation is best described as a grouping of noncontiguous database objects. Fragmentation usually means extra resources are consumed (disk I/O, rotational delay of the disk drives, dynamic extensions, chained blocks, and so on) to perform the requested database function. The only good fragmentation is intentional fragmentation: either disk striping or Oracle partitioning. The objective with *disk striping* is to take little pieces of a file and spread them evenly over a hard disk or a series of hard disks (RAID drives do this) because not all users will be accessing the same part of the file. If the spreading is effective, about the same I/O is required on a busy system as on a smaller load on the same system. *Oracle partitioning* takes parts of a table or index object and spreads them across several tablespaces because not all users will be accessing the same part of the object at the same time.

An *extent* is a unit of storage at the object level and is a contiguous group of data blocks. The `INITIAL EXTENT` and `NEXT EXTENT` options in the `storage` clause (the default `storage` clause of the tablespace or specified in the `storage` clause when the object is created) control the size of the initial allocation and the subsequent allocations of tablespace space to a particular object. This extent method reserves space for future use, space that other objects cannot use. When objects use up all the data blocks in the initial extent, Oracle creates the next extent, based on the parameters set at the `storage` clause, and the object then begins storing data in this next extent. This extent becomes available for other objects only if all the rows within this extent are deleted. The associated data blocks are removed from the object and this space is then available for other objects to use.

Adding extents is known as *dynamic allocation*. Oracle always make an attempt to use any empty extents found in the tablespace first. Oracle first looks for an empty extent that is the same size as the extent being requested. If this exact match is not found, Oracle makes a second pass, looking for a larger extent (of which it will use only the part needed, leaving behind some space that will probably not be reused). If it does not find a larger free extent, Oracle rounds down the size of the extent being requested and performs this search again.

This searching is time consuming. If an application is subject to deletes that will empty data blocks (for example, a date-oriented delete), all objects in this particular tablespace should use the same initial and next extent sizes. Based on the previously mentioned dynamic allocation, reusing the space and not wasting any space would be easier for Oracle if all the objects used the same extent size in the application.

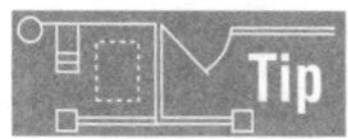

Set up the default storage parameters at the tablespace level and do not include initial and next extent sizes when creating tables and indexes. This will ensure a uniform extent size for all objects in a particular tablespace.

Deletes can leave unused space behind in data blocks and leave smaller disk segments unused in the tablespace, wasting tablespace space. The Oracle process PMON (Process Monitor) periodically *coalesces* contiguous unused smaller extents into single, larger available extents but does not reshuffle used extents so that all free space in the tablespace is together. The only way to fix wasted space in blocks is to re-create the object and copy all its data to the new object. This is accomplished by either using syntax, such as CREATE TABLE <new table name> AS SELECT * FROM <existing table name>, or exporting the data, dropping the object, re-creating the object, and then importing the data back. The only way to recapture various unused extents between objects in a tablespace is to reorganize the whole tablespace and perform the process just described for all the objects in the tablespace at the same time.

Coalesce—In Oracle terms, a method of joining two or more empty adjoining extents in the tablespace into a single larger extent.

Reorganization is a good time to review I/O distribution and possibly relocate some objects to other tablespaces. You must consider many factors when reorganizing objects or entire tablespaces. Any code, such as database triggers, will need to be re-created, and any PL/SQL procedures or functions that made reference to the objects being dropped will need to be recompiled. Additionally, indexes must be re-created, and referential integrity will need to be re-established. The table objects should all be locked in exclusive mode during this process to prevent a user from making changes that would invalidate the constraint when they are re-created. Grants and permissions also must be re-applied. The rebuild takes time and must be performed at a time when the objects are not available to the application. Extent *interleaving* occurs when two or more data objects in the same tablespace are dynamically growing in such a way that the newly added extents are not next to the existing extent, much like a checkerboard. Oracle performs best with a minimal number of extents and when extents are next to each other. This is because the fewer the extents, the fewer trips Oracle must make to the data dictionary to find out where the next extent is. Objects involved in this interleaving should be reorganized. Extent interleaving can be completely eliminated by putting tables with static or very little growth together in a tablespace and placing each dynamically growing object in a tablespace by itself. This increases tablespace maintenance but eliminates this type of fragmentation.

Two particularly bad kinds of fragmentation will have a direct, negative impact on performance. Row chaining and row migration cause Oracle to have to perform extra I/Os per row to retrieve the data being requested. The more I/Os that Oracle must perform, the longer a user waits for the requested data.

Row chaining is caused when a row being inserted is larger than the Oracle block size. When this occurs, Oracle will *chain*, or link by block number, an additional block(s) to hold the remaining data from the row. This chained block is not indexed and cannot be referenced without first referencing the original block. This greatly slows the data access because Oracle has to wait for an additional I/O process to retrieve the chained block. Therefore, if significant chaining occurs, performance can be seriously affected. The only way to correct this kind of chaining is either to export the whole database, re-create the database with a larger block size, and then import the whole database, or to locate the object and its data into an Oracle database that already has a larger block size.

Chaining can also occur when a row is being updated and the block doesn't have enough free space to contain the new row with the update.

Row migration is caused by an update in which the block doesn't have enough free space to contain the new row. If the object has several indexes, moving the row can cause a significant amount of updating to these indexes because the underlying `ROWID` for the row will have changed. Oracle version 7 introduced row migration in which the updated row relocates the updated row to a different block where it completely fits, leaving a `ROWID` pointer in the original block that references the new row location in another block. In this method, the indexes do not need to be updated, and unlike chaining, the row is in a regular data block being used by other rows of the same object. Similar to chaining, however, it always requires extra I/O (there is no reason this row would have been migrated several times) to find the actual row. Another similarity it shares with row chaining is that no other way exists to access this row in the new location except to access the original location first. Once again, Oracle must wait for an additional disk I/O to retrieve the new row. During the update that migrates the row, Oracle will also have to search for a block with enough free space to hold it. This, too, can be a time-consuming process for Oracle.

Row migration and row chaining caused by updates can be limited by making adjustments to the `PCTFREE` parameters in the `storage` clause. `PCTFREE` is the amount of space left in each Oracle block after insertions for the purpose of accommodating future updates. However, altering the `PCTFREE` clause will not have any effect on any existing migrated rows. Therefore, the table will have to be reorganized as mentioned previously.

Discovering Database Fragmentation

The SQL statement in Listing 5.15 monitors growth, the number of extents, and the maximum number of extents assigned.

Listing 5.15—Extent Allocation by Tablespace

```
SELECT  tablespace_name "TABLESPACE",
        segment_name "SEGMENT",
extents "EXTENTS",
        max_extents "MAX EXTENTS",
        bytes "SIZE",
        owner "OWNER"
 FROM   dba_segments
WHERE   owner not in ('SYS','SYSTEM','SCOTT','NET_CONF')
  and   extents > 1
ORDER BY tablespace_name,owner,segment_name;
```

Row chaining and row migration can be discovered by using the ANALYZE command. ANALYZE TABLE <table name> LIST CHAINED ROWS populates the CHAINED_ROWS table with the row IDs of the chained rows. SELECT COUNT(*) FROM chained_rows WHERE table_name = '<table name>', on the other hand, gives an indication of the amount of chaining occurring. The CHAINED_ROWS table also contains the row IDs of the offending rows. An easy way to fix limited amounts of chaining is to copy these rows from the original table to a temporarily created table (using CREATE TABLE <table name> AS <select * with a subquery based on table CHAINED_ROWS), delete the rows from the original object, and copy the rows back from the recently created table with just the offending rows. Be sure you drop the newly created table when finished with this process.

CHAINED_ROWS is part of the utlchain.sql script found in the ORACLE_HOME/rdbms/admin directory.

Summary

This chapter introduced you to the concept of tuning the Oracle8i database environment. Tuning, or making an application perform at its peak performance on any given hardware platform, is not the easiest of tasks, and with the Oracle database product, many different areas can cause performance issues. Many of these issues were discussed in this chapter. You should now have a good understanding of the Oracle8i System Global Area (SGA), how to change its characteristics, and how to monitor for issues that might require adjusting. This chapter also introduced you to the concept of where the various application objects are on disk and how this relates to performance. Finally, this chapter discussed how Oracle records its data, the concept of row chaining and row migration, the effects this has on performance, and how to correct these issues.

Next Steps

After you have the SGA set up correctly and the database objects separated according to the application needs, the next step is to actually understand how the SQL statement is interpreted by Oracle8i, how to tell Oracle8i what to do with specific parts of a SQL statement, and how this can affect performance as well. Chapter 6 is an in-depth study of the Oracle optimizers (how Oracle makes read/write decisions on each SQL statement), how to see the decisions Oracle has made for a particular SQL statement, and how to understand the various parts of this decision-making process. I will also share some of my tips on tuning SQL statements.

In this chapter

- *What Is the SQL Explain Plan?*
- *SQL Coding Guidelines*

Chapter 6

Tuning the Sales Tracking Application

In this chapter, we will discuss how to monitor SQL statements, add indexes, and make the changes necessary to produce top-performing Oracle-based applications.

What Is the SQL Explain Plan?

The *explain plan* illustrates the *execution plan* for any SQL statement. It shows the tables and indexes Oracle will use when processing a SQL statement, as well as the order in which the tables and indexes will be used. The execution plan is the order of events that Oracle will follow to access data and process the SQL statement. The explain plan and execution plan are determined when SQL is presented to Oracle for execution. If a SQL statement's actual code does not change and the SQL statement is still in the library cache, Oracle will simply reuse the original execution plan (discussed in Chapter 5, "Monitoring the Sales Tracking Application"). Oracle8i enables you to store and reuse this execution plan, which is known as *stored outlines*. If you develop and tune a SQL statement in a test environment to use a very specific execution plan in the production environment, stored outlines enable you to guarantee that a particular SQL statement used a certain execution plan.

Oracle8i supports two optimizers, a rule-based optimizer and a cost-based optimizer. The *optimizer* determines which explain plan is best for any SQL statement. It is possible that the same explain plan will be generated differently with subsequent submissions of a SQL statement not previously found in the library cache. The stored outlines come in handy, therefore, if the same execution plan is desired.

The Oracle Optimizers

As mentioned previously, the optimizers tell Oracle the best execution path for a particular SQL statement. The rule-based optimizer is the original Oracle optimizer and makes decisions based on how the SQL statement is physically coded and the existence of indexes. The cost-based optimizer, on the other hand, was introduced with Oracle6 and makes its decisions based on statistics gathered by the `ANALYZE` command.

The Rule-Based Optimizer

The rule-based optimizer uses 19 rules to determine the execution path for a SQL statement (see Listing 6.1). The lower the rank (the rules are ranked from 1–19, with 1 being the best), the better the SQL statement should perform. Changing the execution plan (*tuning*) is accomplished by forcing the rule-based optimizer to make different selections. For example, adding an index to a column in the `WHERE` clause would alter the rank. If you don't want to use an index, you can add a function to an indexed field in a `WHERE` clause, which changes the rank and effectively disables the use of the index for this particular SQL statement. How the SQL statement is physically coded, particularly the order of the tables listed in the `FROM` clause, has a dramatic effect on the rule-based optimizer. For example, consider the concept of a driving table, or the table that is compared to the others in a `join` SQL statement (multiple tables listed in the `FROM` clause). Because Oracle parses SQL statements from back to front, the driving table in a rule-based optimized SQL statement is the last one listed in the SQL statement. A few other dependencies can affect this decision, but for the most part, substantial performance gains can be gotten just by changing the order of the tables in the `FROM` clause.

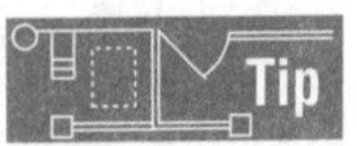

The *driving table* is the table that is accessed first and then used to look up information in the other tables in the `join` condition. The driving table always should be the smaller table or the table with the greatest degree of selectivity in the `WHERE` clause. The `join` columns in the other non-driving tables should have a unique index to ensure optimal performance.

Oracle offers no guarantee that between releases these rules will remain the same or that the rule-based optimizer will make the same decisions as in prior releases. Therefore, testing applications when moving to newer versions of Oracle software is important.

Listing 6.1—Rule-Based Optimizer Rules

```
Rank    Where Clause Rule
1       ROWID = constant
2       unique indexed column = constant
3       entire unique concatenated index = constant
4       entire cluster key = cluster key of object in same cluster
5       entire cluster key = constant
6       entire nonunique concatenated index = constant
7       nonunique index = constant
8       entire noncompressed concatenated index >= constant
9       entire compressed concatenated index >= constant
10      partial but leading columns of noncompressed concatenated index
11      partial but leading columns of compressed concatenated index
12      unique indexed column using the SQL statement BETWEEN or LIKE options
13      nonunique indexed column using the SQL statement BETWEEN or LIKE options
14      unique indexed column < or > constant
15      nonunique indexed column < or > constant
16      sort/merge
17      MAX or MIN SQL statement functions on indexed column
18      ORDER BY entire index
19      full table scans
```

Sort/merge—An execution plan function that can be used when joining two or more tables together in a SQL statement. A *full table scan* is when all the rows are returned from a table by processing the table from beginning to end.

The Cost-Based Optimizer

The cost-based optimizer makes its decisions based on a cost factor derived from statistics for the objects in the SQL statement. The `ANALYZE` SQL statement is used to collect these statistics. Because larger objects take longer to collect the statistics, Oracle offers an `ESTIMATE` option on the `ANALYZE` command so that only a percentage of rows are used to gather the statistics. The cost-based optimizer bases its execution-path decisions strictly on these collected statistics, so it is important to keep the statistics fresh, particularly with objects that have many DML-type SQL statements.

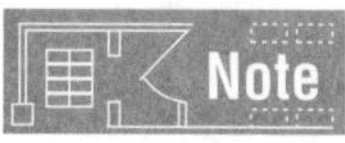

The rule-based optimizer has supported few new indexing, partitioning, or performance features since Oracle version 7.3. Options such as partitioned tables, index-only tables, reverse indexes, histograms, hash joins, parallel query, and bitmapped indexes are supported only by the cost-based optimizer.

You can enable the cost-based optimizer by running the `ANALYZE` command to collect statistics. The `INIT.ORA` parameter `OPTIMIZER_MODE` must be set to `CHOOSE` or `COST`, or it can be set at the user-session level with the `ALTER SESSION` command. You can disable the cost-based optimizer easily by either resetting the `INIT.ORA` parameter

OPTOMIZER_MODE or deleting the statistics. If the shared pool has any current SQL statements that have execution plans based on newer statistics, Oracle will invalidate the SQL in the shared pool, allowing it to be re-prepared using the new statistics the next time the SQL statement is executed.

The database must be shut down and restarted for any INIT.ORA parameter file changes to take effect. The ALTER SESSION command takes effect immediately.

The ANALYZE command sorts the rows in the table and can be a time-consuming, resource-intensive process for larger objects. The ESTIMATE option of the ANALYZE command gathers a sampling of information from the object on which to base its statistics. Figure 6.1 shows the SQL*Plus help text for the ANALYZE command.

Figure 6.1

The ANALYZE command.

```
Oracle SQL*Plus
File Edit Search Options Help

ANALYZE {INDEX | TABLE | CLUSTER}
        [schema.]{index [PARTITION (partition_name)]
                  | table [PARTITION (partition_name)]
                  | cluster}
  { COMPUTE STATISTICS [FOR for_clause]
  | ESTIMATE STATISTICS [FOR for_clause]
                        [SAMPLE integer {ROWS | PERCENT} ]
  | DELETE STATISTICS
  | VALIDATE REF UPDATE
  | VALIDATE STRUCTURE [CASCADE]
  | LIST CHAINED ROWS [INTO [schema.]table] }

for_clause
  [ FOR TABLE
  | FOR ALL [INDEXED] COLUMNS [SIZE integer]
  | FOR COLUMNS [SIZE integer] column | attribute [SIZE integer]
                            [column | attribute [SIZE integer] ] ...
  | FOR ALL [LOCAL] INDEXES]

For detailed information on this command, see the Oracle8 Server SQL
Reference.
```

Hints are used to influence the cost-based optimizer and can be used to control the optimizer's goal, access methods, join conditions, parallel option, and partitioning option. Hints are specified in the SQL statement syntax. Listing 6.2 illustrates an ALL_ROWS hint in the SCOTT.EMP table.

Listing 6.2—Hints in SQL Statements

```
select /*+ ALL_ROWS */ ename, sal from EMP where SAL > 1000
```

Listing 6.3 shows most of the hints for controlling the execution plan available in Oracle8i. The cost-based optimizer also has the driving-table mechanism in join conditions. The ORDERED hint causes the driving table to be the first table in the FROM clause of the SQL statement.

The optimizer goal hint controls one of three modes: RULE forces the rule-based optimizer; FIRST_ROWS is the quickest at returning initial rows; and ALL_ROWS, which is the best overall, uses the cost-based optimizer and forces the optimizer to the desired goal.

Listing 6.3—Access Control Hints

```
Hint            Description
AND_EQUAL       Use the AND_EQUAL hint when more than one equality criterion
                exists on a single table.
CACHE           Use the CACHE hint to place the entire table in the buffer
                cache. The table is placed at the most recently used end of
                the buffer cache. This hint is good for small tables that
                are accessed often.
CLUSTER         Use the CLUSTER hint to access a table in a cluster without
                the use of an index.
FULL            Use the FULL hint to perform a full table scan on a table.
HASH            Use the HASH hint to access a table in a hashed cluster
                without the use of an index.
INDEX           Use an INDEX hint to instruct ORACLE to use one of the indexes
                specified as a parameter.
INDEX_COMBINE   The INDEX_COMBINE forces the use of bitmap indexes.
NOCACHE         Use the NOCACHE hint to place the blocks of the table at the
                beginning of the buffer cache so as not to age any  blocks out.
NOPARALLEL      Use the NOPARALLEL hint to not use multiple-server processes to
                service the operations on the specified table.
ORDERED         Use the ORDERED hint to access the tables in the FROM clause in
                the order they appear.
PARALLEL        Use the PARALLEL hint to request multiple server processes to
                simultaneously service the operations on the specified table.
PUSH_SUBQ       The PUSH_SUBQ evaluates subqueries earlier, rather than as a
                filter operation.
ROWID           Use the ROWID hint to access the table by ROWID.
STAR            STAR hint invokes the STAR query feature.
USE_HASH        Use the USE_HASH hint to perform a hash join rather than a
merge

                join or a nested loop join.
USE_MERE        Use the USE_MERGE hint to perform a merge join rather than a
                nested loop join or a hash join.
```

Say you have a table full of names, with an index on the last name. Let's also say that this table has proportionately more occurrences of Jones and Smith than most of the other rows. A *histogram* would be useful in this example because data won't be evenly distributed throughout the table object. Prior to histograms, the Oracle optimizer assumed even distribution of values throughout the object.

Histogram—Part of the cost-based optimizer used to manage uneven data distribution in table objects.

Figure 6.2 illustrates a histogram as a series of buckets. Two kinds of histograms are available, width balanced and height balanced. *Width-balanced* histograms have values that are divided up into an even number of buckets, enabling the optimizer to easily determine which buckets have higher counts. In *height-balanced* histograms, however, each bucket has the same number of column values, but a column value can span more than one bucket. Figure 6.2 illustrates what the EMP table might look like in each of these types of histograms.

Figure 6.2

The EMP table in a histogram.

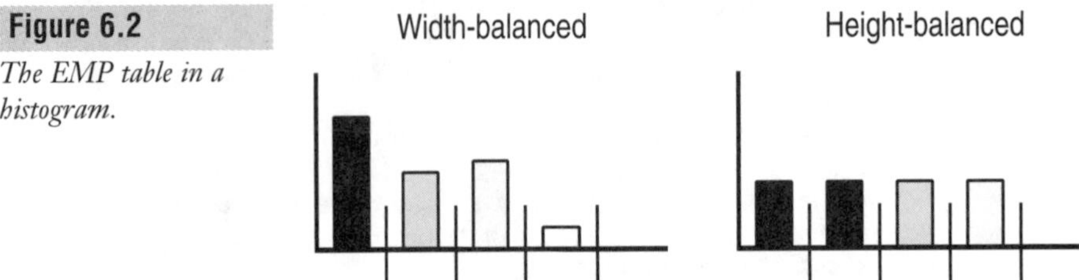

Histograms are implemented by using the `ANALYZE` command and specifying the `column` parameter. Histograms default to 75 buckets, with a maximum of 255 defined buckets, and they can be created for indexes, tables, or clusters.

When two or more tables are joined together, Oracle must pull the columns from each table, creating a *result set*, which is a temporary table of sorts. This result set is created in the TEMPORARY tablespace and contains the combination of rows. The Oracle optimizer chooses one of five methods to perform this join: a nested-loop join, a sort-merge join, a hash join, a cluster join, and (new with Oracle8i) an index join. The most common joins are the first three listed here.

A *nested-loop* join reads the first row from the driving table, or outer table, and checks the other table, called the inner table, for the value. If the value is found then the rows are placed into the result set. Nested-loops work best when the driving table is rather small and a unique index is defined on the inner table's joined column.

A *sort-merge* join sorts both of the joined tables by the join column and then matches the output from these sorts. Any matches are subsequently placed into the result set. The big difference between this join and the nested-loop is that in the sort-merge, no rows are returned until after this matching process completes, whereas the nested-loop returns rows almost immediately. Nested-loops are a good choice when the first few rows need to be returned almost immediately. In contrast, sort-merge joins work better with larger amounts of data, or situations in which the two joining tables are roughly the same size and most of the rows will be returned.

Hash joins can dramatically increase the performance of two joined tables in situations in which one table is significantly larger than the other. The hash join works by splitting two tables into partitions and creating a memory-based *hash table*. This hash table is then used to map join columns from the other table, eliminating the need for a sort-merge. In the hash join method, all tables are scanned only once. Hash joins are implemented by the `INIT.ORA` parameters `HASH_JOIN_ENABLED`, `HASH_MULTIBLOCK_IO_COUNT`, and `HASH_AREA_SIZE`. A star query involves a single table object being joined with several smaller table objects, where the driving table object has a concatenated index key and each of the smaller table objects is referenced by part of that concatenated key. The Oracle cost-based optimizer recognizes this arrangement and builds a memory-based cluster of the smaller tables.

Hash table or hash index—Results when the column being indexed is applied to a calculation and a unique address is returned. A hash table has a predetermined number of slots allocated for these hash keys. The advantage of using hash tables is that the data can be accessed quickly with one or two I/Os to the database. The downside is that the amount of data must be predetermined. In the previously mentioned hash join, the statistics have the row counts for the tables and the hash table can be built quickly.

Cluster joins are used instead of nested-loops when the join condition is making reference to tables that are physically clustered together. The Oracle cost-based optimizer recognizes this condition and uses the cluster join when the tables being joined are in the same cluster. Tables are candidates for clustering when they are joined together and no other queries are typically run against one or the other. Clustering physically aligns the joined column rows together in the same data block, which is why cluster joins are so efficient—the data is already being accessed with a single I/O to the database.

Index joins work on the concept that if all the information required for the SQL statement is found in the index, the underlying table structure is not accessed or referenced in the execution plan.

Figure 6.3 illustrates the differences in the times of the three main kinds of join conditions. Notice that the nested-loop starts out very fast, but the more rows processed, the slower it becomes. The sort-merge join starts off the slowest because it must sort and merge the columns before returning any rows; however, its overall performance is pretty consistent. The hash join, on the other hand, starts out quickly and has the overall best performance because all the columns in the join conditions have a hash key in the hash table, enabling very quick access to the data.

Which method is best? Once again, it depends on the application, the amount of data being joined, and so on.

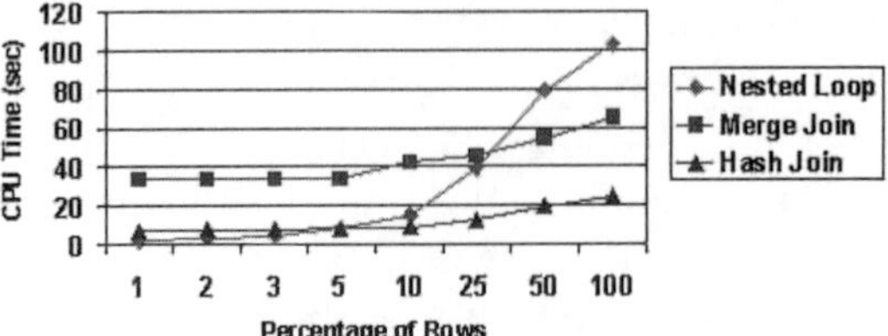

Figure 6.3

CPU time comparisons between nested-loop, sort-merge, and hash joins.

CPU Time (sec) - Parse & Execute

Percentage	Nested Loop	Merge Join	Hash Join
100	103.26	65.63	25.06
50	79.26	54.34	19.16
25	39.01	45.85	12.40
10	15.22	42.26	8.99
5	8.10	34.33	8.50
3	4.54	34.25	7.95
2	3.15	33.47	7.63
1	1.74	33.59	7.60

Tuning the Sales Tracking Application SQL Statements

When we tune SQL statements at the application level, it is important that we are able to monitor and capture long-running, or very I/O-intensive, SQL statements. The old 80/20 rule generally applies here: 20% of the SQL statements are consuming 80% of the system resources. Being able to identify and tune the 20% is critical.

Oracle supplies a product called TKPROF, which is a character-mode tool used to interpret the contents of trace files. *Trace files* contain all the SQL statements and statistics for a particular trace session. Traces can be created by an `INIT.ORA` parameter or more importantly, by setting the `trace` function to on at the application level. For example, one of the options when starting an Oracle form is to trace the form. Traces also can be created by setting a session-level trace to on with a SQL statement, such as `ALTER SESSION SET SQL_TRACE TRUE;`.

The Oracle `trace` facility captures all the SQL statements, but TKPROF is not a tool for the novice, and finding specific poorly performing SQL statements might be difficult. Oracle also provides an explain plan facility, activated by running the script `<ORACLE_HOME>/rdbms/admin/utlxplan.sql`, for each user wanting to visualize explain plans (see Listing 6.4). A single explain plan table can be created and given public access, but if several people are performing SQL statement tuning, it is more convenient for them to simply create their own explain tables. Figure 6.4 illustrates using Quest Software SQLab Xpert to submit a SQL statement and the resulting explain plan. SQLab Xpert is very good at monitoring and finding poorly performing SQL statements across the system or for a particular session but also is an excellent SQL tuning environment. Notice that the resulting explain plans are very similar, but the SQLab, being a GUI environment, has many more features for actually tuning the SQL statement.

Listing 6.4—Oracle Explain Plan Using PLAN_TABLE

```
SQL> l
  1  EXPLAIN PLAN INTO plan_table FOR
  2  select sum(bt_time * staff_billing_rate)
  3  from st_bill_time, st_staff
  4  where st_bill_time.bt_inv_id = 14
  5* and st_bill_time.bt_staff_id = st_staff.staff_id
SQL> /

Explained.

SQL> SELECT cost, operation, options, object_name
  2  FROM plan_table;

     COST OPERATION                     OPTIONS      OBJECT_NAME
--------- ----------------------------- ------------ ---------------------
        3 SELECT STATEMENT


          SORT                          AGGREGATE


        3 HASH JOIN


        1 TABLE ACCESS                  FULL          ST_STAFF
        1 TABLE ACCESS                  FULL          ST_BILL_TIME
```

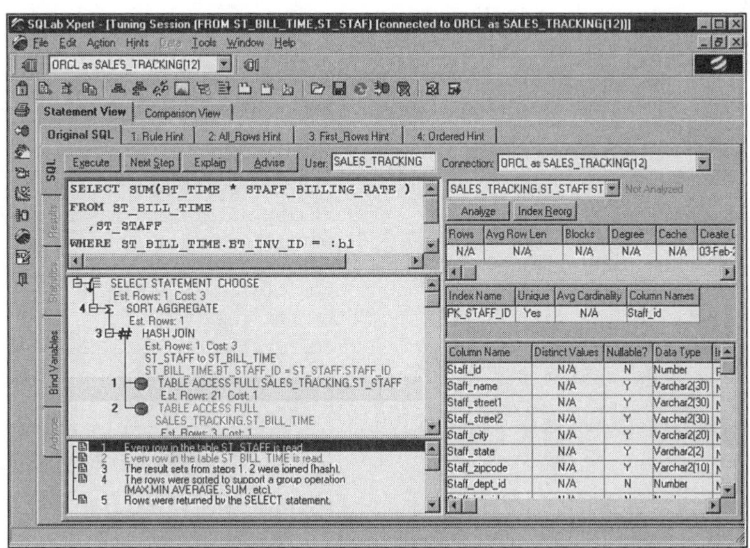

Figure 6.4

SQLab Xpert SQL tuning session.

Understanding the explain plan is a necessity for tuning SQL statements for both the rule-based and cost-based optimizers. Explain plans can be difficult to interpret, but indenting the explain steps greatly aids in understanding the order of the explain steps. The more common explain steps are discussed in Listing 6.5.

Listing 6.5—Common Explain Plan Symbols

```
Explain Symbol                  Description
AND-EQUAL                       Index values will be used to join rows.
CONCATENATION                   SQL statement UNION command.
FILTER                          FILTERs apply 'other criteria' in the query to
                                further qualify the matching rows. The 'other
                                criteria' include correlated subqueries, and
                                HAVING clause.
FIRST ROW                       SQL statement will be processed via a cursor.
FOR UPDATE                      SQL statement clause 'for update of' placed row
                                level locks on affected rows.
INDEX (UNIQUE)                  SQL statement utilized a unique index to search
                                for a specific value.
INDEX (RANGE SCAN)              SQL statement contains a nonequality or BETWEEN
                                condition.
HASH JOIN                       SQL statement initiated a hash-join operation.
MERGE JOIN                      SQL statement references two or more tables,
                                sorting the two result sets being joined over the
                                join columns and then merging the results via
                                the join columns.
NESTED LOOPS                    This operation is one form of joining tables.
                                One row is retrieved from the row source
                                identified by the first (inner) operation, and
                                then joined to all matching rows in the other
                                table (outer).
NONUNIQUE INDEX (RANGE SCAN)    The RANGE SCAN option indicates that ORACLE
                                expects to return multiple matches (ROWIDs) from
                                the index search.
PARTITION (CONCATENATED)        SQL statement will access a partitioned object
                                and merge the retrieved rows from the accessed
                                partitions.
PARTITION (SINGLE)              SQL statement will access a single partition.
PARTITION (EMPTY)               The SQL statement makes reference to an empty
                                partition.
SORT (ORDER BY)                 SQL statement contains an ORDER BY SQL command.
SORT (AGGREGATE)                SQL statement initiated a sort to resolve a MIN
                                or MAX function.
SORT (GROUP BY)                 SQL statement contains a GROUP BY SQL command.
TABLE ACCESS (FULL)             All rows are retrieved from the table without
                                using an index.
TABLE ACCESS (BY ROWID)         A row is retrieved based on ROWID.
TABLE ACCESS (CLUSTER)          A row is retrieved from a table that is part of
                                a cluster.
UNION                           SQL statement contains a DISTINCT SQL command.
```

Oracle version 8 has introduced three new columns: PARTITION_START, PARTITION_STOP, and PARTITION_ID. These three new fields will help in the tuning of SQL statements that access partitioned objects. PARTITION_START and PARTITION_STOP show the range of partitions affected by this explain step, and the PARTITION_ID is the identification number for that particular explain step.

The largest performance gains can be obtained by tuning the top four or five steps of the explain plan. Figure 6.5 illustrates one of the sales tracking SQL statements (from the Profit/Loss Calculation button in the ST_INVENTORY form). SQLab Xpert provides quite a bit of information—notice the indexes listed on the right side and all the column attributes listed as well. This particular SQL statement was captured via monitoring, which is discussed in Chapter 5. Notice that SQLab set up five scenarios using hints: Original SQL, and then Rule Hint, All_Rows Hint, First_Rows Hint, and Ordered Hint. SQLab also has the capability to compare each of these scenarios.

In the SQL explain plan, SQLab indents and highlights each of the explain steps (see Figure 6.5). For the novice, SQLab also provides a meaningful explanation—in the box under the explain plan—of what each step really means. On the highlighted explain plan line, notice the `Table Access Full`, or a full table scan. Also notice the statistics, primarily the number of rows affected. Normally, a full table scan is a bad thing, but when only 21 rows are being affected, a full table scan is actually a good thing. Having an index would only increase the number of I/Os to retrieve this data, which is probably all in the same data block. In addition, notice the hash join in step 3 of the explain plan.

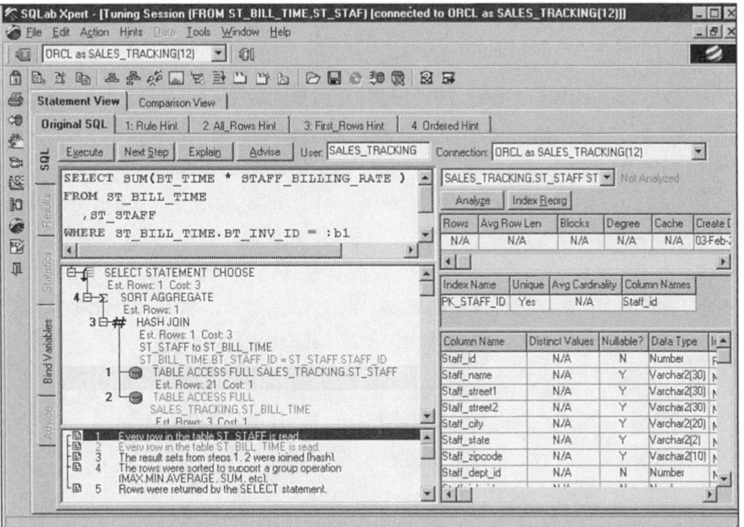

Figure 6.5

SQLab Xpert SQL tuning session.

The example in Figure 6.6 is the same tuning session as in Figure 6.5, except the Rule Hint tab is the current tab. Using the rule-based optimizer, the optimizer picked a nested-loop join operation in step 5 of the explain plan because the rule-based optimizer does not support hash joins.

Sometimes SQL statement performance is better with the rule-based optimizer. Do not automatically rule it out.

Figure 6.6

SQLab Xpert SQL tuning session Rule Hint tab.

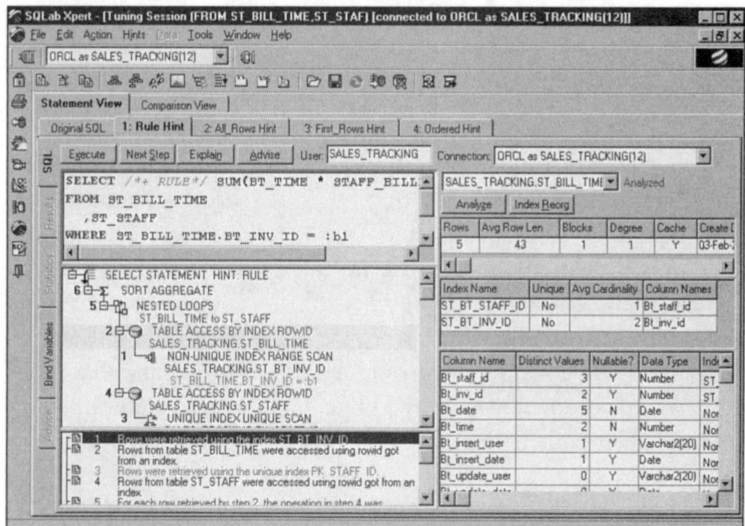

SQLab can actually give advice on how to rewrite the SQL statement. In Figure 6.7, the Advice tab on the left side of screen shows that SQLab is recommending to drop the indexes. This recommendation comes because, in this case, the indexes will probably slow down the processing of this SQL statement due to the extra I/Os required to access the indexes. Notice that it is also advising either to analyze all the tables or to have none of them analyzed. Finally, this SQL statement recommends creating indexes on the foreign keys. The Generate SQL button will generate a SQL script to implement any of the recommendations selected.

The final SQLab example in Figure 6.8 illustrates another way of viewing the explain plan, in a flowchart mode. SQLab enables the user to toggle between the regular explain display mode and the flowchart mode, which provides a nice way to view the relationships in the explain plan.

Figure 6.7

SQLab Xpert SQL tuning session expert advice tab.

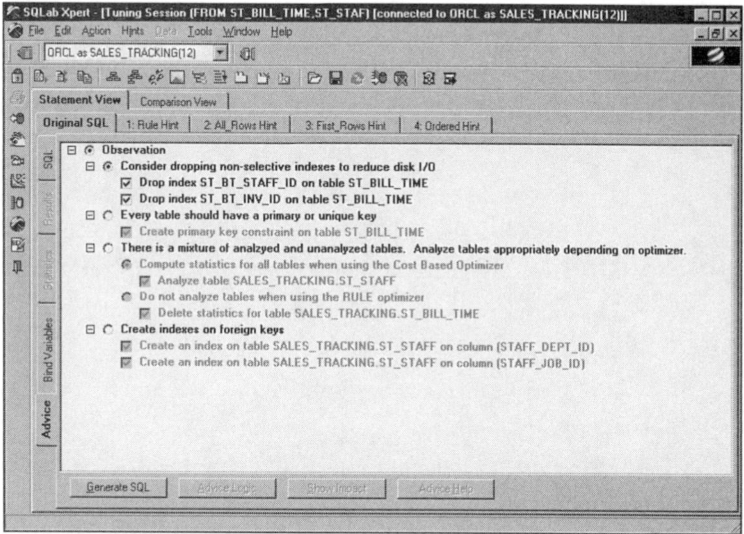

Figure 6.8

SQLab Xpert SQL tuning session in flowchart mode.

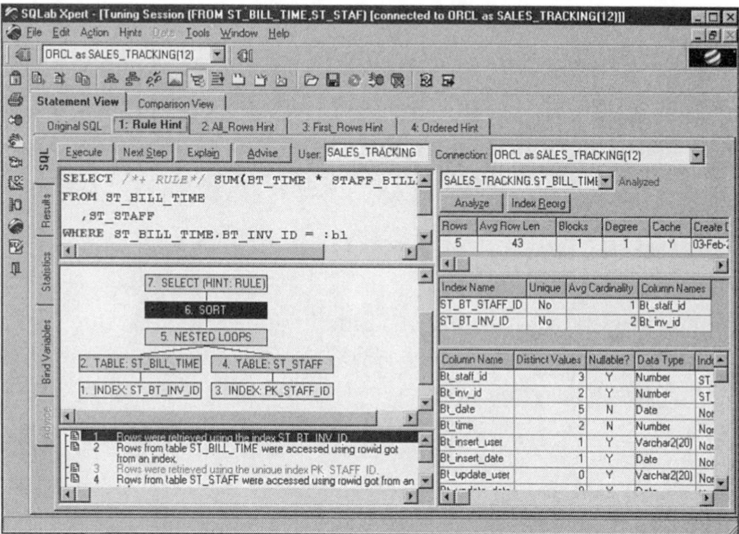

Any change to the SQL statements in any tuning session must be copied back into the program, function, or procedure where it originated.

SQL Coding Guidelines

Finally, we'll discusses some good and poor ways to code SQL statements. The following are some guidelines for SQL statement coding that will help both the rule-based and cost-based optimizers:

- **Do** use the `IN` operator instead of `NOT`. Try to avoid using the `NOT` command by using >=, <=, and so on.
- **Do** use array processing whenever possible (Export, and Pro*C applications).
- **Do** use hints to ensure the desired execution plan results.
- **Don't** use calculations in the `WHERE` clause on indexed columns. Unless the intended behavior is to disable index use, any function on indexed columns will ignore the index.
- **Don't** use an index if more than 20 percent of the rows will be returned by the query.
- **Don't** use subqueries if other solutions exist (PL/SQL loop, for example).
- **Don't** write applications that use SQL execution plan defaults. Oracle Corporation makes no guarantees that default behavior will be maintained in future releases, or even between different hardware platforms.

Array processing—A method in a C program to select groups of rows into the program over SQL Net; it's much faster than processing one row at a time.

Summary

This chapter concentrated on understanding the explain plan, a key ingredient to tuning the SQL statements found in our Sales Tracking Application. We discussed the two Oracle optimizers, how to control both, and how to interpret the output explain plans from both.

Next Steps

In the next chapter, we'll discuss the files that we should back up for our Sales Tracking Application, the options we have available in Oracle8i, and the backup and recovery issues our Sales Tracking Application might encounter.

Chapter 7

In this chapter

- *Why Back Up My Oracle8i Database?*
- *Basic Oracle8i Backup and Recovery*
- *Which Backup Method Is Best?*

Oracle8i Backup and Recovery

Why Back Up My Oracle8i Database?

Any computer is subject to a variety of hardware or software issues that can cause a loss of stored data. Natural disasters, power outages (the plug falling out of the wall), computer program problems (fields getting updated incorrectly), and machine failures are hard to predict. In addition, other issues that need to be considered are accidental and intentional corruption of data.

Each application has specific data requirements. Some applications are data entry–oriented, such as merchandise sales on a cash register or terminal, whereas others are just information retrieval–oriented, such as a typical data warehouse. In the event of software or hardware failure, the ability to restore the data after the failure is corrected is vital. A *backup* in computer terms entails making an electronic copy of your data and programs on removable media. The frequency and extent of backups depend on the application and business needs of the data in the application. For example, a database loaded from computer system files every evening might not require that any backups be performed—for example, some data warehouse applications work this way. In contrast, data entry applications might not have any acceptable data loss or downtime—for example, banking applications.

A backup can entail the copying of all programs and data, with configuration files, to a removable medium such as magnetic tape or disks. *Partial* backups or *incremental* backups copy to a removal medium only those items that have changed since the last backup. The Oracle8i environment has many backup and recovery options to cover the various application scenarios that might be encountered.

Many types of solutions such as *RAID*, *UPS*, and *standby databases* are available. These features can be important but are beyond the scope of this book. We will discuss the important files to back up, some of the options available in Oracle8i, and the backup and recovery issues the Sales Tracking Application might encounter.

A RAID (Redundant Array of Inexpensive Disks) contains many disk drives, but the computer views the whole device as a single disk drive. A key feature of RAID is that it can make copies of its internal disks, so if one goes bad, the computer never knows. RAID automatically recovers from the error and the data is safe.

The UPS (Uninterruptible Power Supply) is made up of batteries or a generator. UPS is designed to power the computer in the event of a power outage. For example, notebook computers have a battery that acts as a UPS, enabling the power cord to be removed from the computer and the computer to keep running as if nothing happened. UPS options range from battery systems with enough power to enable the normal shutdown operations of the computer to fancy generators designed to power the computer, any room air conditioning it might require such as for mainframes, and so on for days.

The last solution available to us is an Oracle standby database. It's a redundant database in recovery mode waiting for archive logs from the in-use Oracle database to become available. Standby databases easily can be brought into use if a failure occurs on the primary database. This ensures very little downtime for an application, but at the expense of duplicate, or identical, computer systems.

When deciding how to back up and recover an Oracle application, such as the Sales Tracking Application, you must understand the business needs of the data. These needs include acceptable downtime, which is how long a firm can do without access to the data, and acceptable data loss, which is whether the data already entered can be easily re-created or will be lost for good in the event of a failure (such as in a Web-based application that is taking orders for merchandise). Each of these scenarios has drastically different backup and recovery needs. Recovery needs must be taken into account, as well. Maybe total duplicate hardware is too expensive or recovering from a tape backup will take too long. Backup and recovery procedures require careful consideration of the application's business and technological contexts. The section "Which Backup Method Is Best?" found later in this chapter, discusses the various backup needs of our Sales Tracking Application.

Basic Oracle8i Backup and Recovery

The Oracle8i database environment has many operating system–level files associated with it. This section gives a brief description of each file, its relative importance, and the methods of backing it up.

Figure 7.1 illustrates the various components of the Oracle8i environment with the computer files associated with those components.

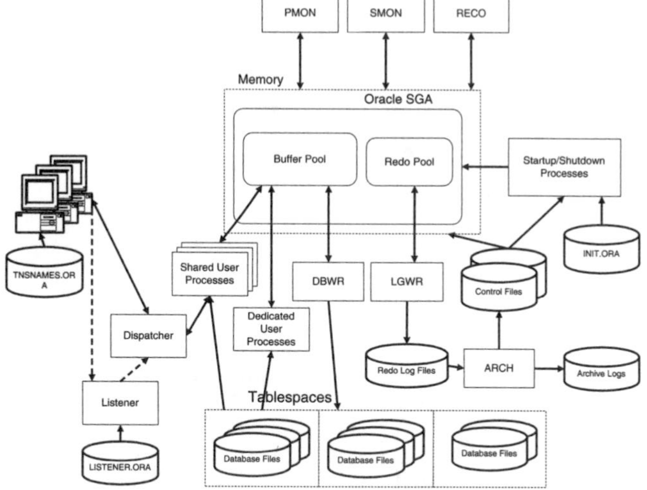

Figure 7.1

Oracle8i architecture with related data files.

The control file that was created at installation is probably the most important file to the Oracle8i database. This file contains the locations of all the other Oracle files, important recovery information, important startup and shutdown information, and—if Recovery Manager is implemented—the recovery files. If the control file is missing or corrupted in any way, the Oracle database cannot be started. Oracle allows as many control files to be maintained on disk as desired (preferably on different physical hard drives). These files are listed, with their operating system full path specifications, in the `INIT.ORA` parameter file, which is the second most important file to the Oracle database. It is the parameter file that Oracle refers to on startup to tell it how to create various memory structures, control tuning features, and so on.

The Oracle data dictionary and all application data are assigned to one or more tablespaces. These are the main files to be backed up, and Oracle supports two methods of backing them up—cold backups and hot backups. A *cold backup* occurs when the Oracle8i database is in a complete shutdown and inaccessible mode. A *hot backup* involves copying the files associated with a particular tablespace while the Oracle8i database is completely functional and the users of applications accessing the database have no knowledge of this backup activity. All database files can be viewed easily with the SQL statement `select name from v$datafile` (see Figure 7.2).

Figure 7.2

Data files associated with the Sales Tracking database.

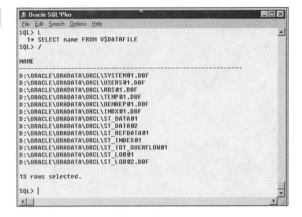

```
Oracle SQL*Plus
File Edit Search Options Help
SQL> L
  1* SELECT name FROM V$DATAFILE
SQL> /

NAME
------------------------------------------------------------
D:\ORACLE\ORADATA\ORCL\SYSTEM01.DBF
D:\ORACLE\ORADATA\ORCL\USERS01.DBF
D:\ORACLE\ORADATA\ORCL\RBS01.DBF
D:\ORACLE\ORADATA\ORCL\TEMP01.DBF
D:\ORACLE\ORADATA\ORCL\OEMREP01.DBF
D:\ORACLE\ORADATA\ORCL\INDX01.DBF
D:\ORACLE\ORADATA\ORCL\ST_DATA01
D:\ORACLE\ORADATA\ORCL\ST_DATA02
D:\ORACLE\ORADATA\ORCL\ST_REFDATA01
D:\ORACLE\ORADATA\ORCL\ST_INDEX01
D:\ORACLE\ORADATA\ORCL\ST_IOT_OVERFLOW01
D:\ORACLE\ORADATA\ORCL\ST_LOB01
D:\ORACLE\ORADATA\ORCL\ST_LOB02.DBF

13 rows selected.

SQL> |
```

The redo log files are used to record all changes made to the database. Appendix D, "Advanced SQL Queries," discusses read consistency and Appendix B, "Learning SQL—A Complete Tutorial," discusses commit and rollback. These files enable users to see the database at the time their query started (read consistency), and these same files also enable DML-type statements to be rolled back if necessary. In addition, these files are used during Oracle8i startup to roll forward any committed changes to the data files and roll back any uncommitted changes, in the event that Oracle8i stopped abnormally or via a shutdown with immediate or abort options. At least two of these redo logs are online and available for the Oracle environment to record changes to data and schemas. If ARCHIVE LOG MODE is activated, the contents of these logs are saved to operating system files called *archive logs* before being made available for reuse by the Oracle8i environment.

It is important to copy the redo log files as part of a cold backup but *not* during a hot backup. Restoring these files at any time other than during a cold backup could and will corrupt the database environment.

The redo log files are very important to the operation of the Oracle environment, and for this reason, Oracle provides a method to mirror these files—as many times as needed—to other disk drives. A complete list of assigned redo log files can be viewed with the SQL statement `select member from v$logfile` (see Figure 7.3).

A cold backup is a convenient time to capture almost any operating system file associated with Oracle8i. Other files to consider backing up at this time are the SQL Net configuration files `TNSNAMES.ORA`, `LISTENER.ORA`, and `TNSNAMES.ORA`. Another rather important file is the `INIT.ORA` file, which is the database startup parameter file.

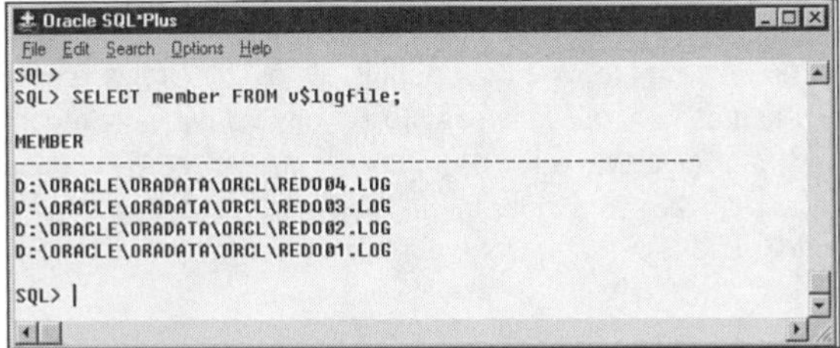

Figure 7.3

Log files associated with the Sales Tracking database.

Cold backups are performed when the Oracle RDBMS is in a down state and all the physical files and initialization files are backed up. This method can be supplemented with Oracle's Export and Import utilities to perform incremental backups of changed objects, or better yet, to supplement Oracle's Log Archive Mode. Incremental backups are discussed later in this chapter in the section "Incremental Backups."

Hot backups are concerned only with the data files associated with the particular tablespace being backed up. They utilize the archive log files to store all writes, which is DML activity, while the physical tablespace files are being backed up. Although, when they utilize the archive log files, Archive Log Mode must be implemented. In the event of a database recovery, the unaffected tablespaces are online and available. In recovery mode, Oracle8i prompts the person performing the recovery for the necessary archive logs, by name, to restore the tablespace.

Cold backups should include the redo log files for any instance recovery required from the previous shutdown of the database. Hot backups, on the other hand, should *avoid* the redo log files for this very reason. If the database is in an online status, the redo log files play no role in any future media recovery scenario.

Implementing archive redo log mode, or archive logs, is easy. Two `INIT.ORA` parameters control this mode of operation. To implement it, set `ARCHIVE_LOG_MODE = True` and set `LOG_ARCHIVE_DEST = <operating system full path name>`. Then, you must shut down the database and restart it. The log files will be created in the `LOG_ARCHIVE_DEST`, defined in the `INIT.ORA` parameter file. These log files have predetermined names and sequence numbers and are used by the hot backup in recovery and in recovery at Oracle startup. The recovery process will prompt the computer operator for these log files by their names. The size of these online redo logs has a direct impact on the amount of time needed to restart the Oracle8i database. The smaller the files, the faster the recovery, but the more frequently archive logs will be created.

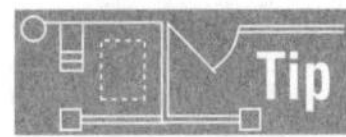

Archive log files are important in almost all Oracle recovery scenarios. Mirroring the archive log files is easy to set up and is highly recommended. Set the `INIT.ORA` parameter `LOG_ARCHIVE_DUPLEX_DEST = <operating-system full path name>` to a different physical disk drive from that of the original archive logs.

The frequency at which these archive log files are created easily can be controlled by the size of the online redo files or by entering the SQL command `alter database switch log file`. An Oracle8i *checkpoint* is a process in which all database buffers are written to disk and a mark (a checkpoint) is recorded in the log as a quiet point in the database where all transactions are committed or rolled back. More frequent checkpoints can greatly reduce the time of a recovery startup. However, checkpointing can have a negative impact on overall application performance if performed too frequently. Checkpoint frequency should be balanced against the amount of data in the logs being written. The `INIT.ORA` parameter `LOG_CHECKPOINT_INTERVAL = <integer>` controls the frequency of checkpoints. The integer is the number of megabytes written in the online redo logs between checkpoints. A checkpoint always occurs at a log switch, during the process of Oracle having filled one online redo log and beginning to use the next available online redo log. Archive log files are created as a part of the log switch process, as well. The online redo logs must be large enough to hold complete transactions but small enough to fit recovery-time requirements.

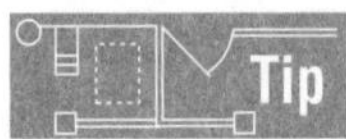

On active systems, make sure the online redo logs can hold enough data to fit the recovery-time window and set the `LOG_CHECKPOINT_INTERVAL` to a size larger than the largest online redo log. This will ensure that checkpointing does not slow down the active system.

Several SQL commands will indirectly cause a checkpoint to occur. The obvious ones are any log file switch command, but other commands that will cause a checkpoint are `alter tablespace begin backup`, `alter tablespace offline`, and `instance shutdown`.

Cold Backup and Restore

Cold backups occur in an Oracle8i shutdown state. Therefore, all the physical files that make up the database should be copied to a removable media. Listing 7.1 illustrates a useful script that utilizes some of the SQL*Plus reporting techniques to provide a list of the tablespace files required for a cold backup and their associated sizes. This script is executed through the SQL*Plus interface and utilizes information stored in the data dictionary table SYS.DBA_DATA_FILES. The total size of these files is important so that the correct number of tapes, or other removable magnetic media, can be available.

The script illustrated in Listing 7.1 must be run using the SYSTEM user ID. Lines 12–15 turn off the SQL*Plus display output, whereas lines 16–19 apply simple SQL*Plus headings and column formatting. Line 20 computes a total for each tablespace, and line 21 computes a total of all the tablespaces. Line 24 opens an operating system file to store the formatted results of the query in lines 25–27. Finally, line 29 closes the operating system file. Listing 7.2 illustrates the tablespace files report.

Listing 7.1—Tablespace Files SQL*Plus Script

```
1:  rem
2:  rem    Tablespace Listing/Sizing Report for Cold Backups
3:  rem        Oracle8i From Scratch
4:  rem            by Dan Hotka
5:  rem         Que Publications March 2000
6:  rem         All Rights Reserved
7:  rem
8:  rem File:  "tablespace_size.sql"
9:  rem
10: rem Tablespace file and size report by Dan Hotka 2/15/1998
11: rem
12: set feedback off
13: set verify off
14: set termout off
15: set echo off
16: ttitle 'Oracle Tablespace Physical Files'
17: column tablespace_name format a20 heading 'Tablespace'
18: column file_name format a40 heading 'File Name'
19: column bytes format 999,999,999 heading 'File Size'
20: compute sum of bytes on tablespace_name
21: compute sum of bytes on report
22: break on tablespace_name skip 2
23: break on report skip 2
24: spool tablespace_files.out
25: SELECT tablespace_name, file_name, bytes
26: FROM sys.dba_data_files
27: ORDER BY tablespace_name
28: /
29: spool off
30: exit
```

7

Listing 7.2—Tablespace Files Report

```
Wed Feb 23                                                               page      1
                          Oracle8i Tablespace Physical Files

Tablespace            File Name                                        File Size
--------------------  ----------------------------------------  ------------
INDX                  D:\ORACLE\ORADATA\ORCL\INDX01.DBF                2,097,152
OEM_REPOSITORY        D:\ORACLE\ORADATA\ORCL\OEMREP01.DBF              5,242,880
RBS                   D:\ORACLE\ORADATA\ORCL\RBS01.DBF                26,214,400
ST_DATA01             D:\ORACLE\ORADATA\ORCL\ST_DATA01                 1,048,576
ST_DATA02             D:\ORACLE\ORADATA\ORCL\ST_DATA02                 1,048,576
ST_INDEX01            D:\ORACLE\ORADATA\ORCL\ST_INDEX01                5,242,880
ST_IOT_OVERFLOW01     D:\ORACLE\ORADATA\ORCL\ST_IOT_OVERFLOW01        10,485,760
ST_LOB01              D:\ORACLE\ORADATA\ORCL\ST_LOB01                  1,048,576
ST_LOB01              D:\ORACLE\ORADATA\ORCL\ST_LOB02.DBF             10,485,760
ST_REFDATA01          D:\ORACLE\ORADATA\ORCL\ST_REFDATA01                512,000
SYSTEM                D:\ORACLE\ORADATA\ORCL\SYSTEM01.DBF            167,772,160
TEMP                  D:\ORACLE\ORADATA\ORCL\TEMP01.DBF                2,097,152
USERS                 D:\ORACLE\ORADATA\ORCL\USERS01.DBF              34,603,008
                                                                    ------------
sum                                                                  267,898,880
```

Cold backups should have all the online redo logs, the tablespace files, and the control file. Listing 7.3 shows a SQL*Plus listing, run with the `SYSTEM` user account, that will extract these files with their full operating system file path. This list then can be used to back up these Oracle8i required database files. Other files to include in this backup are the SQL Net files and the `INIT.ORA` files. The locations of these files are not stored in the database.

Listing 7.3 creates a list of these database files, and Listing 7.4 illustrates the list produced. The output from Listing 7.3 will simply be a list of the Oracle database files currently being utilized by the Oracle RDBMS environment. In Listing 7.3, line 13 opens the operating system file `cold_back.lst`. Lines 14–25 are the SQL that retrieves the various data, control, and log file names. In these lines, the `UNION` command is useful when selecting rows from different tables. And lastly, line 26 closes the `cold_back.lst` file.

Listing 7.3—Cold Backup File List SQL*Plus Script

```
1:  rem
2:  rem    Cold Backup File List
3:  rem        Oracle8i From Scratch
4:  rem            by Dan Hotka
5:  rem         Que Publications March 2000
6:  rem         All Rights Reserved
7:  rem
8:  set feedback off
9:  set verify off
```

```
set termout off
set echo off
set head off
spool cold_back.lst
SELECT file_name
FROM sys.dba_data_files
UNION
SELECT name
FROM v$datafile
UNION
SELECT name
FROM v$controlfile
UNION
SELECT member
FROM v$logfile
/
spool off
exit
```

Listing 7.4—Cold Backup File List

```
D:\ORACLE\ORADATA\ORCL\CONTROL01.CTL
D:\ORACLE\ORADATA\ORCL\CONTROL02.CTL
D:\ORACLE\ORADATA\ORCL\INDX01.DBF
D:\ORACLE\ORADATA\ORCL\OEMREP01.DBF
D:\ORACLE\ORADATA\ORCL\RBS01.DBF
D:\ORACLE\ORADATA\ORCL\REDO01.LOG
D:\ORACLE\ORADATA\ORCL\REDO02.LOG
D:\ORACLE\ORADATA\ORCL\REDO03.LOG
D:\ORACLE\ORADATA\ORCL\REDO04.LOG
D:\ORACLE\ORADATA\ORCL\ST_DATA01
D:\ORACLE\ORADATA\ORCL\ST_DATA02
D:\ORACLE\ORADATA\ORCL\ST_INDEX01
D:\ORACLE\ORADATA\ORCL\ST_IOT_OVERFLOW01
D:\ORACLE\ORADATA\ORCL\ST_LOB01
D:\ORACLE\ORADATA\ORCL\ST_LOB02.DBF
D:\ORACLE\ORADATA\ORCL\ST_REFDATA01
D:\ORACLE\ORADATA\ORCL\SYSTEM01.DBF
D:\ORACLE\ORADATA\ORCL\TEMP01.DBF
D:\ORACLE\ORADATA\ORCL\USERS01.DBF
```

If the Oracle8i application utilizes externally stored Bfiles (LOBs), it is important to back up these files with the cold backup. The SQL*Plus script in Listing 7.5 is useful for listing the operating system directory path in which these externally stored LOBs would be stored. The Sales Tracking Application does not utilize LOBs stored outside the database, but many applications do.

The script in Listing 7.5 must be run with the `SYSTEM` user account, too. Lines 13–16 select and format the external directory structure stored in the table SYS.DBA_DIRECTORIES.

Listing 7.5—Bfile Directory Location List

```
rem
rem    Externally Stored Binary File Directory Location
rem        Oracle8i From Scratch
rem            by Dan Hotka
rem         Que Publications March 2000
rem         All Rights Reserved
rem
set feedback off
set verify off
set termout off
set echo off
set head off
spool binary_file_location.lst
SELECT directory_path || '\' || directory_name
FROM sys.dba_directories
/
spool off
exit
```

Listing 7.6 is for users of UNIX raw partitions. Consult your DBA before running this script. This code can be used for UNIX raw partitions, placing one raw partition on a single tape.

Listing 7.6—Copying UNIX Raw Partitions to a Tape Backup

```
Unix> rawpartition_backup.sh <<EOF
#!/bin/sh

tar for j in \`cat cold_back.lst\`
do
    echo "Put tape in tape device 0"
    pause "Hit Return to continue..."
    dd if=$j if=/dev/rmt0
done

EOF
Unix>
```

The following steps are required for a cold backup from an Oracle8i RDBMS:

1. Determine the amount of backup space required by running the script in Listing 7.1.
2. Create a list of Oracle data files to be backed up using the script in Listing 7.3.
3. Use the script in Listing 7.5 if LOBs are stored outside Oracle8i.
4. Back up the other Oracle8i support files. The INIT.ORA files and the SQL Net files can be found in the following locations:

```
<ORACLE_HOME>/dbs/init*.ora
<ORACLE_HOME>/admin/*/pfile/*.ora
<ORACLE_HOME>/network/admin/*.ora
```

5. Shut down the instance of Oracle8i to be backed up.
6. Copy all identified files to a removable medium.
7. Start up the instance of Oracle8i.

Cold backup recovery is accomplished by first taking the Oracle8i RDBMS completely down. Next, connect as SYSTEM using SQL*Plus and enter shutdown abort. After the system error or hardware failure is corrected, restore all the physical tablespace files, control files, INIT.ORA parameter files, and possibly the SQL Net configuration files. Then, after all the backed-up files have been restored to their original locations on the computer's file system, connect as SYSTEM using SQL*Plus, and enter startup. Remember that all the work since your last cold backup is lost unless some form of incremental backup has been performed.

Hot Backup and Restore

Hot backups differ from cold backups in that only one tablespace is backed up at a time and while the database is still online and available for use. Applications such as banking applications or Web-based sales applications that cannot have any unavailability time would use this method to back up the database.

Recovery is accomplished by restoring the damaged files and initiating a recovery for that particular tablespace. During recovery, Oracle8i prompts the user performing the recovery for the required archive log files. These files must be in the LOG_ARCHIVE_DEST location as defined in the init.ora file.

A control file can always be created with the SQL statement alter database backup controlfile to c:\temp\<Oracle SID>.ctl. The location and names of the currently maintained control files can be viewed with the SQL statement select name from v$controlfile.

When performing hot backups (backups with the database online and available), it is important to use the alter database backup controlfile to c:\temp\<Oracle SID>.ctl command to create a backup copy of the control file, *not* the control file that is currently on the disk. The only time the real control files should be backed up is during a cold backup.

The script in Listing 7.7 is similar to that in Listing 7.1 except that this script will prompt the user for a tablespace name and the output will list only information about that particular tablespace. Listing 7.8 illustrates the output from this SQL*Plus report. Run the script in Listing 7.7 with the `SYSTEM` user account.

Listing 7.7—Tablespace Files SQL*Plus Script

```
rem
rem    Tablespace Listing/Sizing Report for Hot Backups
rem         Oracle8i From Scratch
rem             by Dan Hotka
rem          Que Publications March 2000
rem          All Rights Reserved
rem
rem File:  "tablespace_size.sql"
rem
rem Tablespace file and size report by Dan Hotka 2/15/1998
rem
set feedback off
set verify off
ACCEPT TNAME PROMPT 'Tablespace to be HOT backedup'
set termout off
set echo off
ttitle 'Oracle Tablespace &TNAME Physical Files'
column tablespace_name format a20 heading 'Tablespace'
column file_name format a40 heading 'File Name'
column bytes format 999,999,999 heading 'File Size'
compute sum of bytes on report
break on report skip 2
spool tablespace_files.out
SELECT tablespace_name, file_name, bytes
FROM sys.dba_data_files
WHERE tablespace_name = &TNAME
/
spool off
exit
```

Listing 7.8—Tablespace Files Report

```
Wed Feb 23                                                              page     1
                           Oracle8i Tablespace Physical Files

Tablespace          File Name                                        File Size
------------------- ---------------------------------------- ------------
ST_DATA01           D:\ORACLE\ORADATA\ORCL\ST_DATA01                 1,048,576
                                                             ------------
sum                                                                  1,048,576
```

Start the hot backup by first running the SQL*Plus script in Listing 7.8 to obtain a list of the physical files assigned to the tablespace needing to be backed up. Log in to SQL*Plus with the `SYSTEM` user account and issue the following command: `alter tablespace <TABLESPACE NAME> begin backup;`. Copy the files identified by the script in Listing 7.8 to a removable magnetic medium. When the copy is complete, log in to SQL*Plus again as the `SYSTEM` user and issue the following command: `alter tablespace <TABLESPACE NAME> end backup;`.

If any externally stored LOBs are associated with any data in this tablespace, now would be a good time to back those up as well. Use the SQL*Plus script (log in as user `SYSTEM`) in Listing 7.5 to identify the directory location of these LOBs.

LOBs (Long Objects)—An Oracle8I data type that enables the storage of long, unstructured binary type data such as pictures, video clips, and so on.

When performing hot backups, it is important to immediately capture the archive log files associated with the hot backup, especially the ones that were being used while the tablespace files were being backed up. To accomplish this, log in to SQL*Plus with the `SYSTEM` user account and enter `alter system switch logfile;` and then enter `alter database backup controlfile to c:\temp\<oracle instance>.ctl;`. Back up the control file created in `c:\temp` and all the archive log files in the `LOG_ARCHIVE_DEST` (see the `INIT.ORA` parameter file for operating system directory location).

Hot backup recovery is accomplished by recovering the damaged or lost tablespace files and applying the necessary archive log files. If a restore of a tablespace is needed, it should be offline already; however, the following syntax will ensure that it is indeed offline. Log in to SQL*Plus using the `SYSTEM` user account and enter `alter tablespace <TABLESPACE NAME> offline normal;`. Copy the tablespace physical files from the backup medium back to the original operating system directory. The following syntax will begin the recovery process on the tablespace in question:

```
set autorecovery on;
alter database recover tablespace <TABLESPACE NAME>;
 ***SQL*Plus will prompt the user for the archive log files needed***
alter tablespace <TABLESPACE NAME> online;
```

Incremental Backups

In addition to hot and cold backups, Oracle's Export and Import utilities provide a different method of backing up and recovering database objects. They also provide many functions to the Oracle RDBMS environment. These utilities are useful in moving individual objects or entire groups of objects owned by a single user from one Oracle RDBMS to another. Plus, these same utilities provide the Oracle8i environment with a way of incrementally backing up only those objects that have changed since the prior incremental backup. The hot and cold backup methods concentrate on copying the database files assigned to the tablespaces. In contrast, the incremental backup method using Export and Import concentrates on copying the objects out of the tablespace and has nothing to do with the database files assigned to the tablespaces.

The three levels of Export for object backup and recovery are complete export, cumulative export, and incremental export. The level of the export is controlled by a parameter on the command line or in the export parameter file. In addition, three objects track the time and type of export backup: `SYS.INCEXP`, `SYS.INCFIL`, and `SYS.INCVID`, which are optionally created by the `CATEXP.SQL` file at database install time. Consult your DBA if you have a question about whether this `CATEXP.SQL` script was installed or not.

Different settings exist for the export to support this incremental backup mode. These options are `FULL=Y` and `INCTYPE = COMPLETE` (or `CUMULATIVE` or `INCREMENTAL`).

The three levels of export backup all build on one another. *Incremental* backups have changes made only to objects from the most recent incremental or cumulative export, in this order. *Cumulative* backups have all changes made to objects from the most recent cumulative or complete export backup. *Complete* backups have all changes made to objects from the next previous complete export. The three levels of export supersede each other in that, when a complete export is performed, all prior complete, cumulative, and incremental backups become obsolete. Similarly, when a cumulative export is done, all incremental exports to the next most recent cumulative export become obsolete. Incremental backups are the lowest level of export in this backup scenario.

Figure 7.4 illustrates a typical incremental backup scenario utilizing the Export process. Point A on the time line is the complete backup. Point B is the first incremental backup and contains all the changed objects from Point A to Point B. The next point, Point C, is the first cumulative backup. At this point, the cumulative file contains all the changed objects to the database from Point A, including those changed objects captured in the incremental backup of Point B. At Point C, the incremental backup from Point B is no longer of any value. The same is true of the relationship of Point C to Point F. Point F will contain all the changed objects to the database from Point C, the last most previous incremental backup at the same level. Each level (Complete, Cumulative, or Incremental) will contain the changed objects from the last incremental export of the same level.

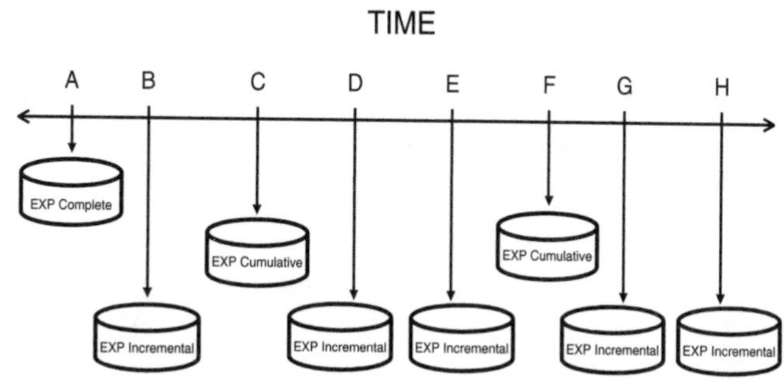

Figure 7.4
Incremental backup scenario.

The reason for all these levels is time—it takes longer to perform the complete export than to perform the cumulative or incremental exports. This system was designed to work best with the following scenario: Perform complete exports once a month, perform cumulative exports on each of the following weekends, and perform incremental exports daily. Each cumulative export will contain all the changes to the database from either the previous cumulative or the complete export. The incremental exports will contain the changes made on that particular day. This scenario is best used in a development environment or an environment with many end users performing their own object manipulation. This method of export/import gives the DBA great flexibility to restore single objects or data that was inadvertently dropped or deleted.

7

Listing 7.9 illustrates two weeks' worth of backups. This scenario performs a complete export, which begins with an F, on the first of the month and cumulative backups on the weekends. An incremental backup is performed daily, with each of the incrementals containing only changes from the prior complete (F) or cumulative (C). The cumulative contains all the changes from the last cumulative or the last complete.

Listing 7.9—Complete, Cumulative, and Incremental Backup Scenario

```
F_day1.exp
I_day2.exp
I_day3.exp
I_day4.exp
I_day5.exp
I_day6.exp
C_day7.exp
I_day8.exp
I_day9.exp
I_day10.exp
.
.
.
```

When restoring a series of exported files, it is important to perform the last export first with the `INCTYPE=SYSTEM` to restore the Oracle8i data dictionary. This parameter must be performed first to restore any changes to objects owned by SYS. An `INCTYPE = RESTORE` restores all other objects except those owned by SYS. Run these non-SYS restores in the order in which they were created.

The recovery scenario in Listing 7.10 is based on the same backups illustrated in Listing 7.9. For the example, let's say a user's table got dropped on the 11th and was last updated on the 7th. The recovery scenario in Listing 7.10 would recover that lost object. The last backup must be run first with the `INCTYPE = SYSTEM` first, and then the series of export files needs to be recovered with Import using the `INCTYPE = RESTORE`.

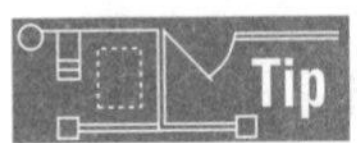

When the `INCTYPE = SYSTEM`, only those objects that have changed and are owned by SYS are restored, thus restoring the Oracle data dictionary first. This is important so that the incremental objects can find the correct object settings when they run and load data.

Listing 7.10—Incremental Recovery Using Oracle Import

```
IMP system/manager FULL=Y INCTYPE=SYSTEM FILE=I_day10.exp
IMP system/manager FULL=Y INCTYPE=RESTORE FILE=C_day7.exp
IMP system/manager FULL=Y INCTYPE=RESTORE FILE=I_day8.exp
IMP system/manager FULL=Y INCTYPE=RESTORE FILE=I_day9.exp
IMP system/manager FULL=Y INCTYPE=RESTORE FILE=I_day10.exp
```

Which Backup Method Is Best?

Which backup method is best depends on the business requirements of the particular application. A single Oracle8i database easily can have more than one type of application. These applications could even have quite different backup and recovery needs. In this scenario, the backup method that would be utilized would be dictated by the application with the strictest business requirements.

The size and recovery time also are major factors that must be considered in a backup and recovery plan. The larger the database, the longer it will take to perform a cold backup. If a database were solely dependent on a cold backup, it would need to be recovered, and it would take the same amount of time to restore the cold backup as it took to create the cold backup initially. The larger the database, the more the hot backup option should be considered.

For smaller or ad hoc type systems, in which the users have their own tables and small applications, the export/import incremental backup might be the perfect solution. The nature of the incremental backup captures all the objects that have changed since the last incremental level backup.

Other issues include acceptable data loss. How much data loss is acceptable in the event that a disk drive suddenly goes bad? If the answer is no data loss, then use the ARCHIVE_LOG_MODE and be sure you mirror the redo logs to at least one other disk drive.

A standby database should be considered if a very minimal amount of downtime is desired. This is an expensive solution that requires complete duplicate computer hardware systems.

The best method for our Sales Tracking Application is probably a mix of incremental backups performed daily and a cold backup performed on the weekends. The data availability needs of the Sales Tracking Application really depend on the size of the dealership using our application. If a dealership works only from 8 a.m. to 5 p.m. and occasional Saturdays, there is probably more than enough time to perform cold backups each night. The daily incremental backups would more than likely pick up only the ST_INVENTORY, ST_PARTS, and ST_BILL_TIME objects—the table objects with daily inserts and changes. This backup would take less time to perform than a cold backup.

As you can see, many business practices, data volumes, recovery times, and so on need to be considered to determine what is best for any given business application.

The best backup and recovery method is based solely on the business requirements of the applications. Oracle8i has enough features to cover most of the recovery scenarios.

Summary

This chapter covered important application-level backup and recovery issues. As stated clearly in the previous paragraph, each application's needs for backup and recovery times are clearly dependent on the business needs of both the data and the application. No two applications will have the same exact needs. I introduced you to a variety of methods of both backup and recovery as well as a discussion on when each might be appropriate. Sometimes a mix of methods is best for a particular application.

Next Steps

Coming up, we'll take a look at some of the Oracle8i index and partitioning features. We'll discuss how to keep your Sales Tracking Application users happy and your application humming.

Chapter 8

In this chapter

- *Understanding Indexes*
- *What Is a B-Tree Index?*
- *What Is an IOT?*
- *Implementing IOTs in the Sales Tracking Application*
- *What Is Partitioning?*
- *Oracle8i Partitioning Options*
- *Range Partitioning*
- *Hash Partitioning*
- *Composite Partitioning*
- *Oracle8i Index Partitioning Options*

Understanding Oracle8i Index and Partitioning Features

The more quickly rows can be returned to the requesting application, the happier the end users are. As computers' storage devices (that is, disk drives) become larger and less expensive, more data must be stored and easily accessed. It is common to find *data warehouse* applications that have data storage requirements in the *terabytes*. Oracle has always provided the basic b-tree index (discussed in depth in the next section). These larger data requirements have brought additional changes to the Oracle database. Many new indexing methods accommodate various data-access needs. Partitioning was introduced in Oracle8. A *regular* table (non-partitioned) is assigned to a tablespace, whereas a *partitioned* table is assigned to two or more tablespaces (based on key values). This is useful for large tables that have millions of rows. Partitioning enables all the tablespace features, such as backup and recovery, to be performed on smaller volumes of data and assists Oracle in retrieving data more quickly. Indexes can be partitioned as well, providing better performance by using smaller pieces of the whole table or index.

Terabyte—A trillion bytes of information.

Data warehouse—Usually a large volume of rather undefined data, available for the end user to query and process with various query tools.

Understanding Indexes

An *index* is a data structure that can greatly reduce the time it takes to find particular rows in the associated table. A table object can have one or more indexes assigned to it. Figure 8.1 shows the syntax for creating an index on a table. Indexes can be created on one or more table columns. These columns, when relating to indexes, are known as *key fields*, or *keys*. A *composite* key uses more than one table column in a single index. Indexes are automatically created for the primary key constraint and can be unique—that is, have only one key value stored—or can have many keys with the same value. The more unique the key, the faster the access to the rows in the table.

Figure 8.1

*SQL*Plus Help text about Create Index syntax.*

```
Oracle SQL*Plus
File Edit Search Options Help
CREATE INDEX
------------

Use this command to create an index on:

  *  one or more columns of a table, a partitioned table, or a
     cluster
  *  one or more scalar typed object attributes of a table or a
     cluster
  *  a nested table storage table for indexing a nested table column

An index is a schema object that contains an entry for each value
that appears in the indexed column(s) of the table or cluster and
provides direct, fast access to rows. A partitioned index consists
of partitions containing an entry for each value that appears in the
indexed column(s) of the table.

CREATE [UNIQUE | BITMAP] INDEX [schema.]index
ON { [schema.]table ( column [ASC | DESC]
                    [, column [ASC | DESC] ] ...)
   | CLUSTER [schema.]cluster}
   [ physical_attributes_clause
   | {LOGGING | NOLOGGING}
   | {TABLESPACE tablespace | DEFAULT}
   | {NOSORT | REVERSE} ] ...
   [ GLOBAL PARTITION BY RANGE (column_list)
     ( PARTITION [partition_name]
     | VALUES LESS THAN (value_list)
     [ physical_attributes_clause
     | {LOGGING | NOLOGGING} ], ...)
   | LOCAL [(PARTITION [partition_name]
     [ physical_attributes_clause
     | {LOGGING | NOLOGGING} ], ...) ] ]
   [ PARALLEL parallel_clause ]
```

Each row in a table has a unique identifier called *ROWID*. This row ID is a *pseudocolumn* (false column) that contains the exact location of a row within the database. It also contains the following information: object ID, data file ID, block ID, and row ID. In addition, ROWID is the fastest way to access a row in any version of Oracle. Any time the row is moved, exported, imported, and so on, this row ID changes because the physical location of the row has changed. Indexes store ROWID along with the index key fields, and Oracle automatically updates all references to ROWID if and when a row is inserted or moved.

Pseudocolumn—A column that can be selected with standard SQL syntax but does not occupy any space in the database. ROWID is a pseudocolumn that is really an exact physical location of that particular row.

Using indexes greatly enhances the response time of most SQL statements. The rule of thumb here is if more than 20% of the rows of a table are going to be returned, you should consider not using indexes. The next sections cover the various indexing features of Oracle8i. Understanding the various available indexing options is important in order to choose the optimal indexing method for a given SQL statement.

What Is a B-Tree Index?

A *b-tree (balanced tree structured object)* index is the default indexing method of Oracle8i. The index structure resembles a tree in that the top block is read first, then a block in the next layer—which is known as a *branch* block—is read, and so on, until the index block (known as a *leaf* block) that contains the actual row ID is retrieved. This balancing-structure approach helps minimize I/O. Oracle8i keeps this type of index in order by sorting on its key, splitting the blocks if necessary, to keep the structure balanced so it will take the same number of read operations to retrieve any table row, whatever the size of the table structure. Figure 8.2 illustrates how these branch blocks and leaf blocks might look using the EMP table. Notice that the branch blocks simply point to other blocks associated with this same index, in which the leaf blocks (along the bottom) contain an actual row ID. Larger indexes have many rows or levels of branch blocks. The example in Figure 8.2 would have three levels, and each level could represent an I/O to the database.

Figure 8.2

B-tree index illustration on the EMP.ENAME column.

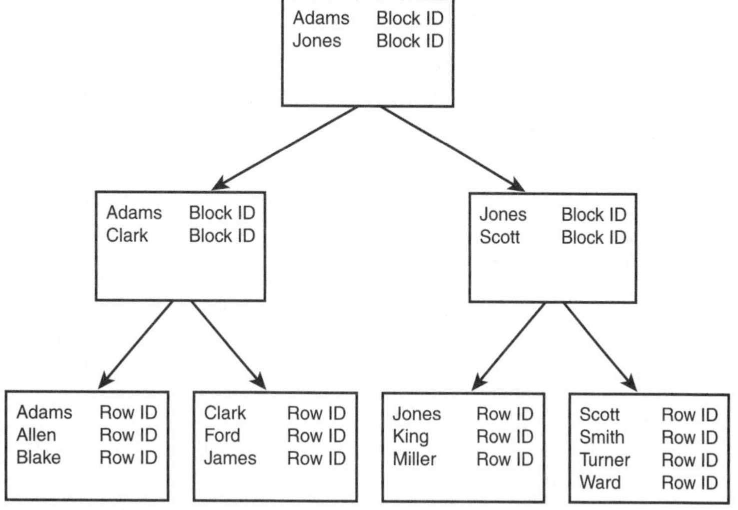

The SQL script illustrated in Figure 8.3 shows a good way to monitor the growth of indexes. The height is the number of levels an index contains. The fewer the levels, the better the index performance is. On larger indexes, a good time to reorganize the index is when the height changes. Indexes can be reorganized by either dropping them and re-creating them or using the `alter index <INDEX NAME> rebuild` command. To use this command, you must have enough room in the tablespace to hold both indexes. This method guarantees that an index is available for application use while the index is being rebuilt.

8

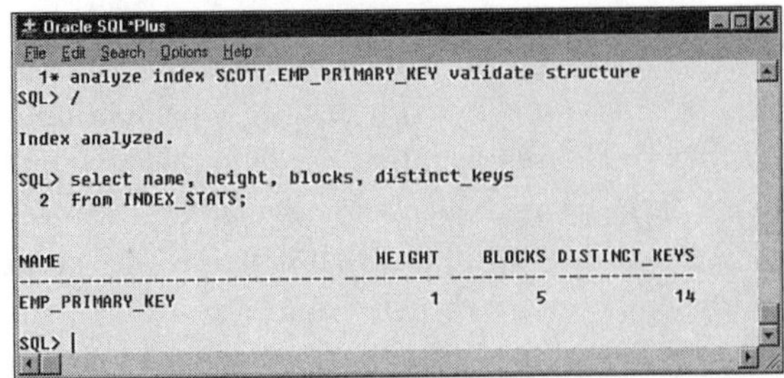

Figure 8.3

Query to monitor the levels and sizes of indexes.

If the tables being accessed by indexes contain gigabytes of data, you might want to consider using a larger default block size when creating the database. The larger the block size, the more of these index pointers can be read into the SGA with a single read operation. The more quickly these index pointers are read into memory, the more quickly the row(s) can be located for the application.

B-tree indexes can be based on a single column of a table or on multiple columns of a table. A key comprised of multiple columns of a table is a composite key. If the data requirements for a SQL statement are satisfied from information in an associated index, the table structure is not accessed. This is where the idea of an index-organized table (IOT) originated.

What Is an IOT?

An *index-organized table* is a b-tree index structure that acts like a table. All the data is stored within the b-tree structure or in an overflow tablespace. Listing 8.1 illustrates the basic syntax for an IOT. Notice everything is pretty much the same, down to the `organization index` clause. This tells Oracle that this is an IOT. The `pctthreshold` tells Oracle to store the remainder of the row in the defined overflow tablespace if a row is larger than this percentage of the block size. This ensures that multiple key values exist in each index block. If the b-tree index block contains only a few rows, it would be more efficient not to have an index, defeating the purpose of an index—fast access to rows.

The advantage, in regards to storage, is that the key values are not stored twice, once in the underlying table and again in the index. As mentioned in the previous section, sometimes the underlying table is never accessed if the results of the SQL statement can be achieved with information stored in the index. This is the main reason for the development of the IOT.

Listing 8.1—IOT Syntax

```
create table <TABLE NAME>
(field descriptions
     .
     .
<FIELD NAME>
primary key (<KEY FIELDS>))
organization index tablespace <TABLESPACE NAME>
pctthreshold 20
overflow tablespace <TABLESPACE NAME>
```

In Oracle8, IOTs had no ROWID, so it was not possible to add more indexes. Oracle8i supports a logical ROWID so that additional columns in an IOT can have their own indexes as well.

What Are the Oracle8i Indexing Options?

Oracle8i supports several indexing options that improve on the traditional b-tree indexes. Oracle7 introduced bitmap indexes, star queries, histograms, and hash joins, whereas Oracle8 introduced index-organized tables and reverse-key indexes. Oracle8i, on the other hand, has introduced the function-based index.

Bitmap Indexes

Bitmap indexes were introduced with Oracle v7.3. Each bit location in a bitmap index relates to a ROWID within the table object. If a row contains the key value, a 1 is stored in the index row for that value. Bitmap indexes can be very fast because all Oracle has to do is search for the presence of a 1 to know it must retrieve this row. Also, this is not a b-tree index structure, so the goal is that the row can be located with a single read of the bitmap index structure. This indexing option is intended for columns with low cardinality of data, such as color, sex, and so on. If too many values are found in a column, additional I/Os are necessary to find the table row ID, defeating the purpose of this kind of index. Figure 8.4 illustrates how the EMP table (bitmap index on DEPTNO) object might look in a bitmap index.

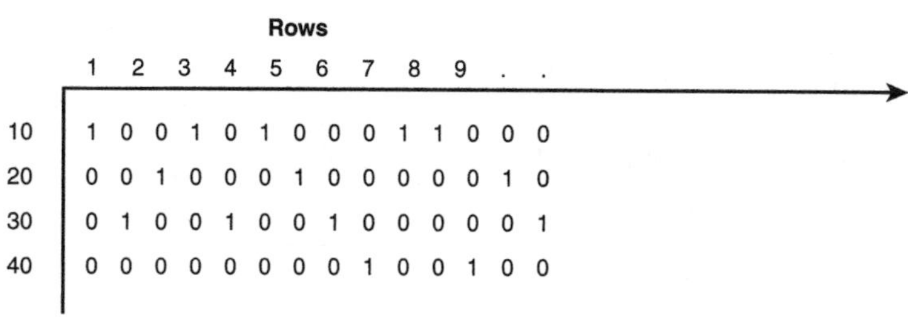

Figure 8.4

Bitmap index illustration.

Listing 8.2 can help identify table columns for possible bitmap index consideration.

Listing 8.2—Candidates for Bitmap Indexes

```
select owner "Owner", index_name "Index Name", distinct_keys "Distinct Keys"
from DBA_INDEXES
where distinct_keys < 15
```

Reverse-Key Indexes

The *reverse-key* index introduced in Oracle8 reverses the order of the bytes of a numeric key. It therefore provides a good way to help keep all the leaf blocks of a b-tree index structure more evenly populated with values. Candidates for reverse-key indexes are keys with a sequence number or incremental-type keys. Listing 8.3 illustrates how to make regular indexes reversed and change the reverse key back to a regular key.

Reverse-key indexes are only used to return individual rows and cannot perform range searches.

Listing 8.3—Reverse-Key Index Syntax

```
create index <INDEX NAME> on <TABLE NAME> (<COLUMN NAME(S)>) reverse
alter index <INDEX NAME> rebuild noreverse/reverse
```

Function-Based Indexes

If a function is used in the `where` clause on an indexed column, Oracle does not use the index. For example, if you were giving all the SCOTT.EMP employees in dept 10 a raise, and an index existed on column DEPTNO, the statement in Listing 8.4 would result in reading all the rows from the SCOTT.EMP table. By creating a *function-based* index with the `where` clause calculation, the index is used and only the rows meeting the `where` criteria are returned (see Listing 8.5). Function-based indexes can also be created as bitmap indexes.

Listing 8.4—SCOTT.EMP Access Via Function

```
UPDATE scott.emp
SET sal = sal * 1.10
WHERE (sal * 1.10) > 1000;
```

Listing 8.5—Function-Based Index

```
CREATE INDEX emp_raise_idx ON scott.emp (sal * 1.10);
```

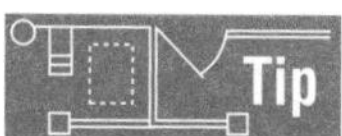

Oracle will not use a function-based index if a `WHERE` clause is not specified. For example, in the case of the SCOTT.EMP table, if you wanted to use the index to return the rows in the order of the index using `SELECT * FROM EMP ORDER BY UPPER(ename)`, to ensure that the function-based index created on this same function was used, you would use `SELECT * FROM EMP WHERE UPPER(ename) IS NOT NULL ORDER BY UPPER(ename)`.

Implementing IOTs in the Sales Tracking Application

Several of the Sales Tracking table objects are good candidates for IOTs. A good candidate is a table with infrequent updates but frequent use of some of the columns. The ST_VENDOR table (see Listing 8.6), as well as the ST_CUSTOMER table, lends itself well to IOTs. Both tables have frequent read access with just the ID and names fields being frequently accessed. Notice the `INCLUDING` clause lists the vendor_name field. This field is frequently accessed by the ST_INVENTORY application when the vendor_id field is used to verify the accuracy of information entered onscreen.

Listing 8.6—ST_VENDOR Index-Organized Table

```
CREATE TABLE st_vendor
    (vendor_id              NUMBER(6)      PRIMARY KEY,
    vendor_name             VARCHAR2(30)      NOT NULL,
    vendor_street1         VARCHAR2(30),
    vendor_street2          VARCHAR2(30),
    vendor_city             VARCHAR2(20),
    vendor_state            VARCHAR2(2),
    vendor_zipcode          VARCHAR2(10),
    vendor_tax_id           VARCHAR2(20)      NOT NULL)
    ORGANIZATION INDEX
    TABLESPACE st_data02
    PCTTHRESHOLD 20 INCLUDING vendor_name
    OVERFLOW TABLESPACE st_iot_overflow01
    STORAGE (INITIAL 5K
        NEXT 5
        MINEXTENTS 5
        MAXEXTENTS 100);
```

What Is Partitioning?

Some applications have tremendous amounts of data stored in tables. The larger the table, the longer it takes to perform certain administrative functions, such as backup and recovery. In addition, the larger the index associated with a table, the longer it takes to read through the leaf blocks to locate the row ID of the row or rows being accessed.

Partitioning is a way of spreading tables and indexes physically, by keys, across two or more tablespaces. The Oracle cost-based optimizer is smart enough to recognize partitions and identify the best way to return rows. Partitioning also aids in backups and recovery by being capable of performing these functions on significantly less data, which means it takes far less time to back up a tablespace as well as recover it (should the need arise).

It has been my experience that the more one can divide up the disk I/O across disk drives, the better Oracle will perform. The best reason for partitioning Oracle tables and indexes is to break an otherwise large object into smaller, more manageable pieces, both from a data-access point of view and from an availability point of view.

Oracle8i Partitioning Options

Oracle8 introduced table partitioning with a feature known as *range partitioning*. Range partitioning means separating the rows from a table into various predefined tablespaces by a key, known as the *partition key*. The table can be accessed like any other table by its table name, or each partition can be accessed individually. An example of this is a quarterly report on a particular quarter in which the table is partitioned by date so that a quarter's worth of data resides in each tablespace. This report, knowing that it was going to use only data from this one "quarterly" tablespace, could just access this one tablespace, saving the optimizer and Oracle some work.

Each tablespace can be backed up and restored independently from the others.

Oracle8i built on this partitioning feature by offering hash partitioning and composite partitioning. *Hash* partitioning is an alternative to range partitioning when no predictable data pattern, such as a date field, exists. Hash partitioning evenly distributes the rows, based on a hash key, across the defined tablespaces.

Composite partitioning, on the other hand, is a combination of range and hash partitioning. In this process, the table is first distributed across tablespaces based on a range of keys, and then each of these range partitions is further subdivided across subpartitions (where the partition is actually divided a predetermined number of times). Then, rows are evenly allocated across these subpartitions by a hash key.

Oracle8i partitioning does not support long data types.

Range Partitioning

Range partitioning organizes rows in the various assigned tablespaces based on a column(s). As illustrated in Figure 8.5, a partitioned table is a logical table physically stored across many tablespaces.

Figure 8.5

ST_SALES range partitioned table.

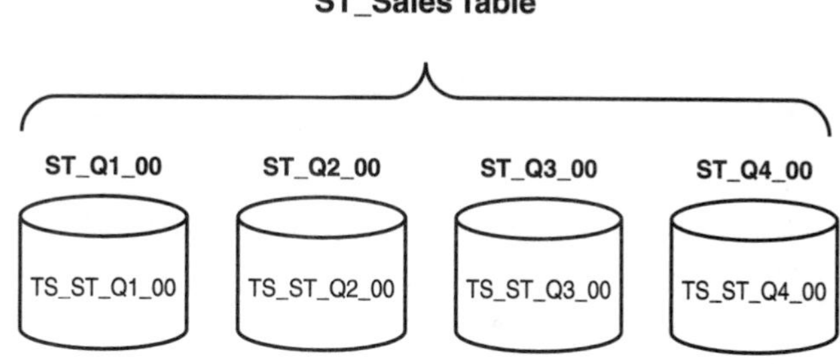

The ST_SALES partitioned table is not implemented with the other Sales Tracking objects because of the lack of physical disk drives on the author's NT platform and the lack of example data. Partitioning is useful for tables with hundreds of thousands of rows, or even millions of rows.

Listing 8.7 illustrates the `CREATE TABLE` syntax that creates the ST_SALES table illustrated in Figure 8.5. Notice the `PARTITION BY RANGE` with the key field on which the partitioning will be based. More than one column can be listed with this clause. Each partition then has a `LESS THAN` clause that tells Oracle which rows to place in which tablespaces. It is good practice to always use the `MAXVALUE` clause, as illustrated in the last `PARTITION` statement in Listing 8.7.

8

Listing 8.7—Sales Tracking ST_SALES Range Partition Table Example

```
CREATE TABLE st_sales
    (sales_customer_id        NUMBER(6),
    sales_sale_amt        NUMBER(9,2),
    sales_sale_date        DATE)
    PARTITION BY RANGE(sales_sale_date)
        (PARTITION st_q1_00 VALUES LESS THAN ('01-APR-2000')
            TABLESPACE ts_st_q1_00,
        (PARTITION st_q2_00 VALUES LESS THAN ('01-JUL-2000')
            TABLESPACE ts_st_q2_00,
        (PARTITION st_q3_00 VALUES LESS THAN ('01-OCT-2000')
            TABLESPACE ts_st_q3_00,
        (PARTITION st_q4_00 VALUES LESS THAN (MAXVALUE)
            TABLESPACE ts_st_q4_00
        );
```

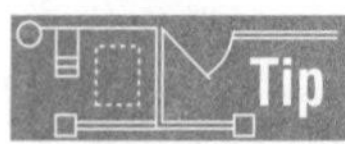

This table easily can be created by first creating the tablespaces, then following the example in Listing 8.7, and finally adding a `postupdate` and/or a `postinsert` trigger to execute from the ST_INVENTORY table when the Inv sale date field is not null.

Each partition can have its own defined storage clause.

Each partition can be accessed independently from the others. The SQL statement `SELECT sales_customer_id, sales_sale_amt from ST_SALES PARTITION (st_q2_00)` would only access the rows in the `st-q2-00` tablespace.

As new quarters are encountered, the DBA can simply add new partitions. Because the ST_SALES quarterly data is no longer needed, the tablespace can be backed up and then dropped, easily dropping all the rows. However, the rows can be easily re-established if business needs require it. Listing 8.8 shows the valid partitioning tablespace syntax options.

It is advised that you do not use the keyword `MAXVALUE` on the last partition of data-sensitive partitioning, such as the date field used in this example. It is easier to use the date for the partitioning and add another partition when the business requires it rather than to have to split, rename, and so on the last partition to accommodate a new range of dates.

Partitions can be easily dropped with the command `ALTER TABLE ST_SALES DROP PARTITION st_q1_00`. New tablespaces also can easily be added (unless the `MAXVALUE` clause has been specified) by using `ALTER TABLE ST_SALES ADD PARTITION st-q1-01 VALUES LESS THAN '01-APR-2001' TABLESPACE st_q1_01`.

Listing 8.8—Sales Tracking ST_SALES Partitioned Table Example

```
ALTER TABLE ADD PARTITION
ALTER TABLE DROP PARTITION
ALTER TABLE MOVE PARTITION
ALTER TABLE SPLIT PARTITION
ALTER TABLE TRUNCATE PARTITION
ALTER TABLE EXCHANGE PARTITION
```

Notice in Figure 8.5 that the partitions have meaningful names. Accessing the data by partition might be necessary for good reason. However, with hash partitioning, no real reason exists to access the data by partition, although the Oracle syntax does allow for this.

Hash Partitioning

Hash partitioning is similar to range partitioning except that the partition key is hashed and the rows spread evenly across the assigned tablespaces. This kind of partitioning is convenient when the distribution of the rows might not be even, or no well-defined grouping of the key fields exists (as in the situation of the date field in the range partitioning example). Figure 8.6 illustrates how the tablespaces might appear for a hash-partitioned table, and Listing 8.9 shows the syntax needed to support the example in Figure 8.6. Notice no MAXVALUE clause exists with hash partitioning.

Hashing algorithm—Takes a key field and applies a calculation to it that always equals a real number. This number then becomes the position in the table or index for the row or key value. In any kind of hash organization, you almost always need to know about how big the object will be so that Oracle can allocate enough hash positions to hold all the possible key values.

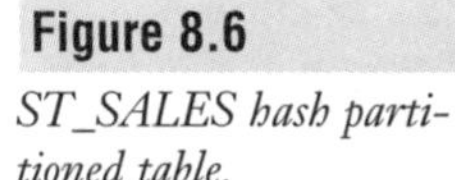

Figure 8.6

ST_SALES hash partitioned table.

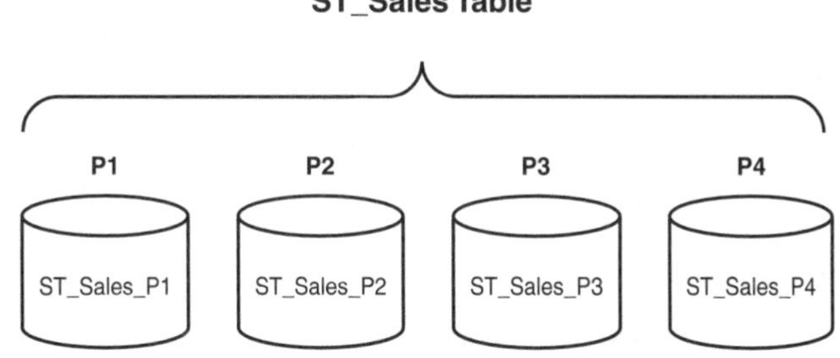

Listing 8.9—Sales Tracking ST_SALES Hash Partition Table Example

```
CREATE TABLE st_sales
    (sales_customer_id        NUMBER(6),
    sales_sale_date           DATE,
    sales_sale_amt            NUMBER(9,2))
    PARTITION BY HASH(sales_customer_id)
        (PARTITION p1 TABLESPACE ST_SALES_p1,
         PARTITION p2 TABLESPACE ST_SALES_p2,
         PARTITION p3 TABLESPACE ST_SALES_p3,
         PARTITION p4 TABLESPACE ST_SALES_p4
        );
```

Composite Partitioning

Composite partitioning is a combination of range and hash partitioning. Notice in Figure 8.7 that each partition is now subdivided into four additional subpartitions. Listing 8.10 is the syntax used to support Figure 8.7. Each partition named P1, P2, P3, and P4 would contain the range of dates as defined by the `STORE IN` clause. The `SUB PARTITIONS 4` clause subdivides each of these partitions into four logical units. The `SUBPARTITION BY HASH` clause, on the other hand, equally divides the rows that meet the range criteria, using the ST_CUSTOMER_ID as the hash key to evenly distribute the rows throughout these four subpartitions.

This example gives the ST_SALES object a total of 16 partitions for even row distribution.

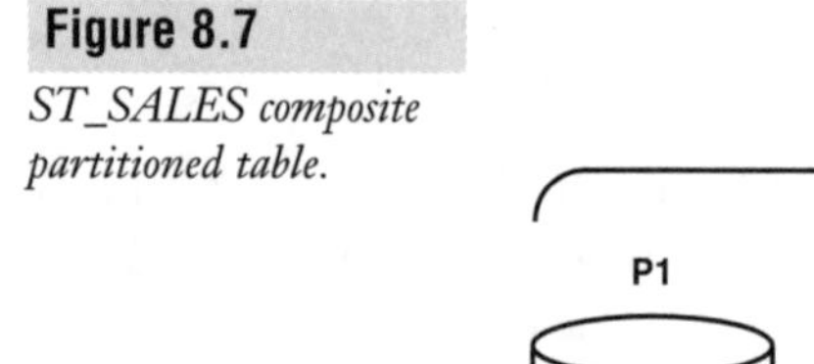

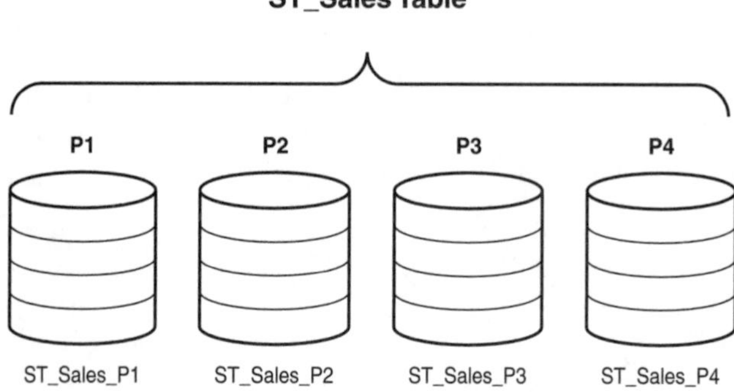

Figure 8.7

ST_SALES composite partitioned table.

Listing 8.10—Sales Tracking ST_SALES Composite Partition Table Example

```
CREATE TABLE st_sales
    (sales_customer_id          NUMBER(6),
    sales_sale_date          DATE,
    sales_sale_amt          NUMBER(9,2))
    PARTITION BY RANGE(sales_sale_date)
    SUB PARTITION BY HASH (sales_customer_id)
    SUB PARTITIONS 4
    STORE IN (ST_SALES_p1, ST_SALES_p2, ST_SALES_p3, ST_SALES_p4)
        (PARTITION p1 VALUES LESS THAN ('01-APR-2000'),
        (PARTITION p2 VALUES LESS THAN ('01-JUL-2000'),
        (PARTITION p3 VALUES LESS THAN ('01-OCT-2000'),
        (PARTITION p4 VALUES LESS THAN (MAXVALUE)
        );
```

Oracle8i Index Partitioning Options

Similar to table partitioning, *index* partitioning is a method of intelligently breaking larger indexes into smaller pieces across many tablespaces. The two types of index partitioning are local and global. *Local-partitioned* indexes have the same partitioning key values, number of tablespaces, and partitioning rules as the underlying table, whereas *global-partitioned* indexes have a `PARTITION BY RANGE` clause that enables the partitioning values, number of partitions, and tablespaces themselves to all be defined and vary from the underlying table partitioning structure. These indexes can either be *prefixed* (meaning they contain a leading part of the index key) or *nonprefixed* (meaning they're index partitioned on a value different from the indexing column).

Indexes can be partitioned even if the table being indexed is not partitioned. By default, this would be a global index because you would have to define the `PARTITION BY RANGE` clause.

Oracle8i does not support a nonprefixed, global-partitioned index. An error is returned if the partition range value is different from the leading column defined in the `INDEX` clause.

Types of Index Partitioning

8

A local index is one in which a single index partition's key values reference table rows in a single table partition. Listing 8.11 is an index example based on the ST_SALES table range partitioning example from Listing 8.7. The range partition key on the underlying table, ST_SALES, is sales_sale_date. A locally defined index is said to be *equi-partitioned*, meaning it has the same number of partitions with the same rules of partitioning. All local indexes are equi-partitioned by default. Notice that the locally defined index in Listing 8.11 has no `PARTITION BY RANGE` clause because Oracle automatically uses the same number of partitions, as well as the same partitioning rules. In addition, the `PARTITION` clause is used in Listing 8.11 to enable you to control the names of the index partitions.

If the `PARTITION` clause is omitted, Oracle creates system-generated partition names. If the `TABLESPACE` clause is omitted, Oracle places the index partition in the same tablespaces as the underlying table.

Listing 8.11—Sales Tracking ST_SALES Local Partition Index Example

```
CREATE INDEX st_sales_Date_Idx on st_sales (sales_sale_date)
    LOCAL
    (PARTITION st_i_q1_00 TABLESPACE ts_st_i_q1_00,
     PARTITION st_i_q2_00 TABLESPACE ts_st_i_q2_00,
     PARTITION st_i_q3_00 TABLESPACE ts_st_i_q3_00,
     PARTITION st_i_q4_00 TABLESPACE ts_st_i_q4_00
    );
```

A global-partitioned index has a partitioning structure (and probably partitioning keys) that differ from the table being indexed. Listing 8.12 illustrates the syntax for a global-partitioned index on the ST_SALES table, as previously discussed in Listing 8.7. Notice that the indexed column and the PARTITION BY RANGE columns are the same. Also notice that having the same number of partitions as the underlying table is unnecessary.

Listing 8.12—Sales Tracking ST_SALES Global Prefixed Partition Index Example

```
CREATE INDEX st_sales_Customer_ID_Idx on st_sales (customer_id)
    GLOBAL
    PARTITION BY RANGE(customer_id)
        (PARTITION st_i_p1 VALUES LESS THAN 1000
            TABLESPACE ts_st_i_p1,
        PARTITION st_i_p2 VALUES LESS THAN 2000
            TABLESPACE ts_st_i_p2,
        PARTITION st_i_p3 VALUES LESS THAN (MAXVALUE)
            TABLESPACE ts_st_i_p3
        );
```

Prefixed Versus Nonprefixed Partitioned Indexes

A local-partitioned index can be created on a column other than the partitioning key of the underlying table. Listing 8.13 shows a nonprefixed index being created on the CUSTOMER_ID column. A local index cannot have a `PARTITION BY RANGE` clause (because it would not be a local-partitioned index), so the same partitioning rules from the underlying table apply here. The index will be created based on the Customer ID field, but the index values will be partitioned by sales_salp date as defined in the underlying table.

Listing 8.13—Sales Tracking ST_SALES Local, Nonprefixed Partition Index Example

```
CREATE INDEX st_sales_Customer_ID_Idx on st_sales (customer_id)
    LOCAL
    (PARTITION st_i_q1_00 TABLESPACE ts_st_i_q1_00,
     PARTITION st_i_q2_00 TABLESPACE ts_st_i_q2_00,
     PARTITION st_i_q3_00 TABLESPACE ts_st_i_q3_00,
     PARTITION st_i_q4_00 TABLESPACE ts_st_i_q4_00
    );
```

If the underlying table is hash-partitioned and the STORE IN clause is not specified on the CREATE INDEX clause, Oracle uses the same tablespaces as the underlying tables. If the underlying table is composite-partitioned, the same holds true. This default can be overridden by specifying STORE IN and new SUBPARTITION definitions in the CREATE INDEX clause.

Oracle8i supports bitmap-partitioned indexes.

Evaluating the Index Partitioning Options

A local, prefix-partitioned index relationship to the base table is illustrated in Figure 8.8. Notice that a local partition is equi-partitioned and the index has the same partitioning structure and rules as the underlying table.

Local, prefixed-partitioned indexes are the most efficient of the partitioned indexes because the optimizer knows that the rows in the underlying table will be indexed in a single partition. Oracle therefore does not have to scan all the partitions to satisfy the SQL statement request.

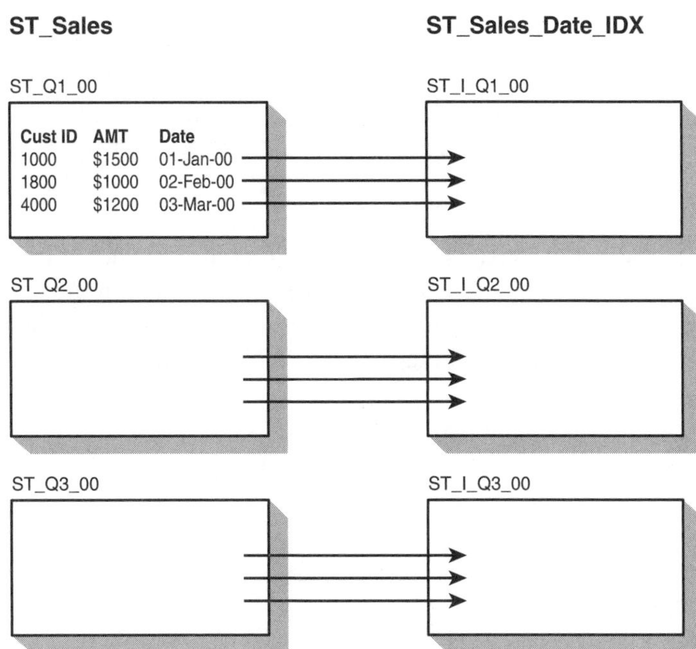

Figure 8.8

Local prefix-partitioned index relationship illustration.

8

A local, nonprefix-partitioned index is more work for Oracle because it must scan each of the partitions looking for values. In Figure 8.9, the index is created on the CUSTOMER_ID column, but the index leaves are still organized by the date field as defined by the underlying ST_SALES table. The CUSTOMER_ID leaves can be in any of the partitions. This type of index is best suited for parallel-processing Oracle environments in which each processor working on the SQL statement can search a partition.

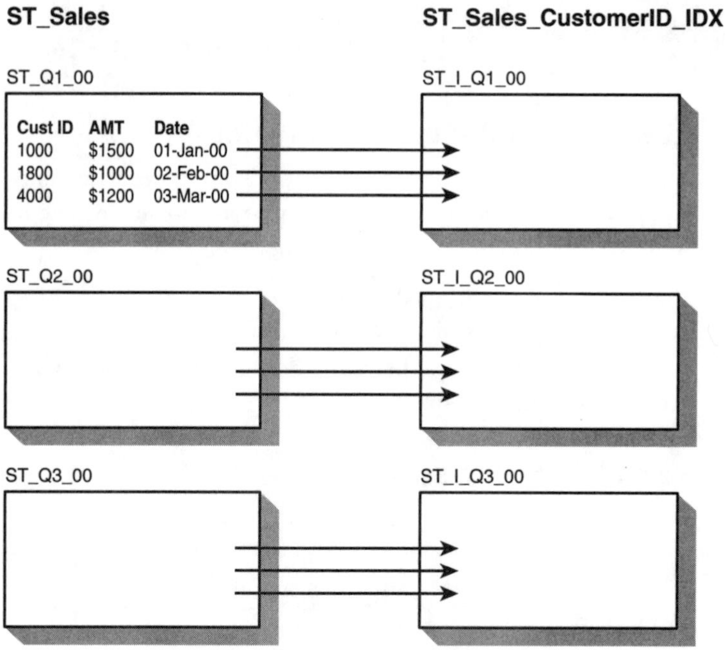

Figure 8.9

Local, nonprefixed-partitioned index relationship illustration.

Global, prefix-partitioned indexes are best for any kind of range-scan–type processing. This kind of an index groups the rows together in the same partition, and the cost-based optimizer knows in which partition to look for the range of values being requested. Figure 8.10 illustrates the relationship of a global index to its underlying table.

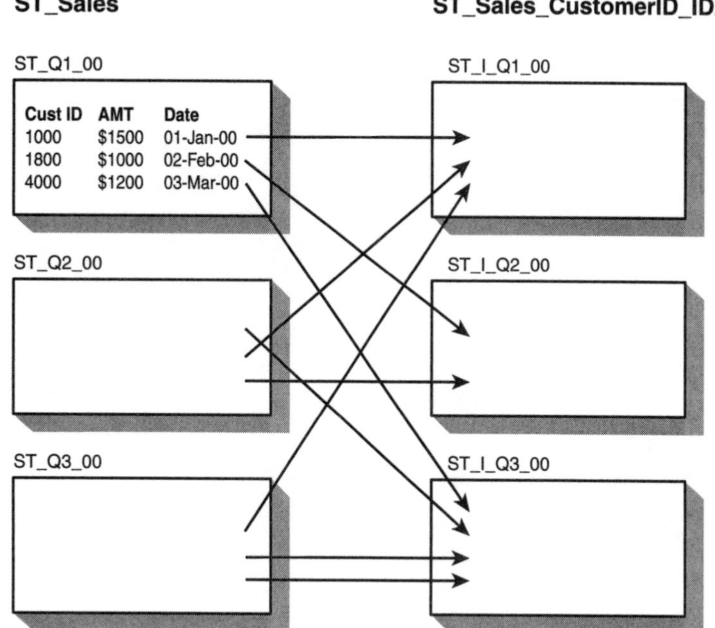

Figure 8.10

ST_SALES composite-partitioned table relationship illustration.

Summary

This chapter introduced you to the various Oracle8i indexing features. These examples were highlighted with example usage in the Sales Tracking Application. This chapter also discussed all the Oracle8i partitioning features, examples of good uses of each, and illustrations using these partitioning features in the Sales Tracking Application.

The remainder of this book covers using Oracle8i with the Web and the Internet.

Chapter 9

In this chapter

- *Sales Tracking Application Web Site—Buying a Car*
- *What Is OAS?*
- *Converting the Sales Tracking Forms to Web Pages*
- *Web-Based Strategies*

Planning the Sales Tracking Web Site

Several ways are available to process *HTML (Hypertext Markup Language)*, the language that Web browsers understand. Figure 9.1 illustrates the typical static Web environment in which all the files are generated ahead of time in an HTML format that contains tags telling the Web browser how to display various items. Each computer hosting a Web server has an *HTTP* listener or a Web listener—these are the same. An HTTP or Web listener is assigned to a specific *TCP/IP* port on the computer and listens for *URLs* addressed to that particular computer and port.

URL—Stands for Uniform Resource Locator, which is the addressing mechanism of the World Wide Web. It contains the computer's TCP/IP address (or a name that translates to the computer's TCP/IP address), the port number on that computer, and the resource to be first accessed. When `WWW` is part of a URL, this name is registered with a nameserver that interprets this WWW URL address (such as `www.oracle.com`) into the computer's name (known as a hostname) and the port for the listener.

TCP/IP—A common computer network, which also supports the World Wide Web.

HTTP (Hypertext Transfer Protocol)—The communication layer between the Web browser and the HTTP or Web listener. HTTP is a transmission protocol that works over TCP/IP and the Internet.

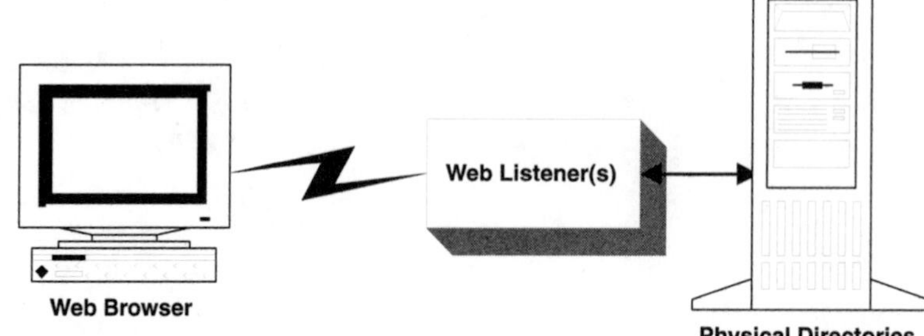

Figure 9.1
Web browser accessing an HTML file.

HTML (Hypertext Markup Language)—Used to build Web pages by specifying various display attributes, accessing computer files for display, and using tags. These tags tell the Web browser whether to bold, highlight, link, access computer files, and so on.

Another method for creating and processing Web requests is through a *CGI* program, illustrated in Figure 9.2. In Figure 9.2, where a computer system file containing HTML is being accessed, the CGI method executes a program that can be written in almost any language and produces files (in HTML format, or referenced by an HTML-formatted file) that are returned to the Web browser. This method consumes quite a bit more resources than the one shown in Figure 9.1 because a program has to start, execute, possibly log in to a database, and perform some work there (such as data extraction) before it can return anything to the Web browser. In addition, each Web listener request starts a new program. You can see that if this method is employed on a popular Web site, it could create quite a load on the computer system.

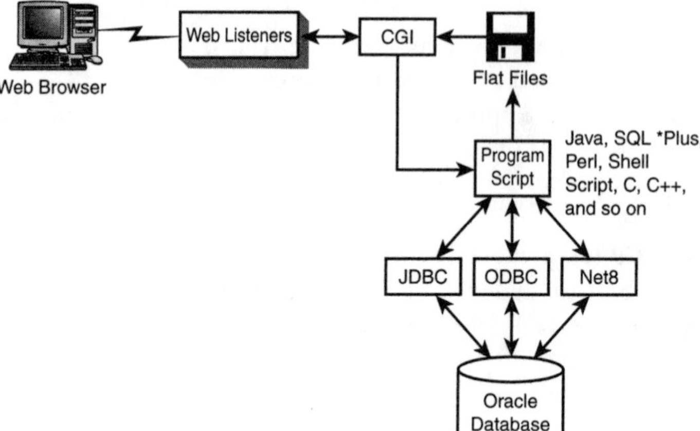

Figure 9.2
Web browser accessing a CGI interface.

CGI (Common Gateway Interface)—Usually a program being accessed instead of a computer file, as in Figure 9.2.

Applets are Java programs that are parts of Web pages. They are downloaded through the listener to a compliant Web browser (Netscape and Microsoft Explorer both support applets) and are executed on the client machine. *Servlets* are host-based Java programs that build dynamic Web pages that are then passed back to the Web browser. A series of servlets remains running to handle requests from the Java Web server. Two versions of Java Database Connectivity (JDBC) exist—thin JDBC and thick JDBC. *Thin* JDBC is used by applets and provides database connectivity for a particular client session. *Thick* JDBC is used to maintain connectivity for the duration of the servlet process. Both kinds of JDBC connect to Oracle8i via Net8. Figure 9.3 illustrates how the servlets work and how the applets work. The applet is downloaded to the client's Web browser via a Web page; it then connects and processes Java requests from the client's computer. Servlets maintain connectivity and are designed to be shared across requests coming through the Java Web server.

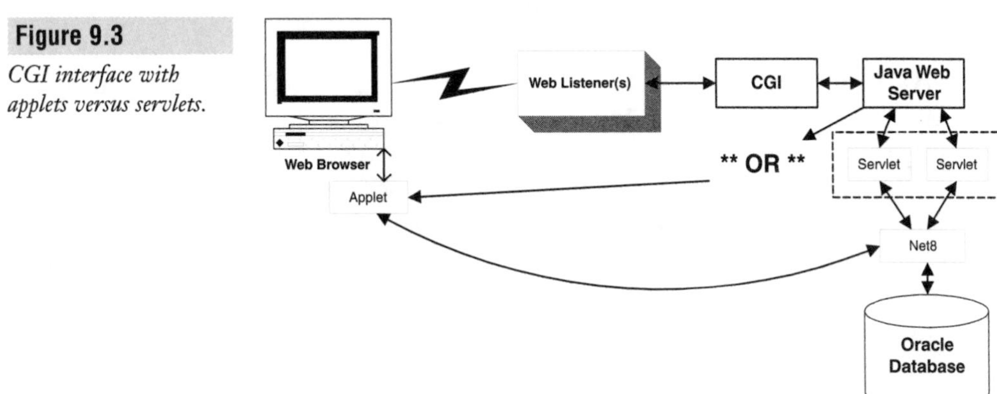

Figure 9.3

CGI interface with applets versus servlets.

The HTTP or Web listener can be one of many products, such as Microsoft IIS, Netscape FastTrack, or Oracle Web Server. Each complete URL contains many parts. The first part up to the first `/` is the machine address. Somewhere along the way, this WWW name gets relayed back to a host and domain name and a TCP/IP address and port number for a particular computer. On that computer is a listener process waiting for requests for that computer. What follows the first `/` is the virtual address. Figure 9.4 shows how that virtual address relates to a physical location on the particular computer. Whatever follows the final `/` is what is accessed, started, or executed on that computer. If nothing follows the final `/`, a default, such as `Index.html`, is used.

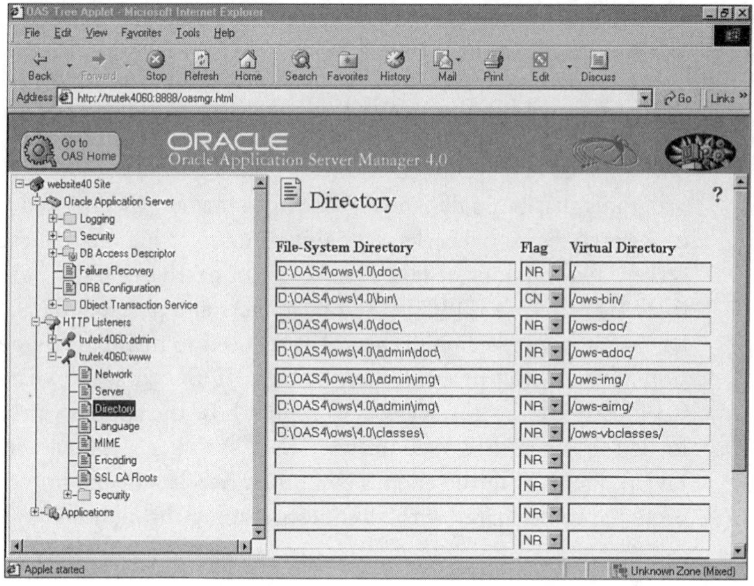

Figure 9.4

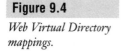

Web Virtual Directory mappings.

Several different kinds of URLs exist. An HTTP URL is used to connect with a Web server that handles HTML documents (Web pages)—for example, `http://www.quest.com/`, which accesses the Quest Web server and returns the HTML document `Index.HTML`. Other URLs are used for file transfer, such as `ftp://www.some_ftp_server.com/`, which uploads or downloads files using the FTP program and protocol. In addition, many kinds of servers are available, each with its own protocol, such as Usenet (uses the News URL), and so on.

URLs can also contain parameters. Parameters begin following a `?`, where the parameters are then named and values passed. A URL with parameters might look like this:

```
http://yourdomain.com/virtual_path_for_plsqlcart/stored_proc?param=1
```

Sales Tracking Application Web Site—Buying a Car

As cars are prepared for sale, they are added to the ST_CARS_FOR_SALE table (see Figure 9.5). This object tracks the inventory ID, the description of the car, and the location of the picture image on disk. HTML output can pick up images from only the disk, so all you need to do is store the location of the image in the database, not necessarily the whole picture. If the picture is stored in the database, the `get_lob` PL/SQL built-in procedure can be used to extract it to a specific location with a specific name, which can then be referenced by the HTML output. An additional

Oracle form could be added to maintain the ST_CARS_FOR_SALES, and of course, a report or form would be needed to display or process the BUYER information when offers are made.

Figure 9.5

Sales Tracking Cars For Sale object.

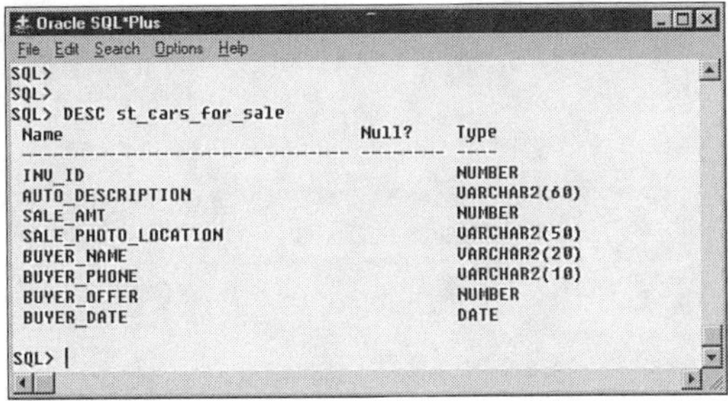

```
SQL>
SQL>
SQL> DESC st_cars_for_sale
 Name                            Null?    Type
 ------------------------------- -------- ----
 INV_ID                                   NUMBER
 AUTO_DESCRIPTION                         VARCHAR2(60)
 SALE_AMT                                 NUMBER
 SALE_PHOTO_LOCATION                      VARCHAR2(50)
 BUYER_NAME                               VARCHAR2(20)
 BUYER_PHONE                              VARCHAR2(10)
 BUYER_OFFER                              NUMBER
 BUYER_DATE                               DATE

SQL>
```

The Sales Tracking Web site dynamically displays auto information on those vehicles that have been added to the ST_CARS_FOR_SALE table object. Figure 9.6 shows the `1990 Camry Deluxe` auto information that is in the ST_CARS_FOR_SALE object. This is the information that will be pulled from the database to be displayed on the actual Web site.

Figure 9.6

ST_CARS_FOR_SALE data.

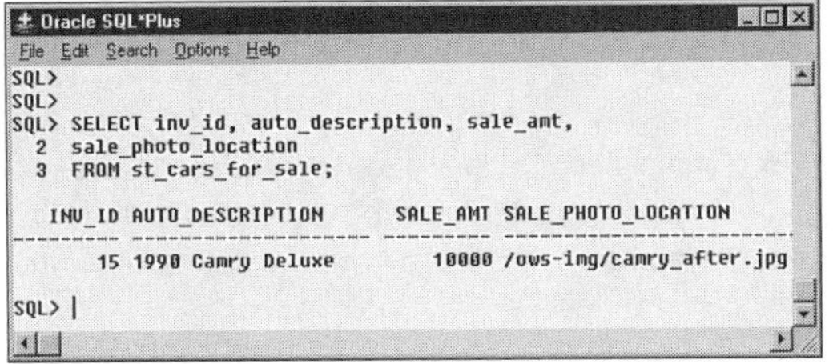

```
SQL>
SQL>
SQL> SELECT inv_id, auto_description, sale_amt,
  2  sale_photo_location
  3  FROM st_cars_for_sale;

   INV_ID AUTO_DESCRIPTION       SALE_AMT SALE_PHOTO_LOCATION
--------- -------------------- ---------- --------------------------
       15 1990 Camry Deluxe         10000 /ows-img/camry_after.jpg

SQL>
```

The Web site will then be capable of displaying information stored in this table object. Figure 9.7 shows the Web site that will be built in Chapters 10, "Building the Web Site with PL/SQL," and 11, "Building the Web Site with Java." Three buttons control the navigation of this Web page: Previous, Next, and Buy This Car (shown in the main screen in the upper-left window). The Previous and Next buttons display information from the previous or next row in the ST_CARS_FOR_SALE object. For example, clicking the Next button displays the Camry information as illustrated in the upper-right window. If you click the Place Offer button here, you then see the entry boxes displayed on the Web page in the bottom-left window. After you enter the offer information and click Place Offer, you will see the summary information displayed as in the bottom-right window. The Browse Inventory button in this panel then returns the Web user back to the original screen, as seen in the upper left.

Figure 9.7

These four windows (starting at the upper left) show the navigation of the actual Sales Tracking Web site.

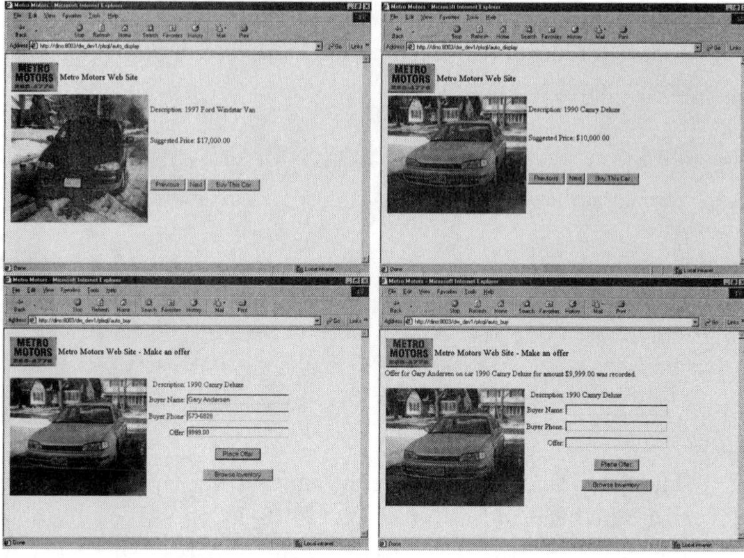

Figure 9.8 shows the data stored in ST_CARS_FOR_SALE after the Place Offer button has been clicked. This shows the information from the Web page has been written into the database.

This is a sample application. A real application that takes offers over the Web would collect as many offers as possible, storing them in yet another table object. The author is interested in showing functionality in these examples.

Figure 9.8

ST_CARS_FOR_SALE offer data recorded.

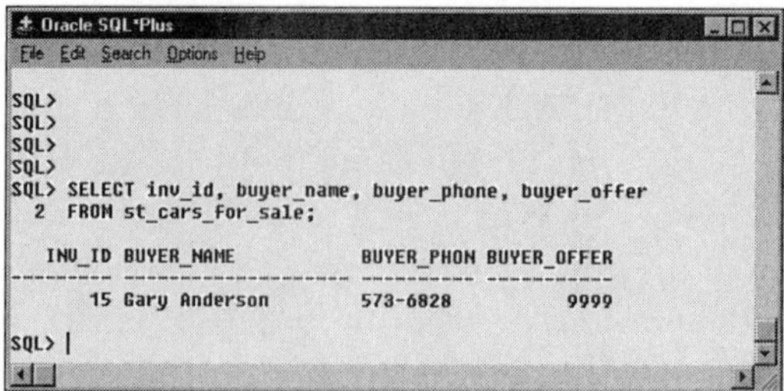

What Is OAS?

Oracle Application Server (OAS) is Oracle Corporation's integrated Web server. Figure 9.9 illustrates Oracle's Web server technology. When a listener receives an HTTP transaction from a Web browser (end user), the transaction is passed to the Object Request Broker (ORB). The ORB processes the URL and converts the virtual mappings into the computer mappings (as per entries illustrated in Figure 9.4). The ORB also determines the type of resource being requested, such as a Java program, and passes the request to the appropriate cartridge. Within the ORB is the *Web Request Broker (WRB)*, which is the piece that actually handles the incoming HTTP transactions from the Web browsers and returns HTTP headers with the HTML generated from the cartridge or program being accessed.

Figure 9.9

Web browser accessing Oracle Application Server.

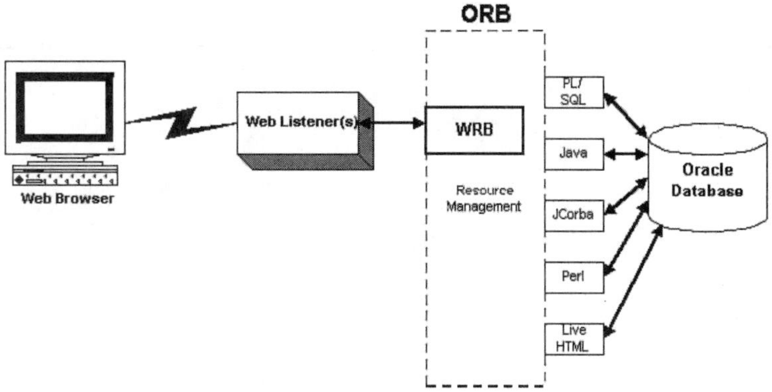

Virtual Mappings—The part of the URL that can specify a location after the computer's address. This location is virtual in that it is converted by the Web listener process into a real computer directory location on the computer hosting the Web server. This virtual address can be named anything because it is simply a name to be looked up and converted by the Web listener.

The Web Request Broker maintains a pool of resources (processes) that are already running and have logged on to the Oracle database. This alone is much more efficient than the CGI process because these processes are already logged in to the database. The WRB also contains a dispatcher that keeps track of the processes being used, passes the requests from the listeners to these processes, and returns the results to the appropriate listener, which in turn forwards the request to the original Web browser. The WRB can *load balance* requests across the available processes. Figure 9.10 shows the pool of processes for each cartridge type. These processes are initiated by the cartridges and are actually logged in to the Oracle database. In addition, they are a pool of resources for the WRB dispatcher to assign incoming HTTP requests and return results from. These processes are started when the OAS process is started.

These processes are part of each cartridge that was installed when the Oracle Application Server was installed. Various kinds of cartridges are available, such as the PL/SQL cartridge, the Java cartridge, and so on. The incoming URL will have a virtual mapping to one of these cartridges, as in Figure 9.11. This is how Oracle knows what kind of request is coming into it.

Figure 9.10

WRB cartridge pool resources.

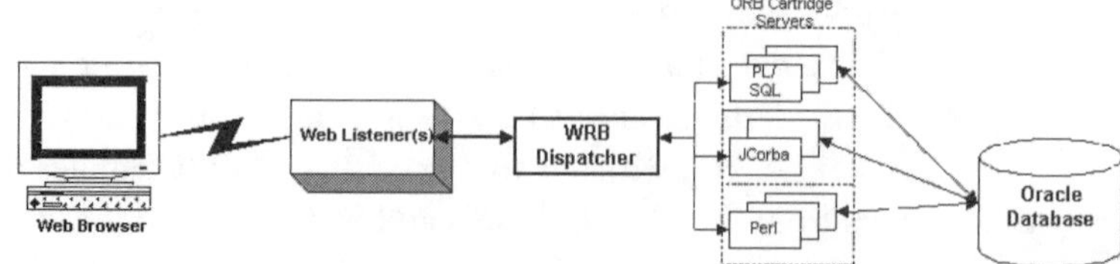

Figure 9.11

Virtual mappings for the Oracle cartridges.

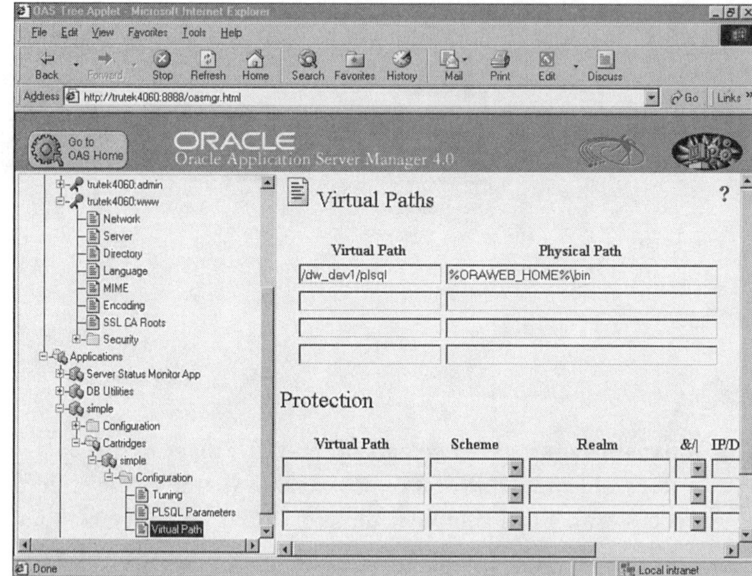

More than one listener process per computer is possible, which is a useful way of handling larger volumes of user requests.

Figure 9.9 is an illustration of how OAS v3.0 is implemented with a single cartridge model. The concept of *cartridge servers*, on the other hand, is the capability to have multiple processes working on behalf of each cartridge (refer to Figure 9.10). This allows for a greater amount of throughput because multiple processes can perform work for the same cartridge.

The OAS ORB has load balancing features. OAS v4.0 can evenly distribute the incoming requests across multiple processors that comprise an Oracle instance (Oracle Parallel Server) and evenly distribute requests among the active cartridge servers. OAS v4.0 Enterprise Edition has additional load balancing features. OAS Manager (part of OAS v4.0 Enterprise Edition) can load balance across nodes (similar to the non-enterprise version) and can give a weight to the processor type, enabling additional requests to be processed on faster servers instead of the even distribution that the non-enterprise edition allows.

Basic OAS Features

The Oracle Application Server enables you to develop Web-based applications using a variety of languages. The cartridge architecture (each cartridge is logged into the Oracle database) enables a close relationship between the Web-based application using OAS and the Oracle database.

OAS v4.0 comes with five different cartridges. Cartridges can be created and added based on the type of resources the computing environment needs to support. For example, a COBOL cartridge could be written to enable COBOL programs to be interpreted and executed by the OAS.

The five cartridges are Enterprise Java Beans, Jcorba, LiveHTML, Perl, and PL/SQL. Sun Microsystems developed *Enterprise Java Beans*, a method that is useful in larger, Web-based applications and enables the distribution of various components across many computers (see Figure 9.12). *Jcorba* is a standard programming methodology that enables various components to easily communicate with one another regardless of location or computing environment, whereas *LiveHTML* enables you to combine scripts (such as Perl) with Web applications. *Perl*, on the other hand, is a common scripting language similar to UNIX shell scripts. Lastly, *PL/SQL* is Oracle's proprietary procedural programming language that has been adapted to support the Web environment with extensions that support HTML.

Figure 9.12

Enterprise Java Beans computing environment.

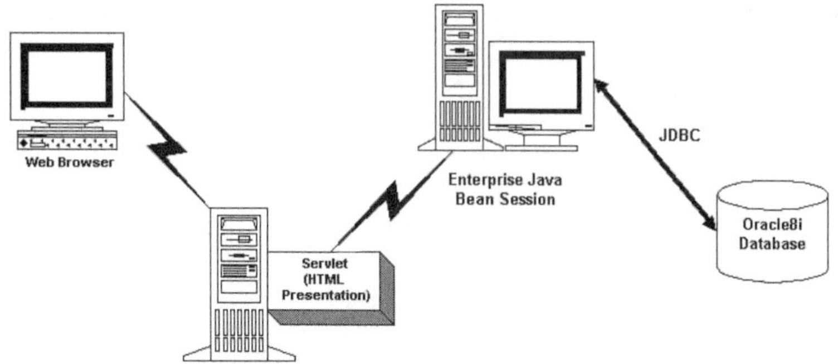

Basic OAS Administration

Configuring the Oracle Application Server v4.0 is made simple with the OAS Manager. The previously mentioned virtual addresses are also configured and maintained using the OAS Manager. Figure 9.13 illustrates how the OAS Manager appears and the various points of configuration available.

9

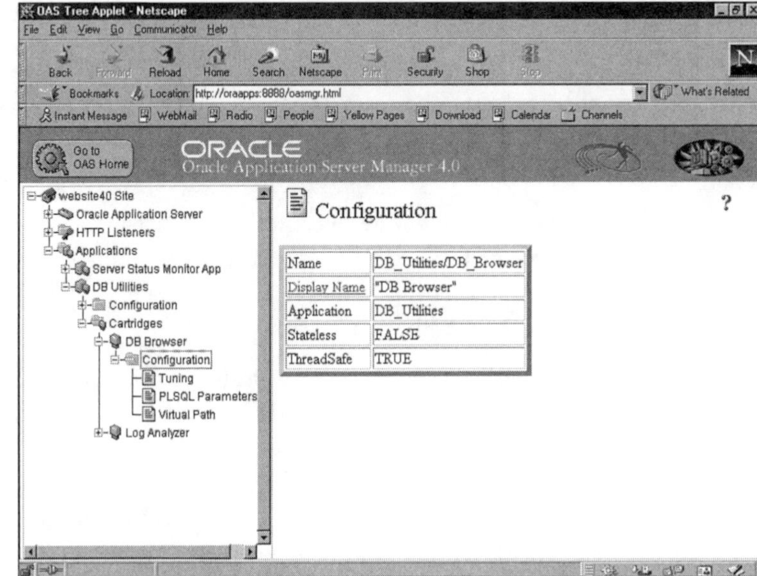

Figure 9.13

Oracle Application Server Manager v4.0.

Converting the Sales Tracking Forms to Web Pages

Converting the Oracle Forms–based applications to HTML is simple. Figure 9.14 illustrates how the ST_BILL_TIME application looks running in Java. To run Forms Developer applications on the Web, you must install two components: the Forms Client and the Forms Server from the Forms Developer v6.0 Installation Media.

The Forms Client is a Java applet downloaded to a user's Web browser when a Forms Developer application is being accessed. This applet maintains a login and serves as an interface between Forms Server software installed and the Web browser.

These applications have their own URLs that access the Forms Client applet and begin the interaction with the Forms Server. The Forms Server also has its own listener process, communicates with the Oracle database via SQL*Net or Net8, and manages the interaction between end users and the Forms Server. The Forms Client receives bundles of interface commands from the Forms Server and translates them (in sets) into interface objects for the end user. Some interface events handled by the Forms Server Runtime Engine in a client/server implementation, such as typing characters in a text field or moving around a dialog box, occur only on the Forms Client in the Web implementation, with no interaction with the Forms Server Runtime Engine.

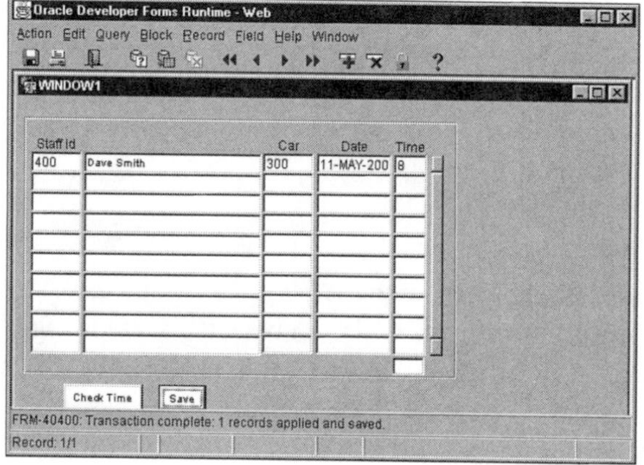

Figure 9.14

ST_BILL_TIME converted to a Web page.

Web-Based Strategies

This book considers three different strategies for creating Web sites that will access the Sales Tracking database. Chapter 10 introduces you to creating Web pages with PL/SQL; Chapter 11 introduces you to creating Web pages with Java; and Chapter 12, "Building Web-Based Forms with WebDB," introduces you to creating Web pages with WebDB. Each strategy has its purpose and has different levels of efficiency.

PL/SQL

PL/SQL is Oracle's proprietary procedural language. The Web Toolkit has given PL/SQL Web extensions by supplying an additional set of built-in procedures that handle the various aspects of HTML.

Advantages

The only advantage of using PL/SQL to build Web pages is

- Lower learning curve

PL/SQL is a fairly straightforward programming language with which many Oracle programmers are already familiar.

Disadvantages

Disadvantages of using PL/SQL to build Web pages include the following:

- Is less flexible
- Performs more slowly than Java
- Is proprietary to Oracle databases

PL/SQL is less flexible than full-featured languages such as Java. The execution of the PL/SQL code is still run-time interpreted; that is, it is not compiled into machine language as many programming languages are. PL/SQL is also proprietary to the Oracle database environment. If a possibility ever exists that the application being coded will be required to run in a different database environment, PL/SQL should not be used; one of the other languages available should be used instead to code the application.

Java

Java is an open language, meaning it is not constrained to a particular database or computing environment. Java is also an object-oriented language that can be difficult for some folks to understand. However, it is capable of easily handling Web page HTML needs as well as a variety of other computer tasks.

Advantages

Advantages of using Java to build Web pages include

- Code execution time is faster as compared to PL/SQL.
- It's a full-featured programming language.
- Code is portable between database and computing environments.
- Java resources are possibly easier to find.
- It's useful if Oracle might not be the only database environment for the application.

Java compiles into intermediate code that executes much more quickly in most computing environments when compared to PL/SQL. Java is a full-featured programming language with a lot more capability than PL/SQL. Additionally, when coded correctly, Java is portable between computing environments and even between different kinds of databases. This is the purpose of philosophies such as Enterprise Java Beans, JDBC, and so on. Because Java covers many database and computing environments, Java programmers might be easier to find than PL/SQL programmers. And, Java would be useful if the database environment might not always be Oracle.

Disadvantages

Disadvantages of using Java to build Web pages include

- Possible steep learning curve
- Still have to use PL/SQL

Java is an object-oriented language that is much more powerful than PL/SQL. Being a full-featured programming language, Java might be too much for some to learn for one or two Web-based projects. When using Java for Oracle triggers and so on, the Java code needs to be called by a PL/SQL procedure. This is known as wrapping the Java in PL/SQL.

WebDB

WebDB is Oracle's wizard-based Web application and Web site building environment. Although it is still in its infancy, WebDB can quickly build Web-based applications and Web sites with very little knowledge of the Web environment.

Advantages

Advantages of using WebDB to build Web pages include the following:

- Virtually no learning curve
- Ease of use

The WebDB wizard walks the Web page builder through all the steps necessary to build complete, functional applications and Web sites. The wizard-based development takes all the guesswork out of building Web-based applications.

Disadvantages

Disadvantages of using WebDB to build Web pages include the following:

- There's no flexibility in appearance.
- Performance is slow as compared to Java.

The appearance of WebDB applications is not flexible. The WebDB wizard builds rather generic-looking Web pages whose appearance (as of this writing) is not subject to change. The WebDB wizard builds PL/SQL behind-the-scenes, so the same performance issues and previously listed PL/SQL disadvantages exist with WebDB.

Summary

In this chapter, you learned what the Oracle Application Server is. The first part of this chapter provided an in-depth overview of how a Web browser can interact with a host computer. The topics of applets and servlets were introduced, as well as how the Oracle Application Server works to provide services (HTML output) to requesting Web browsers. This chapter also summarized the three Web-based programming environments that will be covered in the remainder of this book: PL/SQL, Java, and WebDB. The final section of this chapter summarized the uses and differences of these three programming environments as they apply to Web page development.

Next Steps

The next chapter will introduce you to PL/SQL with HTML extensions. You first will learn the PL/SQL Web page basics by building several modules that will then be used throughout the remainder of the chapter. You will also learn how to build the Sales Tracking Web site that was outlined in this chapter.

In this chapter

- *Using PL/SQL*
- *Building the Web Site*

Chapter 10

Building the Web Site with PL/SQL

The "Using PL/SQL" section of this chapter builds a basic `HelloWorld` display-type Web page using simple PL/SQL HTML-type commands. The `HelloWorld` example begins with passing text strings from PL/SQL to the HTML output (and subsequently being passed back to a Web browser). We will then build on the example by building a heading and displaying a picture. We will learn by updating the `HelloWorld` example to include either a parameter being passed or the Web page prompting the user for the parameter. Then, the "Building the Web Site" section of this chapter uses these skills from the `HelloWorld` example to build the Sales Tracking Web site.

Using PL/SQL

The Oracle Application Server (OAS) processes requests from users (Web browsers) and replies to these users with an HTML document. This document can be built either using a variety of methods, such as Java (see Chapter 11, "Building the Web Site with Java"), or using the PL/SQL cartridge of the Oracle Application Server.

The incoming URL has a virtual mapping to the PL/SQL cartridge in the Web server. Figure 9.11 in Chapter 9, "Planning the Sales Tracking Web Site," illustrates how the Oracle Application Server knows to use the PL/SQL cartridge to process incoming requests from Web browsers. Listing 10.1 shows the simplest of PL/SQL Web sites, the classic "Hello World" message. Notice that this PL/SQL procedure is created in the normal manner with the `CREATE OR REPLACE` syntax. Two types of PL/SQL built-in packages handle the HTML code. The *HTP* package contains

PL/SQL procedures that generate HTML output, whereas the *HTF* package contains PL/SQL functions that return HTML code as the return value. The `HTP.` syntax tells PL/SQL that this is an HTML command and is passed through to the HTML output. The `htp.htmlOpen` syntax tells PL/SQL that this is the beginning of the HTML document, and `htp.htmlClose` tells PL/SQL that this is the end of the HTML document. The same is true of `htp.bodyOpen` and `htp.bodyClose`. The `htp.p` command, on the other hand, is used to print or place items in the HTML document. In this example, `htp.p` is used to display the `HelloWorld` message. Figure 10.1 shows how to access this procedure through a Web browser, as well as display the output of the PL/SQL procedure. Notice the URL used to access the `HelloWorld` PL/SQL procedure.

Listing 10.1—`HelloWorld` PL/SQL Procedure Syntax

```
CREATE OR REPLACE PROCEDURE helloworld
AS
BEGIN
    htp.htmlOpen;
    htp.bodyOpen;
    htp.p('HelloWorld');
    htp.bodyClose;
    htp.htmlClose;
END;
/
```

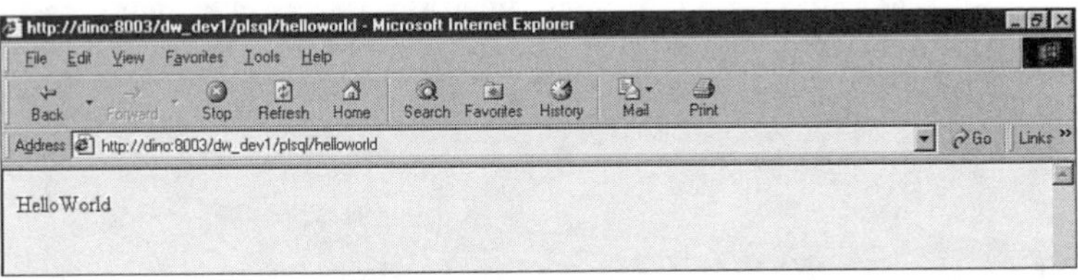

Figure 10.1

`HelloWorld` PL/SQL procedure.

Notice that Listing 10.2 shows the actual HTML code generated by the `HelloWorld` PL/SQL procedure. Also notice how the `htp.htmlOpen` syntax in Listing 10.1 generated the <HTML> document tag in Listing 10.2.

Listing 10.2—HTML Output Created by the `HelloWorld` PL/SQL Procedure

```
<HTML>
<BODY>
HelloWorld
</BODY>
</HTML>
```

Listing 10.3 shows how the `htp.p` command can be used to pass HTML tags to the HTML output. In Listing 10.1, `htp.htmlOpen` was used to generate the `<HTML>` tag, whereas Listing 10.3 illustrates how `htp.p` can be used to pass the text `<HTML>` to the HTML output.

Listing 10.3—`HelloWorld` PL/SQL Procedure Using Just `htp.p`

```
CREATE OR REPLACE PROCEDURE helloworld
AS
BEGIN
    htp.p('<HTML>');
    htp.p('<BODY>');
    htp.p('HelloWorld');
    htp.p('</HTML>');
    htp.p('</BODY>');
END;
/
```

The `owa_util.showpage` package can be used to display the HTML output in SQL*Plus. Figure 10.2 illustrates how to execute the `HelloWorld` procedure in SQL*Plus and then immediately use the `owa_util.showpage` package to display the HTML output generated by the `HelloWorld` procedure.

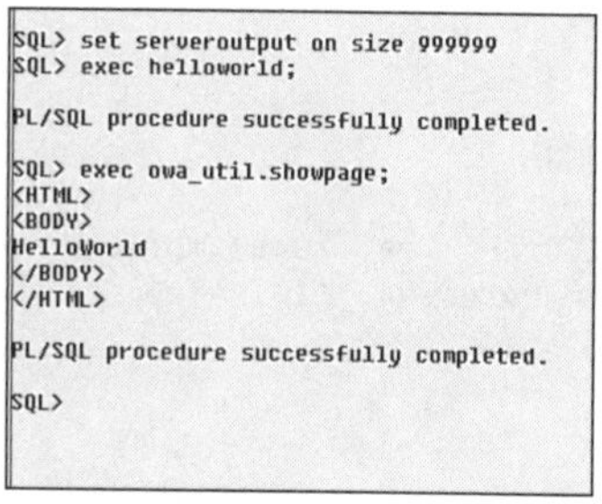

Figure 10.2

*Showing the `HelloWorld` PL/SQL procedure's HTML output in SQL*Plus.*

```
SQL> set serveroutput on size 999999
SQL> exec helloworld;

PL/SQL procedure successfully completed.

SQL> exec owa_util.showpage;
<HTML>
<BODY>
HelloWorld
</BODY>
</HTML>

PL/SQL procedure successfully completed.

SQL>
```

Displaying Pictures with PL/SQL and HTML

Creating simple PL/SQL procedures that display common things, such as banner information and default items, on a Web page is easy. This gives the Web page a consistent look and enables PL/SQL to be coded once and reused many times.

Listing 10.4 builds on Listing 10.3 by adding the code to create the banner Web page information, as illustrated by Figure 10.3. Notice the `htp.tableOpen` and the `htp.tableRowOpen` syntax in lines 9 and 10. Within the table row, also notice that two references to `htp.tableData` exist (lines 14 and 22). Each of these `tableData` references is creating a column in the HTML table. This gives the HTML output the capability to display text and images in a very specific and consistent position.

The first column gets the `metro_motors.jpg` image file (lines 14 through 21). The `htf.img` function is used to return the location of the picture (in this case the Metro Motors jpeg file) stored in the virtual location `ows-img`. Refer to Figure 9.4 in Chapter 9 and notice that `ows-img` maps to the computer directory `D:\OAS4\ows\4.0\admin\img\`. The `metro_motors.jpg` must be in this physical location for the `htf.img` function to find it, and the `htf.img` function generates an `<IMG>` tag that tells HTML where an image is stored in the virtual path. The second column receives the text `Metro Motors Web Site` (lines 22–25).

Listing 10.4—`HelloWorld` PL/SQL Procedure Displaying a Banner (`helloworld2.sql`)

```
1: CREATE OR REPLACE PROCEDURE helloworld
2: AS
3: BEGIN
4:     htp.htmlopen;
5:     htp.bodyOpen;
6:     -- -----------------------------------------------
7:     -- start of our heading / banner
8:     -- -----------------------------------------------
9:     htp.tableOpen;
10:    htp.tableRowOpen
11:    (
12:        cvalign => 'CENTER'
13:    );
14:    htp.tableData
15:    (
16:        cvalue      => htf.img
17:                        (
18:                        curl        => '/ows-img/metro_motors.jpg'
19:                      , cattributes => 'WIDTH=100'
20:                        )
21:    );
22:    htp.tableData
23:    (
24:        cvalue  => htf.big('Metro Motors Web Site')
25:    );
26:    htp.tableRowClose;
27:    htp.tableClose;
28:    -- -----------------------------------------------
29:    -- End of our heading / banner
30:    -- -----------------------------------------------
31:    htp.p('HelloWorld');
32:    htp.bodyClose;
33:    htp.htmlClose;
34: END;
35: /
```

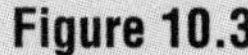

Figure 10.3

Metro Motors Web site banner page.

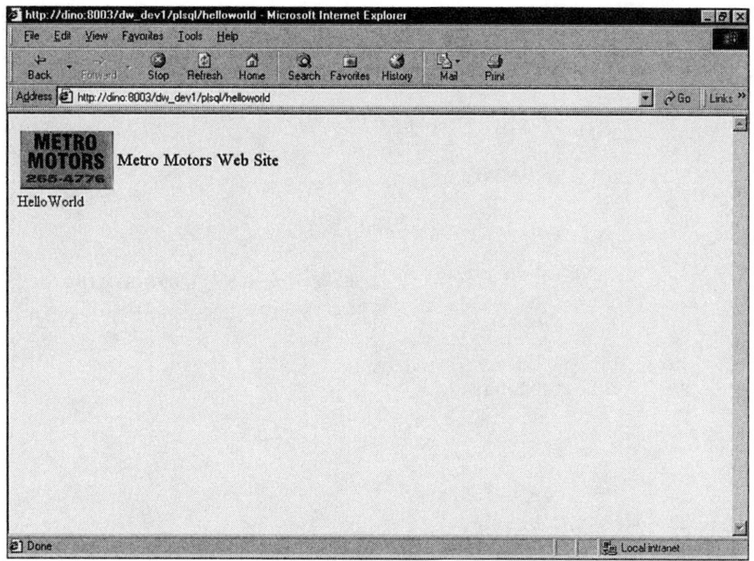

If your browser does not show the graphic, check your OAS virtual mappings to ensure that the jpg image file is in the directory for which the virtual directory is configured (illustrated in Figure 9.4 in Chapter 9).

Now, creating a procedure called `display_banner` and calling it whenever we create a new Web page is easy and enables the banner information to be coded once and then reused throughout the Web application. If a change to the banner information needs to be made, one procedure is changed and the change is then automatically reflected throughout the application upon its next Web browser access.

To do this, review the `display_banner` procedure in Listing 10.5, and you will see that it is very similar to the code in Listing 10.4. Notice that lines 7–25 in Listing 10.5 are very similar to lines 9–27 in Listing 10.4. The only real difference is at lines 3 and 22—the `p_caption` variable replaces the hard-coded Metro Motors banner text so this procedure can be used for any banner by simply inserting `?p_caption=`*`<some text>`* on the URL line.

Listing 10.5—DISPLAY_BANNER PL/SQL Procedure (display_banner.sql)

```
1: CREATE OR REPLACE PROCEDURE display_banner
2: (
3:     p_caption   IN VARCHAR2 DEFAULT 'Metro Motors Web Site'
4: )
5: AS
6: BEGIN
7:     htp.tableOpen;
```

Listing 10.5—continued

```
    htp.tableRowOpen
    (
        cvalign => 'CENTER'
    );
    htp.tableData
    (
        cvalue      => htf.img
                         (
                         curl        => '/ows-img/metro_motors.jpg'
                      ,   cattributes => 'WIDTH=100'
                         )
    );
    htp.tableData
    (
        cvalue  => htf.big(p_caption)
    );
    htp.tableRowClose;
    htp.tableClose;
END;
/
```

Note that we added an input parameter `p_caption` to the procedure. This enables us to specify a caption other than just `Metro Motors Web Site`.

Now we can change our `HelloWorld` procedure to call the `display_banner` procedure, as shown in Listing 10.6.

Listing 10.6—`HelloWorld` PL/SQL Procedure Using `display_banner` Procedure (`helloworld3.sql`)

```
CREATE OR REPLACE PROCEDURE helloworld
AS
BEGIN
    htp.htmlopen;
    htp.bodyOpen;
    -- -------------------------------------------------
    -- start of our heading / banner
    -- -------------------------------------------------
    display_banner
    (
        p_caption => 'Metro Motors Web Site'
    );
    -- -------------------------------------------------
    -- End of our heading / banner
    -- -------------------------------------------------
    htp.p('HelloWorld');
    htp.bodyClose;
    htp.htmlClose;
END;
/
```

Both versions of this procedure, outlined in Listings 10.4 and 10.6, produce the same identical output as illustrated in Figure 10.3. If you were to look at the HTML output as illustrated in Figure 10.2, you would notice that the HTML output is also identical. The `display_banner` procedure creates the same HTML output, and it is now easy to use in other Web pages related to this application to give the identical visual attributes without having to add the code to each additional Web page.

Passing Parameters from PL/SQL to HTML

The final example in this section can accept a parameter from the URL and also accepts data from a field. Listing 10.7 illustrates the `HelloWorld` PL/SQL procedure with the additional code necessary to create a frame for data entry, as well as to process a parameter passed to the procedure. Lines 19–24 process any information in variable `p_name`. This value is populated if a parameter is passed from the URL (see Figure 10.4); otherwise, the generic message `HelloWorld` is displayed (see Figure 10.5).

Lines 26–30 in Listing 10.7 create an HTML `form` tag. This form is further defined by lines 31–43, where a submit button is defined (lines 33–36) and an entry box is defined (lines 38–43).

The HTML form tag has two parameters. `curl` defines the procedure to call when the form is submitted, whereas `ctarget` is the Web page where the results of the procedure should be displayed. This field is intentionally set to blank so the results are displayed on the same Web page.

The submit button contains only one value, `cvalue`, which will contain any text to place inside the button.

The entry field has three parameters. `cname` is the variable name where the contents of the entry field will be placed after the submit button is clicked. `csize` is the maximum length of the entered value to be placed in `cname`, and `cmaxlength` is the total width of the entry box being displayed.

Listing 10.7—`HelloWorld` PL/SQL Procedure Accepting a Parameter/Prompting for a Parameter (`helloworld4_num.sql`)

```
1:  CREATE OR REPLACE PROCEDURE helloworld
2:     (
3:          p_name IN VARCHAR2 DEFAULT NULL
4:     )
5:  AS
6:  BEGIN
7:          htp.htmlopen;
8:          htp.bodyOpen;
9:          -- ------------------------------------------------
10:         -- start of our heading / banner
11:         -- ------------------------------------------------
```

Listing 10.7—continued

```
12:      display_banner
13:       (
14:           p_caption => 'Metro Motors Web Site'
15:       );
16:       -- ------------------------------------------------
17:       -- End of our heading / banner
18:       -- ------------------------------------------------
19:       IF p_name IS NULL THEN
20:          htp.p('HelloWorld');
21:       ELSE
22:           htp.p('Hello '||p_name||'. The time here is '
23:                ||TO_CHAR(SYSDATE,'HH24:MI:SS'));
24:       END IF; -- p_name IS NULL
25:
26:       htp.formOpen
27:       (
28:           curl        => 'helloworld'
29:       ,   ctarget     => ''
30:       );
31:       htp.hr;
32:
33:       htp.formSubmit
34:       (
35:         cvalue      => 'Say Hello to '
36:       );
37:
38:       htp.formText
39:       (
40:           cname       => 'p_name'
41:       ,   csize       => 30
42:       ,   cmaxlength  => 20
43:       );
44:
45:       htp.formclose;
46:       htp.bodyClose;
47:       htp.htmlClose;
48:    END;
49:    /
```

Line 3 of Listing 10.7 identifies the `p_name` parameter, defines it as a variable length character field, and gives it the default value `NULL`. The reason for the default value is that this procedure might not have a parameter passed to it. If the parameter did not have a default value, we would be forced to always provide one on the URL line:

`http://`*`yourdomain`*`.com/`*`virtual_path_for_plsqlcart`*`/helloworld?p_name=Dave`

If this parameter was not passed, the missing parameter error would be returned to the Web browser, as illustrated by Figure 10.4.

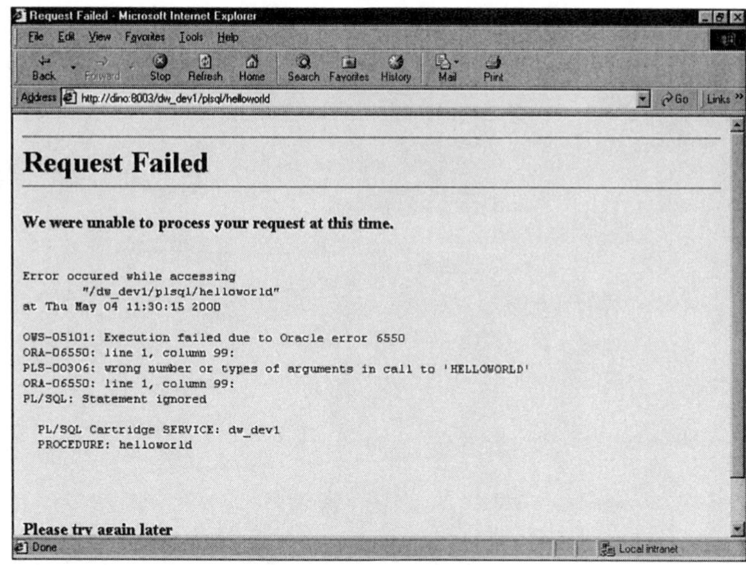

Figure 10.4

Parameter missing Web error.

Figure 10.5 shows the `HelloWorld` procedure with the just-added enterable field. Enter the value `Dave` in the text entry field and click the Say Hello to button. The Web page illustrated in Figure 10.6 will appear.

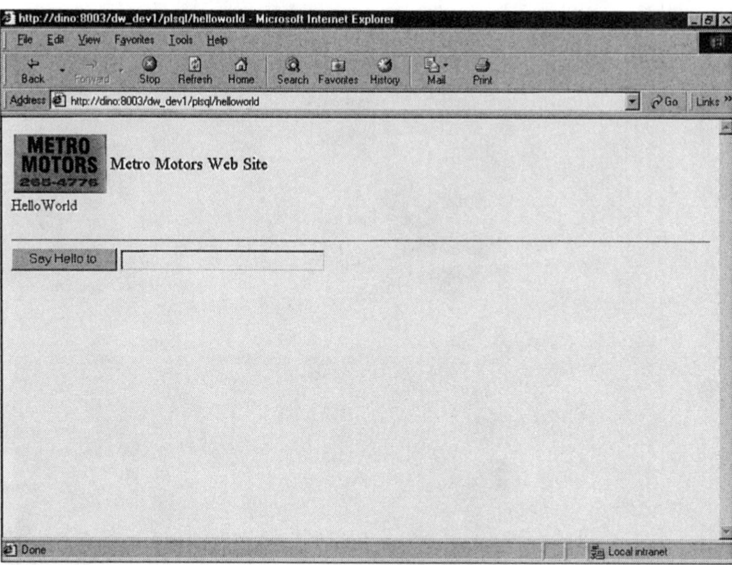

Figure 10.5

`HelloWorld` procedure prompting for input.

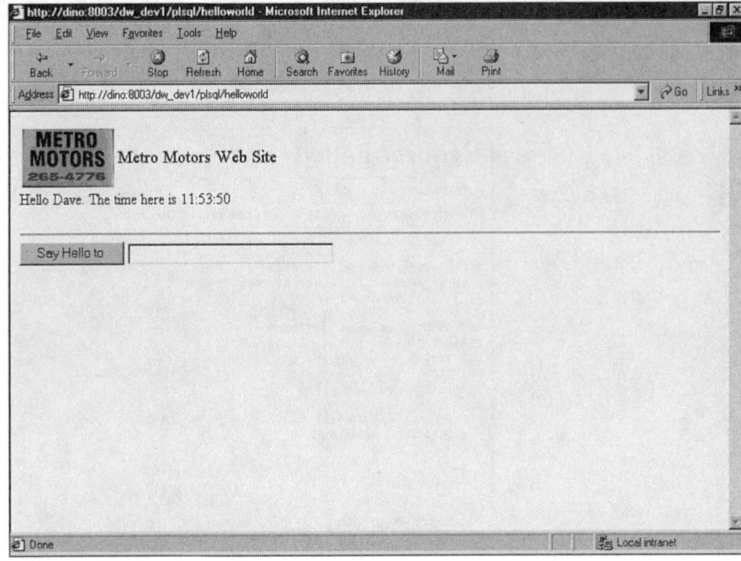

Figure 10.6

`HelloWorld` procedure displaying results.

Building the Web Site

Note

The remainder of this chapter builds the Web site illustrated in Figure 9.7, reprinted here.

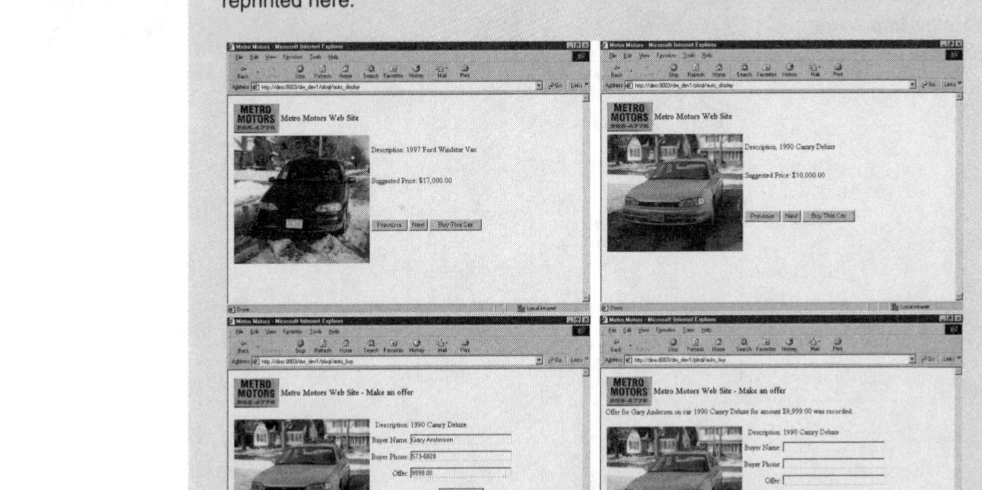

Figure 9.7

The Sales Tracking Web site will be based on two PL/SQL procedures: `auto_display` (see Listing 10.9) and `auto_buy` (see Listing 10.10). The Web site will also reuse the `display_banner` PL/SQL procedure built in Listing 10.5 and make reference to the PL/SQL procedure `display_error` used in Listing 10.8.

The `display_error` PL/SQL procedure (see Listing 10.8) is a simple Web page that accepts a parameter, `p_text`, (see line 3) and displays this text on the Web page at line 15. The `show errors` syntax in line 23 is a SQL*Plus command that's useful in displaying any errors that might have occurred when creating the procedure.

> The procedures detailed in this chapter can also be created using the Quest SQL Navigator tool.

Listing 10.8—DISPLAY_ERROR PL/SQL Procedure Syntax

```
1: CREATE OR REPLACE PROCEDURE display_error
2: (
3:    p_text  IN VARCHAR2 DEFAULT NULL
4: ) IS
5: BEGIN
6:     htp.htmlopen;
7:     htp.headOpen;
8:     htp.title('Error Page');
9:     htp.headClose;
10:    htp.bodyOpen;
11:
12:    htp.big('An Error has occurred');
13:
14:    htp.hr;
15:    htp.p('The following error occurred: '||p_text);
16:    htp.br;
17:    htp.p('Please contact Metro Motors directly at: 265-4776');
18:
19:    htp.bodyClose;
20:    htp.htmlClose;
21: END;
22: /
23: show errors
```


The main page of our Web site relies on the `auto_display` PL/SQL procedure. Because each car has a unique inventory number (INV_ID), easy access to the rows in the ST_CARS_FOR_SALE table object is enabled. This INV_ID column also makes a convenient parameter to look up a specific row if a parameter is passed to this Web page. The page should allow us to browse forward and backward through our entire inventory and should display a link to the auto_buy screen—so that customers can make an offer on the car. This is accomplished with lines 26–69 in Listing 10.9.

Lines 1–5 highlight the procedure and the parameters that can be passed to it. The procedure accepts a source (`p_source`), which tells the Web page to go to the next or previous record in the ST_CARS_FOR_SALE table object. The `p_source` parameter defaults to `DISPLAY_NEXT` if no parameter is passed. As discussed earlier in this chapter, this Web page can be called with parameters or with no parameters without causing any kind of parameter passing violation. The other parameter that can be passed is an inventory number (`p_inv_id`) that provides the row in the ST_CARS_FOR_SALE table object from which to perform the previous or next row function. The URL for this Web page is `http://<computer name or IP address>/virtual_path/auto_display`, which, with no parameters, will display the first auto in the ST_CARS_FOR_SALE table object.

Listing 10.9 shows the entire code for the `display_auto` PL/SQL procedure. Lines 6–14 are a cursor that selects the information about the next car in our inventory. If the inventory ID passed is `NULL`, the Web page starts at the beginning of the ST_CARS_FOR_SALE table object. Lines 15–23 are a cursor that selects the information about the previous row in ST_CARS_FOR_SALE. If the inventory ID passed is `NULL`, this procedure starts with the last row in the ST_CARS_FOR_SALE table object. Line 24 declares a PL/SQL record for the cursor defined in lines 6–23. When this cursor is opened, Oracle returns the row identified by the SQL `select` statement. Lines 26–30 verify that any passed parameters are valid. If any passed parameters are not found to be valid, the PL/SQL procedure `display_error` is then called at line 31. Lines 39–69 determine the row (previous or next) and use the appropriate cursor to select the correct row from ST_CARS_FOR_SALE.

Line 75 begins to build the actual Web page. Lines 81–84 call the `display_banner` PL/SQL procedure that we created in the previous section of this chapter (refer to Listing 10.5). This displays the standard Metro Motors banner at the top of the Web page. Review Figure 9.7 and you will notice that the picture is on the left with the description, pricing, and navigational buttons on the right. To accomplish this, an HTML table with 4 columns and 3 rows is used. The picture takes up column 1 and rows 1–3. The description takes up row 1 and columns 2–4. The price takes up row 2 and columns 2–4. The navigation buttons take up row 3 and each button takes up one column. Lines 89–113 display the information from the database stored in sale_row (see line 24). Lines 117–139 create the Previous button, and lines 141–166 create the Next button. Finally, lines 171–193 create the Buy This Car button. This button is created in a similar fashion to the Previous and Next buttons except that it calls the `auto_buy` PL/SQL procedure.

Listing 10.9—AUTO_DISPLAY PL/SQL Procedure Syntax

```
CREATE OR REPLACE PROCEDURE auto_display
 (
     p_source        IN VARCHAR2 DEFAULT 'DISPLAY_NEXT'
 ,   p_inv_id        IN NUMBER DEFAULT NULL
 ) AS
 CURSOR next_CUR
 (
     p_inv_id IN NUMBER
 ) IS
    SELECT inv_id, auto_description
      ,   sale_amt, sale_photo_location
      FROM st_cars_for_sale
      WHERE inv_id > NVL(p_inv_id,0)
      ORDER BY inv_id ASC;
 CURSOR prev_CUR
  (
     p_inv_id IN NUMBER
  ) IS
      SELECT inv_id, auto_description
      ,   sale_amt, sale_photo_location
      FROM st_cars_for_sale
      WHERE inv_id < NVL(p_inv_id,10000000)
      ORDER BY inv_id DESC;
  sale_row prev_CUR%ROWTYPE;
  BEGIN
      IF p_source NOT IN
      (
          'DISPLAY_NEXT'
      ,   'DISPLAY_PREV'
      ) THEN
          display_error
          (
              p_text  => p_source
          );
    ELSE
          -- ------------------------------------------------
          -- Retrieve the car that we want to display
          -- ------------------------------------------------
          IF p_source = 'DISPLAY_NEXT' THEN
              OPEN next_CUR
              (
                  p_inv_id
              );
              FETCH next_CUR INTO sale_row;
              IF next_CUR%NOTFOUND THEN
                  OPEN prev_CUR
                  (
                      p_inv_id
                  );
                  FETCH prev_CUR INTO sale_row;
                  CLOSE prev_CUR;
```

Listing 10.9—continued

```
                END IF; -- next_CUR%NOTFOUND
                CLOSE next_CUR;
            ELSIF p_source = 'DISPLAY_PREV' THEN
                OPEN prev_CUR
                (
                    p_inv_id
                );
                FETCH prev_CUR INTO sale_row;
                IF prev_CUR%NOTFOUND THEN
                    OPEN next_CUR
                    (
                        p_inv_id
                    );
                    FETCH next_CUR INTO sale_row;
                    CLOSE next_CUR;
                END IF; -- prev_CUR%NOTFOUND
                CLOSE prev_CUR;
            END IF; -- p_source = 'DISPLAY_NEXT'

            -- -----------------------------------------------------
             -- Now that we have the auto to display lets
            -- build our display screen
            -- -----------------------------------------------------
            htp.htmlopen;
            htp.headOpen;
            htp.title('Metro Motors');
            htp.headClose;
            htp.bodyOpen;

            display_banner
            (
                p_caption    => 'Metro Motors Web Site'
            );

            -- -----------------------------------------------------
            -- Display the dynamic content - the selected car
            -- -----------------------------------------------------
            htp.tableOpen;
            htp.tableRowOpen;
            htp.tableData
            (
                cvalue       => htf.img
                 (
                 curl     => sale_ROW.sale_photo_location
                            ,   cattributes => 'WIDTH=300'
                 )
            ,   crowspan     => 3
            );
            htp.tableData
             (
```

```
                cvalue => 'Description: '||sale_ROW.auto_description
                ,   ccolspan    => 3
                );
            htp.tableRowClose;
            htp.tableRowOpen;
            htp.tableData
              (
              cvalue => 'Suggested Price:'||TO_CHAR(sale_ROW.sale_amt,'$999,990.00')
              ,   ccolspan    => 3
              );
              htp.tableRowClose;
              htp.tableRowOpen;
              -- ----------------------------------------------
              -- previous button
              -- ----------------------------------------------
              htp.p('<TD>');
              htp.formOpen
              (
                 curl         => 'auto_display'
              ,   cmethod      => 'post'
              ,   ctarget      => ''
              );
              htp.formHidden
              (
                  cname        => 'p_source'
              ,   cvalue       => 'DISPLAY_PREV'
              );
              htp.formHidden
              (
                  cname        => 'p_inv_id'
              ,   cvalue       => TO_CHAR(sale_ROW.inv_id)
              );
              htp.formSubmit
              (
                  cvalue       => 'Previous'
              );
              htp.formClose;
              htp.p('</TD>');

              -- ----------------------------------------------
              -- next button
              -- ----------------------------------------------
              htp.p('<TD>');
              htp.formOpen
              (
                  curl         => 'auto_display'
              ,   cmethod      => 'post'
              ,   ctarget      => ''
              );
              htp.formHidden
              (
```

Listing 10.9—continued

```
                cname       => 'p_source'
            ,   cvalue      => 'DISPLAY_NEXT'
            );
            htp.formHidden
            (
                cname       => 'p_inv_id'
            ,   cvalue      => TO_CHAR(sale_ROW.inv_id)
            );
            htp.formSubmit
            (
                cvalue      => 'Next'
            );
            htp.formClose;
            htp.p('</TD>');

            -- -------------------------------------------------
            -- Buy this car
            -- -------------------------------------------------
            htp.p('<TD>');
            htp.formOpen
            (
                curl        => 'auto_buy'
            ,   cmethod     => 'post'
            ,   ctarget     => ''
            );
            htp.formHidden
            (
                cname       => 'p_source'
            ,   cvalue      => 'MAKE_OFFER'
            );
            htp.formHidden
            (
                cname       => 'p_inv_id'
            ,   cvalue      => TO_CHAR(sale_ROW.inv_id)
            );
            htp.formSubmit
            (
                cvalue      => 'Buy This Car'
            );
            htp.formClose;
            htp.p('</TD>');

            htp.tableRowClose;
            htp.tableClose;


            htp.bodyClose;
            htp.htmlClose;
        END IF; -- p_source NOT IN
    END auto_display;
    /
```

The auto_display PL/SQL procedure is accessed by pointing a Web browser to http://<computer name or IP address>/virtual_path/auto_display. Notice that the Web page functions perfectly when no parameters are passed. This same Web page (bottom-left panel of Figure 9.7) also processes parameters correctly, as in this example:

```
http://<computer name or IP address>/virtual_path/auto_display?p_
➥source=DISPLAY_PREV&p_inv_id=15
```

The auto_buy PL/SQL procedure is called from the Web page auto_display and updates the BUYER information in the ST_CARS_FOR_SALE table object (see bottom-left panel of Figure 9.7).

Lines 1–8 name the procedure (auto_buy) and define the parameters it will accept. Note that all the parameters have a default value that will allow this procedure to be called without having to supply any parameters at all. Lines 20–24 check to see whether any supplied parameters are correct and display an error (using the display_error routine built earlier in this chapter) if they are not (lines 25–28).

Lines 33–45 select the car from inventory (based on the passed p_inv_id). If the car is not found, the user is directed again to the error page.

Line 46 checks to see whether the p_source variable is set to RECORD_OFFER. If it is, the UPDATE statement in lines 47–72 is executed.

Lines 46–72 check to see whether our source should record our offer or not. If the variable p_source does not contain RECORD_OFFER, the MAKE_OFFER Web page is displayed (roughly the remainder of this PL/SQL procedure). Notice that line 101 sets the p_source variable to RECORD_OFFER so that, when the Web page is returned, this UPDATE code is then executed.

If any Oracle error codes are returned, the failure message at lines 50–53 is shown.

Lines 54–56 check the parameters to make sure that a person making the offer has filled out the name, phone, and amount fields.

Lines 58–63 are the actual UPDATE to the ST_CARS_FOR_SALE table object.

If this were a realistic situation, we would insert a record in a separate table so that multiple buyers and offers could be tendered. This example is just to show functionality between the Web page and the Oracle database.

Lines 64–67 set the status message indicating that the offer was successfully recorded.

Lines 68–69 catch any Oracle errors that might have occurred from the `UPDATE` statement. If an error does occur, the new status message is not set and we are left with the failure message.

Lines 76–203 create the HTML output. Lines 82–85 display the Metro Motors standard banner, whereas lines 87–90 display the status message (if one was created) from lines 50–69. Lines 92–107 open up an HTML form and set some hidden values (parameters) that are not to be displayed but are important to the Web page when it is returned. Lines 113–195 generate the main structure of the HTML table, laying out elements similar to the way `auto_display` was laid out.

Notice in lines 143 and 166 that the `htp.p` procedure is used to hard code the HTML `<TD>` tags. Lines 144–149 call the `htp.formtext` procedure, which generates a text input box.

Lines 196–216 create a second HTML form and button that take the Web user back to the `display_auto` page.

Listing 10.10—AUTO_BUY PL/SQL Procedure Syntax

```
CREATE OR REPLACE PROCEDURE auto_buy
 (
     p_source        IN VARCHAR2 DEFAULT 'MAKE_OFFER'
 ,   p_inv_id        IN NUMBER DEFAULT NULL
 ,   p_buyer_name    IN VARCHAR2 DEFAULT NULL
 ,   p_buyer_phone   IN VARCHAR2 DEFAULT NULL
 ,   p_buyer_offer   IN VARCHAR2 DEFAULT NULL
 ) AS
 CURSOR inv_CUR
  (
      p_inv_id IN NUMBER
  ) IS
      SELECT inv_id, auto_description
      ,   sale_amt, sale_photo_location
      FROM st_cars_for_sale
      WHERE inv_id = p_inv_id;
  inv_ROW inv_CUR%ROWTYPE;
 v_status_msg VARCHAR2(200);
  BEGIN
     IF p_source NOT IN
      (
          'MAKE_OFFER'
      ,   'RECORD_OFFER'
      ) THEN
         display_error
          (
              p_text  => p_source
          );
      ELSE
```

```
         -- --------------------------------------------------
         -- get the car they are interested in
         -- --------------------------------------------------
         OPEN inv_CUR
         (
            p_inv_id
         );
         FETCH inv_CUR INTO inv_ROW;
         IF inv_CUR%NOTFOUND THEN
             CLOSE inv_CUR;
             display_error
             (
             p_text  => 'The auto selected could not be found'
             );
         ELSE
             CLOSE inv_CUR;
             IF p_source = 'RECORD_OFFER' THEN
    -- --------------------------------------------------
    -- update the table with the offer
    -- --------------------------------------------------
  v_status_msg := 'Offer could not be recorded at this time for '
  ||p_buyer_name||'.<BR> Please make sure the name and phone '
  ||' are filled in and that the offer ('||p_buyer_offer
  ||') is a number.<BR> Please correct your data and try again.';
          IF p_buyer_name IS NOT NULL
             AND p_buyer_phone IS NOT NULL
             AND p_buyer_offer IS NOT NULL THEN
             BEGIN
                UPDATE st_cars_for_sale
                SET buyer_name = p_buyer_name
                ,   buyer_phone = p_buyer_phone
                ,   buyer_offer = TO_NUMBER(p_buyer_offer)
                ,   buyer_date = SYSDATE
                WHERE inv_id = p_inv_id;
         v_status_msg := 'Offer for '||p_buyer_name||' on car '
             ||inv_ROW.auto_description||' for amount '
             ||TO_CHAR(TO_NUMBER(p_buyer_offer),'$999,990.00')
             ||' was recorded.';
              EXCEPTION WHEN OTHERS THEN
              NULL; -- leave the original status message as is...
              END;
         END IF; -- p_buyer_name IS NOT NULL AND ...
    END IF; -- p_source = 'RECORD_OFFER'
    -- --------------------------------------------------
    -- display the offer form...
    -- --------------------------------------------------
              htp.htmlopen;
              htp.headOpen;
              htp.title('Metro Motors');
              htp.headClose;
              htp.bodyOpen;
```

Listing 10.10—continued

```
                display_banner
                  (
            p_caption    => 'Metro Motors Web Site - Make an offer'
                  );

              IF v_status_msg IS NOT NULL THEN
                    htp.p(v_status_msg);
                    htp.br;
              END IF; -- v_status_msg IS NOT NULL

                htp.formOpen
                (
                    curl         => 'auto_buy'
                ,   cmethod      => 'post'
                ,   ctarget      => ''
                );
                htp.formHidden
                (
                     cname       => 'p_source'
                 ,   cvalue      => 'RECORD_OFFER'
                 );
                 htp.formHidden
                 (
                     cname       => 'p_inv_id'
                 ,   cvalue      => TO_CHAR(p_inv_id)
                 );



                 htp.tableOpen;

                 htp.tableRowOpen;
                 htp.tableData
              (
                     cvalue      => htf.img
                        (
                        curl    => inv_ROW.sale_photo_location
                    ,   cattributes => 'WIDTH=300'
                        )
            ,    crowspan    => 5
                 );

                 htp.tableData
                (
                     cvalue      => 'Description: '
                 ,   calign      => 'RIGHT'
                 );
                 htp.tableData
                 (
                     cvalue      => inv_ROW.auto_description
```

```
                  ,   calign      => 'LEFT'
                  );

                  htp.tableRowClose;

                  htp.tableRowOpen;
                  htp.tableData
                  (
                      cvalue      => 'Buyer Name:'
                  ,   calign      => 'RIGHT'
                  );
                  htp.p('<TD ALIGN=LEFT>');
                  htp.formText
                  (
                      cname       => 'p_buyer_name'
                  ,   csize       => 30
                  ,   cmaxlength  => 20
                  );
                  htp.p('</TD>');
                  htp.tableRowClose;

                  htp.tableRowOpen;
                  htp.tableData
                  (
                      cvalue      => 'Buyer Phone:'
                  ,   calign      => 'RIGHT'
                  );
                  htp.p('<TD ALIGN=LEFT>');
                  htp.formText
                  (
                      cname       => 'p_buyer_phone'
                  ,   csize       => 30
                  ,   cmaxlength  => 10
                  );
                  htp.p('</TD>');
                  htp.tableRowClose;

                  htp.tableRowOpen;
                  htp.tableData
                  (
                      cvalue      => 'Offer:'
                  ,   calign      => 'RIGHT'
                  );
                  htp.p('<TD ALIGN=LEFT>');
                  htp.formText
                  (
                      cname       => 'p_buyer_offer'
                  ,   csize       => 30
                  ,   cmaxlength  => 10
                  );
                  htp.p('</TD>');
                  htp.tableRowClose;

```

Listing 10.10—continued

```
                htp.tableRowOpen;
                htp.tableData
                (
                    cvalue      => ''
                );
                htp.p('<TD ALIGN=CENTER>');
                htp.formSubmit
                (
                    cvalue      => 'Place Offer'
                );
                htp.formClose;
                htp.formOpen
                (
                    curl        => 'auto_display'
                ,   cmethod     => 'post'
                ,   ctarget     => ''
                );
                htp.formHidden
                (
                    cname       => 'p_source'
                ,   cvalue      => 'DISPLAY_NEXT'
                );
                htp.formHidden
                (
                    cname       => 'p_inv_id'
                ,   cvalue      => '0'
                );
                htp.formSubmit
                (
                    cvalue      => 'Browse Inventory'
                );
                htp.formClose;
                htp.p('</TD>');
                htp.tableRowClose;


                htp.tableClose;

                htp.bodyClose;
                htp.htmlClose;
           END IF; -- inv_CUR%NOTFOUND
        END IF; -- p_source NOT IN
    END auto_buy;
    /
```

Summary

This chapter introduced you to the creation of PL/SQL procedures, which create HTML output that will be returned to a Web browser. You were able to use simple but effective techniques to understand basic Web page building techniques. You then learned how to use these techniques to build the Sales Tracking Web site using PL/SQL and HTML.

Next Steps

The next chapter introduces you to Java, another language useful in creating Web pages. You will learn how to use JDeveloper v3.0 to learn the basics of JDeveloper and Java, as well as how to build a simple Web page using Java. Similar to this chapter, you

Chapter 11

In this chapter

- *Java VM*
- *Java Development Tools*
- *Using Java*
- *Building the Web Site*

Building the Web Site with Java

Oracle8i supports procedures, functions, packages, and triggers to be coded in Java instead of PL/SQL. Because Java is a much more open language (supported by many platforms and databases) than the Oracle proprietary language, PL/SQL, it should provide Oracle environment performance improvements.

Java can perform any task that PL/SQL can perform. The `AS LANGUAGE JAVA` syntax is added to the Oracle procedure, function, package body, or trigger. In addition, these procedures, functions, and packages are executed in the same manner as their PL/SQL equivalents.

Java stored procedures execute much more quickly than their PL/SQL counterparts. Java stored procedures with SELECT or DML type SQL statements typically execute 20 to 40 percent faster, and Java stored procedures without any SQL statements run about 10 times faster than their PL/SQL counterparts.

Java VM

Java is a cross–operating-system, cross-database language. This versatility is accomplished by the Java Virtual Machine (JVM), which is *ported* to each specific hardware platform and database that supports Java. The JVM enables Java code to be entirely portable across various computers and database environments. In addition, JVM is the Java interpreter that eliminates the need for a Java compiler for specific computing environments. Plus, it is part of the Oracle8i database, which makes it possible to have either Java-based procedures or PL/SQL-based procedures (or both). One JVM exists for each Oracle Application Server (OAS), and it is started when the OAS is started.

Port—To have a *port* of software means to have a version that runs in a particular computing environment. Previously in this book, I referred to *runtime* interpreters. A port exists for each of these for each computing environment that will support a particular software.

Java Development Tools

Chapter 9, "Planning the Sales Tracking Web Site," discusses various methods of deploying Java-based programs across a computing network. The *applets*, *servlets*, and Java-based programs all must be developed with some kind of Java development language. Many of these are available on the market today, such as Visual Cafê, Visual Age, and JBuilder.

Applet—When accessed, it is loaded to the user's Web browser and run on the local PC or workstation.

Servlet—When accessed, it is run on the server, returning the output to the user's Web browser.

This chapter uses Oracle's JDeveloper v3.0.

Using Java

This part of the chapter explains and illustrates building a servlet, a server-side Java program that will be accessed by using the OAS. To review how these pieces fit together, please refer to Figure 9.3 and its accompanying description in Chapter 9.

Building a Java Servlet with JDeveloper v3.0

Figure 11.1 shows the JDeveloper interface. Access the Project Wizard from the File, New Project menu item. This wizard guides you through all the necessary pieces to build a server-side Java program that will access the EMP demonstration table.

After you click the Next button, the Project Wizard begins a three-step project setup. You must name the project and tell JDeveloper where to store it on your computer's hard disk. Notice in Figure 11.2 that the name of the new servlet is `Empservlet.jar`. Also notice that DbServlet is selected from the A Project containing a new option. Step 2 of 3 defines the project name, where to store the actual servlet code, and the Java classes code. Step 3 of 3 tracks where the project is documented. None of these fields is actually required, but the information might be convenient for others who might be making future changes to this program.

Figure 11.1

JDeveloper v3.0 Project Wizard.

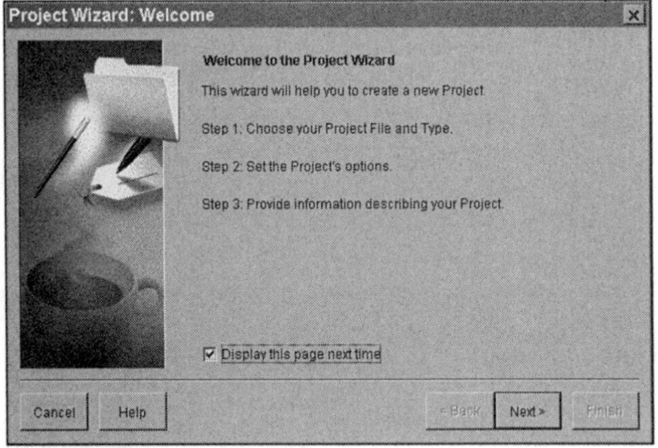

.jar file—It's being created by JDeveloper and contains all the code necessary for the Web browser to access and run this particular Java program. Jar stands for Java archive file.

Figure 11.2

JDeveloper v3.0 project setup steps 1–3.

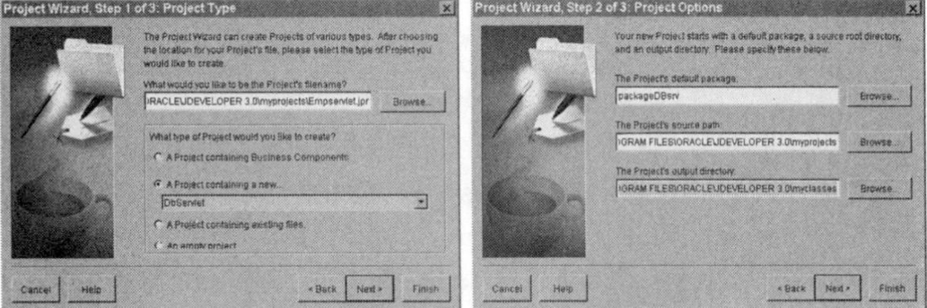

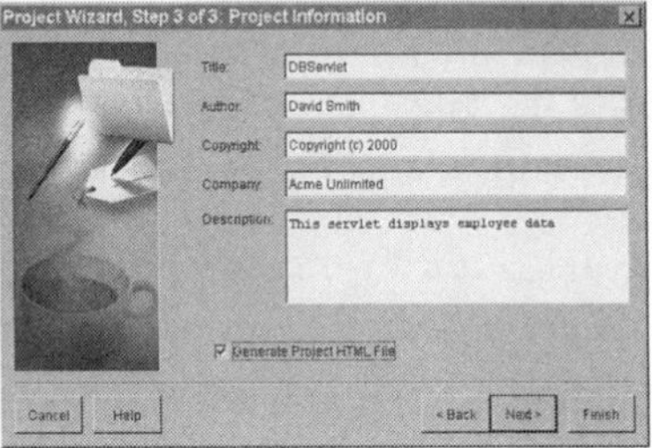

Figure 11.3 shows all the recently entered project information. If this information is correct, click Finished. If this information is not correct, use the Back button to return to where the incorrect information was entered and correct it.

If you have clicked Finish and you later find that some of the information is incorrect, you probably should start again. JDeveloper uses some of this information inside various components being generated. Some of the options, such as source path and output directory, can be changed via the preferences selection in the menu bar.

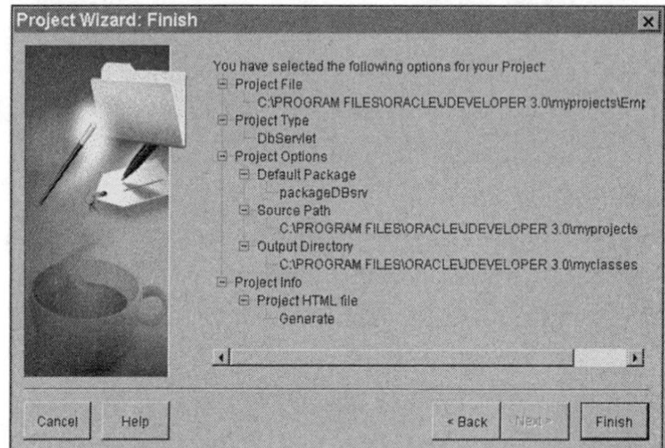

Figure 11.3

JDeveloper v3.0 project setup finish.

The DbServlet Wizard automatically starts based on selections made in the Project Wizard. This wizard can also be started from the menu bar by selecting File, New, DbServlet. This wizard actually builds the Java code needed to access a database table. It automatically stores its resulting code in the project that is highlighted—if the wizard started automatically, it will be stored in the project you just created. If you have to manually start the wizard, be sure to highlight the project for which you want to create the DbServlet. The wizard walks you through the process of creating the DbServlet with the following five steps:

1. In the first wizard window, be sure to select whether this is an individual table or a master-detail relationship type database access. Click Next.
2. Next, name the actual servlet and establish the type of connection to the database (see Figure 11.4). Notice that the DBServlet connection type is selected. This fills in the default URL needed to access this Java servlet from a Web browser. Also notice the check box designed to prompt the user for a valid password. Click Next.
3. In this step you define the database object the servlet will reference. Notice in Figure 11.5 that the user SCOTT is used. When you click the Tables check box, the table objects appear in the window. Highlight the EMP table by clicking.

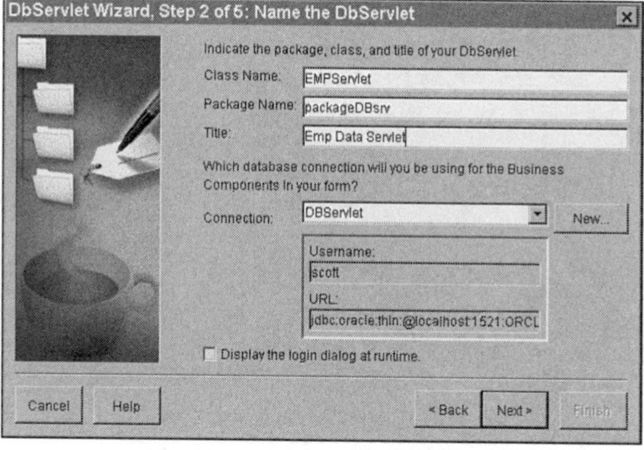

Figure 11.4

DbServlet Wizard Step 2—name and connection information.

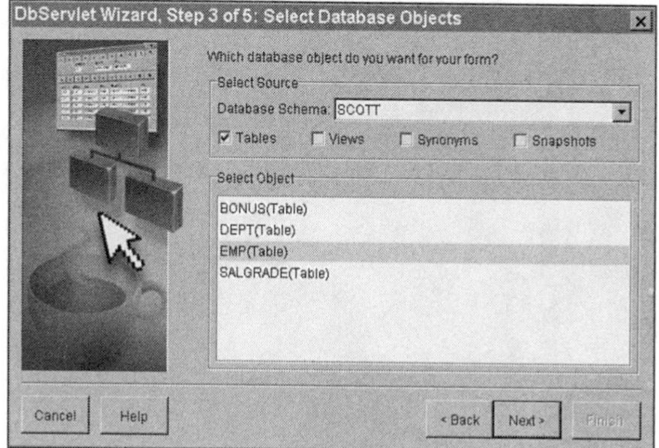

Figure 11.5

DbServlet Wizard Step 3—database object selection.

4. Next, the available database columns are displayed. Use the >> button to select all the columns, as shown in Figure 11.6. When all the desired columns are moved to the Selected Attributes column, click Next.
5. Figure 11.7 shows the final step, which is to select a color pattern for the servlet. When you have chosen your desired color theme, click Next. The final step is the DBWizard Completion screen. This lists all the pertinent information about the name, the table being accessed, and the name and full path of the project where all these items will be stored. To exit the wizard, click Finish.

Select File, Save As to save the JDeveloper workspace (see Figure 11.8). Notice the items in the recently created project in Figure 11.9. The HTML file will be accessed by the Web browser. This file contains the necessary HTML code to access the Empservlet.java program.

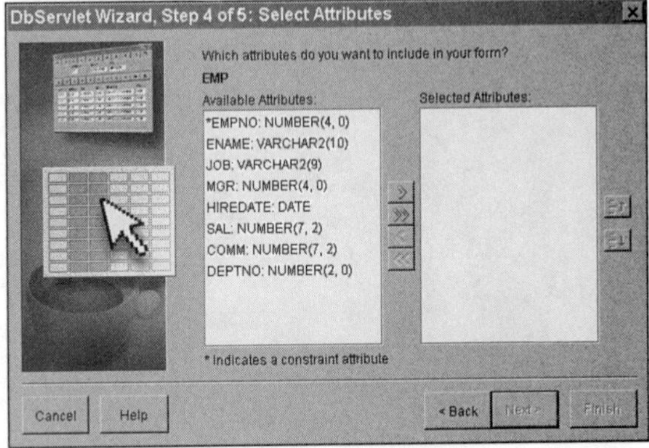

Figure 11.6

DbServlet Wizard Step 4—database column selection.

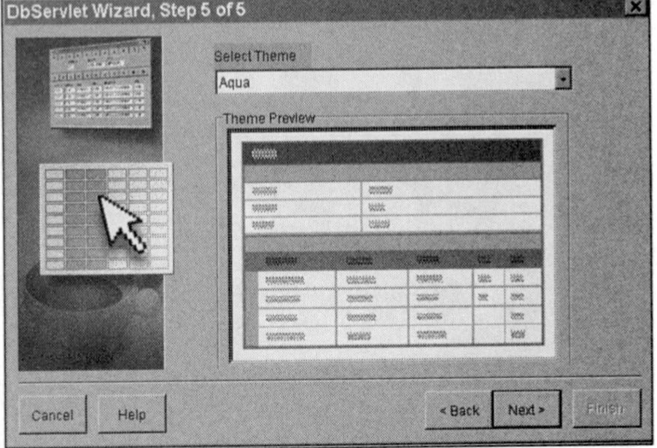

Figure 11.7

DbServlet Wizard Step 5—form template layout selection.

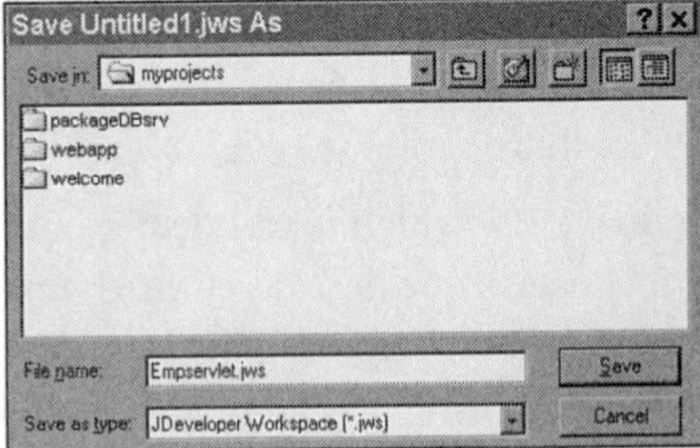

Figure 11.8

Items developed with JDeveloper.

Deploying the Java Servlet Application

Because this is a server-side piece of code, it needs to be copied to the computer that has the Oracle Application Server with the Java cartridge. This is accomplished by using the deployment feature of JDeveloper.

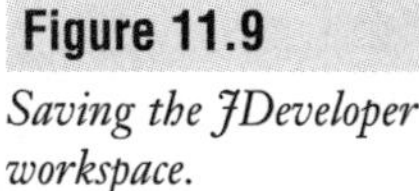

Figure 11.9

Saving the JDeveloper workspace.

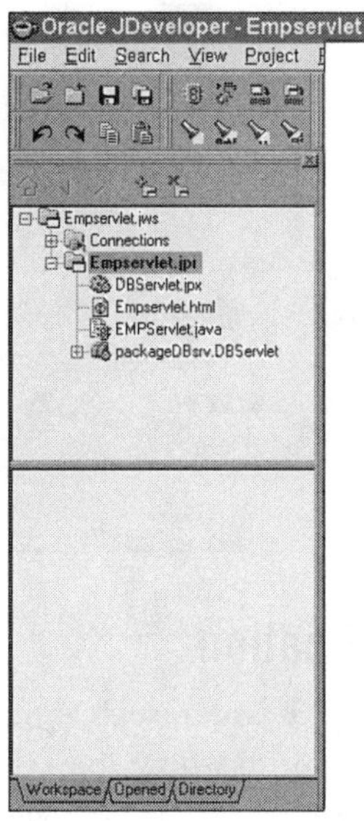

Figure 11.10 shows the EmpServlet project with the DBServlet package inside. From the menu, select Project, Deploy to start the Deployment Wizard. Walk through the wizard and complete the information as it pertains to your computing environment. Figure 11.11 shows the actual deployment. Make sure to check this screen for any errors that might have occurred.

Figure 11.10

Deploying the Java DBServlet.

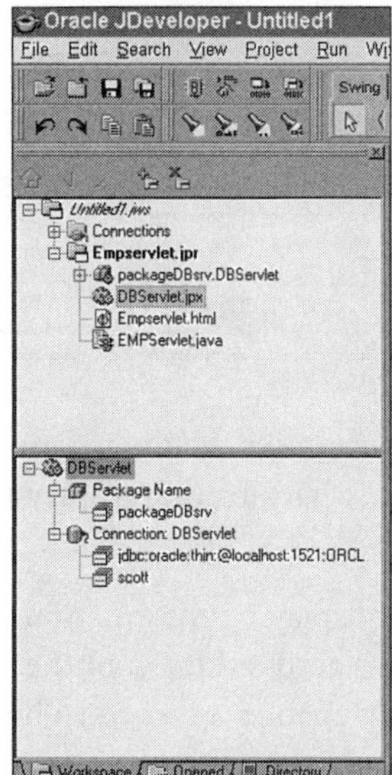

11

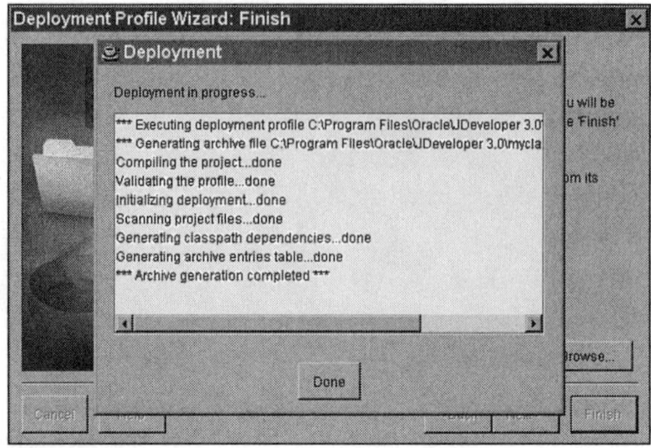

Figure 11.11

Deployment Wizard finished screen.

Running the Java Servlet Application

Chapter 9 covered some basic administrative issues, such as virtual paths. Figure 11.12 uses one of these virtual paths to point to where the DBServlet was deployed. Notice the URL in Figure 11.12. You see the http://<IP Address>:<Port Number> of the computer with the Oracle Application Server. Servlets is the virtual path that will be translated by OAS into a directory path on this computer, and DBServlet is the name of the previously created and deployed servlet that will be found in this virtual path. Because this servlet is using the JDBC thin drivers, it will prompt the Web browser user for a user ID and password.

Figure 11.12

Netscape browser accessing the DBServlet.

DBServlet then prompts the Web browser user for the information to be displayed from the EMP table. Notice the pick list buttons that display the various options in Figure 11.13.

Figure 11.14 illustrates the DBServlet displaying information from the SCOTT.EMP table. Notice the buttons across the top of the displayed form. The + enables a record to be added, and the X enables a record to be deleted. The next set of blue buttons controls the capability to access the next or previous records in the table, and the key buttons enable the Web browser user to lock a record or unlock a record for update purposes.

Figure 11.13

DBServlet query screen.

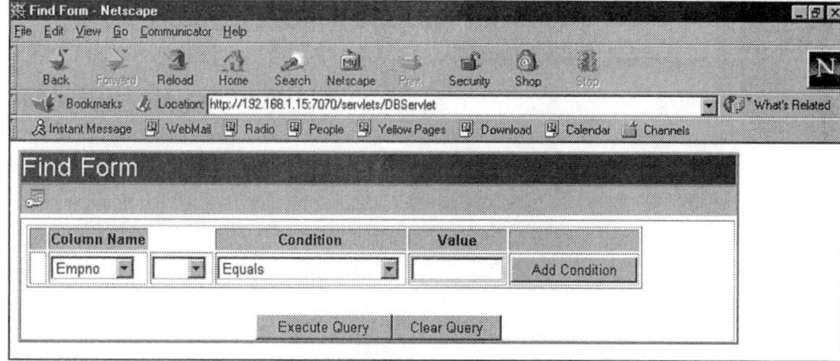

Figure 11.14

DBServlet displaying SCOTT.EMP table information.

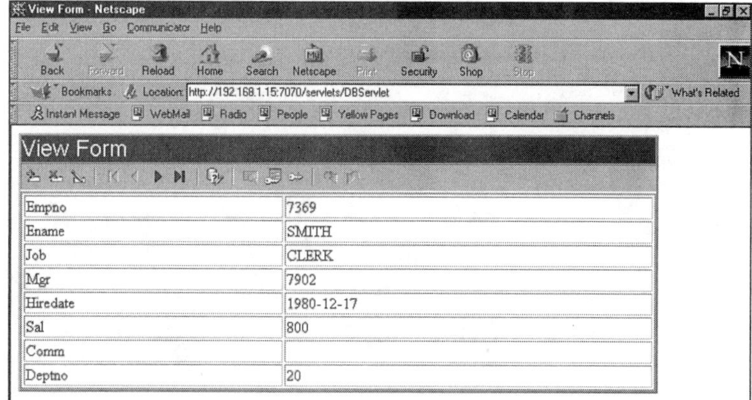

OAS and Java Setup

The OAS environment needs to know about the servlets it is to manage, how to access the database (the DAD configuration), and even the installation and setup of the Java cartridge.

Figure 11.15 shows the configuration of the DAD in the OAS Server Manager. This database descriptor is used by servlets to make automatic connections to the database when the DAD name is referenced in the URL.

Figure 11.16 shows the virtual path mapping configuration of the `samplej` virtual path. Notice the URL in Figure 11.17. The hostname `trutek4060` matches the description of the DAD, and the virtual path `samplej` is also illustrated when accessing a `HelloWorld` servlet (which will be built in the next section of this chapter).

Figure 11.15

DAD configuration for Web site examples.

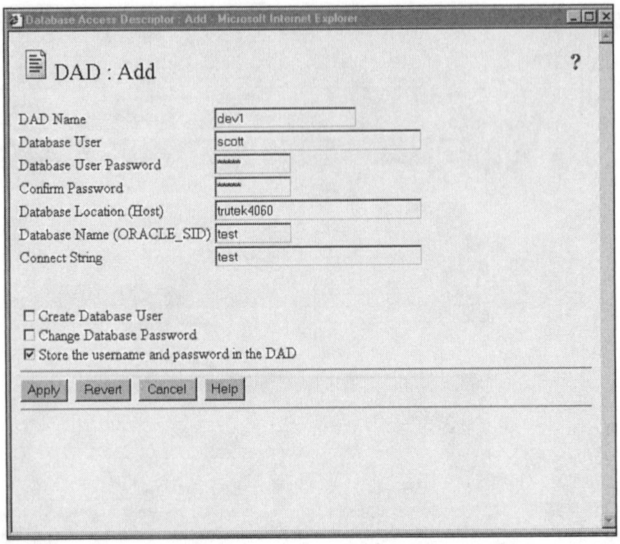

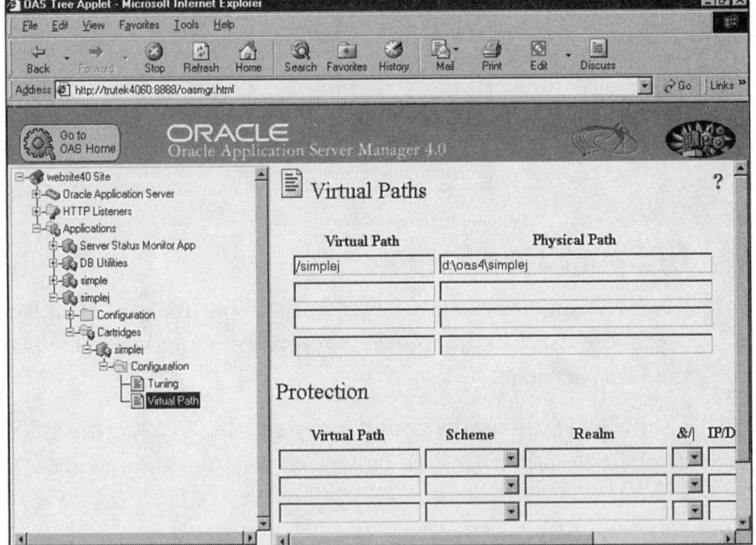

Figure 11.16

Virtual path configuration for Web site examples.

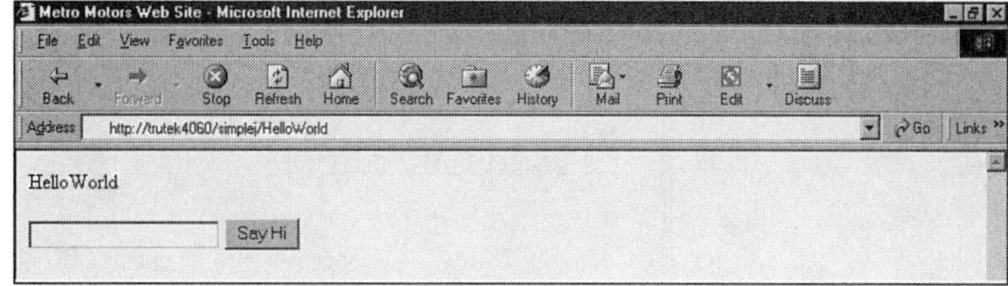

Figure 11.17

URL example for Web site examples.

Figure 11.18 illustrates the `simplej` Java cartridge configuration area. The `simplej` in this case is both a virtual path and an indication to the OAS that this is Java code that will need to be passed to the Java cartridge.

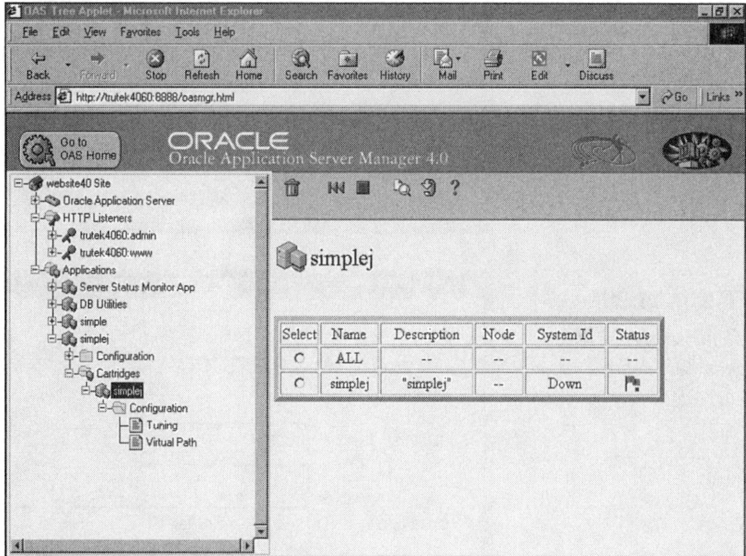

Figure 11.18

`simplej` *Java cartridge configuration.*

Figures 11.19 and 11.20 illustrate how to manually configure a Java cartridge. Notice in Figure 11.19 that the manual radio button is selected and that in Figure 11.20 that the cartridge is named (`test`, in this example) and is assigned a virtual path.

To test the Java cartridge, build the `HelloWorld` servlet illustrated in Listing 11.1, locate the output in the physical path as defined by the virtual path configuration (refer to Figure 11.16), and use the URL (as defined in Figure 11.17) to display the output as shown in Figure 11.17. Listing 11.2 shows the generated HTML output by the `out.println` code in Listing 11.1. This can be seen from your browser by displaying Source Code.

Figure 11.19

Manually defining a Java cartridge.

Cartridge: Add - Microsoft Internet Explorer
Add Cartridge
?
Configure Mode
From File
Manually
Apply
Revert
Cancel
Help

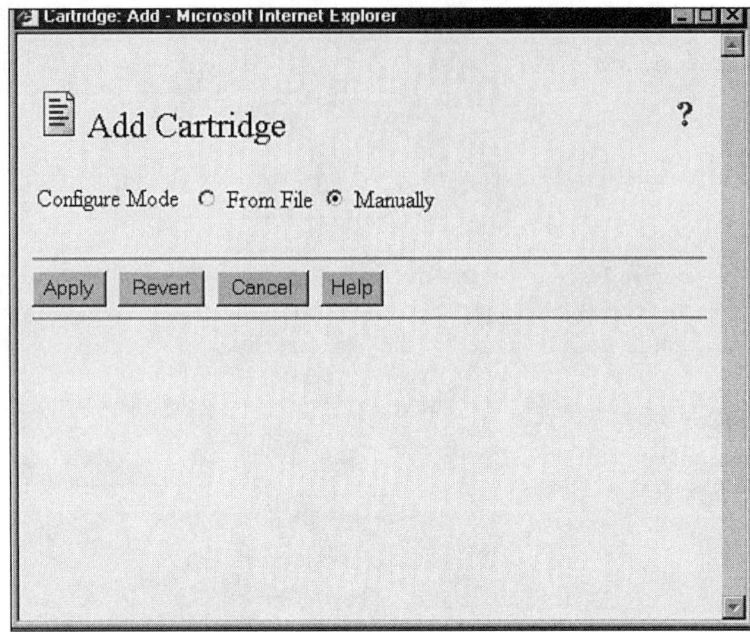

Figure 11.20

Configuring the manually defined Java cartridge.

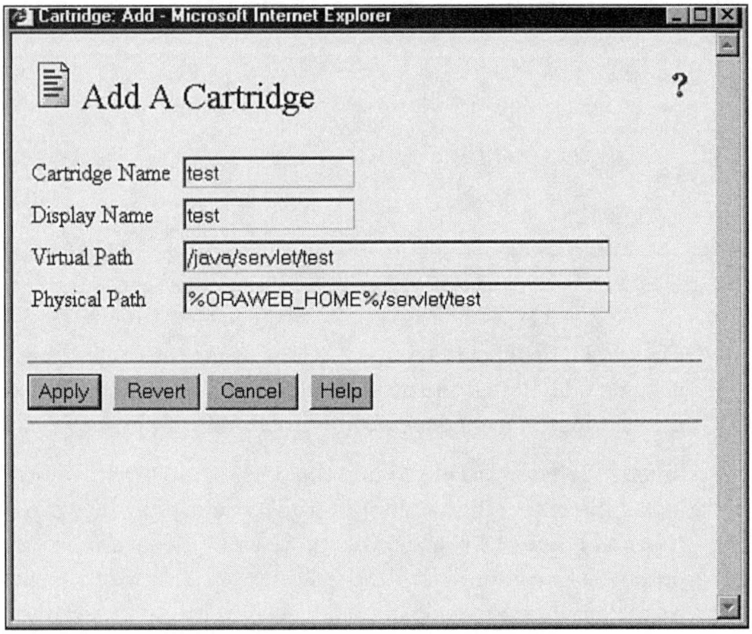

Cartridge: Add - Microsoft Internet Explorer
Add A Cartridge
?
Cartridge Name
test
Display Name
test
Virtual Path
/java/servlet/test
Physical Path
%ORAWEB_HOME%/servlet/test
Apply
Revert
Cancel
Help

Listing 11.1—`HelloWorld` Java Servlet Syntax

```
import java.io.*;
import java.sql.*;
import javax.servlet.*;
import javax.servlet.http.*;
import java.util.*;

public class HelloWorld extends HttpServlet {


  public void doGet(HttpServletRequest req, HttpServletResponse res)
        throws ServletException, IOException{

    res.setContentType("text/html");
    PrintWriter out = res.getWriter();
    out.println("<HTML>");
    out.println("<BODY>");
    out.println("Hello World!");
    out.println("</BODY>");
    out.println("</HTML>");
  }
}
```

Listing 11.2—HTML Output from `HelloWorld` Java Servlet

```
<HTML>
<BODY>
HelloWorld
</BODY>
</HTML>
```

Displaying Pictures and Passing Parameters with Java

Parameters are passed to Java from the URL in the same manner as parameters are passed to any other Web process:

```
http://yourdomain.com/virtual_path_for_servlet/servlet?param=1
```

Listing 11.3 expands on the `HelloWorld` example by building the Metro Motors banner page (see Figure 11.21) and prompts the Web browser user for input if a parameter is not supplied. Notice that `req.getParameter` in line 12 retrieves a parameter, `p_name`, and puts this parameter's contents into the variable `myname`. If the parameter does not exist on the URL line, `myname` is set to null. `myname` is then used later in the program in line 29. Notice that this will be displayed only if something exists in `myname`. This enables the program to have a parameter or to continue without error even if no parameter is supplied.

Lines 16–26 process the Metro Motors banner. Notice line 21 makes reference to the virtual address `ows-img` where the `metro_motors.jpg` file should be located.

Line 36 defines the input text box, and line 37 defines the submit button.

Listing 11.3—`HelloWorld` Displaying Metro Motors Banner and Accepting a Parameter

```
1:  import java.io.*;
2:  import java.sql.*;
3:  import javax.servlet.*;
4:  import javax.servlet.http.*;
5:  import java.util.*;
6:
7:  public class HelloWorld extends HttpServlet {
8:
9:  public void doGet(HttpServletRequest req, HttpServletResponse res)
10:        throws ServletException, IOException{
11:
12:    String myname = req.getParameter("p_name");
13:
14:    res.setContentType("text/html");
15:    PrintWriter out = res.getWriter();
16:    out.println("<HTML>");
17:    out.println("<HEAD><TITLE>Metro Motors Web Site</TITLE></HEAD>");
18:    out.println("<BODY>");
19:    out.println("<TABLE><TR VALIGN=CENTER>");
20:    out.println("<TD>");
21:    out.println("<IMG WIDTH=100 SRC=/ows-img/metro_motors.jpg>");
22:    out.println("</TD>");
23:    out.println("<TD>");
24:    out.println("<B>Metro Motors Web Site</B>");
25:    out.println("</TD>");
26:    out.println("</TR></TABLE>");
27:
28:    if ( myname != null ) {
29:      out.println("Hello " + myname);
30:    }
31:    else {
32:      out.println("HelloWorld");
33:    }
34:
35:    out.println("<FORM URL=HelloWorld METHOD=get>");
36:    out.println("<INPUT TYPE=TEXT NAME=p_name maxlength=20>");
37:    out.println("<INPUT TYPE=SUBMIT VALUE='Say Hello to'>");
38:    out.println("</FORM>");
39:    out.println("</BODY></HTML>");
40:  }
41: }
```

Figure 11.21

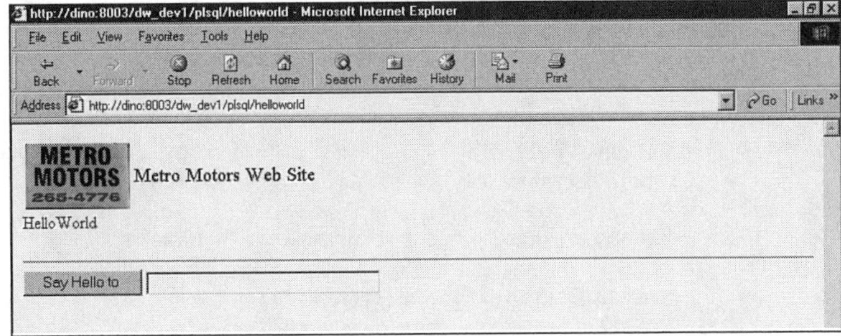

HelloWorld Java servlet.

Java Code Reuse

Java enables the easy reuse of code in the form of modules or public classes. Notice that lines 7–14 in Listing 11.4 is the same code as lines 19–26 in Listing 11.3.

Listing 11.4—Java `stcarsutil` Public Class

```
1:  import java.io.*;
2:
3:  public class stcarsutil {
4:
5:  public static void banner(PrintWriter out, String caption) {
6:
7:     out.println("<TABLE><TR VALIGN=CENTER>");
8:     out.println("<TD>");
9:     out.println("<IMG WIDTH=100 SRC=/ows-img/metro_motors.jpg>");
10:    out.println("</TD>");
11:    out.println("<TD>");
12:    out.println("<B>" + caption + "</B>");
13:    out.println("</TD>");
14:    out.println("</TR></TABLE>");
15:   }
16: }
```

To use the new public class, notice line 20 in Listing 11.5 makes reference to the class `stcarsutil` and the routine `banner` and passes the text string `Metro Motors Web Site`. As in the PL/SQL example of Chapter 10, "Building the Web Site with PL/SQL," this routine or Java class can now be used to give constant visual attributes to our Web site, without having to add the same code to each Web page.

Listing 11.5—Java `HelloWorld` Calling Public Class `stcarsutil.banner`

```
1: import java.io.*;
2: import java.sql.*;
3: import javax.servlet.*;
4: import javax.servlet.http.*;
5: import java.util.*;
6:
```

11

Listing 11.5—continued

```
public class HelloWorld extends HttpServlet {


  public void doGet(HttpServletRequest req, HttpServletResponse res)
        throws ServletException, IOException{

    String myname = req.getParameter("p_name");

    res.setContentType("text/html");
    PrintWriter out = res.getWriter();
    out.println("<HTML>");
    out.println("<HEAD><TITLE>Metro Motors Web Site</TITLE></HEAD>");
    out.println("<BODY>");
    stcarsutil.banner(out,"Metro Motors Web Site");
    if ( myname != null ) {
      out.println("Hello " + myname);
    }
    else {
      out.println("HelloWorld");
    }

    out.println("<FORM URL=HelloWorld METHOD=get>");
    out.println("<INPUT TYPE=TEXT NAME=p_name maxlength=20>");
    out.println("<INPUT TYPE=SUBMIT VALUE='Say Hello to'>");
    out.println("</FORM>");
    out.println("</BODY></HTML>");
  }
}
```

Building the Web Site

The remainder of this chapter builds the Sales Tracking Web site as defined in Chapter 9 in Figure 9.7 (reprinted here). Figure 11.22 illustrates that Java can build the same Web site as was built in Chapter 10 using PL/SQL. Notice the URL, in Figure 11.22, makes reference to the `simplej` virtual path and Java cartridge (as defined in Figures 11.16 and 11.18).

The final example for this chapter illustrates two servlets—`stcarsforsale` and `stcarsforsalebuy`—to match the two Web pages of the Web site. Each will use the `stcarsutil.banner` to provide a consistent banner. These Java servlets also will select and update the ST_CARS_FOR_SALE table object, illustrated in Chapter 9 (Figures 9.5 and 9.6).

The Java code will be listed and can be accessed and compiled using the Oracle JDeveloper v3.0 environment, discussed earlier in this chapter. This chapter also discusses the Java examples and the specific code necessary to build the Web site. Java is a complex code, and it is beyond the scope of this one chapter to discuss the intricacies of the Java language.

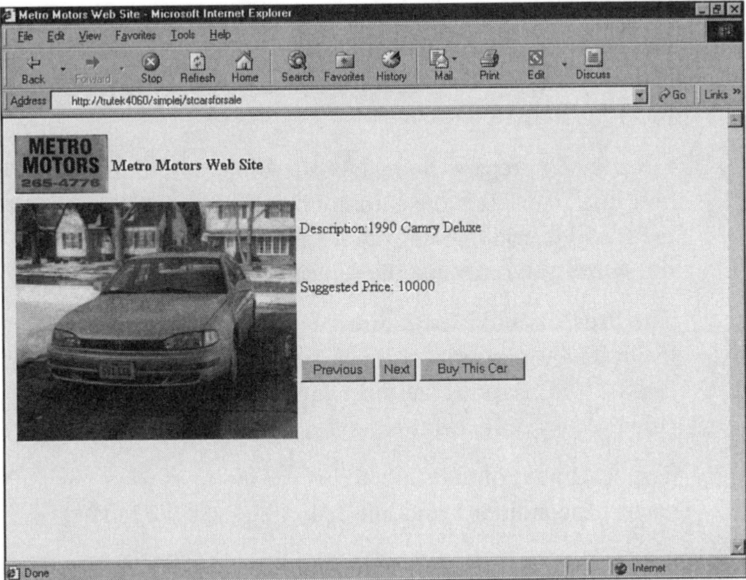

Figure 11.22
Sales Tracking Web site.

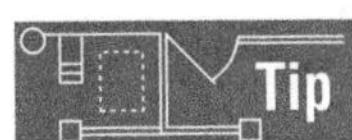

Tip

Many good books about the Java language are available, including *Java from scratch* by Que.

The `stcarsforsale` Java servlet builds the Web page as illustrated in Figure 11.22. Lines 15 and 16 retrieve specific parameters coming in from the URL. If no parameters are passed, the `inv_id` and `direction` variables are set to null.

Lines 20–22 begin the HTML output. Notice in line 23 the call to `stcarsutil.banner` (from Listing 11.4) to display the Metro Motors banner page.

Line 31 connects to the database using the JDBC thin driver and connects to an Oracle database with a Net8 name of `test`, using the sales_tracking user ID and password. Remember from Chapter 9 that the thin connection will be maintained only for a single session initiated by a single Web browser access.

Some tasks, such as cursor management (retrieving a group of rows from the database and moving forward and backward through the rows), are best handled by PL/SQL. This Java servlet shows interaction between Java and PL/SQL (see line 33). The `get_car` PL/SQL procedure is similar to the `auto_display` PL/SQL developed in Chapter 10 (refer to Listing 10.9) in how it selects rows to be displayed. In Java, the `CallableStatement` routine is used to build the `call` statement and process any parameters. The six question marks (`?`) in line 33 are parameter placeholders: There are two input variables to this procedure and four variables returned. Lines 34–37 define the parameters that will be returned from the PL/SQL procedure, and lines 39–45 do some checking for the existence of URL input parameters. If they exist, they will be passed to the PL/SQL routine. Line 46 calls the PL/SQL routine.

Lines 48–84 prepare the bulk of the Web page illustrated in Figure 11.22. Notice how line 50 displays the automobile photo (its path was returned in variable 6 from the PL/SQL routine: line 66 of Listing 11.7) by defining an image `IMG` and making the source `SRC` reference the return variable from the PL/SQL `get_car` procedure.

The Previous and Next buttons are defined in lines 59–62 and lines 66–69, respectively. The `URL` is set to this Java servlet, whereas the Buy This Car button's URL (lines 73–75) is set to the other Java servlet, `stcarsforsalebuy`. This is how access to either Web page is defined.

The remainder of the code in this servlet, lines 87–99, is used to catch and handle any error conditions, and line 101 completes the HTML output.

Listing 11.6—`stcarsforsale` Java Servlet

```
1:  import java.io.*;
2:  import java.sql.*;
3:  import javax.servlet.*;
4:  import javax.servlet.http.*;
5:  import java.util.*;
6:
7:  public class stcarsforsale extends HttpServlet {
8:
9:   public void doGet(HttpServletRequest req, HttpServletResponse res)
10:     throws ServletException, IOException{
11:     Connection con = null;
12:     Statement stmt = null;
13:     ResultSet rs = null;
14:
15:      String inv_id = req.getParameter("p_inv_id");
16:      String direction = req.getParameter("p_direction");
17:
18:      res.setContentType("text/html");
19:      PrintWriter out = res.getWriter();
20:      out.println("<HTML>");
21: out.println("<HEAD><TITLE>Metro Motors Web Site</TITLE></HEAD>");
22:      out.println("<BODY>");
23:      stcarsutil.banner(out,"Metro Motors Web Site");
24:
25:      try {
26:      //Register Oracle Driver
```

```
      Class.forName("oracle.jdbc.driver.OracleDriver");

      //Get a Connection to the database
      con = DriverManager.getConnection(
"jdbc:oracle:thin:@localhost:1521:test", "sales_tracking","sales_tracking");

   CallableStatement cstmt = con.prepareCall("{call get_car(?,?,?,?,?,?)}");
      cstmt.registerOutParameter(3,java.sql.Types.FLOAT);
      cstmt.registerOutParameter(4,java.sql.Types.VARCHAR);
      cstmt.registerOutParameter(5,java.sql.Types.FLOAT);
      cstmt.registerOutParameter(6,java.sql.Types.VARCHAR);
      cstmt.setString(1,direction);
      if (inv_id != null) {
      cstmt.setInt(2,Integer.parseInt(inv_id));
      }
     else
       {
         cstmt.setInt(2,0);
     }
       cstmt.execute();

      out.println("<TABLE><TR>");
      out.println("<TD ROWSPAN=3>");
      out.println("<IMG WIDTH=300 SRC=" + cstmt.getString(6) + ">");
      out.println("</TD>");
      out.println("<TD COLSPAN=3>");
      out.println("Description:"+cstmt.getString(4));
      out.println("</TD></TR><TD COLSPAN=3>");
      out.println("Suggested Price: "+ cstmt.getInt(5));
      out.println("</TD></TR>");
      out.println("<TR>");
      out.println("<TD>");
      out.println("<FORM URL=stcarsforsale METHOD=get>");
out.println("<INPUT TYPE=hidden NAME=p_direction VALUE=DISPLAY_PREV>");
out.println("<INPUT TYPE=hidden NAME=p_inv_id VALUE="+cstmt.getInt(3)+">");
      out.println("<INPUT TYPE=SUBMIT VALUE=Previous>");
      out.println("</FORM>");
      out.println("</TD>");
      out.println("<TD>");
      out.println("<FORM URL=stcarsforsale METHOD=get>");
out.println("<INPUT TYPE=hidden NAME=p_direction VALUE=DISPLAY_NEXT>");
out.println("<INPUT TYPE=hidden NAME=p_inv_id VALUE="+cstmt.getInt(3)+">");
      out.println("<INPUT TYPE=SUBMIT VALUE=Next>");
      out.println("</FORM>");
      out.println("</TD>");
      out.println("<TD>");
out.println("<FORM URL=stcarsforsalebuy METHOD=get>");
out.println("<INPUT TYPE=hidden NAME=p_inv_id VALUE="+cstmt.getInt(3)+">");
      out.println("<INPUT TYPE=SUBMIT VALUE='Buy This Car'>");
      out.println("</FORM>");
      out.println("</TD>");

      out.println("");
```

Listing 11.6—continued

```
80:       out.println("");
81:       out.println("");
82:       out.println("");
83:       out.println("</TR>");
84:       out.println("</TABLE>");
85:
86:
87:      }
88:      catch(ClassNotFoundException e) {
89:        out.println("Could not load db driver" + e.getMessage());
90:    }
91:      catch(SQLException e) {
92:        out.println("SQL Error: " + e.getMessage());
93:      }
94:      finally {
95:      try {
96:          if (con != null) con.close();
97:        }
98:        catch (SQLException e) {}
99:      }
100:
101:      out.println("</BODY></HTML>");
102:    }
103: }
```

The PL/SQL procedure `get_car`, Listing 11.7, is similar to Listing 10.9 in how it selects cars from the ST_CARS_FOR_SALE table object. It is passed two input variables. In line 3, the `p_direction` variable has a default value, in case no input values were passed from the Java servlet (Listing 11.6, line 33).

There is no connect string to the database. The Java servlet is already connected to the database and can call this procedure. The output of this procedure is in lines 63–lines 66 and returns information from the current row in the open cursor.

Listing 11.7—`get_car` PL/SQL Procedure `stcarsforsale` Java Servlet

```
1:  CREATE OR REPLACE PROCEDURE get_car
2:  (
3:      p_direction         IN VARCHAR2 DEFAULT 'DISPLAY_NEXT'
4:  ,   p_inv_id            IN NUMBER DEFAULT NULL
5:  ,   x_inv_id            OUT NUMBER
6:  ,   x_auto_description  OUT VARCHAR2
7:  ,   x_sale_amt          OUT NUMBER
8:  ,   x_photo_location    OUT VARCHAR2
9:  ) IS
10: CURSOR next_CUR
11: (
12:     p_inv_id IN NUMBER
13: ) IS
14:     SELECT inv_id, auto_description
15:     ,    sale_amt, sale_photo_location
```

```
    FROM st_cars_for_sale
    WHERE inv_id > NVL(p_inv_id,0)
    ORDER BY inv_id ASC;
CURSOR prev_CUR
(
    p_inv_id IN NUMBER
) IS
    SELECT inv_id, auto_description
    ,   sale_amt, sale_photo_location
    FROM st_cars_for_sale
    WHERE inv_id < NVL(p_inv_id,10000000)
    ORDER BY inv_id DESC;
sale_row prev_CUR%ROWTYPE;
BEGIN
    IF p_direction = 'DISPLAY_NEXT' THEN
        OPEN next_CUR
        (
            p_inv_id
        );
        FETCH next_CUR INTO sale_row;
        IF next_CUR%NOTFOUND THEN
            OPEN prev_CUR
            (
                p_inv_id
            );
            FETCH prev_CUR INTO sale_row;
            CLOSE prev_CUR;
        END IF; -- next_CUR%NOTFOUND
        CLOSE next_CUR;
    ELSE
        OPEN prev_CUR
        (
            p_inv_id
        );
        FETCH prev_CUR INTO sale_row;
        IF prev_CUR%NOTFOUND THEN
            OPEN next_CUR
            (
                p_inv_id
            );
            FETCH next_CUR INTO sale_row;
            CLOSE next_CUR;
        END IF; -- prev_CUR%NOTFOUND
        CLOSE prev_CUR;
    END IF; -- p_direction = 'DISPLAY_NEXT'

    -- Set return values
    x_inv_id          := sale_row.inv_id;
    x_auto_description  := sale_row.auto_description;
    x_sale_amt        := sale_row.sale_amt;
    x_photo_location    := sale_row.sale_photo_location;
END;
/
```

The `stcarsforsalebuy` Java servlet (see Listing 11.8) displays the Web page as illustrated in Figure 9.9 of Chapter 9. This Web page enables the Web browser user to make an offer on a car and record the information in the ST_CARS_FOR_SALE table object. The `UPDATE` statement that performs this task can be found in lines 43–47. If the `UPDATE` was successful (see line 48), the offer information is displayed on the Web page.

The `SELECT` statement (lines 54–56) reread the information being displayed on the original Web page (the `stcarsforsale` Java servlet). The remainder of the code (beginning at line 58) builds the Web page and directs the Web browser to the appropriate servlet for the selections made by the Web browser user, similar to Listing 11.6 (lines 48–84).

Listing 11.8—`stcarsforsalebuy` Java Servlet

```
1: import java.io.*;
2: import java.sql.*;
3: import javax.servlet.*;
4: import javax.servlet.http.*;
5: import java.util.*;
6:
7:
8:
9:
10: public class stcarsforsalebuy extends HttpServlet {
11:
12:  public void doGet(HttpServletRequest req, HttpServletResponse res)
13:       throws ServletException, IOException{
14:   Connection con = null;
15:   Statement stmt = null;
16:   ResultSet rs = null;
17:   int counter = 0;
18:
19:   String inv_id = req.getParameter("p_inv_id");
20:   String buyer_name = req.getParameter("p_buyer_name");
21:   String buyer_phone = req.getParameter("p_buyer_phone");
22:   String buyer_offer = req.getParameter("p_buyer_offer");
23:
24:   res.setContentType("text/html");
25:   PrintWriter out = res.getWriter();
26:   out.println("<HTML>");
27:out.println("<HEAD><TITLE>Metro Motors Web Site Make Offer</TITLE></HEAD>");
28:   out.println("<BODY>");
29:   stcarsutil.banner(out,"Metro Motors Web Site - Make An Offer");
30:
31:   try {
32:   //Register Oracle Driver
33:   Class.forName("oracle.jdbc.driver.OracleDriver");
34:
35:   //Get a Connection to the database
```

```
  con = DriverManager.getConnection(
"jdbc:oracle:thin:@localhost:1521:test", "sales_tracking","sales_tracking");

  stmt = con.createStatement();

  if (buyer_name != null) {
  // update the record with the offer
  counter = stmt.executeUpdate(
  "UPDATE st_cars_for_sale SET buyer_name='" + buyer_name
     + "', buyer_phone='" + buyer_phone + "', buyer_offer="
     + buyer_offer + ", buyer_date=SYSDATE WHERE inv_id = " + inv_id
   );
   if (counter > 0) {
     out.println("Offer for $" + buyer_offer + " recorded<BR>");
     }
   counter = 0;
   }

   rs = stmt.executeQuery("SELECT auto_description, sale_amt,
➥sale_photo_location, inv_id "
    + "FROM st_cars_for_sale WHERE inv_id="+inv_id);

     while (rs.next()) {
       counter++;
       out.println("<TABLE><TR>");
       out.println("<TD ROWSPAN=6>");
       out.println("<IMG WIDTH=300 SRC=" + rs.getString
➥("sale_photo_location") + ">");
       out.println("</TD>");
       out.println("<TD COLSPAN=2>");
       out.println("Description:"+rs.getString
➥("auto_description"));
       out.println("</TD></TR>");
       out.println("<TR>");
       out.println("<TD>");
       out.println("<FORM URL=stcarsforsale METHOD=get>");
 out.println("<INPUT TYPE=hidden NAME=p_direction VALUE=DISPLAY_PREV>");
       out.println("<INPUT TYPE=hidden NAME=p_inv_id
➥VALUE="+rs.getInt("inv_id")+">");
       out.println("Buyer Name:");
       out.println("</TD><TD>");
       out.println("<INPUT TYPE=TEXT NAME=p_buyer_name maxlength=20>");
       out.println("</TD><TD></TR>");
       out.println("<TR><TD>");
       out.println("Buyer Phone:");
       out.println("</TD><TD>");
       out.println("<INPUT TYPE=TEXT NAME=p_buyer_phone maxlength=10>");
       out.println("</TD></TR>");
       out.println("<TR><TD>");
       out.println("Offer:");
       out.println("</TD><TD>");
       out.println("<INPUT TYPE=TEXT NAME=p_buyer_offer maxlength=10>");
       out.println("</TD></TR>");
```

Listing 11.8—continued

```

        out.println("<TR>");
        out.println("<TD COLSPAN=2 ALIGN=CENTER>");
        out.println("<INPUT TYPE=SUBMIT VALUE='Make Offer'>");
        out.println("</FORM>");
        out.println("</TD></TR>");
        out.println("<TR><TD COLSPAN=2 ALIGN=CENTER>");
        out.println("<FORM URL=stcarsforsale METHOD=get>");
        out.println("<INPUT TYPE=hidden NAME=p_inv_id
➥VALUE="+rs.getInt("inv_id")+">");
        out.println("<INPUT TYPE=SUBMIT VALUE='Browse Inventory'>");
        out.println("</FORM>");
        out.println("</TD></TR>");
        out.println("</TABLE>");
        }
      if (counter==0) {
        out.println("Car Not found");
        }

    }
    catch(ClassNotFoundException e) {
      out.println("Could not load db driver" + e.getMessage());
      }
    catch(SQLException e) {
    out.println("SQL Error: " + e.getMessage());
        }
        finally {
            try {
              if (con != null) con.close();
            }
            catch (SQLException e) {}
        }

      out.println("</BODY></HTML>");
   }


}
```

Summary

In this chapter, you learned the basics of Java and the portability of Java across many computing platforms. You learned the basics of JDeveloper v3.0, Oracle's Java procedure building toolkit, while building a basic servlet that created a simple Web page based on the SCOTT.EMP table. You then applied this knowledge to build the Sales Tracking Web site, as illustrated in Chapter 9.

Next Steps

In the next chapter, you will learn about WebDB, Oracle's wizard-based application and Web site building toolkit.

Chapter 12

In this chapter

- *What Is WebDB?*
- *WebDB Administration*
- *Using WebDB in the Sales Tracking Application*
- *Creating a WebDB Sales Tracking Application*

Building Web-Based Forms with WebDB

What Is WebDB?

WebDB is a Web-based tool from Oracle Corp. that is useful for Web-based database administration, database and Web-based application monitoring, Web-based forms access, and content-oriented Web sites.

WebDB installation is simple and is covered in Appendix A, "Installation and Configuration of Oracle8i NT-Based Software." WebDB has its own listener process with an integrated *PL/SQL* cartridge. Basically, WebDB generates *HTML*-related PL/SQL behind the scenes. Figure 12.1 illustrates how WebDB interacts with the browser community and the Oracle database. The WebDB service is the listener process that is listening on a specific port on the computer.

HTML—The Hypertext Markup Language that all Web browsers understand.

PL/SQL—Oracle's own procedural language.

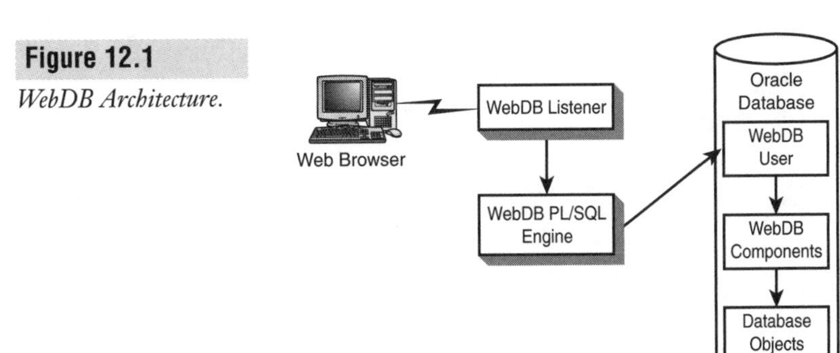

Figure 12.1
WebDB Architecture.

WebDB Administration

Chapter 4, "Basic Oracle8i Administration Tasks," covered how to use WebDB to monitor tablespaces and Web-based application activity, and how to perform basic database administration tasks, such as creating users, assigning privileges, and so on.

On Windows NT, the WebDB Listener is started and stopped through the control panel, as illustrated in Figure 12.2.

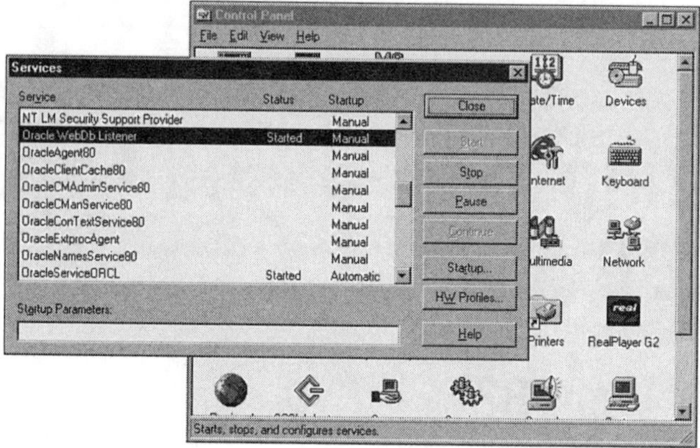

Figure 12.2

WebDB Listener.

The *Database Access Descriptor (DAD)* for WebDB is accessed through the main WebDB panel (see Figure 12.3). This URL is created when the WebDB software is installed. Select Administer, Listener Settings to display the Database Access Descriptor Settings.

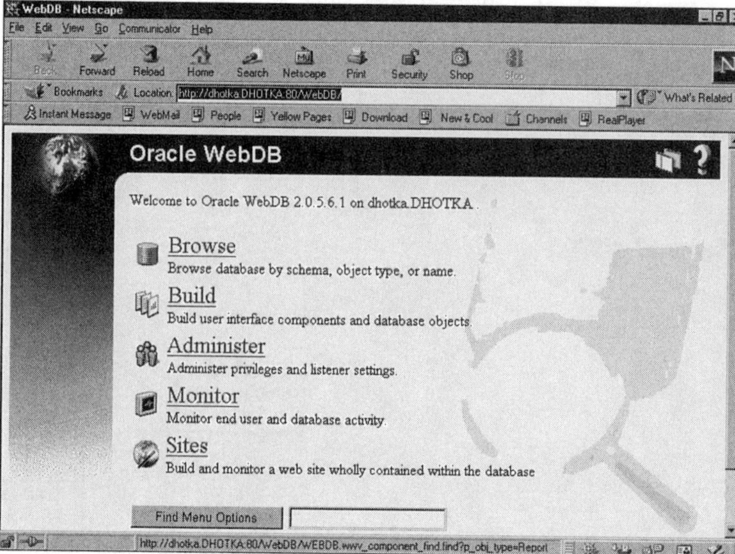

Figure 12.3

WebDB home page.

The DAD Name is the name used on the URL and equates to the Default (Home) Page described later in this DAD. The Oracle User Name and Password fields, on the other hand, are used to access the Oracle database. If left blank, the browser user is prompted for this authentication. You should fill in the Oracle Connect String if more than one local Oracle database exists. This field also can be filled in for documentation purposes. The Default (Home) Page field is the PL/SQL procedure that will be executed from this DAD access. In addition, Document Table is where information to return to the browser is stored, and Document Access Path is used to store any file retrieved from the browser. Finally, Document Access Procedure is any PL/SQL code to be executed after a download is complete.

Database Access Descriptor—A way for a Web listener to interpret a URL from the Internet and relate it to a specific process. In this application, the DAD is pointing to the WebDB home page. In Oracle Application Server, the DAD points to the PL/SQL code that contains the HTML for the particular assigned Web page.

Using WebDB in the Sales Tracking Application

WebDB is capable of producing Web-based forms to access various data objects in the Oracle database and of creating and maintaining *content-oriented Web sites.*

The forms-based WebDB development requires special permissions. In addition, the WebDB Web site installs its own set of PL/SQL procedures and DAD settings for each Web site desired.

Content-oriented Web site—A site in which everything displayed on a browser is predetermined, with no direct access to information in the database.

Creating a WebDB Sales Tracking Application

WebDB is a wizard-based development environment. To begin to build an application, select User Manager (under Administer; refer to Figure 12.3) and enter the Web administrator user ID (WEBDB in this example) as illustrated in Figure 12.4.

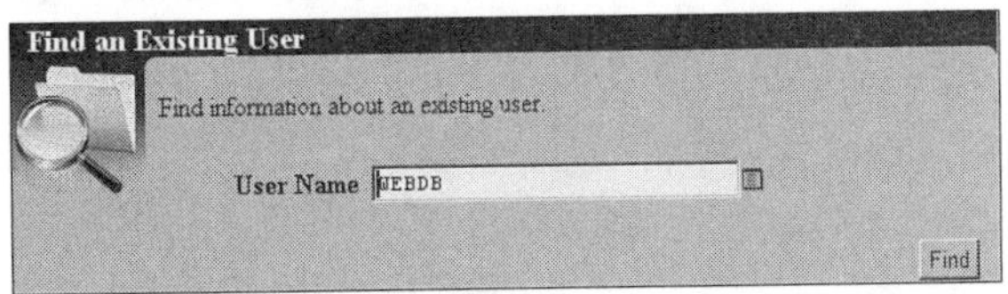

Figure 12.4

Using the WebDB user manager to find an existing user.

Locate the user who will be performing the WebDB development, and click to highlight that user. Highlight the SALES_TRACKING user (see Figure 12.5).

Although this might just be a bug in WebDB release v2.0, the username being used to build WebDB applications must be highlighted in this window.

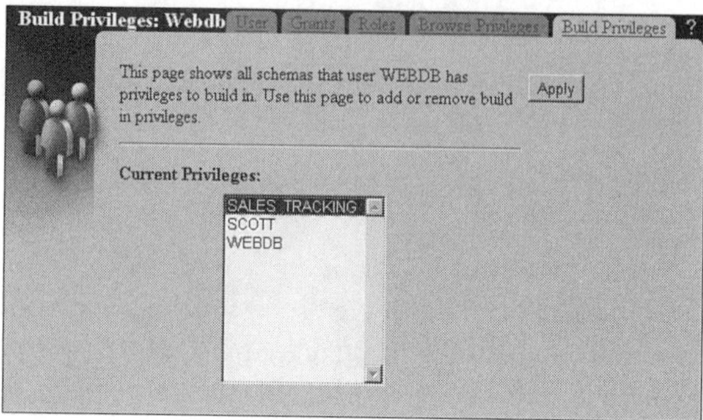

Figure 12.5

WebDB User Manager Build Privileges tab.

Return to the WebDB main menu by using the Web browser Back button; then select Build and select User Interface Components or click the Build UI Components icon, which is the second icon from the left along the bottom of the Web screen. To build a form, click Forms. The wizard in Figure 12.6 should be displayed. Select the radio button Forms on Tables/Views and click the Create button.

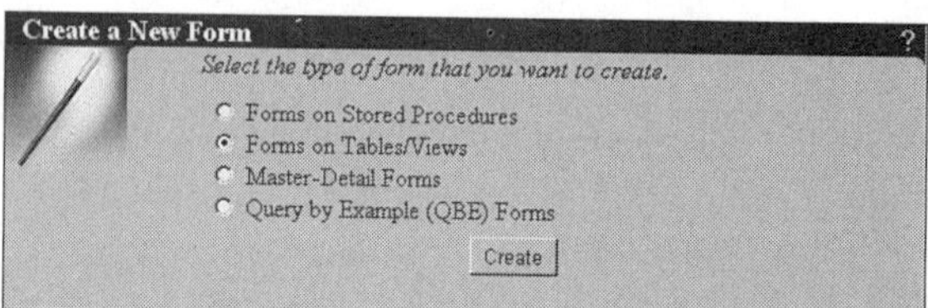

Figure 12.6

WebDB form building.

The SALES_TRACKING user ID already should be in the Schema check box. Give the form a name. The example in Figure 12.7 names the form Webdb_Bill_Time, as we build a Web-based version of the ST_BILL_TIME application. Click the orange arrow to the right on the upper-right part of the browser window. Select the table SALES_TRACKING.ST_BILL_TIME on the next screen and click the orange arrow to the right.

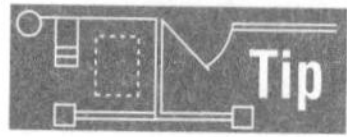

If the Schema list box does not display the correct user (SALES_TRACKING, in this case), return to the User Manager Build Privileges screen and highlight the SALES_TRACKING user, as shown in Figure 12.5.

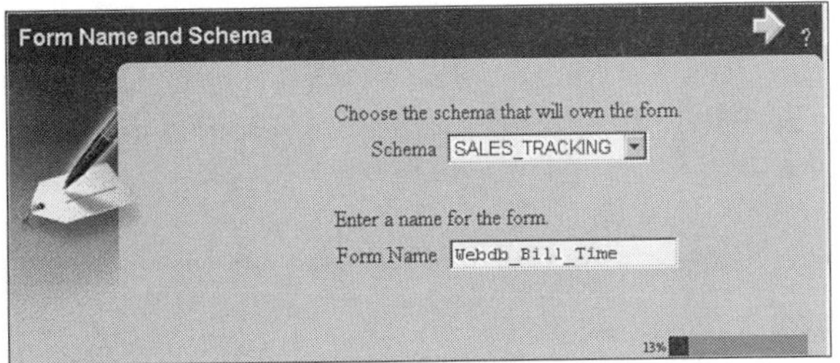

Figure 12.7

WebDB form naming.

Figure 12.8 shows the screen in which the form items are defined. Notice that all the columns from the ST_BILL_TIME table appear in the Columns box. Remove the INSERT_USER/DATE and UPDATE_USER/DATE columns by clicking each one, and then click the Remove button just under this box. These fields are automatically maintained by a database trigger assigned to the ST_BILL_TIME table. Notice as you click each of the remaining fields of this box that their attributes appear on the remainder of the screen. Click each of the attributes and select the options you desire for each field. Do not worry if you make the wrong selections here; it is easy to make adjustments to these selections. Click the orange arrow to the right when your changes are complete.

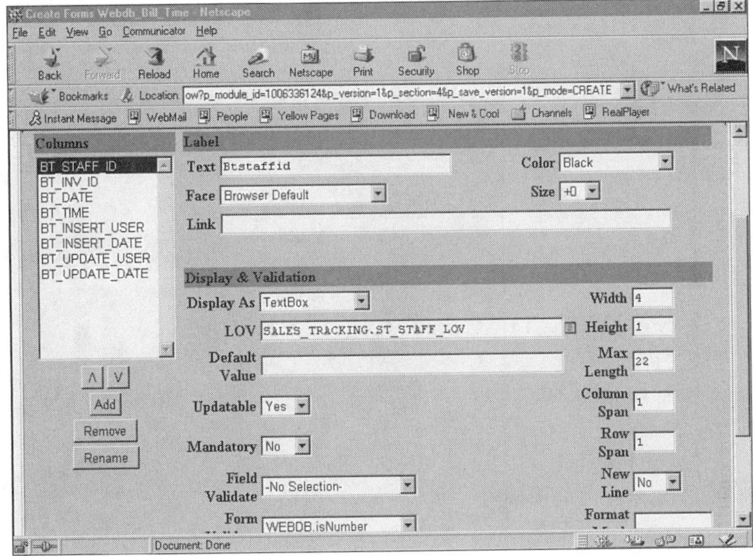

Figure 12.8

WebDB Form Display & Validation screen.

The next few screens enable you to add various text items, to insert PL/SQL code to execute at various points in the screen, and to label the Update and Delete buttons. The final screen says that the Webdb_Bill_Time form will be created as a packaged procedure (see Figure 12.9). This procedure can then be referenced with a Web browser or run from the Manage Component screen (see Figure 12.10). Notice the URL in Figure 12.11. This accesses the newly built form directly from a Web browser.

Figure 12.9

WebDB Create Forms screen.

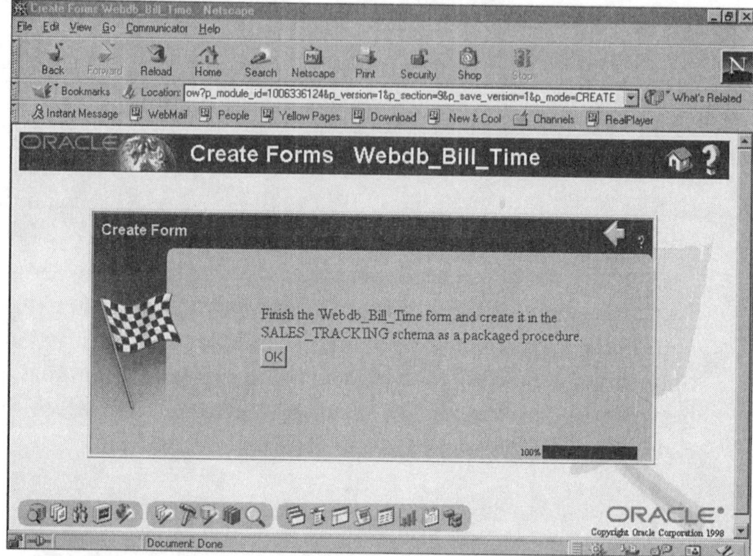

Figure 12.10

Manage Component screen.

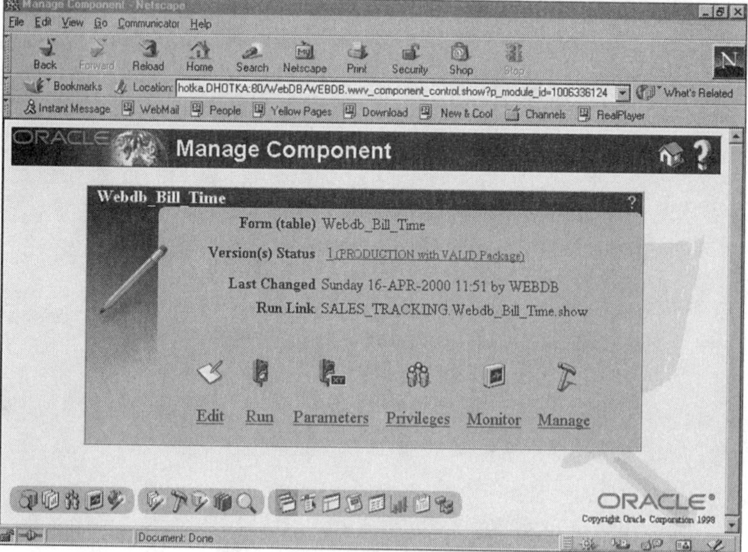

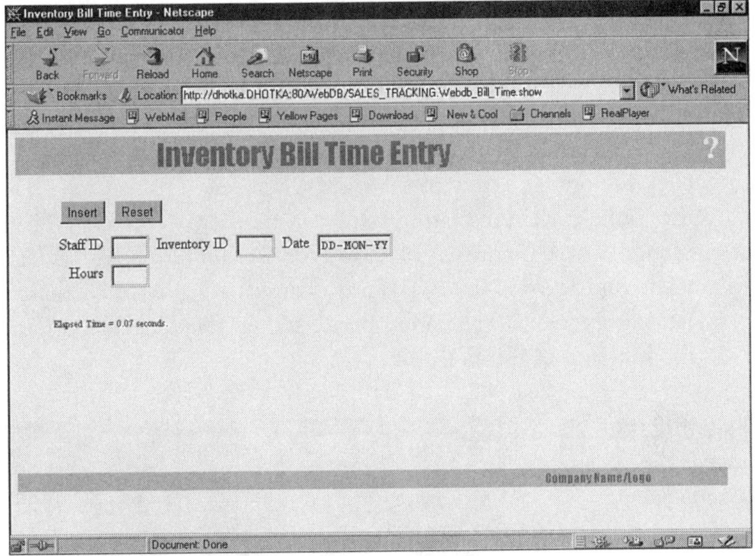

Figure 12.11

WebDB Inventory Bill Time Entry application.

Creating a WebDB Sales Tracking Web Site

WebDB also enables easy building and maintenance of *content* Web sites, or Web pages that do not directly access the database. Select Sites from the Oracle WebDB main menu (refer to Figure 12.3). Click Create in the Site Building box of the Create Site Wizard. Then, enter a Site Name on the next screen of the wizard. In this case, enter **`WEBDB_Buy_A_Car`** and click the orange arrow to the right (see Figure 12.12).

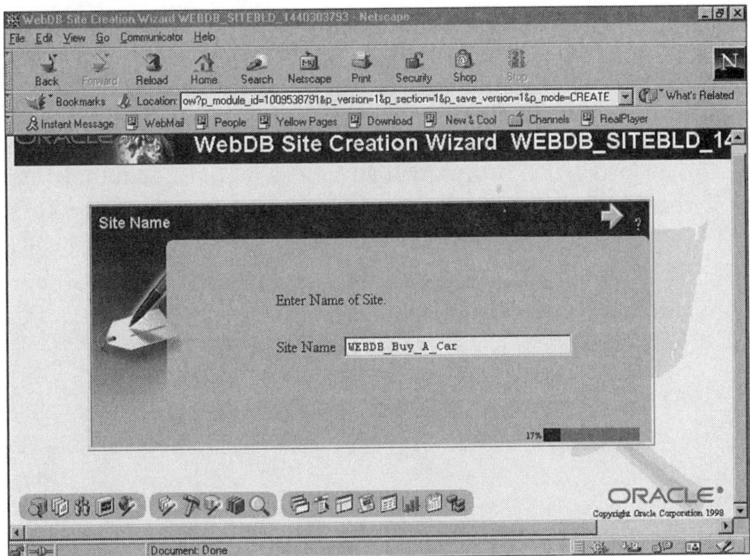

Figure 12.12

WebDB Site Creation Wizard's Site Name screen.

Follow the directions on the next screen to enter a new user ID that will own the new Web site schema. Enter **`Sales_Tracking_WebDB`** and click the orange arrow to the right. Accept the Language default of American (or select the language of your choice), and then click the orange arrow to the right. Select the appropriate table-spaces to hold the new Web site objects on the Select Tablespaces screen. Again, click the orange arrow to the right when ready to continue. Decide whether to put the Traveler demonstration folder on the newly created Web site and then click the orange arrow. Figure 12.13 shows the Create Site pane, which lists all the selections made on the prior screens. If any changes are necessary, click the orange arrow to the left until you are at the appropriate screen for the change. Click Finish to complete the building of the Web site.

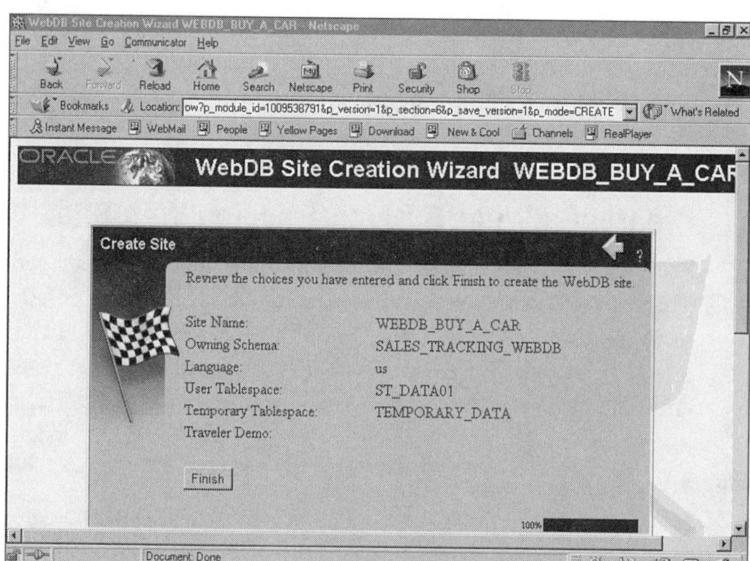

Figure 12.13

WebDB Site Creation Wizard: Finish.

The installation process will take a few minutes. It automatically creates a DAD for the WebDB Listener, as seen in Figure 12.14. Notice the DAD references the name you gave the Web site, SALES_TRACKING_WEBDB, which in turn references the SALES_TRACKING_WEBDB.home procedure (created by the wizard). Notice also that no user ID or password will be required to access this Web page.

The newly created home page is shown in Figure 12.15. Notice the URL in the browser location.

Figure 12.14

New Web site DAD information.

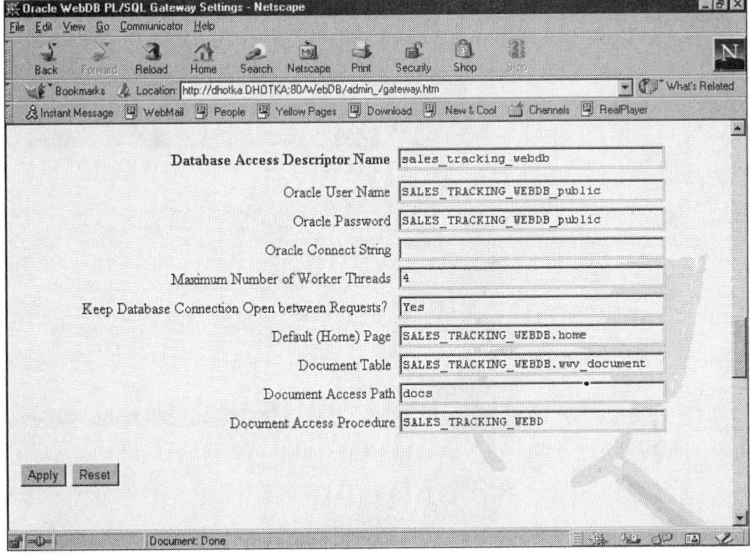

Figure 12.15

The newly created Web site home page.

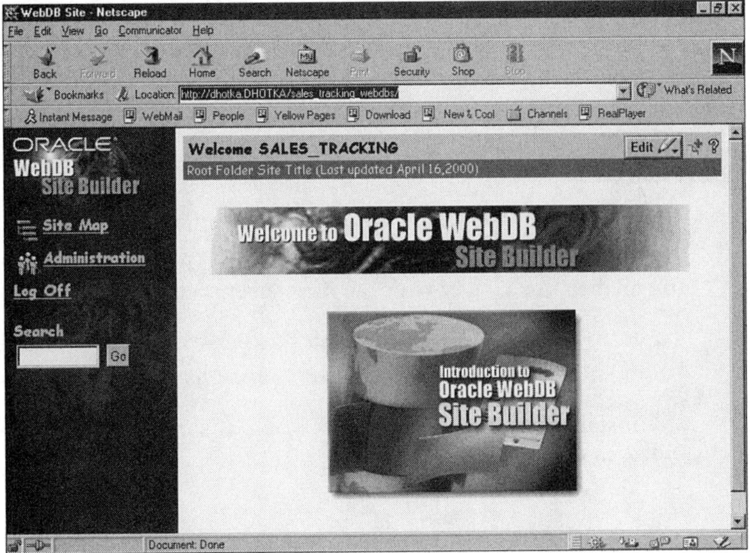

Click Introduction to Oracle WebDB Site Builder, and instructions on how to customize this Web site appear (see Figure 12.16).

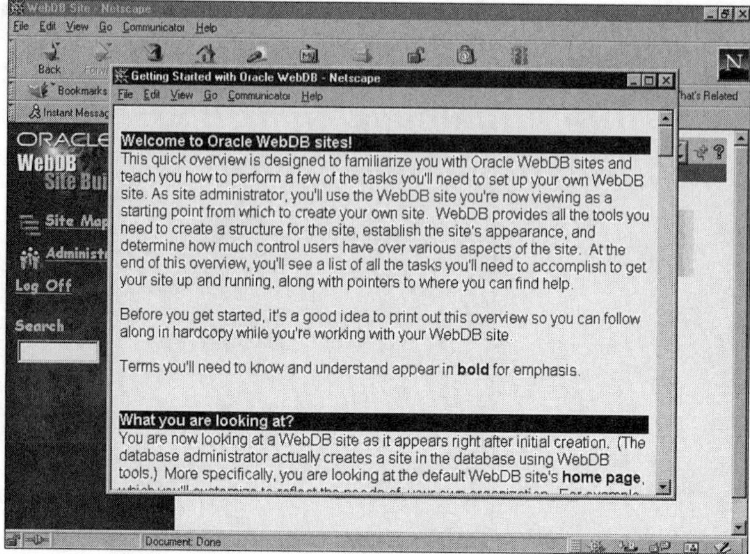

Figure 12.16

WebDB Site Builder Help.

The Administration page enables you to customize this particular Web site, changing the style, adding/changing folders, adding/maintaining users and privileges, and so on. Follow the instructions in Figure 12.16 to customize your new Web site.

Summary

This chapter introduced you to the development side of WebDB. It also covered building interactive forms as well as creating a basic Web site. I expect Oracle Corp. to enhance this facility over the next several years.

I want to thank you for purchasing this book and I hope that, by learning by building, you were able to enhance your skills when working with the Oracle8i database.

Appendix A

In this appendix

- *Oracle8i Architecture*
- *Hardware Requirements*
- *Oracle8i NT Database Software Install*
- *Problem-Solving DBMS Install*
- *Installing the Oracle Development Tools*
- *Installing the Oracle WebDB*
- *Installing the Oracle Application Server*
- *Installing the Quest Software Tools*

Installation and Configuration of Oracle8i NT-Based Software

Oracle8i Architecture

This section describes the basic components of the Oracle8i database software across all computers. It describes the various components (including memory, hardware, and network components) that make up the Oracle8i Relational Database Management System (RDBMS) environment and the interaction between them. Some of the internal mechanisms will be discussed to provide a better understanding of how Oracle8i works.

Computer *memory* is a physical storage device (computer chips) on which instructions (programs) and data (data read from the hard disks) are entered and retrieved when needed for processing. Reading information from memory is literally hundreds of thousands times faster than reading it directly from disk. It is the job of the computer's operating system to read both programs and data from hard disks and place them in memory. The more physical memory that can be allocated to the Oracle RDBMS, the more data can be stored there from the hard disks and the faster the applications will respond to end user requests.

For Oracle, the processes are the Oracle system (background) processes that look after the database and perform the actual access to the database for the users of the database.

In today's computing environment, networking computers together has become a way of life. A *network* is a system of connections between machines that enable one machine to communicate with another and share resources. In addition to the physical wires and components, a network requires a set of rules for communication, known as a *protocol.*

Oracle can support many different types of networks and protocols. If communication between computers running Oracle software is required, the Oracle Net*8 software must be installed on all the computers participating in this network. The Net*8 software hides the complexities (and even the type of network) from the end user. Because the Net*8 software handles all the issues, the end user does not have to do anything to access Oracle from one network type to another. This networking independence is also what makes Oracle applications portable across physically different computers.

The Oracle8i architecture described in this section is the generic architecture that applies to all platforms on which Oracle runs. Subtle differences in the architecture might exist between different platforms, but the fundamentals are all the same.

A *database* is a collection of related data that is used and retrieved together for one or more computer-based applications. The physical location and implementation of the database are transparent to the application programs, and the physical database can be moved without affecting the programs. This is another great feature of the Net*8 software. All the user needs is a connect string (a name given to a particular Oracle database) and Net*8 will know how to find it and connect the user.

Physically, an Oracle database is a set of files somewhere on disk. The physical location of these files is irrelevant to the function of the database. The location of these files can have a significant impact on how quickly requests for data can be supplied to the end user. The files are binary files that you can only access using the Oracle RDBMS.

Logically, the Oracle8i database is divided into a set of user accounts known as *schemas*. Each schema is associated with a user ID that was used to create the objects in the schema. It is good practice to create a super-user–type account (usually with DBA privileges) that owns all the objects for a particular application and also controls the privileges to those same objects. Without a valid username, password, and access privileges, access to information within the database is not possible. The Oracle username and password are different from the operating system username and password. Oracle allows the same operating system username and password to be used to log in to the Oracle environment, which is known as OPS$ Login. Additional information on using this feature can be found in the *Oracle8i Database Administrators Guide.*

Oracle user accounts provide a method of separating applications. It is common practice to have a single application residing in a single Oracle database. The same table name can coexist in two separate Oracle user accounts or schemas. The tables might have the same name, but they are different tables containing different information. Sometimes, the same database is used for holding various versions of tables for the developers, system testing, or user testing, or the same table name is used in different application systems. In Oracle, the schema name is the same as the Oracle user who created the table.

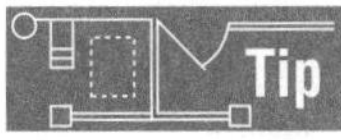

It is a good practice to have a single Oracle user account create all the database objects for a single application.

A good practice is to have an application *test* and a *development* environment on a separate computer from where the users are using the application (the production system).

A test or development environment—Environment in which the programmers actually make changes to the applications and make sure that these changes will work correctly for the end users of the application. A *production system* is the environment where the users are actually doing the application work.

Figure A.1 shows the basic Oracle8i architecture.

Figure A.1

Oracle8i architecture.

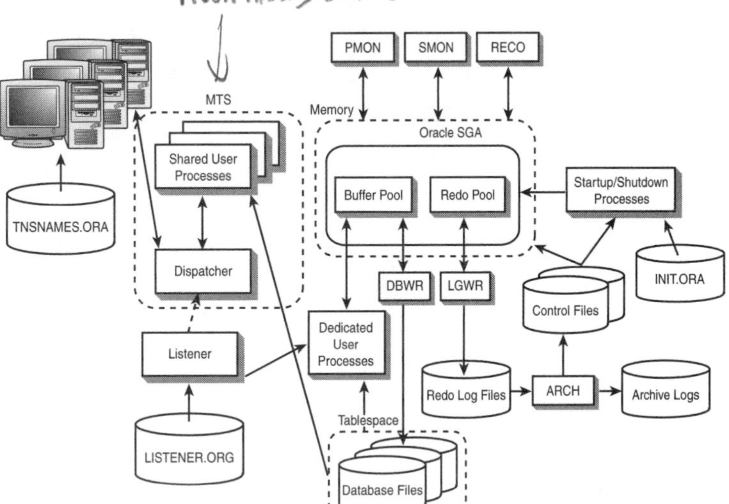

Three sets of files store the actual user data and control the various Oracle8i database functions. These sets—database files, control files, and redo logs—must be present, open, and available to Oracle before any data can be accessed. The most important of these files are the database files, where the actual data resides. The control files and the redo logs support the functioning of the architecture itself.

For the database to be accessible, the Oracle8i system processes and one or more user processes must be running on the computer. The Oracle system processes, also known as Oracle *background* processes, provide necessary functions for the user processes to access the database. These processes are initiated by a Startup function, discussed in Chapter 4, "Basic Oracle8i Administration Tasks." Many background processes are initiated, but as a minimum, only the Process Monitor (PMON), System Monitor (SMON), Database Writer (DBWR), and Log Writer (LGWR) must be up and running for the database to be usable. Other background processes support optional additions to the way the database runs. One option is for each user who logs on to get a background process as well (see Figure A.2). Another option is using the multithreaded server as a way of sharing these user background processes (see Figure A.3). In both cases, the listener process routes the user traffic to the proper Oracle database being requested. In the case of dedicated background processes (see Figure A.2), after the background process is established, the listener is no longer involved with this particular user. In the case of the multithreaded server, on the other hand, the users are passed to a dispatcher and the dispatcher interacts with the user programs to share a pool of dedicated background processes.

Figure A.2

User background processes.

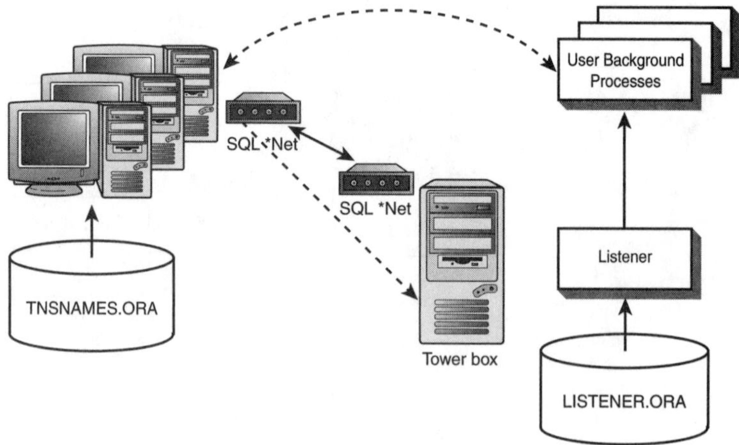

Figure A.3

Multithreaded server: shared background processes.

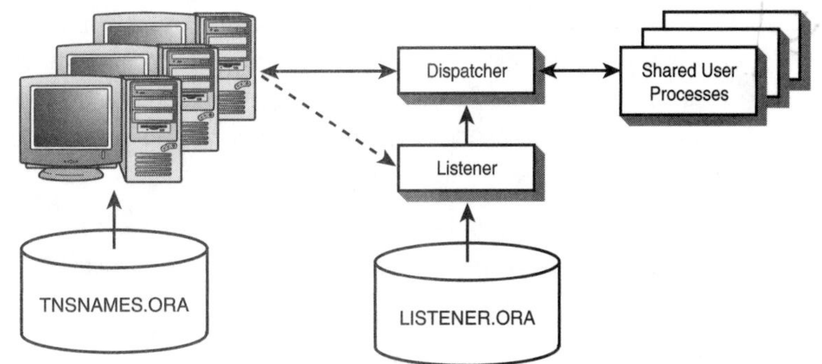

User background processes—Started when a user logs in to Oracle. These processes are used to pass data to and from the user application (that is, SQL*Plus, Forms, and a C program). The multithreaded server (MTS) is a way of sharing a set number of these background processes because each of these background processes takes computer memory and processing time to manage. When a large number of users is on a particular computer (such as 500 or more users accessing a single Oracle database), it might be a better use of memory to use MTS. This MTS uses a queuing mechanism and works on the assumption that not all users are reading or writing the database at the exact same time.

Oracle8i requires a series of memory structures to store and manipulate the data within the data blocks. These memory structures are known as the *System Global Area (SGA)*. The SGA is established upon startup of the Oracle8i database. The `INIT.ORA` file is a parameter file that defines the sizes of these memory structures and many of the options of the Oracle database. The startup process reads this file and builds the various memory structures of the SGA. Figure A.4 illustrates the memory structures that comprise the SGA.

Figure A.4

The Oracle8i System Global Area.

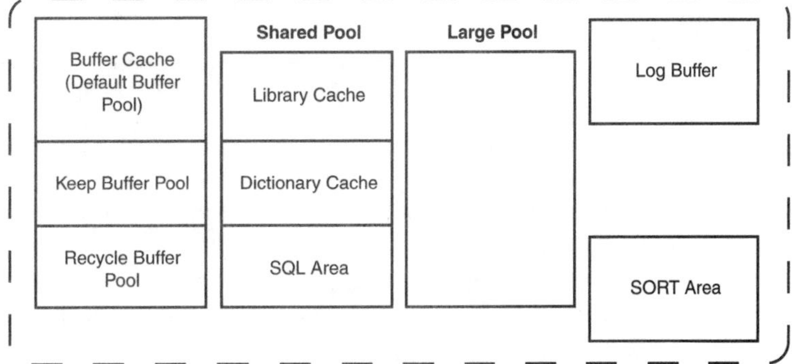

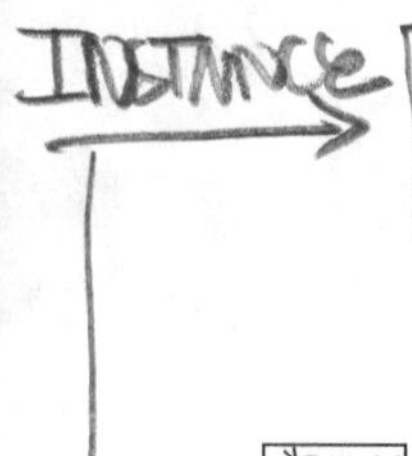

The combination of the SGA and the Oracle background processes makes up an Oracle8i database *instance*. Various features and options affect how many instances can use the same set of database files. An Oracle instance comprises a unique set of Oracle background processes, shared memory, and database files. A single computer can have several Oracle instances running on it.

Oracle instance—A common way to refer to unique Oracle database environments, whether they are on the same physical computer or not.

During the installation process, Oracle8i creates several default database files. These database files are assigned to various tablespaces. Tables and other objects can be stored together in a tablespace. A *tablespace* is similar to a directory or folder on a computer—a point of organization within the Oracle database environment. The database files are created for each tablespace, and each tablespace must have at least one database file assigned to it. Oracle requires at least two very specific tablespaces: SYSTEM and TEMP. The SYSTEM tablespace contains all the objects (tables, indexes, clusters, and so on) that the Oracle8i database uses to keep track of itself. These objects are known as *Data Dictionary objects*. The TEMP tablespace, in contrast, is a work area for many kinds of SQL statements that might be joining data together (such as multiple tables in the `FROM` clause), as well as sorting data.

The control file records the name of the database, the date and time it was created, the location of the various database and redo logs, and information to ensure that, at startup time, all these files are from the same date and time from when this Oracle instance was previously shut down. This is one way that Oracle can tell it might be in a recovery situation. The control file is an important part of the recovery process because all the required recovery information is most likely stored in the control file. If the control file is missing or corrupted, the Oracle instance will not start up. The `INIT.ORA` parameter file enables multiple copies of the control file to be automatically maintained.

The Oracle8i database must have at least one control file. Additionally, at least three control files should be maintained on separate physical disk drives.

The redo log files (sometimes called the *online* redo logs) are the master record of all activity going on in the database: The redo logs record all changes to the user objects or system objects. If any type of failure occurs, such as a loss of one or more database files, the changes recorded in the redo logs is used to recover the Oracle database without losing any committed transactions. If the computer was simply experiencing some problems (loss of electricity, for example), Oracle applies the information in the redo logs automatically. The SMON background process automatically reapplies the committed changes from the redo logs to the database files.

The redo logs are always in use while the Oracle instance is up and running. Changes made to the Oracle instance are recorded to each of the redo logs in turn. When one redo log is full, the other is written to. When the redo log becomes full, the first is overwritten and the cycle continues. If the redo logs don't have enough room for a large update, for example, the error `Snapshot too old` is returned. This means that the end of the transaction has used all the space in the redo logs and has found the beginning of the transaction in the redo logs.

The Oracle8i database must have at least two redo logs. The redo log files are fixed in size and never grow from the size at which they were originally created.

The Oracle RDBMS has the capability to save these redo logs so the information in them can be applied if recovery is required. The names of these logs are stored in the control file. The process is called *Archive Log Mode*, and it can be turned on with a series of manually entered commands. It also can be automatically started within the `INIT.ORA` parameter file. These archive logs are exact copies of the online redo logs that have just been filled and are created when Oracle switches to another online redo log.

Archive Log Mode is turned off by default at database installation time.

Four main Oracle background processes must always be running for the database to be accessible by the users. These processes are DBWR, LGWR, SMON, and PMON.

The DBWR process writes database blocks that have been changed (inserted, updated, or deleted rows) in the SGA to the correct database files. A block that is in the SGA and has a change to it but has not yet been written back to the disk drive is known as a *dirty* block. The DBWR writes only dirty blocks, starting with the oldest block (or the block longest in the SGA) first.

Least-recently-used (LRU)—Used throughout Oracle to describe the process of dealing with the oldest of anything first, or the least-recently-used.

The LGWR process writes the redo information from the SGA's redo log buffer into the online redo log files. When a user or a transaction issues a commit to the Oracle database, it is the LGWR's job to write out the contents of the redo log buffer before acknowledging a successful commit. This ensures, in the event of some kind of computer failure, that all committed transactions can be recovered.

SMON performs a variety of tasks, including the monitoring of multiple users trying to change the same object at the same time, which can lead to a *deadlock* situation. SMON reviews each transaction and rollback and returns an error to the transaction with the least processing time. SMON also performs some space management in the tablespaces and is used to apply the transactions in the online redo log files if the Oracle database was not shut down in a normal manner (including shutdowns that did not wait for transactions to complete or some kind of computer failure that stopped the Oracle processes).

Deadlock—Situations in which transactions are trying to make multiple updates to the same objects. One transaction is trying to lock an object that another transaction already has locked, and that other transaction is trying to get a lock on an object that the first transaction already has a lock on. As you can see, these transactions would wait indefinitely because the locks would never clear.

PMON monitors the user processes, the dispatcher, and shared background processes of the multithreaded server. If any failure occurs with these background user processes (either shared or dedicated), PMON automatically rolls back the work of the user process since the transaction started (anything since the last `COMMIT` or `ROLLBACK`) and releases any locks that the transaction might have been holding.

A series of optional background processes will be started if certain features of the Oracle database are being used. The ARCH process is used in Log Archive Mode to create the archive log files from the online redo log files. Conversely, the RECO process is used if Oracle Replication has been implemented and is used with transactions that span two or more Oracle instances. In the event of a failed transaction, RECO will need to either commit or roll back parts of the transaction that failed. Finally, the LCK process is used by Oracle Parallel Server.

The listener process is similar to a traffic cop between the users connecting to an Oracle instance and the Oracle instance itself. The listener process is not related to any particular Oracle instance and uses the information in the `LISTENER.ORA` file to know to which Oracle instance to route the user traffic. A listener process exists for each type of network being accessed by a particular computer. In a non-MTS environment, the listener actually starts up the background process on the same computer as the requested Oracle instance is running, logs the user in, and returns to listening for new users wanting to connect to Oracle. The users then directly communicate with this background process for the duration of their connection to an Oracle instance. In an MTS environment, however, the listener hands the user request off to an available dispatcher. This dispatcher then handles the user requests between existing background processes, enabling many users to share just a few background processes. The users interact with the dispatcher, and the dispatcher then routes the user requests to a free background process (or starts additional background processes if the user demand is high). MTS is very useful when hundreds or even thousands of users are connecting to a single instance of Oracle. Each user has access to a `TNSNAMES.ORA` file, which contains information about the type of network and the name of the Oracle instance where the connection is desired.

Each Oracle instance has its own SGA. These memory structures are created when the Oracle instance is started, and the memory allocated to these structures is returned to the computer when the Oracle instance is shut down.

The SGA has several areas (refer to Figure A.4).

The *buffer cache* is the work space for data blocks when user processes make requests for data from the tablespaces. Oracle always checks for the existence of a requested data block before performing a read operation to retrieve it. The buffer cache *hit ratio* is a ratio of the number of times that a data block was already in the buffer cache versus the number of times Oracle had to read the requested data block from a tablespace. Listing A.1 shows a SQL statement that can be used to monitor this buffer hit cache ratio. In general, setting the buffer hit cache ratio correctly can have the greatest impact on performance in any Oracle instance. All applications will have different needs, but this buffer cache hit ratio should be above 90% the majority of the time.

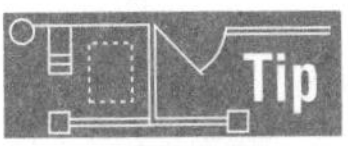

Adjustments to the buffer cache hit ratio can be controlled by setting the DB_BLOCK_BUFFERS in the `INIT.ORA` parameter file.

Listing A.1—Buffer Hit Cache Ratio

```
select round(((sum(decode(name,'db block gets',value))
            +  sum(decode(name,'consistent gets',value)))
             -  sum(decode(name,'physical reads',value))) /
              (sum(decode(name,'db block gets',value))
            +  sum(decode(name,'consistent gets',value))) * 100)
               "Buffer Cache Hit Ratio"
from v$sysstat
```

Oracle8 enables the buffer pool to be subdivided into three additional areas to better control the buffer cache hit ratio. The *keep* pool is designed for those objects that might be referenced many times but with few new inserts, and the *recycle* pool is for those objects that might have quite a bit of insert and update activity that may not be immediately referenced again. Finally, the *default* pool (also known as the *buffer* pool) is for all other objects. Through monitoring and placing various objects in these various pools, objects with frequent read activity can be separated from those that do not spend much time in memory, thus allowing those with frequent read activity to remain in the SGA longer and not be processed out via the LRU (least recently used) process.

The shared pool contains the library cache, dictionary cache, and SQL area. The *SQL area* holds the actual text of the SQL statement. The *library cache* is for the application SQL statements, and the *dictionary cache* is for the data dictionary SQL statements.

The shared pool size is determined by the INIT.ORA parameter SHARED_POOL_SIZE.

The large pool was introduced by Oracle8 to help ease some traffic and contention in the shared pool. The multithreaded server and the Oracle backup processes use space here rather than in the shared pool. The large pool is defined by setting the LARGE_POOL_SIZE and LARGE_POOL_MIN_ALLOC parameters in the `INIT.ORA` parameter file.

Hardware Requirements

For system prerequisites for Intel platforms, check `www.oracle.com`; for all other platforms, check the installation guide for your particular platform.

Oracle8i Server Requirements:

Pentium 133 (Pentium 200 recommended)

64MB Memory (96MB memory recommended)

Disk Space 587MB (720MB disk space recommended)

Operating System: Windows NT 4.0

Oracle8i Client-Side Requirements:

32MB memory (64MB memory recommended)

Disk Space 267MB

Operating System: Windows 95, Windows 98, or Windows NT 4.0.

Oracle WebDB Requirements:

32MB memory

Disk Space 50MB

Operating System: Windows NT 4.0 with Service Pack 3 or 4

Database: Oracle v7.3.4, Oracle v8.0.5, Oracle v8.1.5

Web Browser: Netscape 4.0.7 (or newer) or Microsoft Internet Explorer 4.0.1 with Service Pack 1 (or newer)

Oracle Developer 2.0 Requirements:

Intel 80486/33MHZ processor (or newer)

8MB memory for runtime components

16MB memory for Builder components

Disk Space: 530MB for Developer product

Operating System: Windows 95 or Windows NT 3.51 or newer

Database: Client/Server (two-system installation) Oracle 7.1 or newer (including Oracle8.1.5)

Single System (with Database): Oracle7.3.4, Oracle 8.0.3, or Oracle 8.0.4

Oracle8i NT Database Software Install

Insert the Oracle 8.1.5 CD in to the CD drive and close the drive door. This CD is set up with an autorun feature, and you will see the Oracle8i autorun screen (see Figure A.5). If you do not see this screen, start the Windows Explorer, go to the CD drive on your computer, click the NT folder, and then click the icon named setup.

Figure A.5

The Oracle8i Enterprise Edition install splash screen.

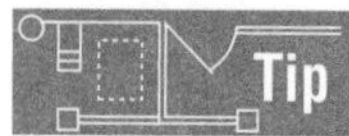

Trial versions of Oracle software, as well as a wealth of Oracle technical information, can be found on the Oracle Technical Network. Registration is simple via the Web site at `http://otn.oracle.com`. A confirmation and password will be emailed to you.

The next screen of the autorun feature is a welcome screen that enables you to see products that are already installed and to remove them. Click Next to move on to the File Locations screen (see Figure A.6). The Oracle Installer has taken some defaults. A `.jar` file should be in the first box onscreen that contains a file from the CD drive. This is the actual installation file the Oracle Installer will use for this install. You have two choices at this time. You can change the `ORACLE_HOME` variable and you can change the (operating system environment–specific full) path for this Oracle home. Click Next to proceed.

You might need to change the Oracle path to reflect an area on your computer's disk drives where more than 500KB of available disk space exists.

Figure A.6

The Oracle8i Installer File Locations screen.

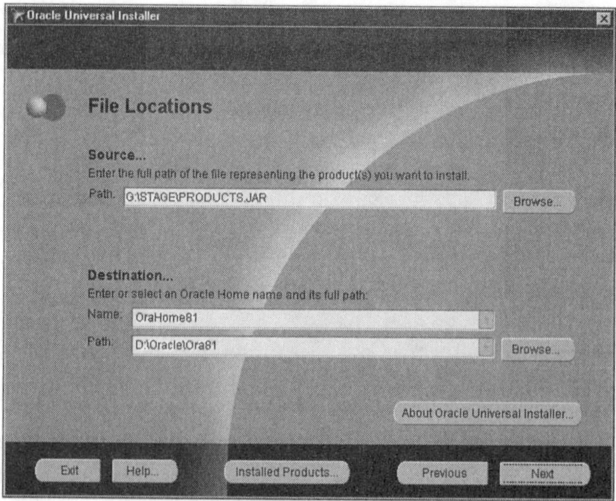

Select the Oracle8.1.5 Enterprise Edition radio button on the Available Products screen and click Next. The next screen is the Installation Types screen. The typical install creates the initial database. The minimum install also creates a database but installs the minimum set of programs necessary to run the Oracle8i environment. The custom install enables you to select the exact Oracle products to install. Make your selection and click Next.

This book assumes an initial install of the Oracle software, and I made the typical install selection.

Select the custom install if upgrading to Oracle8i from a previously installed version of Oracle software.

The next screen asks whether you want the Oracle8i documentation set physically installed on your hard drive. The complete set of Oracle8i RDBMS manuals are on the CD.

Install the documentation files if you have the extra room on your hard drive. This documentation is the entire Oracle Documentation set; having it on your hard drive will eliminate having to have the installation CD whenever you want to reference the documentation.

The next screen is where the Oracle System Identifier (or Oracle SID) is named. This should be a unique name for each instance of Oracle. In addition, your shop might have SID naming conventions. I used the generic ORCL. This SID is also a good name to use when configuring Net*8 because the Net*8 identifier and this SID can (and should) be the same name.

Click Next to begin the actual Oracle installation process. When the process is complete, the Configuration Assistant Alert screen appears (see Figure A.7). This screen contains the default passwords for this new instance of Oracle; these passwords should be changed because these defaults are both common and well known. Chapter 4 illustrates how to change these passwords.

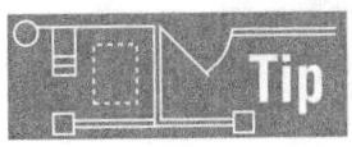

The SYS account owns the Oracle data dictionary. Very few reasons to use the SYS account exist. The SYSTEM account is used to perform many of the standard administrative functions, including adding tablespaces, starting and stopping the database, and so on. The SYSTEM account should also be used to create the user accounts used to create the application objects.

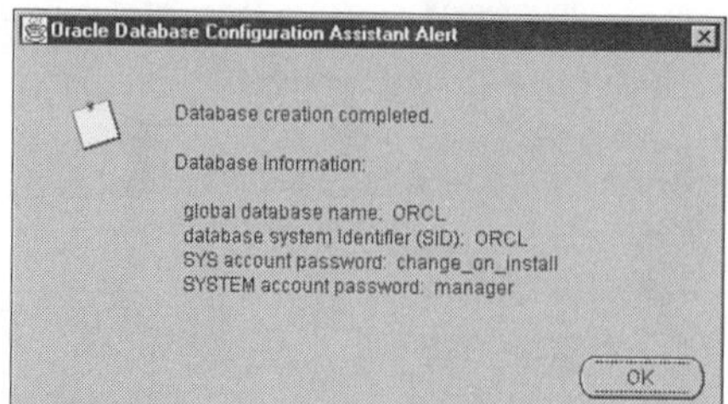

Figure A.7

The Oracle8i instance default user IDs and passwords.

Now is a good time to make sure that Net*8 was configured correctly and that the database is accessible. Click Start, Programs, Oracle for Windows NT, SQL*Plus. Enter the user **SCOTT** with a password of **TIGER** (you can also use the user ID SYSTEM with a password of MANAGER). Use the SID as entered in the installation process. If all is working well, you should receive a SQL> prompt. Enter **EXIT** and press Enter. If an error is returned, verify that you entered the correct SID, and the error message should give some indication as to what occurred in SQL*Plus.

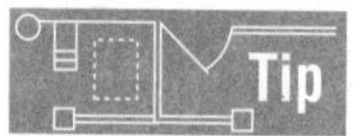

If you get the ORA-12154 TNS: Could Not Resolve Service Name error, the <ORACLE_HOME>/net80/admin directory where the Oracle8i is installed will have a TNSNAMES.ORA file. Try copying the TNSNAMES.ORA file to your local machine's <ORACLE_HOME>/net80/admin directory and try again. Be sure you are using the correct spelling and so on. If your computer has multiple ORACLE_HOMEs, try copying the TNSNAMES.ORA file to each net/80/admin or network/admin directory.

The SQL*Plus Help environment does not automatically install with the database instance installation. If you want to have a SQL help facility available when in SQL*Plus, follow the next few steps. The files required to perform this installation are in the <ORACLE_HOME>/sqlplus/admin/help directory.

If these files did not install from your CD, please contact your Oracle representative or download them from this book's Web site at www.quepublishing.com.

The order of events here is to create the help table (HELPTBL.SQL); then use SQL*Loader to load the three data files (PLUSHELP.CTL, SQLHELP.CTL, and PLSHELP.CTL); and then run the final script (HELPINDX.SQL, which will create the correct indexes on the help table, as well as create the permissions and so on).

Log in to SQL*Plus using the SYSTEM account, and run the following:

```
START HELPTBL.SQL
```

Execute the SQL*Loader process for each of the `*.CTL` files by using the following commands:

```
dir *.ctl  (shows PLUSHELP.CTL, SQLHELP.SQL, and PLSHELP.CTL on my system)
sqlldr userid=system/manager control=plushelp.ctl
sqlldr userid=system/manager control=sqlhelp.ctl
sqlldr userid=system/manager control=plshelp.ctl
```

Complete the SQL*Plus Help Assistant Installation process by running the `HELPINDX.SQL` script:

```
sqlplus system/manager
start helpindx.sql
```

Test the SQL Help Assistant by logging in to SQL*Plus as any user and entering **`HELP`** or **`HELP <topic>`**—for example, **`HELP SELECT`** (as illustrated in Figure A.8). If you see help definitions, everything is installed properly.

Figure A.8

*The SQL*Plus Help Assistant.*

```
Oracle SQL*Plus
File Edit Search Options Help

SQL*Plus: Release 8.1.5.0.0 - Production on Sun Jan 30 16:50:55 2000

(c) Copyright 1999 Oracle Corporation.  All rights reserved.


Connected to:
Oracle8i Enterprise Edition Release 8.1.5.0.0 - Production
With the Partitioning and Java options
PL/SQL Release 8.1.5.0.0 - Production

SQL> help select

 SELECT
 ------

 Use this command to retrieve data from one or more tables, object
 tables, views, object views, or snapshots.

 SELECT
   [ DISTINCT | ALL ]
   { *
   | { [ schema. ]{ table | view | snapshot } .*
     | expr [ [ AS ] c_alias ] }
   [, { [ schema. ]{ table | view | snapshot } .*
```

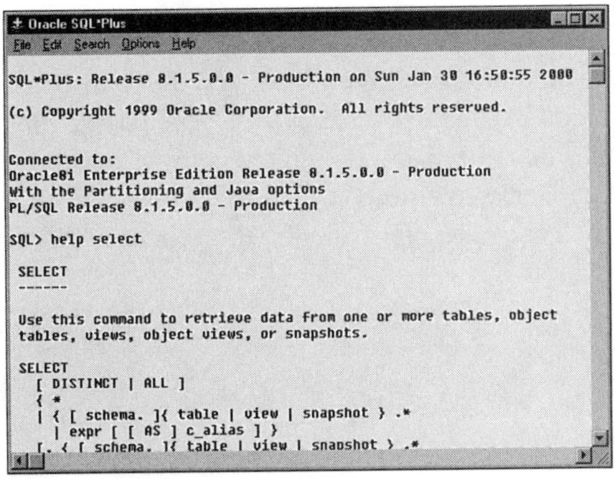

Problem-Solving DBMS Install

`ORACLE_HOME` is a computer environment setting that is set to the directory structure where the Oracle database and Oracle products are installed. For example, if `ORACLE_HOME` (on Windows NT) is set to `c:\OraNT`, all other Oracle product directories will be created under this location.

On Windows NT, Oracle8i does not use the `ORACLE_HOME` directory but relies on Windows NT registry settings.

All Oracle products use the CORE.DLL program. This program uses the directory path from which it was started to determine the registry entry and ORACLE_HOME defined in the NT registry.

Oracle products, however, should not rely on ORACLE_HOME to be set in the computer's environment variables. All Oracle products instead should use the previously described process, using the NT registry, to determine what ORACLE_HOME should be for the program being executed.

Oracle products will use the ORACLE_HOME setting if it exists. However, this can cause problems with programs such as SQL*Plus, especially if ORACLE_HOME and the first Oracle-related path in the environment variable PATH do not match. SQL*Plus will look for its message file, login.sql, in the directory where the program was started. If ORACLE_HOME is defined, SQL*Plus looks for these files in the ORACLE_HOME directory, not the directory where it was started.

The Oracle8i installation and database do not rely on ORACLE_HOME. The Oracle Installer v3 does not set an ORACLE_HOME environment variable. On the other hand, WebDB and Developer v6.0 both use the Oracle Installer v2, which does set an ORACLE_HOME, and their related products do depend on ORACLE_HOME to be set.

This has made for an interesting problem because both Oracle Developer and Oracle WebDB (v2) want to use the default ORACLE_HOME setting. But because many of the Oracle products do not rely on a specific version of the database, each product tends to use different database versions of DLL files, as well. These products cannot be installed on the same computers running the Windows NT operating system.

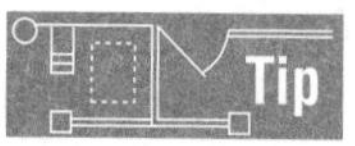

Install each of the Oracle products—Oracle8i, Oracle Web Server, and Oracle Developer—on separate Windows NT computers.

Installing the Oracle Development Tools

I installed this product on a different Windows NT 4.0 computer from the one used to install the Oracle8i database. If you want to install the Oracle Developer v6.0 and the Oracle8.1.5 database software on the same physical machine, please reference Oracle Metalink Bulletin Doc ID: 74131.1 "Installing Developer 6.0 and Oracle8i in the Same Physical Oracle Home." Consult your database administrator (DBA) or Oracle representative if you need assistance in retrieving this document.

Insert the Developer v6.0 CD in your computer's CD drive. Similar to the Oracle8i installation, the Oracle Installer should start automatically. (If it doesn't run automatically, refer to the Windows Explorer instructions in the "Oracle8i NT Database Software Install" section previously in this chapter.) Insert the appropriate Company Name and set the `ORACLE_HOME` directory to a location on your computer that has more than 500MB of available disk space. Click OK when ready to proceed. Select Development Installation on the next screen and click OK.

When the installation is complete, the installation process will have created dozens of icons in the Oracle Developer 6.0 folder (see Figure A.9).

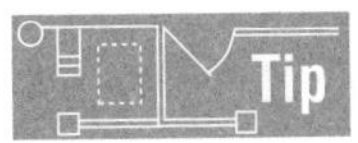

You might find it more convenient to add some of these icons (such as the Forms Builder, Forms Runtime, Report Builder, Report Runtime, and SQL*Plus) to the desktop for your convenience. This is easily accomplished with a drag-and-drop using your mouse.

Figure A.9

Oracle Developer icons.

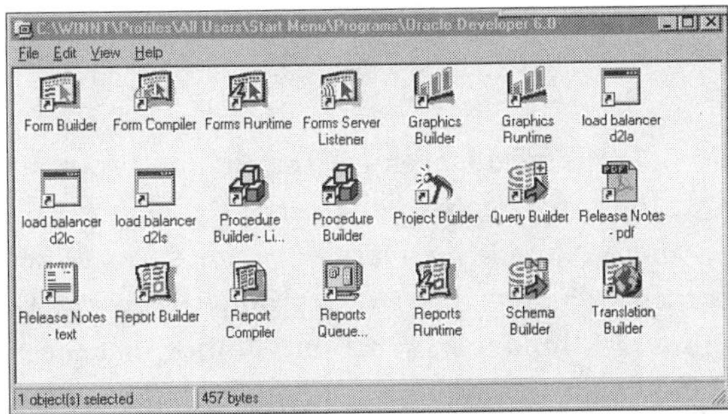

Test SQL*Plus to ensure that the Oracle SID (Host String) is working and that you can successfully connect to the database. If you get the `ORA-12154` error, as illustrated in Figure A.10, you can edit the `TNSNAMES.ORA` file (using Windows Notepad) to see what the valid entries are and to make sure you see a valid Oracle SID for the database to which you want to connect. If not, try copying the `TNSNAMES.ORA` file from the `<ORACLE_HOME>/net80/admin` directory from the database server and connecting again.

The DBA at your site is responsible for maintaining all valid Oracle SIDs in this `TNSNAMES.ORA` file. You might want to consult your DBA before making changes to the `TNSNAMES.ORA` file on your system.

Figure A.10

*Test the SQL*Plus connection to the Oracle8i Server.*

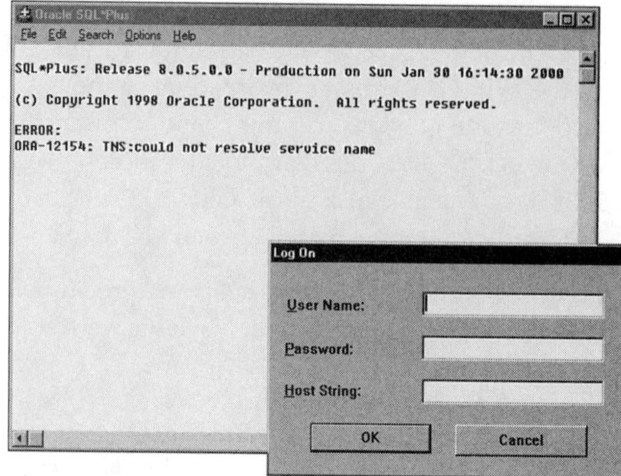

If you have not created the user `Sales_Tracking`, now would be a good time to do so. Consult "Building the Sales Tracking Database" in Chapter 2, "Building the Sales Tracking Application Database," for details on the user `Sales_Tracking`.

The remainder of the Oracle Developer Installation process relies on the previously mentioned SQL*Plus program working correctly. Figure A.11 illustrates the four icons used to maintain the Oracle Developer repository. These icons can be accessed from the Start menu via Start, Developer Admin. Figure A.12 illustrates the Developer Repository Build icon in action. Notice that the SYSTEM account is used to create this repository. Figure A.12 applies all the correct permissions to individual user accounts that will be using the Oracle Developer tools. Be sure to run this item for the `Sales_Tracking` user.

Figure A.11

The Oracle Developer administrative icons.

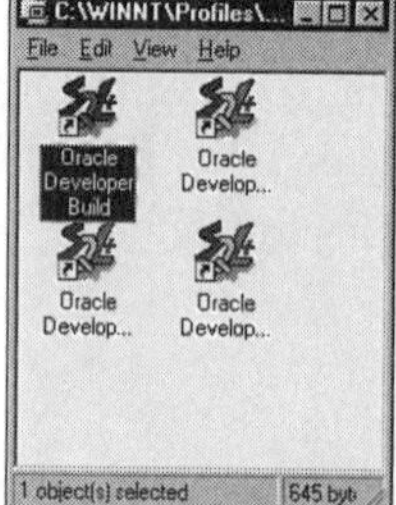

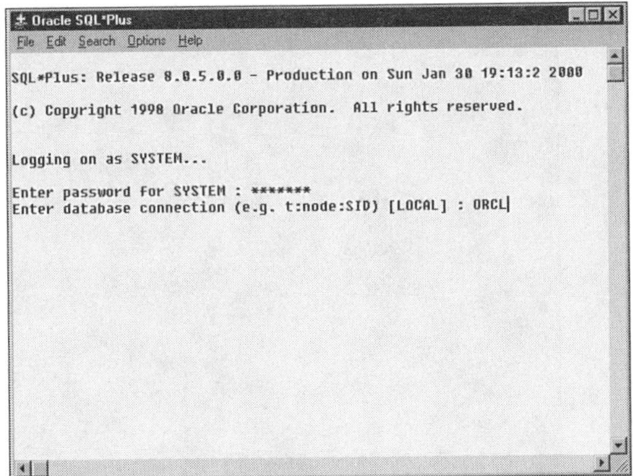

Figure A.12

Building the Oracle Developer Repository

Installing the Oracle WebDB

Installation of the WebDB software takes about half an hour. Insert the WebDB CD in the CD drive and close the drive door. This CD is set up with an autorun feature, so you should see the Oracle Installation Settings screen (see Figure A.13). (If Oracle Installer does not automatically start, start Windows Explorer, go to the CD drive on your computer, click the NT folder, and then double-click the Setup icon.) The first option is to select an Oracle Home for the WebDB software. Click OK when ready to continue. Select Typical Install on the next screen and click OK.

This Oracle Home must be different from the Oracle Home used to install the Oracle8i software. This Oracle Home also conflicts with the Oracle Developer v2.0 installation, which wants the same Oracle Home.

The next screen asks for the SYS account password, the hostname (or machine name), and the port number. The hostname of your computer can be found by clicking Start, Settings, Control Panel, and then double-clicking the Networks Icon. The port number 80 is the default setting. It should probably be 80 unless your DBA has advised you to use a different setting.

Next, specify the database type into which WebDB will be installed. Before beginning, the system warns you that the installation is about to start. It runs for about half an hour, depending on how fast your computer is. When the installation is complete, a screen appears informing you what the base URL is to access the WebDB and the user accounts and passwords needed to use the WebDB software (see Figure A.14).

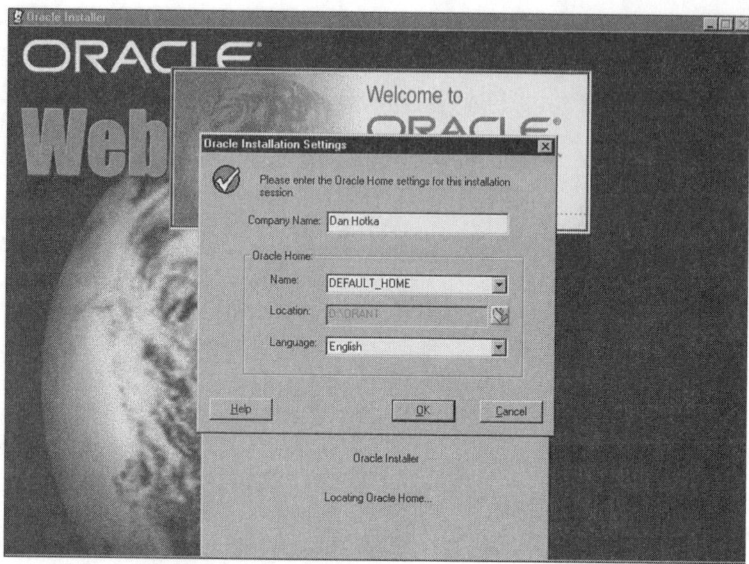

Figure A.13

Oracle home selection for WebDB installation.

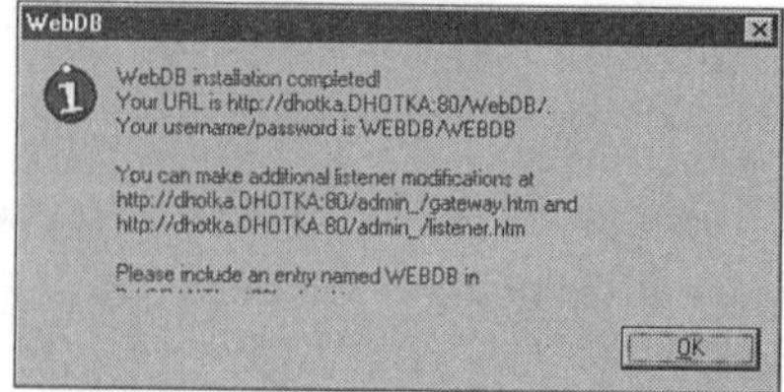

Figure A.14

Installation completion with important information.

Installing the Oracle Application Server

Installation of the Oracle Application Server (also called the Web server) software is easy and straightforward. Insert the Oracle Application Server CD in the CD drive and close the drive door. The installation process should start automatically. (If Oracle Installer does not automatically start, start Windows Explorer, go to the CD drive on your computer, click the NT folder, and double-click the Setup icon.)

The first option is to select an Oracle Home. The Oracle Application Server (OAS) does not seem to conflict with the Oracle8i database software, so select the default Oracle Home. Accept the defaults and click OK. Highlight the Oracle Application Server from the list of Available Products and click Install.

Through the next series of screens, install the Enterprise Edition and make the proper selection for the type of computer hardware configuration you are installing by selecting Custom Install.

The wizard will prompt you for a single-node or multi-node installation. Select the single-node installation unless otherwise instructed by your DBA.

Figure A.15 illustrates the various Web components supported by the OAS. These cartridges are Oracle Corp.'s method for supporting various Web-based languages but not overloading the server with unnecessary software. Select the cartridges required for any application using this OAS. If you are not sure which pieces will be required, select them all.

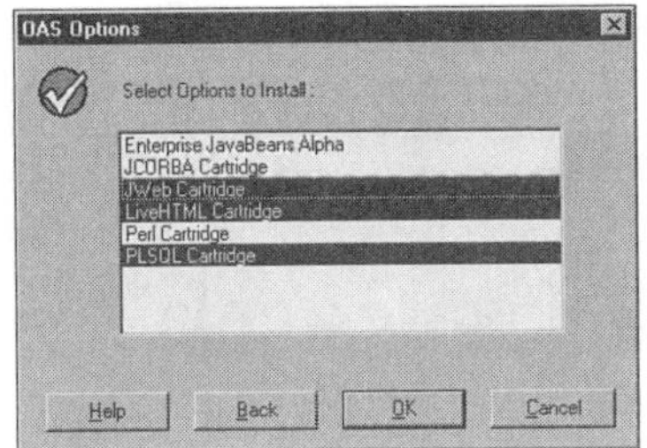

Figure A.15
OAS cartridge selection.

Next, give the Oracle Application Server a name and designate the correct boot port. This becomes an entry for the Web listener and the `TNSNAMES.ORA` file for Net8 access to this server. Figure A.16 illustrates setting up the port number and passwords for the Web listener. Let the port number take the 8888 default and select a password for the admin account for this server.

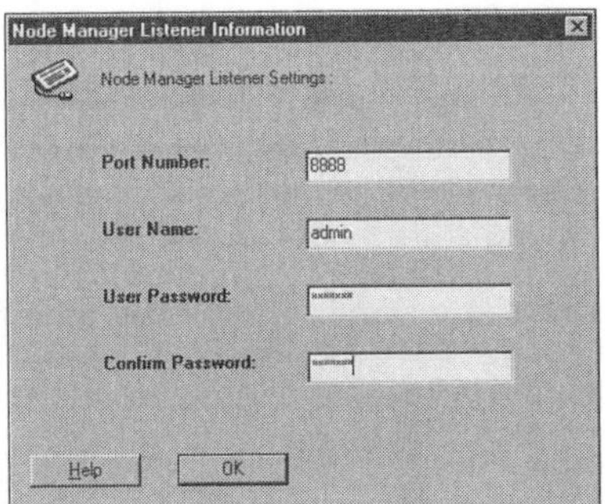

Figure A.16
OAS Listener installation.

In the Administrative Utility Listener Information window, accept the port default of 8889. This listener will be used to make administrative changes to the Web server. The Web listener port number then defaults to 80 in the next screen. If you are also going to be using the WebDB server on this server, make sure this port number does not conflict with the Web listener of the WebDB. If you are not using the WebDB, accept the default. Next, select the JDBC v1.1 drivers (see Figure A.17).

Figure A.17

Oracle8 JDBC drivers.

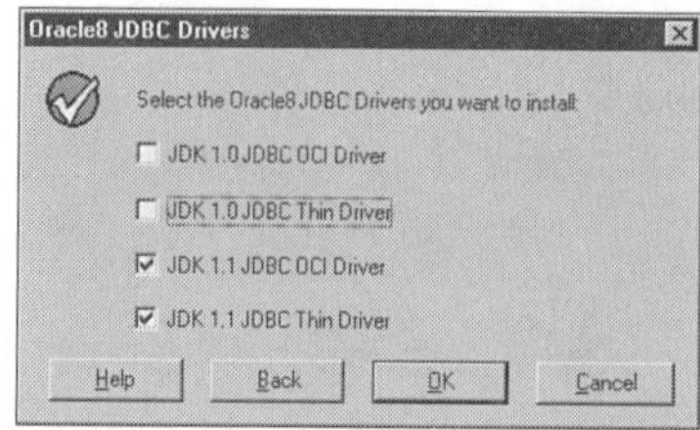

The Oracle Application Server is now installed and configured. This takes about 15 minutes.

On Windows NT platforms, the computer needs to be rebooted for the Oracle Application Server changes to take effect.

Installing the Quest Software Tools

The Quest Software tools used in this book can be downloaded free of charge from the Web site at `www.quest.com`. Thirty-day trial license keys are included in this chapter.

Installing Quest SQL Navigator

Begin the installation process by double-clicking the SQLNav31e5 icon in the `QuestTools\Nav` file of your hard drive. You should be presented with the Quest Software license agreement. Read this screen and click I Accept if you meet the requirements of the license agreement.

Figure A.18 shows the three types of computing environments supported by SQL Navigator. Select the one that best fits your company's environment. If you are not sure, select PC Install and click Next. The next screen is the software installation directory. Change this if necessary and click Next. The next screen is a way of protecting existing files in the case of duplicates. Select Yes and click Next.

The Select Component screen automatically chooses some defaults for you, if you selected the PC installation (see Figure A.19). Select the Reporting Tool option. SQL Navigator and SQLab/Xpert have some overlap in functionality. This book uses the tuning features of SQLab/Xpert, but SQL Navigator has a similar feature. Check this box if you want to install the tuning options of SQL Navigator. Click Next when you are ready to continue.

Figure A.18

Installation Type screen.

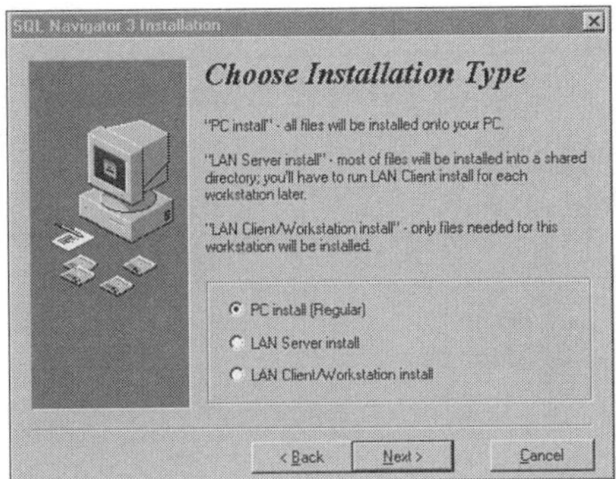

Figure A.19

Select Components screen.

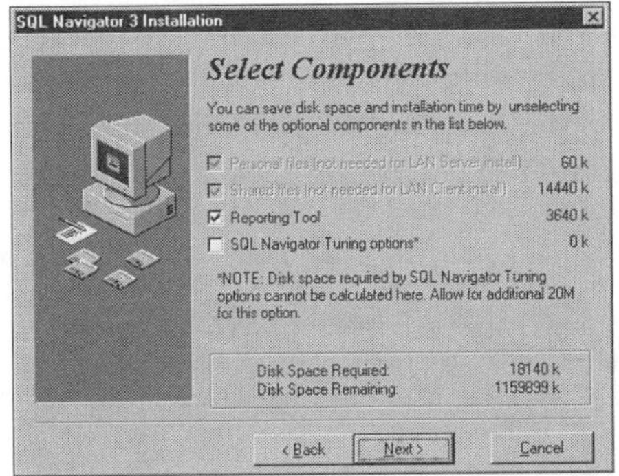

Before the installations begins, you are presented with three options. The first option creates an Icon on your computer, making it a bit easier to start the product. The second option relates all files with a .sql extension to this product so that SQL Navigator will be started if any file with a .sql extension is accessed from Windows Explorer. The final option needs to be performed at some time. This option sets up some objects and permissions on the Oracle database where SQL Navigator will be used. This step takes about five minutes to complete. Click Next to begin the installation process.

The Server Side Installation Wizard first asks whether you want to install the server-side objects or remove them. If your computer has had an earlier version of SQL Navigator installed on it, remove the server-side objects. After this is completed, you will be returned to this screen, where you can select Install Server Side Objects. Click Next. This book uses SQL Navigator to build server-side objects. Therefore, only the first option is necessary. You can select as many scripts to install as you think you might use (see Figure A.20). Click Next after making your selections.

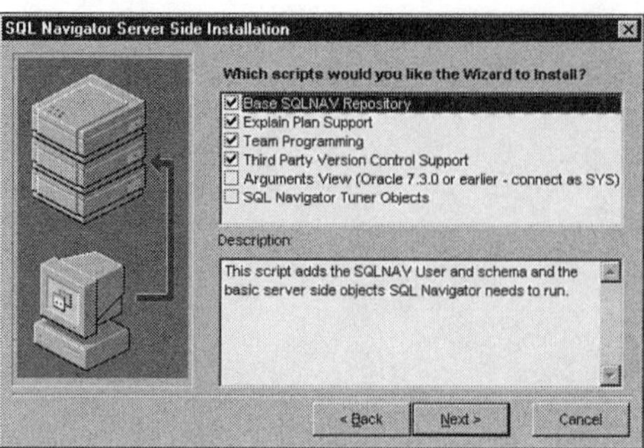

Figure A.20

Server-side installation wizard script selector.

The next screen asks for a user account with DBA privileges, the connect string for the database, and a tablespace for the objects (see Figure A.21). Use the SYSTEM account for this installation with the connect string to the Sales Tracking Oracle database. Select a tablespace with enough room. Be sure to click connect to ensure that the installation wizard can connect to the database. Click Next when you are ready to continue.

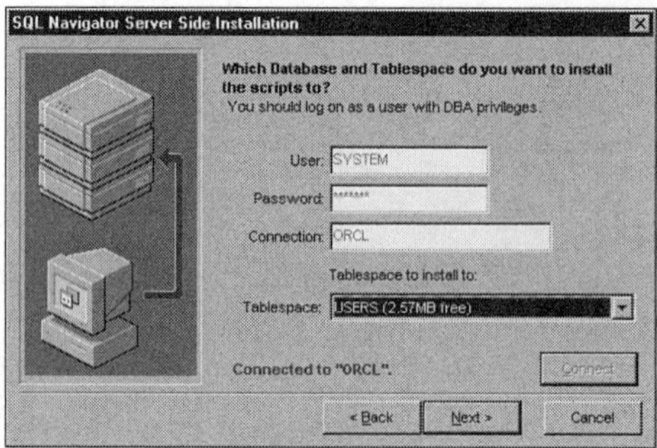

Figure A.21

Account setup and tablespace assignments.

The installation process sets up a user account called SQLNAV and asks for a password for this new account. After the installation is complete, the screen illustrated in Figure A.22 appears. Make sure no errors are reported here and then click Next. The final screen discusses installing the PL/SQL Profiler option that is available for Oracle 8.1.5. This book does not use this feature; however, you might want to install this. Clicking Finish ends the installation process.

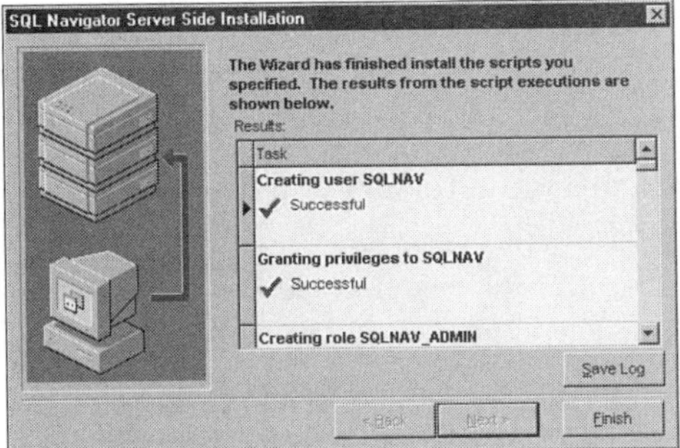

Figure A.22

Installation status.

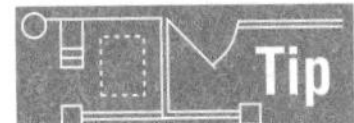

If you are working on just a single computer, not connected to your company's network, you can use the password `SQLNAV`. This makes remembering some of these accounts easy. If you are on a network with other computers, however, consult your DBA for any password standards that might be employed in your environment.

The first time you use SQL Navigator, it prompts you for an authorization key. Use 0-87046-52525-03384-65124, or you can contact Quest Software (800-306-9329) for a 30-day trial key. If the key is entered successfully, you should get the default SQL Navigator screen (see Figure A.23).

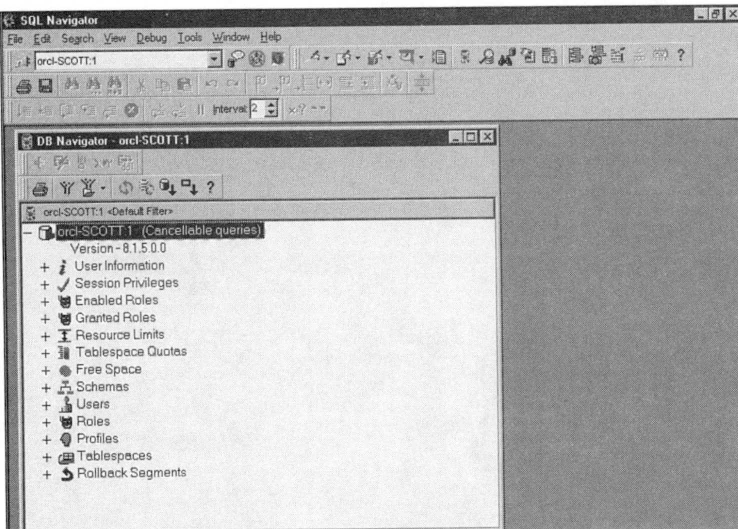

Figure A.23

Quest Software's SQL Navigator.

Installing Quest SQLab/Xpert

The SQLab/Xpert installation is very similar to that of SQL Navigator. Start the installation process via the Windows Navigator by double-clicking the SQLab downloaded file. Make sure this is the version of the software you were expecting and click Next. Select the installation directory on your computer and click Next. Figure A.24 illustrates some installation Options. The desktop icon makes SQLab easy to start. If you have room on your hard disk for the documentation files, select this option. The server-side installation needs to be done before the SQLab software can be used. If you choose to perform this step at a later time, it can be accessed through the Start menu. Make your selections and click Next to continue. The SQLab software is now installed. This process takes about five minutes.

Figure A.24

SQLab installation options.

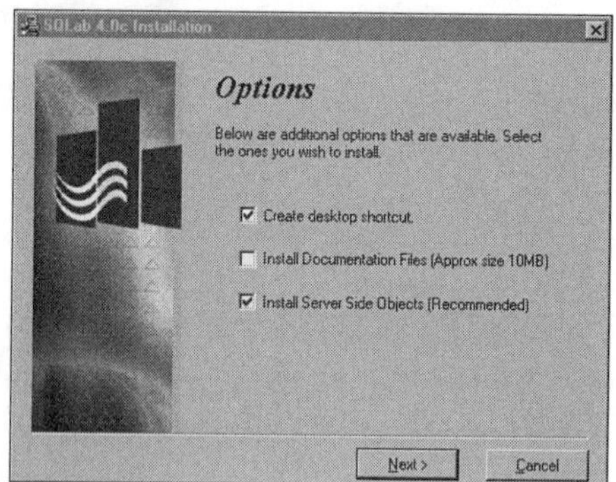

After the software installation process is complete, the server-side installation wizard appears. Use the SYSTEM account and the Sales Tracking database in the connection window. Figure A.25 illustrates some additional options, which include granting SQLab permissions to users (be sure to include the `Sales_Tracking` user account) and selecting a tablespace with enough room for the SQLab repository.

Figure A.25

Server-side installation options.

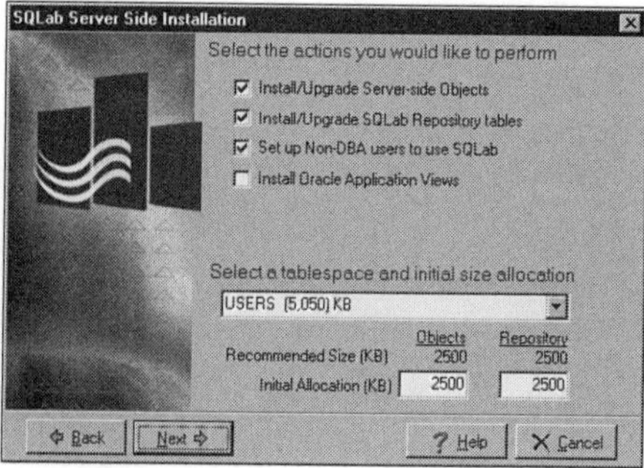

The first time SQLab is accessed, it also prompts you for an authorization key. Use 5-41970-11703-36883-00734, or you can contact Quest Software (800-306-9329) for a 30-day trial key. If the key is entered successfully, you should get the default SQL Navigator screen.

Installing Quest Instance Monitor

The Instance Monitor installation is very similar to that of the other Quest Software products. Start the installation process via the Windows Navigator by double-clicking the Instance Monitor downloaded file. Make sure this is the version of the software you were expecting and click Next to continue. Select the installation directory on your computer on the next screen and select whether you want the installation process to create an icon on your Windows desktop. Click Install when done making selections. The Instance Monitor software is now be installed. This process takes about five minutes.

Quest Instance Monitor will be called Spotlight for Oracle beginning July 2000.

The first time Instance Monitor is accessed, it prompts you for an authorization key. Use 4-14463-84074-26230-15295, or you can contact Quest Software (800 306-9329) for a 30-day trial key. If the key is entered successfully, you should get the Instance Monitor User Setup Wizard. Enter the database connection string and the SYSTEM account login information. Click Next and select Create a new account. Figure A.26 illustrates the options available on this screen. The two check box options are self-explanatory; be careful with the Alter System option because this will give this user account the authority to kill Oracle processes.

Figure A.26

Instance monitor user setup.

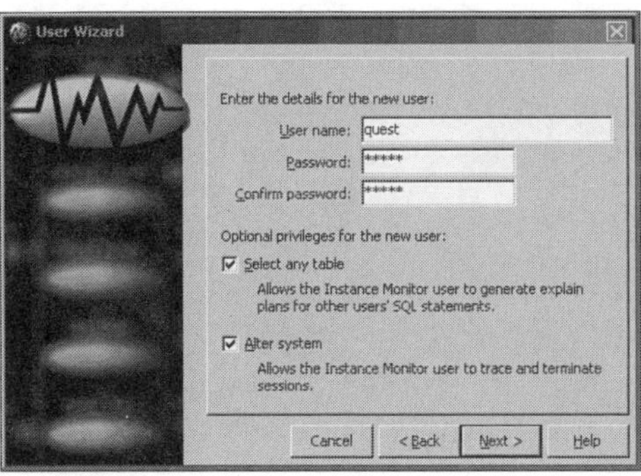

Complete the installation process by selecting a tablespace for the Instance Monitor objects. If the installation is successful, you should get a screen that looks similar to Figure A.27.

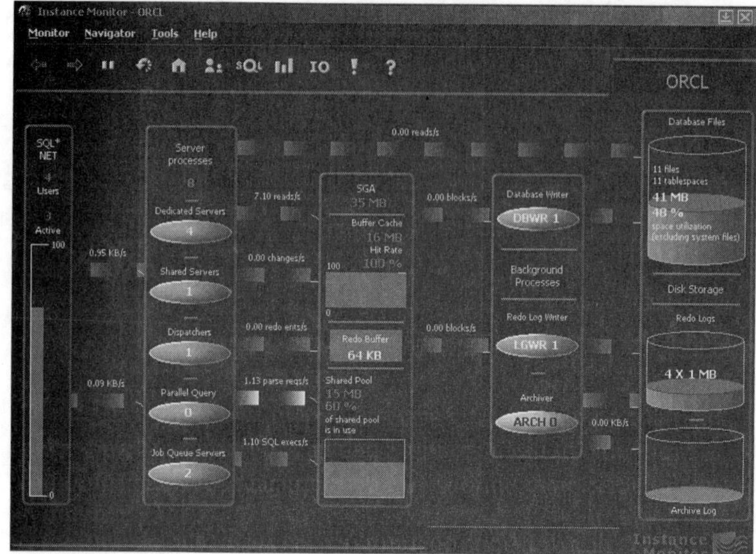

Figure A.27

Quest Software Instance Monitor.

Summary

This appendix covered the installation of all products used in this book. Trial Oracle software can be found by registering for the Oracle Technical Network (`http://otn.oracle.com`), and the Quest Software products can be found on `www.quest.com`.

This appendix discussed the Oracle8i architecture to give you a good understanding of the various processes involved with the Oracle database. Hopefully this was good groundwork to better understand some of the Oracle8i installation terminology, as well as assist in understanding some of the choices that need to be made during the installation process.

Appendix B

In this appendix

- *SQL History*
- *Log In to the Database*
- *The SQL Editor*
- *Introduction to SQL*
- *Advanced SQL Queries*

Learning SQL—A Complete Tutorial

SQL History

Oracle8i is a relational database. All relational databases are based on SQL (Structured Query Language). Therefore, the better you understand SQL, the more productive you can be in the relational world.

SQL actually has three distinct parts: the query language, or `SELECT`; the data manipulation language (DML) that comprises the `UPDATE` and `DELETE` commands; and the data definition language (DDL) that has the `ALTER`, `CREATE`, `RENAME`, and `DROP` commands. Several various other commands perform specific functions, such as `COMMIT`, which tells Oracle that this is desired information and to save it to the database, and `ROLLBACK`, which tells Oracle to discard the changes made by the last SQL statement prior to a `COMMIT`. In addition, a series of commands controls permissions and security, such as `GRANT`, `REVOKE`, and `AUDIT; the data control language (DCL)`. Other SQL commands include `LOCK` and `VALIDATE`.

In this appendix, you will learn the basics of SQL, as well as useful SQL*Plus SQL formatting commands.

Log In to the Database

The syntax conventions used in this book are that words in all uppercase indicate SQL syntax and words in lowercase indicate user-supplied information. Additionally, SQL formatting always places `SELECT`, `FROM`, `WHERE`, `ORDER BY`, and `GROUP BY` on separate lines. SQL syntax enclosed in brackets ([ ]) is optional, and any uppercase SQL syntax that is underlined is the default behavior if no option is specified.

> SQL*Plus is the standard SQL interface to Oracle8i. SQL*Plus is used for ad hoc queries, character-mode/script reporting, and character-mode/script database administration.

Several ways are available to invoke SQL*Plus, the character-mode, SQL-processing utility of Oracle8i. The first method discussed is from a command line. The command line can take the following syntax:

```
sqlplus <userid>/<password>@<dblink> <sqlplus file name> <sqlplus input
variables...>
```

The command line can also take any minimal amount of options, starting from the left of the command. For example, just entering the command `SQLPLUS` starts SQL*Plus and prompts you for a user ID and password. If the SQL*Plus file name option is given with the username and password options, SQL*Plus is started and the SQL and SQL*Plus syntax in the file (called a SQL*Plus script) are processed, passing any of the command-line options listed as well. If the SQL*Plus file name option is used and the username and password are omitted, the first line in the sqlplus file must be a valid username and password (in the format username/password, on a line by itself). See Figure B.1. Figure B.2 shows the SQL*Plus command-line method with supplied username and password.

Figure B.1

*SQL*Plus command-line method prompting for user ID and password.*

```
Command Prompt - sqlplus

C:\>sqlplus

SQL*Plus: Release 8.1.5.0.0 - Production on Thu Dec 30 15:53:07 1999

(c) Copyright 1999 Oracle Corporation.  All rights reserved.

Enter user-name: scott
Enter password:

Connected to:
Oracle8i Enterprise Edition Release 8.1.5.0.0 - Production
With the Partitioning and Java options
PL/SQL Release 8.1.5.0.0 - Production

SQL>
```

The command prompt method can be used on any platform that supports Oracle. In the Windows NT environment, open a DOS window (DOS Prompt from the Start Menu) and enter the command `sqlplus`.

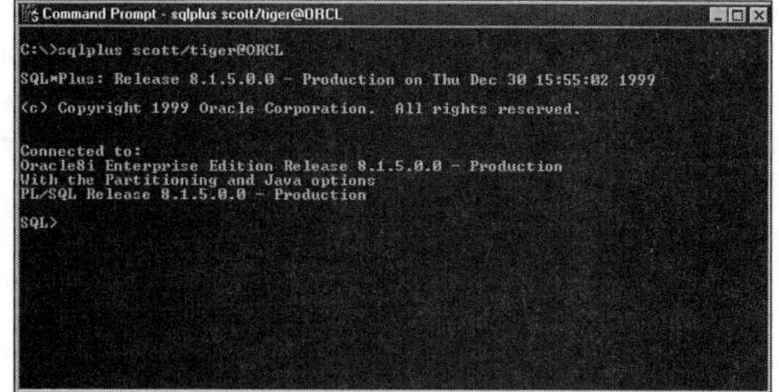

Figure B.2

*SQL*Plus command-line method with user ID and password on the command line.*

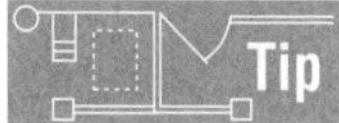

Windows and UNIX both can record a default Oracle System Identifier (sid) that is used when the Host String box is left blank. Oracle always needs to know which database to log in to. In the case of a single Oracle instance on a single Windows NT workstation, you can always leave the host string blank and accept the Oracle default that was set at installation time.

The SQL Editor

The SQL buffer is a work area assigned to the SQL*Plus environment. This buffer contains only SQL or PL/SQL syntax. The contents of this buffer can be loaded, saved, and manipulated with the following commands.

PL/SQL—Pronounced *P-L-S-Q-L*; is an Oracle8i procedural language with SQL embedded in it. This gives the user the ability to perform various tasks based on row-at-a-time or result set processing of the SQL. PL/SQL is useful for performing looping functions and in-depth calculations based on a variety of variables and other tables.

`A or APPEND new text`

The previous command appends text to the end of the current line of the SQL buffer.

`C or CHANGE/target text/new text/`

This command changes the `target text` to the `new text` on the current line in the SQL buffer.

`DEL`

This syntax deletes the current line in the SQL buffer.

`EDIT filename`

The previous syntax uses an operating-system–dependent text editor. To edit the SQL buffer with an operating-system–dependent text editor, simply leave off the *`filename`*. The default editor in Windows NT/95/98 is Notepad (see Figure B.3); in all UNIX environments the default editor is vi. This default editor can be changed in the Windows environments with the `regedit` command (REGEDIT, HKEY_LOCAL_MACHINE, SOFTWARE, Oracle) or by editing the `.profile` file on UNIX.

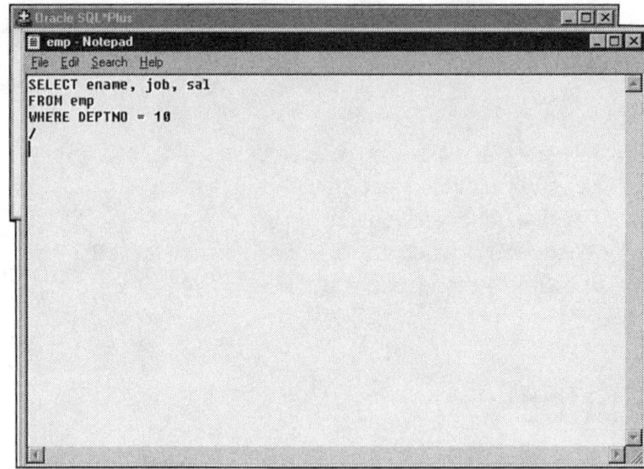

Figure B.3
SQL buffer Notepad editing session.

`GET` *`filename`*

The previous command reads an operating-system–dependent file into the SQL buffer. This command can be used in conjunction with the `EDIT` command to place the contents of the operating-system file editing back into the SQL Buffer (see Figure B.3).

`I` `or` **`INPUT`** *`text`*

This adds the text after the current line in the SQL buffer.

`L` `or` **`LIST`** *`number`* `OR` *`nn nn`*

This syntax displays the contents of the SQL buffer. When the *`number`* syntax is used, `LIST` displays the line number and makes that line the current line in the SQL buffer. The *`nn nn`* option lists the range of lines between the two numbers. `LIST` has been repeatedly demonstrated in this section.

`SAVE` *`filename`*

The previous syntax saves the contents of the SQL buffer to an operating-system–dependent file.

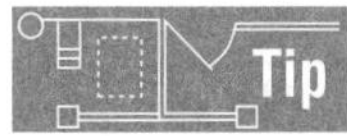

When creating SQL*Plus command files, use these editing features to arrive at the query results desired: SAVE to the operating system, and then edit that file with EDIT to add the formatting and other desired features.

B

START filename param1 param2 ... or @filename param1 param2...

START executes the contents of the SQL*Plus command file named in *filename* and passes any input parameters to the SQL*Plus command file. The difference between START and GET is that GET reads the contents of an operating-system file and places the contents in the SQL buffer. START does the same thing but also executes the contents of the SQL buffer. @ has the same functionality as START.

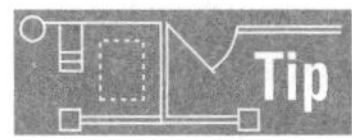

This START feature is used when creating the Sales Tracking tablespaces and the Sales Tracking tables and indexes covered in-depth in Chapter 2, "Building the Sales Tracking Application Database." I have used this command to create INSTALL.SQL scripts used to implement application objects.

/ (forward slash)

The slash is used to execute whatever is in the SQL buffer. This is a convenient way to execute SQL statements in a SQL script file where START is used to run the whole script. The / immediately follows the SQL statement on the next line.

Introduction to SQL

The remainder of this appendix is broken up into various sections, with each section covering important parts of the SQL language. Each section builds on knowledge gained from the prior section. You learn how to create SQL queries; create tables, indexes, and various database objects; set the correct SQL permissions; and learn the basics of SQL*Plus reporting. This SQL primer helps you understand the syntax used to create the Sales Tracking Application table, index, triggers, and referential integrity.

The DESCRIBE command is useful for showing the column names and attributes of specific tables. This same information can be viewed by selecting from user_tab_columns. DESCRIBE, or DESC for short, is easy to remember and gives just the column names and types. These types are covered in detail in the "Creating Tables" section later in this appendix.

VARCHAR2(nn) is a variable length character field, where *nn* is the maximum length. CHAR(nn) is a fixed length character field, and NUMBER(nn,dd) is a numeric field where *nn* is the total length of the field, and, if defined, *dd* is the number of decimal positions. The field TYPEs is covered in the section "Creating Objects with SQL" later in this appendix.

Tables EMP/DEPT Setup

We will use the Oracle demo tables EMP and DEPT throughout this appendix. These tables are synonymous with the Oracle database; they too have been present since at least the Oracle v.4 days. These tables have a minimal amount of data and columns and are therefore perfect for a learning exercise.

Log in to SQL*Plus using the user ID `SCOTT` with a password of `TIGER`. If SQL*Plus complains that this is not a valid user, log in to SQL*Plus as `SYSTEM` and `start` the script `<oracle home>\sqlplus\demo\demobld.sql`. If you want to reset the EMP and DEPT tables to their original state, run the script `demodrop.sql` found in the same operating-system directory and then run `demobld.sql`. Figure B.4 illustrates an NT directory listing showing these two files and the SQL*Plus syntax necessary to run them.

Scott Bruce was one of the early developers working for Oracle Corp. It is believed that *TIGER* was his pet cat!

Figure B.4

Creating EMP/DEPT Oracle tutorial tables.

```
Command Prompt - sqlplus system/manager@ORCL

 Directory of C:\Oracle8\Ora815\sqlplus\demo

12/29/99  11:00p        <DIR>          .
12/29/99  11:00p        <DIR>          ..
01/17/99  03:45p                 2,886 demobld.SQL
01/17/99  03:46p                   477 demodrop.SQL
               4 File(s)          3,363 bytes
                          1,474,539,520 bytes free

C:\Oracle8\Ora815\sqlplus\demo>
C:\Oracle8\Ora815\sqlplus\demo>
C:\Oracle8\Ora815\sqlplus\demo>sqlplus system/manager@ORCL

SQL*Plus: Release 8.1.5.0.0 - Production on Thu Dec 30 16:39:04 1999

(c) Copyright 1999 Oracle Corporation.  All rights reserved.


Connected to:
Oracle8i Enterprise Edition Release 8.1.5.0.0 - Production
With the Partitioning and Java options
PL/SQL Release 8.1.5.0.0 - Production

SQL> start demobld.sql
```

Learning the Basics

The base syntax of a query uses the SQL key words `SELECT`, `FROM`, and `WHERE`. You will also learn the additional syntax `GROUP BY`, `HAVING`, and `ORDER BY`, which is used to control how the rows are returned from a table:

```
SELECT * or column name [alias] [, column name [alias] [,
...][function][arithmetic expression]
FROM table name [, table_name [,...] or [sub-query]
[WHERE [conditional statement] or [sub-query]]
```

Let's begin with the simplest SQL query in the book: `SELECT * FROM emp` (see Figure B.5).

Figure B.5

The simplest SQL query.

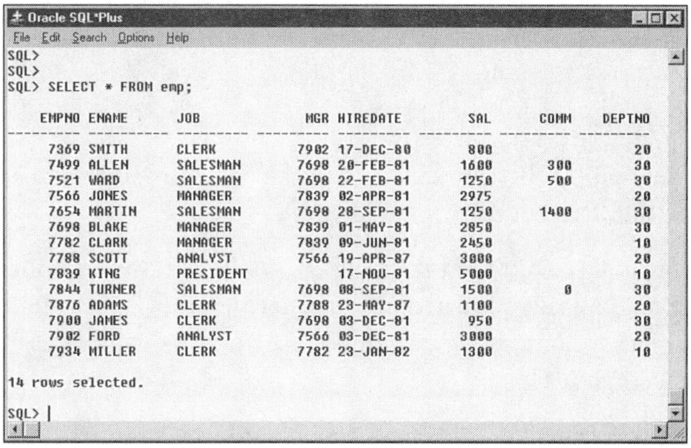

```
Oracle SQL*Plus
File Edit Search Options Help
SQL>
SQL>
SQL> SELECT * FROM emp;

    EMPNO ENAME      JOB             MGR HIREDATE         SAL      COMM    DEPTNO
--------- ---------- --------- --------- --------- --------- --------- ---------
     7369 SMITH      CLERK          7902 17-DEC-80        800                  20
     7499 ALLEN      SALESMAN       7698 20-FEB-81       1600       300        30
     7521 WARD       SALESMAN       7698 22-FEB-81       1250       500        30
     7566 JONES      MANAGER        7839 02-APR-81       2975                  20
     7654 MARTIN     SALESMAN       7698 28-SEP-81       1250      1400        30
     7698 BLAKE      MANAGER        7839 01-MAY-81       2850                  30
     7782 CLARK      MANAGER        7839 09-JUN-81       2450                  10
     7788 SCOTT      ANALYST        7566 19-APR-87       3000                  20
     7839 KING       PRESIDENT           17-NOV-81       5000                  10
     7844 TURNER     SALESMAN       7698 08-SEP-81       1500         0        30
     7876 ADAMS      CLERK          7788 23-MAY-87       1100                  20
     7900 JAMES      CLERK          7698 03-DEC-81        950                  30
     7902 FORD       ANALYST        7566 03-DEC-81       3000                  20
     7934 MILLER     CLERK          7782 23-JAN-82       1300                  10

14 rows selected.

SQL> |
```

The basic syntax of a `SELECT` statement works like this: `SELECT` all columns (by using an `*`) or specifically named columns `WHERE` certain conditions exist or do not exist. This `WHERE` clause can even contain another SQL query.

Single or multiple columns can be selected from a table by specifying the column name after the `SELECT` clause. Each additional column must be separated by a comma, however.

The `WHERE` clause limits the number of rows returned, or returns only certain rows.

Because Oracle8i is a relational database, tables are easily related to other tables by using the `WHERE` clause. Columns with the same data type (or using a function to change the data type discussed in the advanced queries later in this appendix) can easily be related to select columns from two or more tables that have related data. Figure B.6 shows how related data is retrieved from both the EMP and DEPT tables. When joined tables have columns with the same name, column references must be qualified to indicate to which table columns belong. Notice line 4 in Figure B.6 where emp.deptno and dept.deptno are related together.

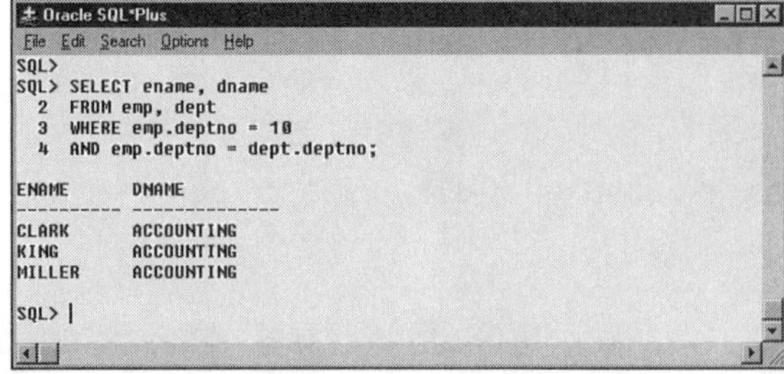

Figure B.6

A simple join between two tables.

SQL Queries

Building on this basic knowledge of the SQL language, you can learn to manipulate the output from queries.

When rows are returned from a SQL statement, they do not have a particular order. They are basically returned in the order that they appear in the underlying Oracle data blocks. There is no guarantee that the rows will be returned in the order that they were inserted.

Therefore, the `ORDER BY` command is used to guarantee a particular order for the rows. The left screen in Figure B.7 shows rows returned from EMP in a random order, and the right screen shows the rows ordered by ename.

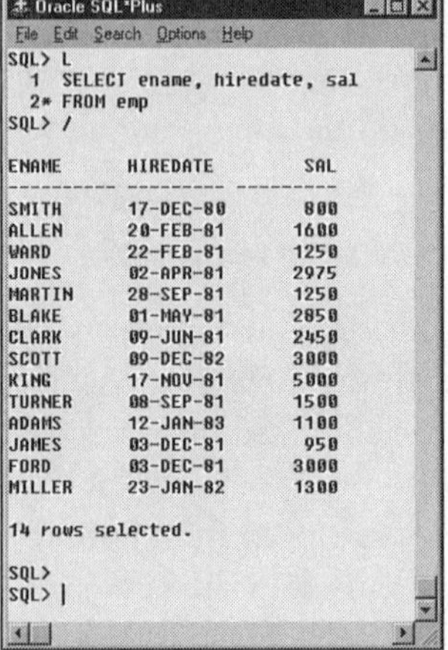


```
SQL> L
  1  SELECT ename, hiredate, sal
  2  FROM emp
  3* ORDER BY ename
SQL> /

ENAME      HIREDATE        SAL
---------- --------- ---------
ADAMS      12-JAN-83      1100
ALLEN      20-FEB-81      1600
BLAKE      01-MAY-81      2850
CLARK      09-JUN-81      2450
FORD       03-DEC-81      3000
JAMES      03-DEC-81       950
JONES      02-APR-81      2975
KING       17-NOV-81      5000
MARTIN     28-SEP-81      1250
MILLER     23-JAN-82      1300
SCOTT      09-DEC-82      3000
SMITH      17-DEC-80       800
TURNER     08-SEP-81      1500
WARD       22-FEB-81      1250

14 rows selected.

SQL>
```

Figure B.7

Random order of rows from EMP and the EMP with `ORDER BY ename`.

You can use `ORDER BY` in various ways. One of the options is to use either `DESCENDING` or `ASCENDING`. The default behavior of `ORDER BY` is `ASCENDING`. The `DESCENDING` option, though, is handy when the highest number is desired first in the list. The order of the columns in the `SELECT` part of the SQL statement can be used as well on the `ORDER BY` line.

You also have various ways to select specific rows. Previously, we discussed how to use the `WHERE` clause to limit the rows returned and how to join two tables (refer to Figure B.6).

Oracle8i supports the whole set of equality and inequality operators:

`=`	Equal to
`!=` or `<>`	Not equal
`>`	Greater than
`<`	Less than
`>=`	Greater than or equal to
`<=`	Less than or equal to

Oracle8i also supports the following SQL syntax:

`IN` (list)	Is equal to any item in the list
`BETWEEN`	Is greater than or equal to *and* less than or equal to
`LIKE %`	Matches parts of character strings
`IS NULL`	Matches on the non-existence of data
`NOT` (previous operators)	Reverses the operation

Some of these options are more efficient for Oracle8i to process than others; this is the topic of discussion in Chapter 6, "Tuning the Sales Tracking Application." Figure B.8 shows the `BETWEEN` operator.

Figure B.8

The `BETWEEN` operator.

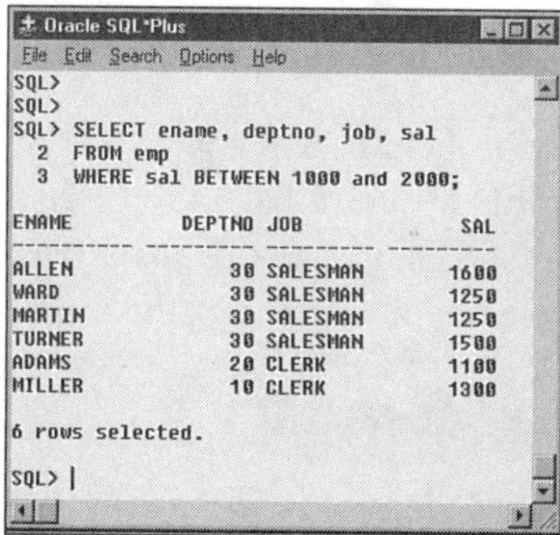

The left screen of Figure B.9 shows the `LIKE` command being used to find all names that end in `S`. The right screen shows how to find names that have `L` in the third and forth positions of the name. Notice that `%` is similar to a global character in that it will skip any number of characters where _ tells Oracle8i to accept anything in a single position.

Figure B.9

The `LIKE` *command finding a trailing* `S` *and* `LIKE` *finding names with* `LL`.

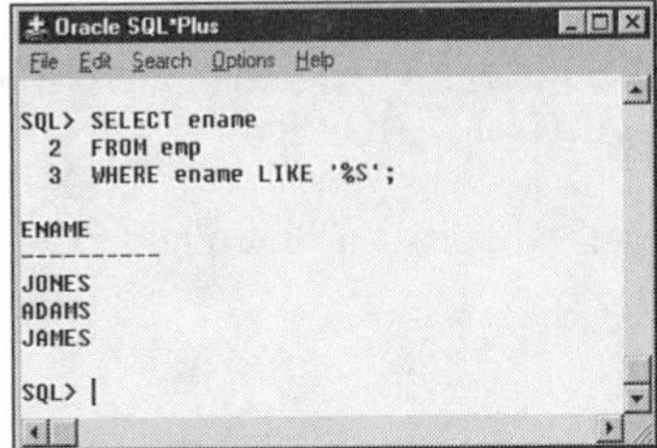

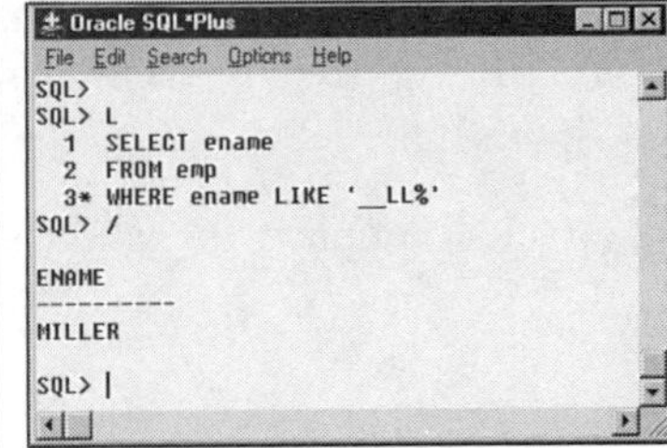

Fields that do not have a value are *not* blank or zero, they are `NULL`, or they have no value assigned. You must use the `NULL` operator to test for the condition of no value in a field. Figure B.10 shows the EMP table's commission field. Note that one row has a `0` commission and several fields have nothing displayed.

Figure B.10

`SELECT FROM emp` *showing the commissions field.*

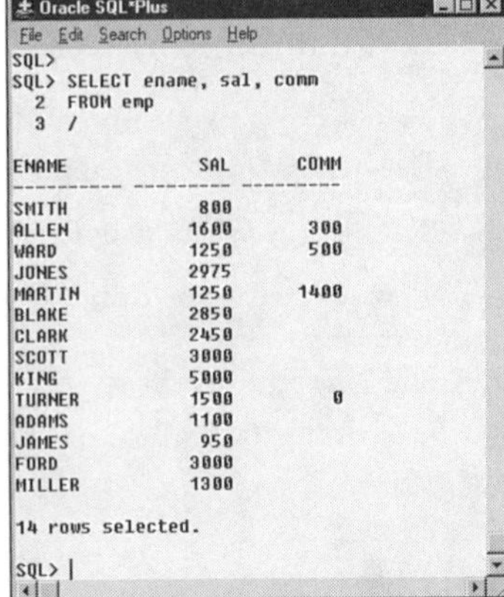

Figure B.11 selects the commission field that is equal to `0`; notice that it found the single row with a `0` commission field. Figure B.12 shows that 10 rows are returned when selecting the commission field that is `NULL`. This proves the previous statement that in regard to numeric fields, `0` and `NULL` are not the same.

Figure B.11

Selecting `WHERE COMM = 0`.

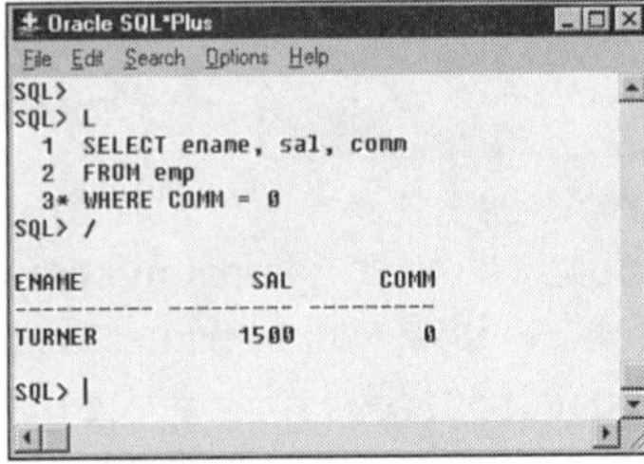

Figure B.12

Selecting `WHERE COMM IS NULL`.

```
SQL> c/= 0/IS NULL/
  3* WHERE COMM IS NULL
SQL> L
  1  SELECT ename, sal, comm
  2  FROM emp
  3* WHERE COMM IS NULL
SQL> /

ENAME            SAL      COMM
---------- --------- ---------
SMITH            800
JONES           2975
BLAKE           2850
CLARK           2450
SCOTT           3000
KING            5000
ADAMS           1100
JAMES            950
FORD            3000
MILLER          1300

10 rows selected.

SQL>
```

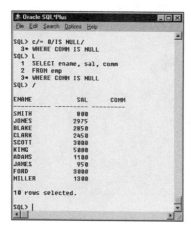

Oracle8i also supports arithmetic operations, which are supported in various parts of a SQL statement, including the `SELECT`, `WHERE`, and `ORDER BY` clauses. Parentheses (`( )`) can be used to control the order of evaluation. For example, `4 * SAL + COMM` does not produce the same results as `4 * (SAL + COMM)`.

Figure B.13 shows various ways to use calculations in a SQL statement. Notice that you can use constants and table columns, such as `(sal * .05)`, or just table columns against table columns. Later when you learn more about joins, you can perform calculations with data from different tables.

Figure B.13

Using calculations in SQL statements.

```
SQL>
SQL>
SQL> SELECT ename, sal, comm, sal * .05
  2  FROM emp
  3  WHERE comm > sal * .05
  4  /

ENAME            SAL      COMM   SAL*.05
---------- --------- --------- ---------
ALLEN           1600       300        80
WARD            1250       500      62.5
MARTIN          1250      1400      62.5

SQL>
```

In addition, multiple conditions can be specified to satisfy the required results. The two main operators are `AND`, which adds additional selection criteria, and `OR`, which separates that selection from one condition or another.

Parentheses (`( )`) can be used to control the order of evaluation. Notice the differences in Figures B.14 and B.15. In this example, the user wants to choose the managers and salespeople in department 30. Figure B.14 does not provide the correct results (notice that a dept 10 and dept 20 show up in the result set), but when parentheses are added in Figure B.15, the correct results are returned.

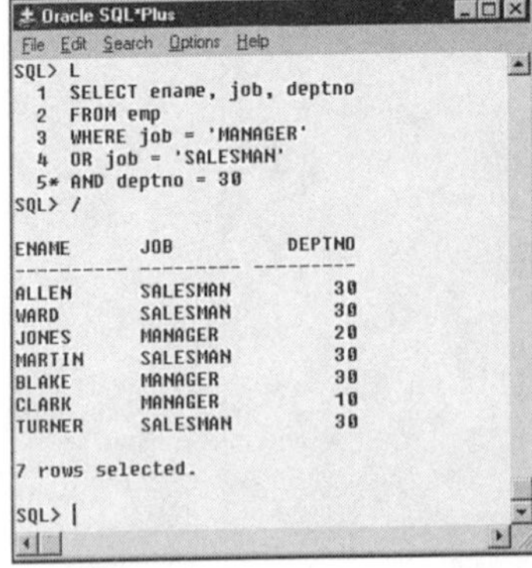

Figure B.14

Using AND *and* OR *in a SQL statement.*

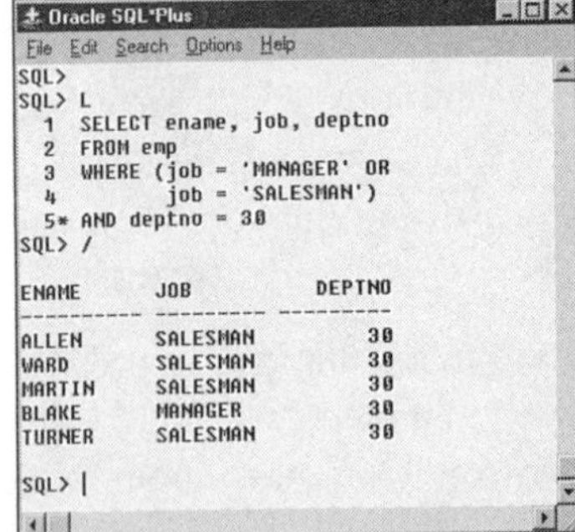

Figure B.15

Using AND *and* OR *in a SQL statement with parentheses.*

SQL Data Manipulation

The SQL language is used to make changes to the data within the tables. This is referred to as *Data Manipulation Language (DML) statements*. Three basic DML statements are available in the SQL language: `INSERT`, `UPDATE`, and `DELETE`.

`INSERT` statements are used to add records to tables. The user must have `UPDATE` privileges to the objects they will be performing DML against. These privileges will be discussed in detail in Chapter 4, "Basic Oracle8i Administration Tasks." The `DESCRIBE` command is also very useful when adding records to an object.

The `INSERT` statement has three basic formats: inserting data into all columns of a table; inserting just a single column or a subset of the columns; and using a `SELECT` statement to select data from another table.

You will learn more about creating tables later in this chapter, but for now, please type in the following command to create a table for use in the next series of examples: `CREATE TABLE test_ch3 (num_field number(5), char_field char(10), date_field date);` (see Figure B.16).

Figure B.16

Creating an example table.

```
Oracle SQL*Plus
File Edit Search Options Help
SQL>
SQL>
SQL>
SQL> CREATE TABLE test_ch3 (num_field number(5), char_field char(10),
  2  date_field date);

Table created.

SQL> |
```

B

The first INSERT format inserts values for each of the columns of a table. If a value for a column does not exist, use the NULL operator to insert a null value. Figure B.17 shows a series of steps for inserting data. The first step is to perform a DESCRIBE of the table to make sure the correct field attributes are used. The first INSERT shows inserting all columns, and the second INSERT shows inserting NULL values and a field called SYSDATE.

Figure B.17

Inserting data into TEST_CH3.

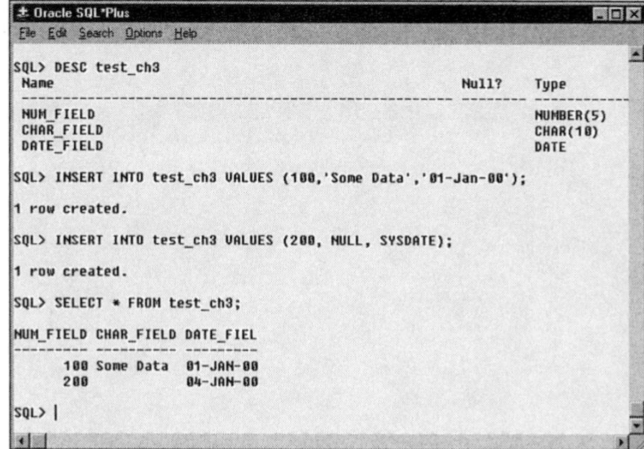

SYSDATE—An Oracle value that always contains the current computer system date and time.

Quotes are necessary to tell Oracle8i that the data within is either character data or a date field. Numeric fields, in contrast, do not need quotes. The default date format is DD-MON-YY and can be changed by the DBA. Check with your DBA if you are unsure of the default date format being used at your company.

Oracle8i is Y2K compliant. When inserting a date of 01-JAN-00, Oracle8i interprets this as the year 2000, not the year 1900.

SQL*Plus supports the use of substitution variables. You will learn more about these in the "Oracle SQL*Plus for Reports" section in Chapter 3, "Building the Sales Tracking Application Forms and Reports." With substitution variables, the user is prompted for each field that begins with an ampersand (&). However, the && prompt the user only once for a value. Figure B.18 demonstrates how these substitution variables work when inserting data into the TEST_CH3 table. Notice that if the substitution variable is not enclosed in quotes for character or date fields, the quotes must be provided with the data. This technique of using substitution variables is a quick way to repeatedly add data to a table. The name of the substitution variable can be anything. The more descriptive the name is, though, the less likely that errors will occur when using this method.

Substitution variables are also very useful in SQL*Plus Reporting, also discussed in this appendix.

Figure B.18

Inserting data into TEST_CH3 using substitution variables.

```
Oracle SQL*Plus
File Edit Search Options Help
SQL>
SQL> INSERT INTO test_ch3 VALUES (&Num_Fld,&&Char_Fld,'&Date_Fld');
Enter value for num_fld: 400
Enter value for char_fld: 'Once'
Enter value for date_fld: 10-JAN-00
old   1: INSERT INTO test_ch3 VALUES (&Num_Fld,&&Char_Fld,'&Date_Fld')
new   1: INSERT INTO test_ch3 VALUES (400,'Once','10-JAN-00')

1 row created.

SQL> /
Enter value for num_fld: 500
Enter value for date_fld: 12-JAN-00
old   1: INSERT INTO test_ch3 VALUES (&Num_Fld,&&Char_Fld,'&Date_Fld')
new   1: INSERT INTO test_ch3 VALUES (500,'Once','12-JAN-00')

1 row created.

SQL> SELECT * FROM test_ch3;

NUM_FIELD CHAR_FIELD DATE_FIEL
--------- ---------- ---------
      100 Some Data  01-JAN-00
      200            04-JAN-00
      300 More Data
      400 Once       10-JAN-00
      500 Once       12-JAN-00

SQL> |
```

The final method for inserting data into a table is by using a query to select data from another table. This technique has many uses, including moving data from a *test environment* to a *production environment* and restoring data from a backup scheme. The SELECT clause must select the same number of columns, in the order listed in the VALUES clause, and be of the same data type as those columns listed in the VALUES clause. Figure B.19 shows how to populate the TEST_CH3 table with values from the EMP table.

Test environment—A computer environment whose sole purpose is to develop applications and test these new applications before deploying them to a production environment. This is a common practice.

Production environment—The computing environment used by the end users of these computer systems.

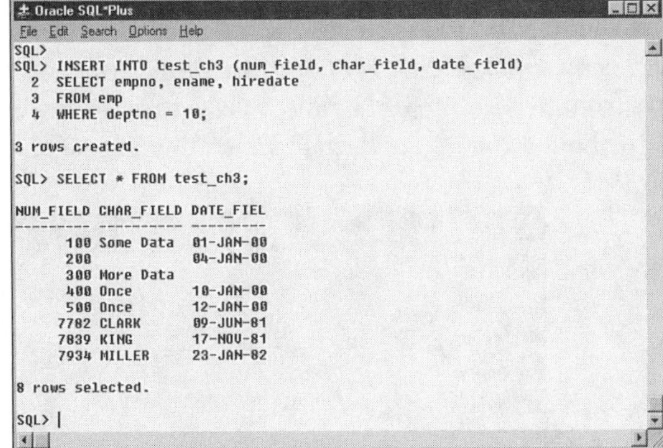

Figure B.19

Inserting data into TEST_CH3 using a SQL query.

UPDATE SQL statements are used to change existing data in the tables. The syntax of the update statement is: UPDATE <table name> SET <col name> = <value or result of a SQL statement> WHERE <conditional expression> (see Figure B. 20). If the WHERE clause is left off, UPDATE will apply the changes to all the rows in the table.

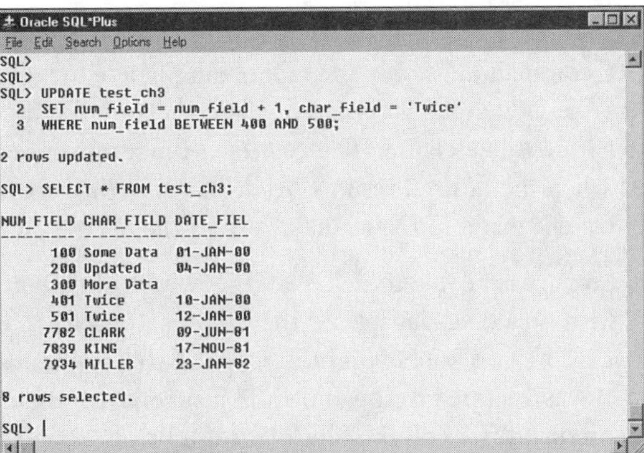

Figure B.20

UPDATE *Statement on Multiple Columns.*

The final DML SQL statement is the DELETE SQL command. Before deleting records from the database, be sure you are deleting the correct records and that you can put the records back if necessary. The COUNT(*) function can be used to run with the WHERE clause that is being considered for a DELETE statement. The other features that are useful when making changes to the database are COMMIT and ROLLBACK. COMMIT actually writes the requested changes to the Oracle8i database, whereas ROLLBACK enables you to undo any changes made before the COMMIT statement back to the last COMMIT statement. SQL*Plus also has a setting called AUTOCOMMIT. By default, AUTOCOMMIT is set to on. Figure B.21 shows a simple scenario that sets AUTOCOMMIT to off, deletes from the TEST_CH3 table, selects to show the empty table, performs ROLLBACK (without a COMMIT), and again shows the original data.

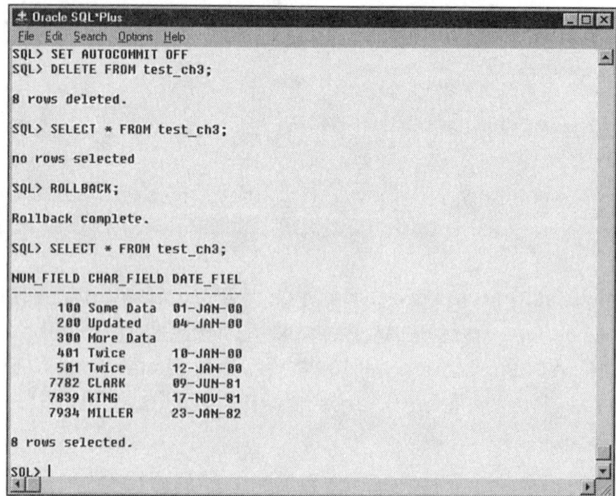

Figure B.21

COMMIT and ROLLBACK example.

The DELETE command has only the table being deleted from and, if some selectivity as to what is being deleted is required, a WHERE clause. Figure B.22 shows the DELETE command with a WHERE clause. The COUNT(*) function is used and shows four rows to be deleted when the desired result is to delete only three rows. Notice the subsequent adjustment made to the WHERE clause of the DELETE statement.

Two easy ways are available to delete all the rows from a table. The first is a DELETE command with no WHERE clause, and the other is a TRUNCATE command. The differences between the two are beyond the scope of this appendix, but put simply: DELETE leaves the blocks assigned to the table and just removes the rows, whereas the TRUNCATE command frees all the blocks for use by other objects. This might be desirable if the application calls for varying amounts of data to be temporarily stored in a table, used for reporting, and then removed. In this case, it would be better to truncate the table. Therefore, when all the rows are being removed from a table, it is invariably better to use the TRUNCATE command.

Figure B.22

The DELETE *command.*

```
Oracle SQL*Plus
File Edit Search Options Help
SQL>
SQL>
SQL> SELECT COUNT(*)
  2  FROM test_ch3
  3  WHERE num_field > 500;

 COUNT(*)
---------
        4

SQL> DELETE FROM test_ch3
  2  WHERE num_field > 501;

3 rows deleted.

Commit complete.
SQL> SELECT * FROM test_ch3;

NUM_FIELD CHAR_FIELD DATE_FIEL
--------- ---------- ---------
      100 Some Data  01-JAN-00
      200 Updated    04-JAN-00
      300 More Data
      401 Twice      10-JAN-00
      501 Twice      12-JAN-00

SQL> |
```

There is no concept of `COMMIT` or `ROLLBACK` with `TRUNCATE`! `TRUNCATE` overrides these safety features. See Figure B.23 for an illustration using `TRUNCATE` with `AUTOCOMMIT` set to off. Notice that all the rows are gone, even after the rollback.

Figure B.23

TRUNCATE *example.*

```
Oracle SQL*Plus
File Edit Search Options Help
SQL>
SQL> SET AUTOCOMMIT OFF
SQL> TRUNCATE TABLE test_ch3;

Table truncated.

SQL> ROLLBACK
  2  ;

Rollback complete.

SQL> SELECT * FROM test_ch3;

no rows selected

SQL> |
```

We are finished with the TEST_CH3 table. So, you can remove the TEST_CH3 table with the command `DROP TABLE test_ch3` when you are done with the examples in this section (see Figure B.24).

Figure B.24

Dropping the exercise table.

```
Oracle SQL*Plus
File Edit Search Options Help
SQL>
SQL>
SQL> DROP TABLE test_ch3;

Table dropped.

SQL>
SQL>
SQL>
```

Creating Objects with SQL

The SQL language is also used to create tables, indexes, and other structures. This is referred to as *Data Definition Language (DDL) statements.*

Database object—In Oracle8i terms, something that exists within the database with which users interact.

Several kinds of database objects are supported by Oracle8i, including the following:

- Tables
- Indexes
- Views
- Sequences
- User-defined data types
- Synonyms
- Clusters
- Constraints
- Tablespaces
- Partitions
- Triggers, packages, procedures, and functions

You will get a basic knowledge of creating tables, indexes, views, sequences, user-defined data types, synonyms, constraints, and tablespaces in this section. These topics will be discussed in depth in Chapter 2, as they pertain to the Sales Tracking Application.

Tables are the relational data storage unit in Oracle8i.

Indexes enable quick access to data within tables. *Index-organized tables* are both a table and an index combined.

Views are *logical* tables in that they act like tables but are really SQL queries. Views are useful in a number of ways, from security (hiding columns or data from certain types of users) to hiding complex SQL access methods from users. A view is accessed with SQL as if it were just a single table.

Sequences are a convenient method of generating sequential numbers. These numbers can be used either to ensure uniqueness of rows or any time an application needs some kind of sequential number.

User-defined data types are definable column attributes, other than the ones that Oracle8i supplies (in other words, number, date, character, and so on). These definable data types are convenient for recurring columns, such as a series of address fields. They are also part of Oracle8i's object-oriented features.

Synonyms provide an easy way to give a table a different or easier name. Synonyms can hide *qualification* and database links from end users.

Qualification—In relational terms, stating a table's full name when the same table name might occur in more than one *schema*. The EMP table's fully qualified name is scott.emp.

Schema—A term used to describe all database objects created by a particular user. Oracle8i creates a schema automatically when creating a user.

Clusters are a way of physically organizing two or more tables that have common key fields and are commonly referenced together in the same SQL statement.

Constraints are rules applied to the data in tables to ensure the accuracy of the data, the accuracy of the data in relation to other tables, and so on.

"*Tablespaces*" is a logical name for the physical operating system files assigned to Oracle8i. All data-oriented objects, such as tables and indexes, are assigned to a tablespace. You will learn how to direct objects to particular tablespaces for performance and organizational needs in Chapter 5, "Monitoring the Sales Tracking Application." Most non–data-oriented objects (such as views, constraints, and so on) are stored in the data dictionary, which is in the SYSTEM tablespace.

Partitions enable data-oriented objects to be split across tablespaces. Remember that physical files are assigned to tablespaces. So, partitioning enables very large tables (tables with millions of rows) to be spread out across several physical disk drives. Many reasons for doing this exist, including easier maintenance (backup and recovery) and performance enhancements.

Triggers, *packages*, *procedures*, and *functions* in Oracle8i can be coded in either PL/SQL or Java. You will learn both coding techniques in this book. They are basically code modules that are referenced by SQL or that occur due to an event—for example, a post-insert trigger on a table would execute the code assigned to it after a row is inserted into a table.

Figure B.25 shows the relationship between a table, a tablespace, and the physical operating system file storage. This example shows the EMP table being created in the C tablespace. The structure of the EMP table is stored in the SYSTEM tablespace in the Oracle8i data dictionary, and the data is stored in the *extent* in tablespace C. It also shows that the EMP tablespace contains one segment or extent that consists of four Oracle8i data blocks.

Figure B.25

Oracle8i object storage overview.

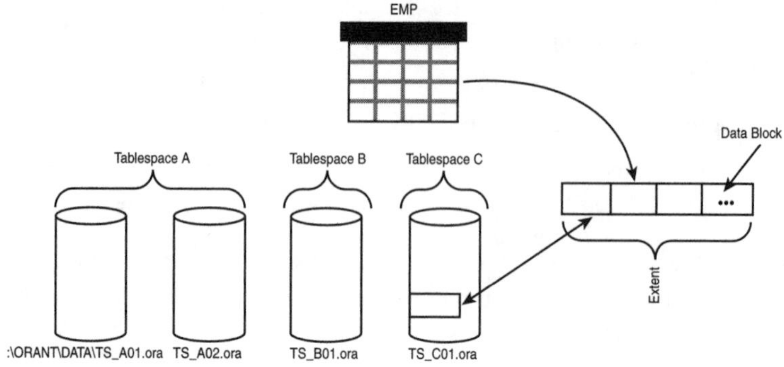

Chapter 1, "Introduction to Oracle8i and the Auto Sales Tracking Application," covers segments and extents. These terms in Oracle8i are basically synonymous with one another. Oracle8i defines a unit of storage as an extent, and this extent can control one or more data blocks.

Extent—A database block or series of contiguous database blocks assigned to the table or index to store rows in.

Creating Tables

The `CREATE TABLE` SQL statement is used to create tables. The basic syntax is as follows:

```
CREATE TABLE table_name (column data type [default expression][constraint][,
...])
[TABLESPACE tablespace name][STORAGE Clause];
```

The items between the `[ ]` are optional.

The `table_name` must be a unique name for this user. In addition, the user must have the `CREATE TABLE` or `CREATE ANY TABLE` privilege or the `RESOURCE` role. These privileges and roles are discussed in Chapter 4. The table name must begin with an alpha character; cannot be an Oracle8i reserved word (any SQL syntax, SQL*Plus command, and so on are all reserved words); and can contain only the character sets A–Z, a–z, or 0–9, or the characters _, $, or #.

The standard Oracle8i data types are as follows:

- CHAR(n)—Fixed-length character field up to 2,000 characters
- DATE—Date field; 1/1/4792 B.C. through 12/31/99 A.D.
- NUMBER(n,m)—Numeric field; up to 38 positions
- VARCHAR2(n)—Variable-length character field up to 4,000 characters

B

In the previous data types, n = length and m = decimal precision.

The large-object storage data types are

- LONG—Variable-length character field up to 2 *gigabytes*
- CLOB—Single-byte character field up to 4 gigabytes
- NLOB—*Double-byte* character field up to 4 gigabytes
- RAW (and LONG RAW)—Raw binary field up to 2,000 bytes
- BLOB—Binary field up to 4 gigabytes
- BFILE—Externally stored binary field up to 4 gigabytes

Gigabyte—A trillion bytes. A *byte* is a single unit of storage that can represent, for example, a character.

The Chinese/Japanese languages require *double-byte*, or two bytes of, storage to represent a single character.

Figure B.26 illustrates the `CREATE TABLE` command. Constraints such as `NOT NULL` in Figure B.26 will be discussed later in the section "Creating Tables." This table will be created in the USERS tablespace because this is the default tablespace assigned to the user SCOTT. However, we could have created the EMP table in a different tablespace by using the `TABLESPACE <tablespace name>` clause. Notice the `NOT NULL` constraint and the `DEFAULT` field value. When rows are inserted into this table, the first field must have a value because of the `NOT NULL` constraint, and the date field will contain the `SYSDATE` at the time of the insert if no other value is supplied.

Figure B.26

CREATE TABLE example.

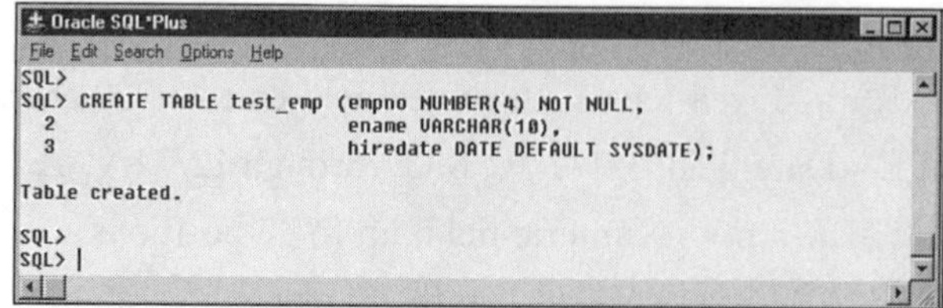

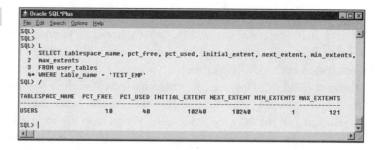

A number of data dictionary views will display all the information about this particular table:

- USER_TABLES—Shows information about the tables owned by the user.
- ALL_TABLES—Shows information about all the tables the user can access.
- DBA_TABLES—Only users with the DBA role can see these tables.

In Figure B.27 you can see a `SELECT` from this view showing the information stored in the Oracle8i data dictionary about our newly created TEST_EMP table. We are interested in only the physical attributes of the TEST_EMP table. Notice that the TEST_EMP table was in fact created in the USERS tablespace and that it also has some storage parameter values. Because we did not supply our TEST_EMP with a *storage clause*, these values were picked up from the default storage clause of the tablespace. When a storage clause is defined at the `CREATE TABLE` statement, it overrides the tablespace storage clause.

Storage clause—Tells Oracle8i how big to make the extents (how many Oracle data blocks to reserve at a time for data storage), how full to fill the blocks, and so on. The storage clause gives you incredible flexibility in the various data storage requirements for various tables and indexes.

Figure B.27

The SELECT FROM user_tables command.

```
SQL>
SQL>
SQL> L
  1  SELECT tablespace_name, pct_free, pct_used, initial_extent, next_extent, min_extents,
  2  max_extents
  3  FROM user_tables
  4* WHERE table_name = 'TEST_EMP'
SQL> /

TABLESPACE_NAME  PCT_FREE  PCT_USED INITIAL_EXTENT NEXT_EXTENT MIN_EXTENTS MAX_EXTENTS
---------------- --------- --------- -------------- ----------- ----------- -----------
USERS                   10        40          10240       10240           1         121

SQL> |
```

Figure B.27 shows the main storage clause fields: `PCT_FREE`, `PCT_USED`, `INITIAL_EXTENT`, `NEXT_EXTENT`, `MIN_EXTENTS`, and `MAX_EXTENTS`. `PCT_FREE` and `PCT_USED` are typically used together to tell Oracle8i how to allocate room in each of the data blocks. When working with these parameters, you must understand the nature of the data in the table. `PCT_FREE` determines the amount of empty space to leave behind in the block for the possibility of accommodating updates to the rows that might fill NULL fields or add length to existing VARCHAR2 fields. PCT_USED, on the other hand, determines when to begin using the block again for UPDATES after this percentage of space exists from deleting rows. In addition, INITIAL_EXTENT tells Oracle8i how many contiguous data blocks to assemble as a unit (EXTENT) and assign to this table. The INITIAL_EXTENT should be large enough to hold all the initial load of rows, as well as about three months of additional rows in the table. The flexibility here is a nice feature of Oracle. Reference tables, such as the abbreviations and names of the 50 states, not only will not change much but are relatively small in size. A table such as this would have PCT_FREE set to 1, and an INITIAL_EXTENT set to 1,000. Tables that hold a name and address list not only might change frequently, but might have growth over a period of time. The amount of space to leave free in each block (PCT_FREE) is really a factor of how many fields are not initially supplied data on the INSERT. The MIN_EXTENTS and MAX_EXTENTS tell Oracle how many extents this table or index might use. MIN_EXTENTS tells Oracle how many extents to initially allocate to the table, whereas MAX_EXTENTS is determined by the data block size used when initially creating an Oracle database. For example, a block size of 2,048 (2KB) has a MAX_EXTENTS of 121. Consult the *Oracle8i Database Administrator's Guide* for all the valid MAX_EXTENT settings. A new extent management command called UNLIMITED EXTENTS can replace the MAX_EXTENTS and enable tables and indexes to have as many extents as necessary. This feature can cause adverse performance issues but is useful for those very large applications with thousands of tables and indexes.

Figure B.28 shows creating a table and populating it with rows with a SQL statement is a good technique for creating test data or for moving tables and data from a test environment to a production environment. This technique is also helpful in making a copy of a table and its contents to refresh a test table quickly.

Figure B.28

CREATE TABLE AS example.

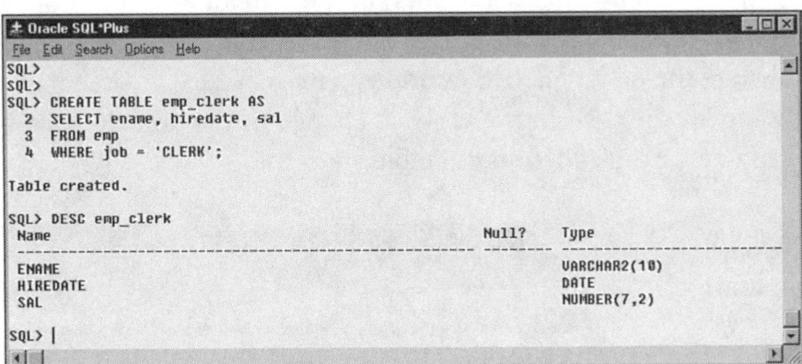

Oracle SQL*Plus
File Edit Search Options Help
SQL>
SQL>
SQL> CREATE TABLE emp_clerk AS
2 SELECT ename, hiredate, sal
3 FROM emp
4 WHERE job = 'CLERK';
Table created.
SQL> DESC emp_clerk
Name Null? Type
ENAME VARCHAR2(10)
HIREDATE DATE
SAL NUMBER(7,2)
SQL> |

SQL enables you to make changes to existing tables. The `ALTER TABLE` command, with the options `ADD`, `MODIFY`, and `DROP COLUMN`, can be used for this purpose. The SQL syntax looks like this:

```
ALTER TABLE table name ADD  (column datatype [default expression][constraint]

[,column datatype[default expression][constraint]][, ...]);
ALTER TABLE table name MODIFY (column datatype [default expression][constraint]
 [, column datatype [default expression][constraint]][, ...]);
ALTER TABLE table name DROP COLUMN column name;
```

The `ADD` column command adds a column or columns to the end of the existing table specs. Figure B.29 builds on a basic EMP_CLERK table by adding two fields. The same column specifications that we learned earlier in this section still apply.

Figure B.29

ALTER TABLE ADD column example.

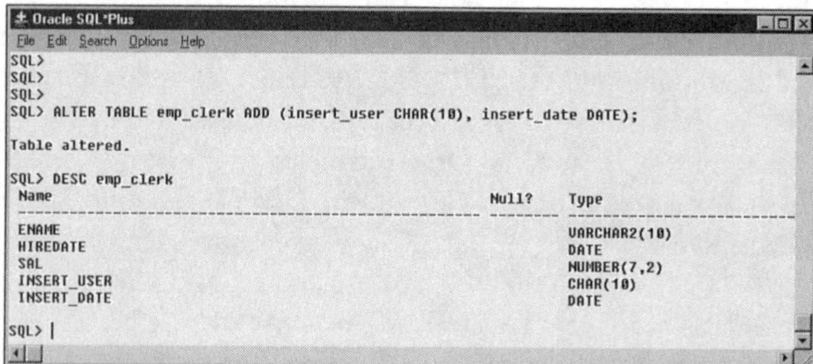

The `MODIFY` column command changes the column attributes of existing columns (see Figure B.30). This command can be used to increase the precision of a numeric field or increase the length of a CHAR or VARCHAR2 field. This command can also change a CHAR to a VARCHAR2 or VARCHAR2 to CHAR *if* either the column does not contain any rows or you are not changing the length of the field. You can decrease the size or precision of a field if the table contains no rows, and you can change the data type (for example, date to VARCHAR2) if the field contains no data in any of the rows in the table. A change to the default value of a column applies to only new rows added to the table.

Figure B.30

ALTER TABLE MODIFY column example.

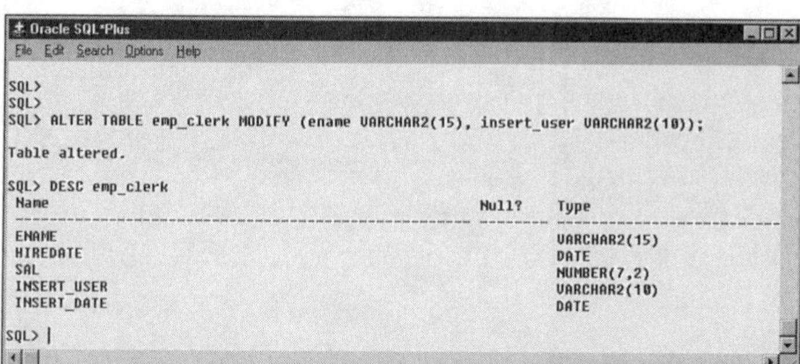

The DROP column command is new to Oracle8i. As the syntax implies, only one column can be dropped at a time, and the column being dropped cannot be the last or only column in the table. The column data is immediately deleted and the space is released to the data blocks to accommodate additional inserts or updates. Another option is to mark the column as UNUSED and then DROP the unused columns at a later time. The column data is not physically removed from the data blocks; however, there is no way to undrop a column. Both commands remove the column from future use. Both commands also allow the same column name to be immediately reused; however, note that this will be a new column, and any data associated with the dropped or unused column will no longer be available. The DROP UNUSED COLUMNS command is used to physically remove the column data from the table's data blocks.

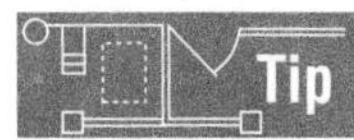

There is no undrop—a dropped column is unrecoverable. Use Oracle Export to make a backup copy of the table prior to the change in case a need arises to get the column and its data back.

The DROP TABLE <table name> command was briefly discussed in the previous section, but it is also quite easy to drop the table and its data. The DROP TABLE command removes the table and its columns from the data dictionary and returns its allocated data blocks back to the tablespace for use with other tables and indexes.

Creating Indexes

An index is a sorted list of commonly accessed data based on one or more columns from the associated table. This data is associated with the ROWID (discussed in Chapter 2), which is a pointer to the block that contains the particular row of data. Maintenance of an index is completely automatic. No difference exists in how the table is accessed or the rows returned whether a particular table column has an index or not. Indexes can be created and dropped with no effect on the table. The main reason for indexes is for faster retrieval of certain rows. This chapter discusses exactly why you would create indexes, how to control their use, and so on. A table column should have an index if the number of rows returned by placing a WHERE clause on the column is less than 5% of the number of rows in the entire table, the column is frequently used in join conditions with other tables, the column contains a wide variety of values, or the column has a large number of NULL values. A distinct trade-off of table insert and update performance exists, depending on the number of indexes on a particular table. In other words, don't create an index on every column of the table, especially if that table will have frequent inserts.

The basic syntax of the INDEX command is

```
CREATE [UNIQUE] INDEX index name ON TABLE table name
  (column name [, column name][, ...]) [TABLESPACE
  tablespace name][STORAGE parameters] ;
```

An index can be created on one or more columns. When the index contains more than one column, this is called a *composite key*. Indexes are automatically created when the PRIMARY KEY CONSTRAINT is specified. If the UNIQUE clause is specified, an error will be returned if you try to insert a row where the index column data already exists.

Indexes are automatically used when the indexed column is specified in the WHERE clause.

Figure B.31 shows the information available from the USER_INDEXES view about a new index or all indexes. Figure B.32, on the other hand, shows specific information from the USER_INDEXES and USER_IND_COLUMNS views. Notice that the new index was created in the USERS tablespace and that the new index is nonunique. Also, the primary key index is a unique index, which is one of the characteristics of a primary key.

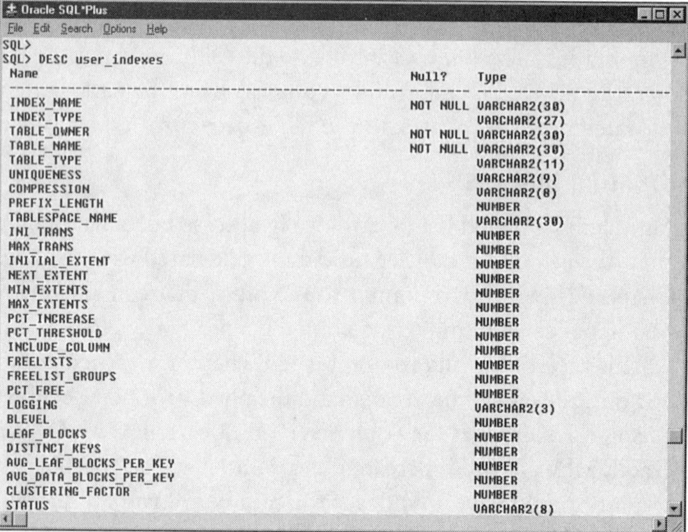

Figure B.31

Index information available from USER_INDEXES.

Creating Views

A view is a selection of one or more columns from one or more tables. A view is nothing more than a query that acts like a table. It does not store data, so it is not assigned to tablespaces and does not require storage parameters. It is simply a stored SQL statement in the Oracle8i Data Dictionary.

Figure B.32

Selecting from USER_INDEXES and USER_IND_COLUMNS.

```
Oracle SQL*Plus
File Edit Search Options Help
SQL>
SQL> SELECT index_name, uniqueness, tablespace_name
  2  FROM user_indexes
  3  WHERE table_name = 'EMP';

INDEX_NAME                     UNIQUENES TABLESPACE_NAME
------------------------------ --------- ------------------------------
EMP_HIREDATE                   NONUNIQUE USERS
PK_EMP                         UNIQUE    USERS

SQL> SELECT index_name,column_name,column_position
  2  FROM user_ind_columns
  3  WHERE table_name = 'EMP';

INDEX_NAME                     COLUMN_NAME     COLUMN_POSITION
------------------------------ --------------- ---------------
PK_EMP                         EMPNO                         1
EMP_HIREDATE                   HIREDATE                      1

SQL> |
```

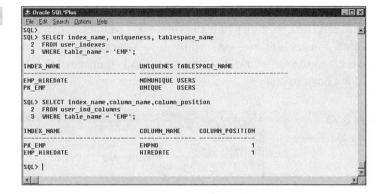

Views can be used to hide complex calculations from users (enabling simple SQL queries to gather complex calculated data), hide certain columns from some levels of users (a good human resource view would be one that displayed name, address, and hire information but not salary/bonus information), and so on.

Two types of views exist—the simple view that is associated with only one table and has no `GROUP BY` clause or functions in SQL and the complex view that is associated with two or more tables and contains functions or `GROUP BY` clauses. The main difference is that the simple view allows for DML, whereas the complex view does not.

All the `NOT NULL` columns must be present in the view to enable `INSERT` activity.

Perform all DML through the base table(s) and use views to restrict column access or provide ease of access to rather complex combinations of information.

The syntax for views is as follows:

```
CREATE [OR REPLACE] [FORCE|NOFORCE] VIEW view name AS sql query
➥[WITH CHECK OPTION] [WITH READ ONLY]
```

The `OR REPLACE` feature enables the same name of the view to be used again in a new (or replacement) view. Another option, the `FORCE|NOFORCE` option, enables a view to be created with or without the underlying tables actually existing. `NOFORCE` is the default behavior, requiring that the table exist before this view can be created. The SQL query can be any valid SQL select statement with an alias and so on. Aliases in views are a convenient way to change the names of the columns. `WITH CHECK OPTION` enables only DML commands on rows displayed by the view, and the `READ ONLY` option is a convenient way to inhibit any DML on this view at all.

Figure B.33 shows the creation of a view on the EMP table, naming the view EMPLOYEES. Notice how the view acts just like a table. This particular view gives users and applications access to the information they need but does not allow them access to the sometimes sensitive salary and compensation information they probably don't need to see.

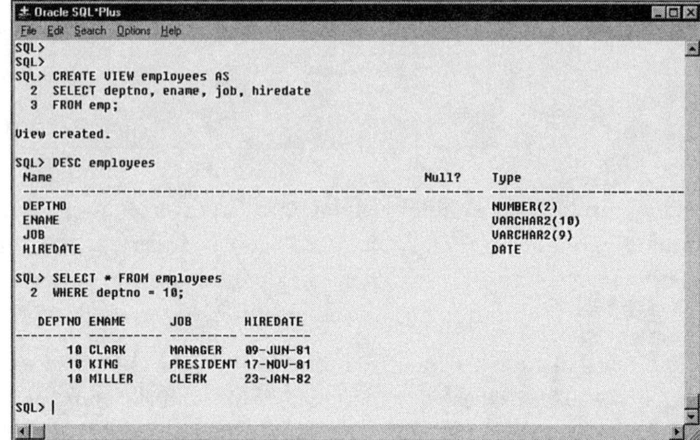

Figure B.33

VIEW usage example.

Creating Sequences

Every application has needs that require either a unique number or a nonassigned number. In Oracle8i, primary keys must be unique. *Sequences* are database objects used to create and maintain a sequence of numbers for tables.

Sequences made their first appearance back in the Oracle6 days. Before sequences, developers used a table to maintain a unique number. Each time a new row was inserted, this table had to be updated and then selected from. This caused considerable overhead, especially when 50 or more users of the same application were all trying to insert records. This single-table approach proved to be quite a performance bottleneck.

Sequences are automatically maintained by Oracle8i, however. The syntax is as follows:

```
CREATE SEQUENCE sequence name [INCREMENT BY n] [START WITH n] [MINVALUE n
|NOMINVALUE] [MAXVALUE n|NOMAXVALUE] [CACHE n|NOCACHE] [CYCLE|NOCYCLE];
```

`name`, `INCREMENT BY`, and `START WITH` are the only required fields. `INCREMENT BY` provides the unit of measure between the numbers, and `START WITH` is the first number of the sequence. The sequence can also maintain a `MINVALUE` (for those sequences that decrease in increments) and a `MAXVALUE`. These values are important when either a business rule dictates the range of values or a field length might be eventually met.

The CACHE option specifies how many sequences will be generated and stored in memory—the default is 20 values. The CYCLE option determines whether the sequence will continue to generate values after the MINVALUE or MAXVALUE has been reached. The default behavior is NOCYCLE.

Remember when creating a sequence for the DEPT table that the table currently has four departments: 10, 20, 30, and 40. The business rule here is to increment by 10. Figure B.34 shows how to receive information on the sequence from the Data Dictionary view USER_SEQUENCES.

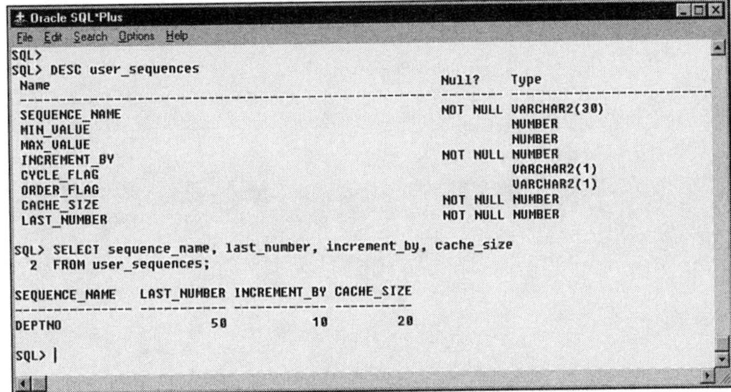

Figure B.34

USER_SEQUENCES available information.

Two values are associated with sequences: CURRVAL and NEXTVAL. NEXTVAL retrieves the next number from the sequence and returns a new value each time it is referenced. On the other hand, CURRVAL contains the last number returned for a particular user session and contains the sequence number from NEXTVAL for the particular user session. These two columns always need to be qualified with the name of the sequence. For example, say Session A, Session B, and Session C are all individual users using the same sequence generator, gen_num, which increments by 1 and starts with 10. Session A inserts a record using gen_num.NEXTVAL; Session B inserts a record using gen_num.NEXTVAL; and Session C inserts a record using gen_num.NEXTVAL. Session A's gen_num.CURRVAL would equal 10; Session B's gen_num.CURRVAL would equal 11; and Session C's gen_num.CURRVAL would equal 11. In addition, the gen_num.CURRVAL would stay constant for this user until the user issues another gen_num.NEXTVAL.

Figure B.35 illustrates how to use the sequence generator deptno in the DEPTNO table. Figure B.36 shows the CURRVAL and USER_SEQUENCES view after this use.

Figure B.35

Using the DEPTNO sequence.

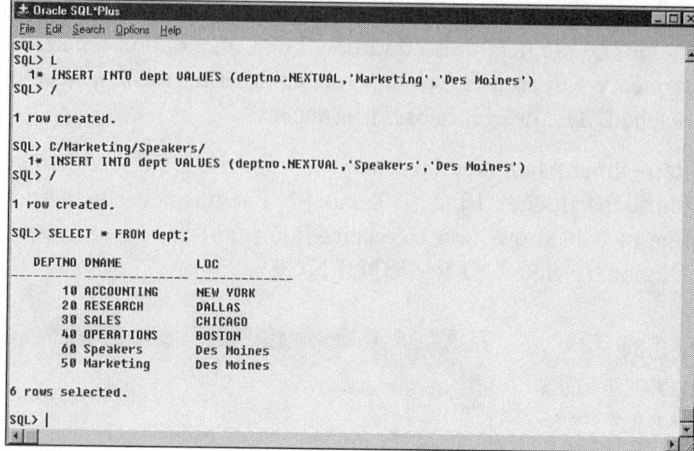

Figure B.36

USER_SEQUENCES available information.

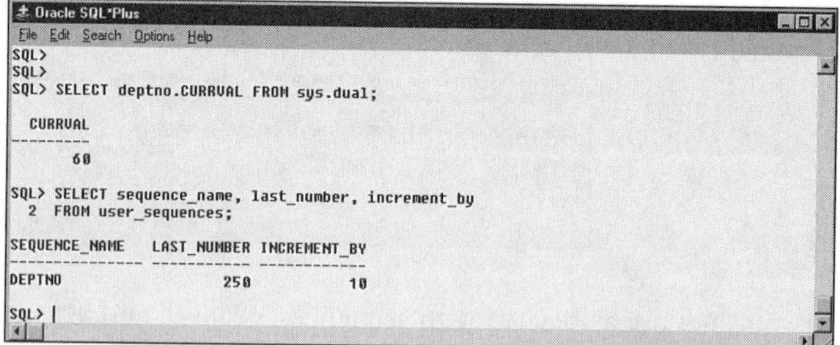

Notice in Figure B.36 that the `LAST_NUMBER` is `250`, but the `CURRVAL` is `60`. Remember that `CURRVAL` is the current value of the sequence for the current user session, whereas `LAST_NUMBER` reflects the number of sequence numbers in the sequence cache. By default, sequences cache 20 values. If we had used the `NOCACHE` option on this sequence, the `LAST_NUMBER` would be `60`.

`DROP SEQUENCE` sequence name removes the sequence. The sequence must be dropped and re-created to make changes to it. However, no `ALTER SEQUENCE` command is available.

Some rules that govern sequences are `CURRVAL` and `NEXTVAL`, which can be used in a `SELECT`, `INSERT`, or `UPDATE` command. But they can't be used in a view, subquery, or default value clause of a column.

User-Defined Data Types

One of the object-oriented features of Oracle8i is the ability to create and use data types that are based on a grouping of other data types. These groupings give a name to commonly used fields, and using them guarantees that their names and lengths are consistent throughout an application. User-defined objects can then appear and be used like any other Oracle8i data type.

Figure B.37 shows how to create a new data type, and Figure B.38 shows how to use this new data type in a `CREATE TABLE` statement. Figure B.39 shows how you would access these columns in an `INSERT` and a `SELECT` statement.

Figure B.37

User-defined data type `CREATE` *example.*

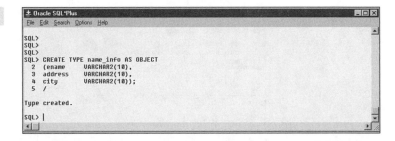

Figure B.38

User-defined data type usage in `CREATE TABLE` *examples.*

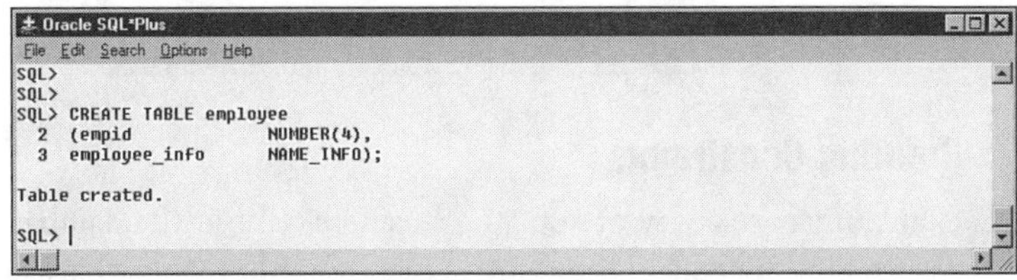

Figure B.39

User-defined data type usage inserting data examples.

```
SQL> INSERT INTO employee VALUES (100,name_info('Dan Hotka',NULL,'Des Moines'));

1 row created.

SQL> SELECT * FROM employee;

    EMPID
---------
EMPLOYEE_INFO(ENAME, ADDRESS, CITY)
--------------------------------------------------------------------------------
      100
NAME_INFO('Dan Hotka', NULL, 'Des Moines')

SQL>
```

To access the individual fields of this new data type requires the use of PL/SQL and REF commands. Refer to the *Oracle8i SQL Reference Manual* for additional details and example code.

Creating Synonyms

Synonyms are simply different names for a table. They provide a simple name to reference a table without having to qualify the table with the schema name or database link name (if the table is located in a different instance of Oracle).

Figure B.40 shows the SYSTEM account trying to access the EMP table without qualifying the name to SCOTT.EMP. The synonym gives the SCOTT.EMP name a public-accessed name (anyone can access EMP) EMP.

Figure B.40

Synonym usage example.

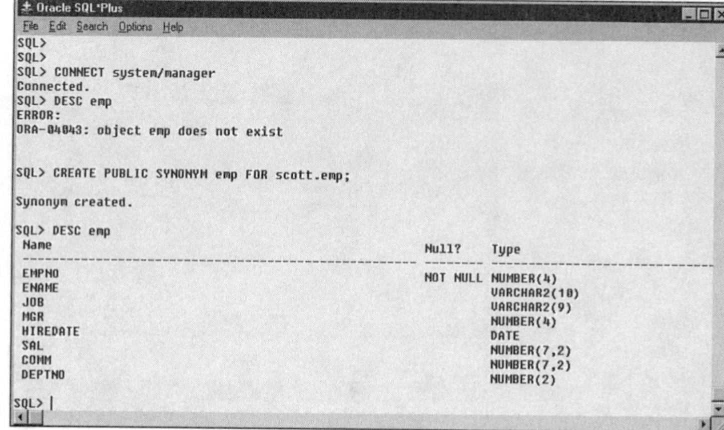

Oracle SQL*Plus
File Edit Search Options Help
SQL>
SQL>
SQL> CONNECT system/manager
Connected.
SQL> DESC emp
ERROR:
ORA-04043: object emp does not exist
SQL> CREATE PUBLIC SYNONYM emp FOR scott.emp;
Synonym created.
SQL> DESC emp
Name Null? Type
EMPNO NOT NULL NUMBER(4)
ENAME VARCHAR2(10)
JOB VARCHAR2(9)
MGR NUMBER(4)
HIREDATE DATE
SAL NUMBER(7,2)
COMM NUMBER(7,2)
DEPTNO NUMBER(2)
SQL>

Creating Constraints

Constraints are a way of applying business rules at the database level. Constraints ensure that the data entered into tables complies with what is expected in the tables. Constraints can be applied at the column level or table level. They can be applied after the table has been created as well.

The two main kinds of constraints are data integrity and referential integrity. The *data integrity* constraints deal with the data that is in the particular column. Examples of such constraints are `NOT NULL`, `UNIQUE`, and `CHECK`. *Referential* constraints, such as primary key/foreign key, deal with the relationship between tables. The `NOT NULL` constraint is obvious and frequently used to ensure that the field does in fact contain a value. `UNIQUE` and `PRIMARY KEY` constraints are similar in that they ensure that the values in a particular column are unique to all the other values in the column. Oracle creates a unique index for each of these as a means to perform the unique check. A `CHECK` constraint enables the column to be checked against certain conditions or a list of values.

Figure B.41 displays several of these constraint types. Notice that the DEPT table has a table-level `PRIMARY KEY` constraint defined on column deptno and that table EMP has a table-level `FOREIGN KEY` constraint on deptno that references the primary key of DEPT. Because only one primary key can exist on a table, it would be redundant to have to name this primary key again in the `FOREIGN KEY` constraint reference. This establishes referential integrity between the DEPT and EMP tables. You cannot insert a record into EMP with a deptno that does not already exist in DEPT.

A column-level `CHECK` constraint is also defined in the EMP table, as well as several column-level `NOT NULL` constraints. The constraint on the MGR column in the EMP table references the EMPNO column, which ensures that the MGR number is a valid employee.

Figure B.41

Constraint examples.

```
Command Prompt - \bin\vi demobld.sql

CREATE TABLE DEPT (
 DEPTNO                 NUMBER(2) NOT NULL,
 DNAME                  VARCHAR2(14),
 LOC                    VARCHAR2(13),
 CONSTRAINT DEPT_PRIMARY_KEY PRIMARY KEY (DEPTNO));

CREATE TABLE EMP (
 EMPNO                  NUMBER(4) NOT NULL,
 ENAME                  VARCHAR2(10),
 JOB                    VARCHAR2(9),
 MGR                    NUMBER(4) CONSTRAINT EMP_SELF_KEY REFERENCES EMP (EMPNO),
 HIREDATE               DATE,
 SAL                    NUMBER(7,2),
 COMM                   NUMBER(7,2),
 CUR_EMPLOYEE           VARCHAR2(1) CHECK (CUR_EMPLOYEE IN ('Y','N')),
 DEPTNO                 NUMBER(2) NOT NULL,
 CONSTRAINT EMP_FOREIGN_KEY FOREIGN KEY (DEPTNO) REFERENCES DEPT (DEPTNO),
 CONSTRAINT EMP_PRIMARY_KEY PRIMARY KEY (EMPNO));

CREATE TABLE PRODUCT (
 PRODID                 NUMBER (6) CONSTRAINT PRODUCT_PRIMARY_KEY PRIMARY KEY,
 DESCRIP                VARCHAR2 (30));
```

Figure B.42 shows valuable information about the constraints in the SCOTT schema. The `USER_CONSTRAINTS` show a variety of information—the constraint name, type of constraint (`P` for primary key and `R` for foreign key), and the table the constraint is on. `USER_CONS_COLUMNS` shows the actual columns that have constraints on them, and the USER_INDEXES view shows the unique indexes created for the primary keys.

Figure B.42

Information on constraints.

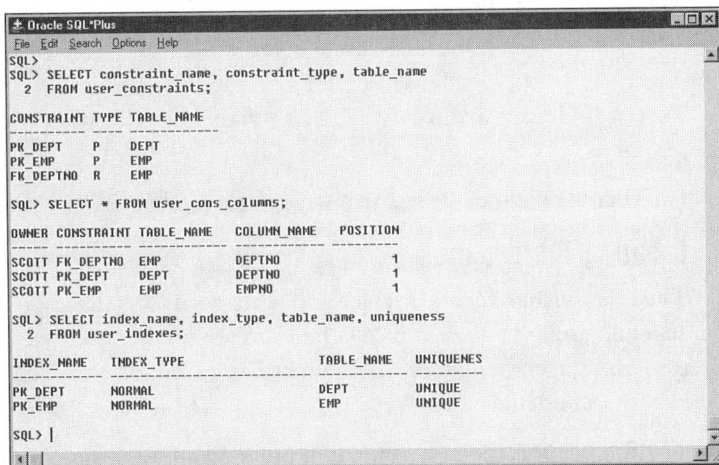

```
Oracle SQL*Plus
File Edit Search Options Help
SQL>
SQL> SELECT constraint_name, constraint_type, table_name
  2  FROM user_constraints;

CONSTRAINT TYPE TABLE_NAME
---------- ---- ------------
PK_DEPT    P    DEPT
PK_EMP     P    EMP
FK_DEPTNO  R    EMP

SQL> SELECT * FROM user_cons_columns;

OWNER CONSTRAINT TABLE_NAME   COLUMN_NAME   POSITION
----- ---------- ------------ ------------- ---------
SCOTT FK_DEPTNO  EMP          DEPTNO                1
SCOTT PK_DEPT    DEPT         DEPTNO                1
SCOTT PK_EMP     EMP          EMPNO                 1

SQL> SELECT index_name, index_type, table_name, uniqueness
  2  FROM user_indexes;

INDEX_NAME   INDEX_TYPE                  TABLE_NAME   UNIQUENES
------------ --------------------------- ------------ ---------
PK_DEPT      NORMAL                      DEPT         UNIQUE
PK_EMP       NORMAL                      EMP          UNIQUE

SQL> |
```

Sometimes loading related data into different tables with the constraints defined can be difficult. Therefore, the `DISABLE` and `ENABLE CONSTRAINT` commands are used for just this purpose—to temporarily disable constraints for data loads or data manipulation. The `ALTER TABLE table name DISABLE CONSTRAINT constraint name [CASCADE]` syntax disables the constraints and any related constraints if the `CASCADE` option is specified. Likewise, the `ALTER TABLE table name ENABLE CONSTRAINT constraint name` syntax reestablishes the constraint and verifies the data named in the constraint.

Constraints can be added and dropped, as well. The `ALTER TABLE table name ADD CONSTRAINT constraint name TYPE (column name)` syntax adds additional table-level constraints, and the `ALTER TABLE table name DROP CONSTRAINT constraint name` syntax removes the constraint from the table.

Another benefit of referential integrity is the ability to remove a *parent row* and all the children records *or* not allow the parent record to be deleted if children records exist. Figure B.43 illustrates how referential integrity protects the data in the related columns. The DEPT record was not deleted because child records still exist in the EMP table. Also, a constraint option exists that will allow `CASCADE ON DELETE` and delete these child records in the EMP table.

Figure B.43

An attempted `DELETE` *from the DEPT table.*

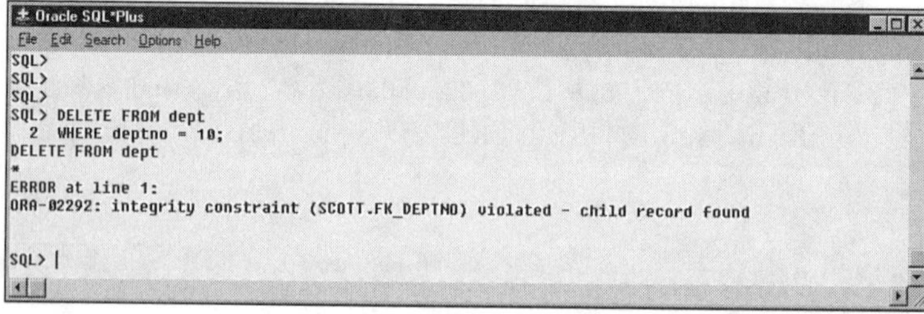
Oracle SQL*Plus
File Edit Search Options Help
SQL>
SQL>
SQL>
SQL> DELETE FROM dept
2 WHERE deptno = 10;
DELETE FROM dept
*
ERROR at line 1:
ORA-02292: integrity constraint (SCOTT.FK_DEPTNO) violated - child record found
SQL> |

geek
speak

Parent table or parent row—The primary key table or row of data in the primary key table.

Child row or children records—The foreign key table and foreign key data.

Creating Tablespaces

The relationship between tables and tablespaces was discussed previously in this appendix (refer to Figure B.25). Tablespaces are the interface between Oracle8i and the operating system–level files. The tablespace is also the place where the default storage parameters are stored.

The following is the base syntax for creating a tablespace:

```
CREATE TABLESPACE tablespace name DATAFILE 'full path operating-system level
file' SIZE n bytes/K/M DEFAULT STORAGE (INITIAL nK, NEXT nK, MINEXTENTS n,
MAXEXTENTS n) ONLINE;
```

Note that the single quotes around the operating system file spec are part of the syntax. The `n` represents a numeric number, and the `SIZE` can be specified in bytes, number of bytes in KB (1024), or number of megabytes (MB).

I always specify a full path for these files. On a single-CPU, desktop configuration of NT, I always place the tablespace files in the same directory as the default database-created tablespace files.

Two data dictionary views are handy for finding information about the tablespaces. Although, you must be logged in to SQL*Plus as SYSTEM or have the DBA role assigned to see the contents of these two views: DBA_TABLESPACES and DBA_DATA_FILES. The view, DBA_TABLESPACES, shows the tablespaces and the default storage parameters of objects created here that did not have a storage parameter defined.

Figure B.44 shows the names of the tablespaces, their underlying operating system files, the size of the files, and their status for use in the Oracle8i database environment.

Notice that a pattern to the naming convention of these files exists in Figure B.44. I recommend naming the physical files assigned to the tablespaces in such a manner that one can easily see which physical files belong to which tablespaces.

Figure B.45 shows the `CREATE TABLESPACE` command in use along with the information from DBA_DATA_FILES to show that the tablespace was created with the specifications from the `CREATE TABLESPACE` command.

Advanced SQL Queries

This section covers a variety of topics related to SQL queries, including functions, advanced queries (joins and subqueries), complex views, and read consistency (Oracle8i locking mechanisms).

Functions

SQL functions perform a variety of tasks, such as date compares; date formatting; a host of character functions, such as string length, substring functions, uppercase/lowercase; and several numerical functions, such as round, truncate, and arithmetic operations.

Figure B.44

Information from DBA_DATA_FILES.

```
Oracle SQL*Plus
File Edit Search Options Help
SQL>
SQL>
SQL> DESC dba_data_files
 Name                                              Null?    Type
 ------------------------------------------------- -------- --------------------
 FILE_NAME                                                  VARCHAR2(513)
 FILE_ID                                                    NUMBER
 TABLESPACE_NAME                                            VARCHAR2(30)
 BYTES                                                      NUMBER
 BLOCKS                                                     NUMBER
 STATUS                                                     VARCHAR2(9)
 RELATIVE_FNO                                               NUMBER
 AUTOEXTENSIBLE                                             VARCHAR2(3)
 MAXBYTES                                                   NUMBER
 MAXBLOCKS                                                  NUMBER
 INCREMENT_BY                                               NUMBER
 USER_BYTES                                                 NUMBER
 USER_BLOCKS                                                NUMBER

SQL> SELECT file_name, tablespace_name, bytes, blocks, status
  2  FROM dba_data_files;

FILE_NAME                                TABLESPACE_NAME     BYTES    BLOCKS STATUS
---------------------------------------- --------------- --------- --------- --------
C:\ORACLE8I\ORADATA\ORCL\USERS01.DBF     USERS             8388608      4096 AVAILABL
C:\ORACLE8I\ORADATA\ORCL\OEMREP01.DBF    OEM_REPOSITORY    5242880      2560 AVAILABL
C:\ORACLE8I\ORADATA\ORCL\INDX01.DBF      INDX              2097152      1024 AVAILABL
C:\ORACLE8I\ORADATA\ORCL\RBS01.DBF       RBS              26214400     12800 AVAILABL
C:\ORACLE8I\ORADATA\ORCL\TEMP01.DBF      TEMP              2097152      1024 AVAILABL
C:\ORACLE8I\ORADATA\ORCL\SYSTEM01.DBF    SYSTEM          146800640     71680 AVAILABL

6 rows selected.

SQL> |
```

Figure B.45

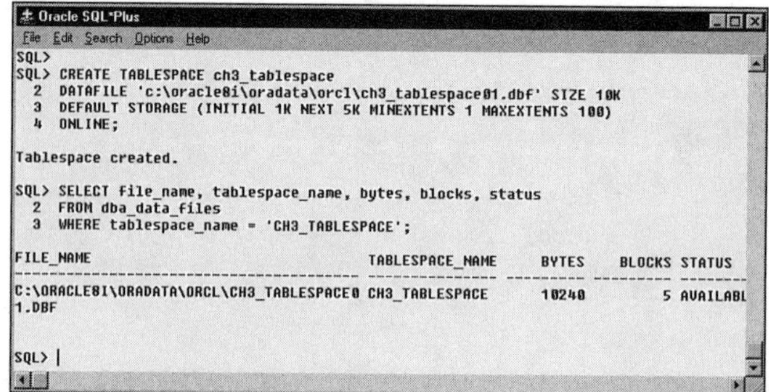

```
Oracle SQL*Plus
File Edit Search Options Help
SQL>
SQL> CREATE TABLESPACE ch3_tablespace
  2  DATAFILE 'c:\oracle8i\oradata\orcl\ch3_tablespace01.dbf' SIZE 10K
  3  DEFAULT STORAGE (INITIAL 1K NEXT 5K MINEXTENTS 1 MAXEXTENTS 100)
  4  ONLINE;

Tablespace created.

SQL> SELECT file_name, tablespace_name, bytes, blocks, status
  2  FROM dba_data_files
  3  WHERE tablespace_name = 'CH3_TABLESPACE';

FILE_NAME                                TABLESPACE_NAME     BYTES    BLOCKS STATUS
---------------------------------------- --------------- --------- --------- --------
C:\ORACLE8I\ORADATA\ORCL\CH3_TABLESPACE0 CH3_TABLESPACE      10240         5 AVAILABL
1.DBF

SQL> |
```

`CREATE TABLESPACE ch3_tablespace` *example.*

SQL functions fall into two categories: single-row functions and multiple-row functions. *Single-row* functions operate on each row, whereas *multiple-row* functions operate on a group of rows.

Single-Row Functions

Several kinds of single-row functions are available. *Character* functions can convert character strings to number or date formats, whereas *number* functions manipulate the returning numeric value. *Date* functions are used to manipulate, compare, and perform calculations between dates. A couple of additional general single-row functions that do not fit into one of these character, number, or date categories are also available.

Character Functions

Character functions convert or change the output of the stored CHAR or VARCHAR2 fields. `UPPER`, `LOWER`, and `INITCAP` are three of the conversion character functions. Figure B.46 shows examples of the `UPPER` and `INITCAP` functions.

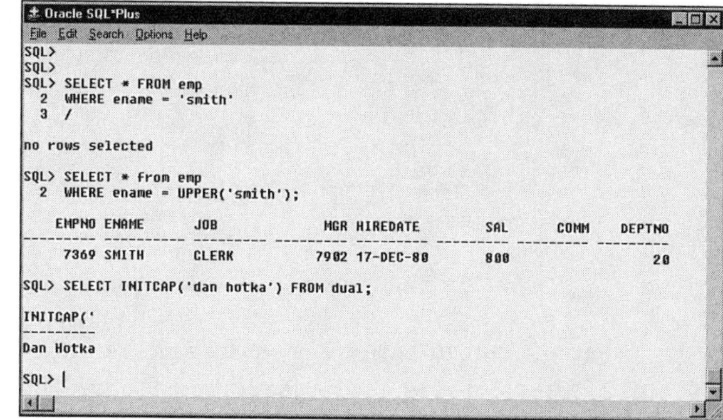

Figure B.46

`UPPER` and `INITCAP` function examples.

DUAL table—Contains one column and one row and is useful for running a function once. Because the DUAL table has only one role, whichever function is run in the `SELECT` statement runs only once.

The character manipulation functions are a powerful way to create desired output. Character manipulation functions include `CONCAT`, `INSTR`, `LENGTH`, `LPAD`, `RPAD`, `SUBSTR`, and `TRIM`. Figure B.45 shows some practical uses for some of these functions.

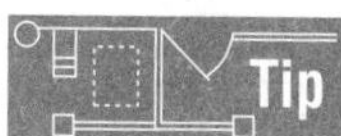

> The || in Figure B.47 also causes *concatenation* between strings and database columns. Notice the handy `DROP` commands created when combining the SQL syntax for dropping a table with that of the table name from the TAB view. Using the `SPOOL` command creates a SQL script that could be used to clean up accounts of employees who have left the company. The `SPOOL` feature is demonstrated while creating SQL*Plus reports in Chapter 3.

Concatenation—When two or more columns are merged together—many times merged with some text items—to form a single column of output.

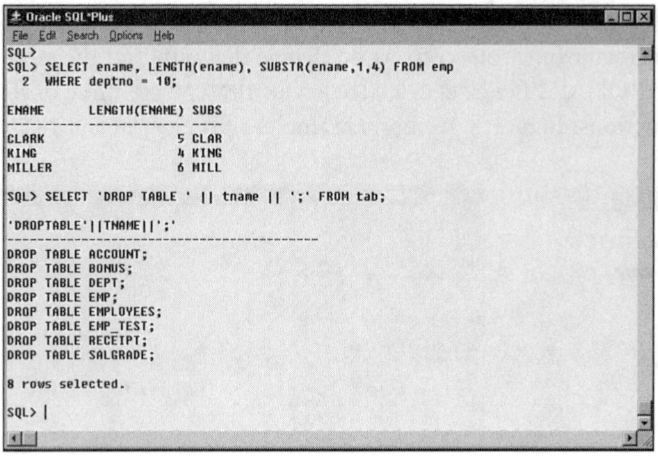

Figure B.47

Character manipulation function examples.

```
Oracle SQL*Plus
File Edit Search Options Help
SQL>
SQL> SELECT ename, LENGTH(ename), SUBSTR(ename,1,4) FROM emp
  2  WHERE deptno = 10;

ENAME      LENGTH(ENAME) SUBS
---------- ------------- ----
CLARK                  5 CLAR
KING                   4 KING
MILLER                 6 MILL

SQL> SELECT 'DROP TABLE ' || tname || ';' FROM tab;

'DROPTABLE'||TNAME||';'
------------------------------------------
DROP TABLE ACCOUNT;
DROP TABLE BONUS;
DROP TABLE DEPT;
DROP TABLE EMP;
DROP TABLE EMPLOYEES;
DROP TABLE EMP_TEST;
DROP TABLE RECEIPT;
DROP TABLE SALGRADE;

8 rows selected.

SQL> |
```

`TO_CHAR`, `TO_NUMBER`, and `TO_DATE` are powerful functions that enable the conversion of one type of data to another and enables different types of date formats for both inserting and query purposes. `TO_CHAR` can be used to format a date into a date format different from the Oracle8i default of DD-MON-YY. Likewise, the `TO_DATE` is used to convert a valid date in almost any format into the date format Oracle8i understands. Lastly, `TO_NUMBER` enables valid numbers stored in character fields to be used in calculations and so on.

The following are some of the valid date and time formats that can be used with both `TO_CHAR` and `TO_DATE`. Consult the *Oracle8i SQL Reference Manual* for all the combinations of date and time formats:

- `DD`—Numeric day of month
- `MM`—Numeric month of year
- `YY`—Two-digit year
- `RR`—Century function (see the following note)
- `YYYY`—Four-digit year
- `Mon`—Three-position month abbreviation
- `DY`—Three-position day abbreviation
- `Day`—Name of day spelled out
- `J`—Julian date
- `MONTH`—Month spelled out
- `YEAR`—Year spelled out

The following is a partial list of time formats:

- `AM` or `PM`—Time of day indicator
- `HH`—Hour of day
- `HH24`—Hour in military time
- `MI`—Minutes
- `SS`—Seconds
- `SSSS`—Seconds since midnight

The `RR` command is used in place of the `YY` function and assists with century identification on two-position years. If the year tested is 00–49 and the current year is between 00 and 49, `RR` returns the current century. If the year tested is 00–49 and the current year is between 50 and 99, `RR` returns the previous century. If the year tested is 50–99 and the current year is between 00 and 49, `RR` returns the next century. If the year tested is 50–99 and the current year is between 50 and 99, `RR` returns the current century:

```
Current year = 1999, Date=01-SEP-96, RR= 1996, YY=1996
Current year = 1996, Date=15-JUL-45, RR= 2045, YY=1945
Current year = 2003, Date=17-MAR-56, RR=1956, YY=2056
```

Date Functions

Six date functions perform various calculations from the number of months between two dates, adding months to a date, getting the next day/previous date, and rounding/truncating dates.

The `MONTHS_BETWEEN(date1,date2)` function returns the number of months between the two dates, and the `ADD_MONTHS(date, n)` returns a date *n* months (both future and past) away from the date given. The `NEXT_DAY(date, char)`, where *`char`* is a day of the week, returns a date of the day of the week in the *`char`* field following the date. `LAST_DAY(date)`, on the other hand, returns the date of the last day in the month of the date. `ROUND(date[,date format]` and `TRUNC (date[,date format])` both perform their functions to the nearest date unless a date format is given—if that occurs, these functions perform the function to the precision referenced in *`date format`*.

Figure B.48 shows some practical examples of DATE functions in use.

Figure B.48

Date function examples.

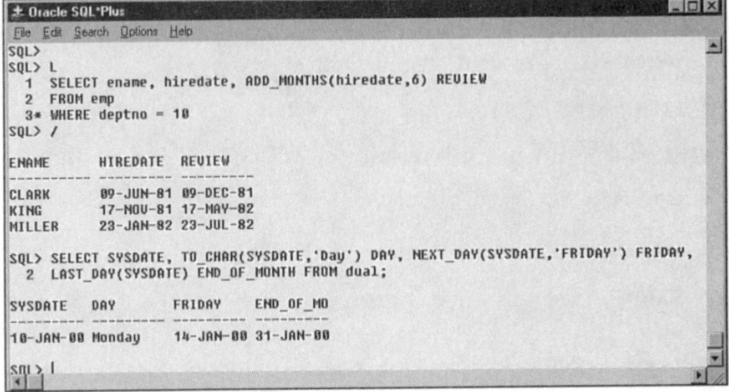

```
Oracle SQL*Plus
File Edit Search Options Help
SQL>
SQL> L
  1  SELECT ename, hiredate, ADD_MONTHS(hiredate,6) REVIEW
  2  FROM emp
  3* WHERE deptno = 10
SQL> /

ENAME      HIREDATE  REVIEW
---------- --------- ---------
CLARK      09-JUN-81 09-DEC-81
KING       17-NOV-81 17-MAY-82
MILLER     23-JAN-82 23-JUL-82

SQL> SELECT SYSDATE, TO_CHAR(SYSDATE,'Day') DAY, NEXT_DAY(SYSDATE,'FRIDAY') FRIDAY,
  2  LAST_DAY(SYSDATE) END_OF_MONTH FROM dual;

SYSDATE   DAY       FRIDAY    END_OF_MO
--------- --------- --------- ---------
10-JAN-00 Monday    14-JAN-00 31-JAN-00

SQL> |
```

Numeric Functions

Several numeric functions are available, such as `ROUND`, `TRUNC`, and `MOD`. The `ROUND(number, precision)` function rounds the value of the number to the desired precision, whereas the `TRUNC(number, precision)` function just drops off the parts past the desired precision. The `MOD(number,number)` function, however, calculates the remainder between two columns.

Other Single-Row Functions

The remaining two functions that do not fit any of the above categories are `NVL` and `DECODE`. `NVL` stands for null value and provides the capability to assign a value to a null field. Figure B.49 shows adding the `SAL` and `COMM` fields to illustrate that when something is added to nothing, you get nothing. The `NVL` function was added to the `COMM` field—notice that the arithmetic then works correctly.

Figure B.49

`NVL` *function example.*

```
Oracle SQL*Plus
File Edit Search Options Help
SQL>
SQL> SELECT ename, sal + comm TOTAL_COMP
  2  FROM emp
  3  WHERE deptno = 10;

ENAME      TOTAL_COMP
---------- ----------
CLARK
KING
MILLER

SQL> 11
  1* SELECT ename, sal + comm TOTAL_COMP
SQL> C/comm/NVL(comm,0)
  1* SELECT ename, sal + NVL(comm,0) TOTAL_COMP
SQL> L
  1  SELECT ename, sal + NVL(comm,0) TOTAL_COMP
  2  FROM emp
  3* WHERE deptno = 10
SQL> /

ENAME      TOTAL_COMP
---------- ----------
CLARK            2450
KING             5000
MILLER           1300

SQL> |
```

> Notice in Figure B.49 that the SQL*Plus buffer editor change command was used to add the `NVL`.

The `DECODE` function is the `IF-THEN-ELSE` logic to SQL. The syntax looks like this:

```
DECODE (col/variable/expression, string1, result1 [, string2, result2][, ...]
[, default value]
```

`DECODE` works like this:

```
if string 1 =<condition> then return result1 else if string2 = <condition> then
return result2 (and so on) else return default value
```

If no default value exists then `NULL` is returned if none of the strings match the original column/variable/expression. Figure B.50 shows how to reference a field value and return a character string based on the value. `DECODE` has many applications that we will discover in Chapter 5.

Figure B.50

DECODE function example.

```
Oracle SQL*Plus
File Edit Search Options Help
SQL> L
  1  SELECT ename, DECODE(deptno,10,'New York',
  2                              20,'Dallas',
  3                              30,'Chicago',
  4                              40,'Boston','Des Moines') Location
  5* FROM emp
SQL> /

ENAME      LOCATION
---------- ----------
SMITH      Dallas
ALLEN      Chicago
WARD       Chicago
JONES      Dallas
MARTIN     Chicago
BLAKE      Chicago
CLARK      New York
SCOTT      Dallas
KING       New York
TURNER     Chicago
ADAMS      Dallas
JAMES      Chicago
FORD       Dallas
MILLER     New York
HOTKA      Des Moines

15 rows selected.

SQL> |
```

Multiple-Row Functions or Group Functions

Several numeric functions are available, such as `MIN`, `MAX`, `SUM`, `AVG`, `STDDEV`, `DISTINCT`, and `COUNT`. These functions, when used by themselves, return one row from the query—the output of the function. For example, `COUNT` is useful for counting the number of rows in a table (or result set). When these functions are used in combination with the `GROUP BY` clause, however, the query returns one row for each unique data grouping. Figure B.51 shows the `GROUP BY` clause with the `HAVING` clause. This `HAVING` clause allows for only those groups that meet certain criteria.

Figure B.51

GROUP BY with a HAVING clause example.

```
SQL>
SQL> L
  1  SELECT job, count(*), MIN(sal), MAX(sal), AVG(sal), SUM(sal)
  2  FROM emp
  3  GROUP BY job
  4* HAVING count(*) > 2
SQL> /

JOB         COUNT(*)  MIN(SAL)  MAX(SAL)  AVG(SAL)  SUM(SAL)
--------- --------- --------- --------- --------- ---------
CLERK              4       800      1300    1037.5      4150
MANAGER            3      2450      2975 2758.3333      8275
SALESMAN           4      1250      1600      1400      5600

SQL>
```

Figure B.52 shows how to use the DISTINCT clause in a query. Notice the first COUNT returns a count for the table, but when included with the DISTINCT clause, it returns the number of unique values.

Figure B.52

DISTINCT function example.

```
SQL>
SQL> SELECT count(job)
  2  FROM emp;

COUNT(JOB)
----------
        14

SQL> SELECT COUNT(DISTINCT(job))
  2  FROM emp;

COUNT(DISTINCT(JOB))
--------------------
                   5

SQL>
```

Using Multiple Functions

These functions can be nested inside one another to provide the result desired. For example, say employees are reviewed six months after they are hired, but these reviews happen only on Mondays. Figure B.53 shows a query that could be used to produce such a list.

Figure B.53

Multiple DATE function example.

```
SQL>
SQL>
SQL> L
  1  SELECT ename, hiredate, NEXT_DAY(ADD_MONTHS(hiredate,6),'MONDAY') Review
  2  FROM emp
  3* WHERE deptno = 10
SQL> /

ENAME      HIREDATE  REVIEW
---------- --------- ---------
CLARK      09-JUN-81 14-DEC-81
KING       17-NOV-81 24-MAY-82
MILLER     23-JAN-82 26-JUL-82

SQL>
```

The `ROUND` function is typically placed outside most calculations to correctly size the result. Similarly, the `NVL` value is included on numeric columns that could contain null values.

Figure B.54 shows `DECODE` being used with a calculation giving those in department 10 a 10% salary increase, department 20 a 20% increase, department 30 a 30% increase, and department 40 a 40% increase.

B

Figure B.54

`DECODE` and `ROUND` function example.

```
Oracle SQL*Plus
File Edit Search Options Help
SQL> L
  1  SELECT ename, sal SALARY, DECODE(deptno,10,ROUND(sal * 1.10),
  2                                          20,ROUND(sal * 1.20),
  3                                          30,ROUND(sal * 1.30),
  4                                          40,ROUND(sal * 1.40)) Raise
  5* FROM emp
SQL> /

ENAME         SALARY     RAISE
---------- --------- ---------
SMITH            800       960
ALLEN           1600      2080
WARD            1250      1625
JONES           2975      3570
MARTIN          1250      1625
BLAKE           2850      3705
CLARK           2450      2695
SCOTT           3000      3600
KING            5000      5500
TURNER          1500      1950
ADAMS           1100      1320
JAMES            950      1235
FORD            3000      3600
MILLER          1300      1430

14 rows selected.

SQL> |
```

Indexing on Functions

In Oracle8 and earlier versions, using a function in a `WHERE` clause (for example, `WHERE UPPER(ename) = 'SMITH'` or `WHERE empno + 10 > 1000`) on an indexed column caused Oracle RDBMS not to use the index but to read all the rows in the table to perform the function. The main reason for having an index is for quick results from tables with thousands of rows. Oracle8i solves this problem of not using indexes on columns with functions. Oracle8i enables indexes to be created and includes the typical function used. This provides a quick result when it is necessary to include a function in a `WHERE` clause.

Summary

The better you understand the SQL language, the more productive you will become when using any relational database. This appendix covered all the SQL features, mostly from the SQL*Plus interface. You should now have a better working knowledge of the SQL language, as well as the SQL*Plus interface.

Appendix C

In this appendix

- *PL/SQL and Why to Use It*
- *PL/SQL Basic Syntax*
- *Debugging Our PL/SQL*
- *Error Handling in PL/SQL*

PL/SQL Basics

PL/SQL and Why to Use It

PL/SQL, or Procedural Language SQL, is Oracle8i's extension to the SQL language. PL/SQL gives SQL many common programming features such as *record processing*, various looping syntax, and data manipulation/calculation capabilities, as well as exception handling.

Record processing—The capability to select one row at a time, manipulate it, and then process the next row. Looping syntax enables you to perform repetitive tasks any number of times.

PL/SQL is what various features of the Oracle8i application environment are coded in. Stored procedures, stored functions, and database triggers are all coded in PL/SQL or Java. Stored procedures and functions are a way of sharing code and performing server-side processing, returning just a result to the application or user at a PC. Figure C.1 shows the network traffic generated by SQL at an application and the network traffic generated by the use of some *server-side code*. Notice that the SQL code must call the rows back to the application (such as Oracle Forms or SQL*Plus) on the PC but the server-side code just sends the result.

Server-side code—Any code that runs where the Oracle8i RDBMS is installed. The database engine actually executes the code and returns just the results, such as a few columns or maybe just the output of a calculation.

A *stored procedure* is a code module that performs some processing and returns a code stating whether the procedure was successful. An example of a stored procedure is to process a group of rows based on a supplied value and perform DML statements on other tables as a result of processing the rows. A *function* is the same as a procedure except it does return a value, such as the result of a calculation. Procedures and functions are an excellent way to perform complex calculations or processing that is not easily done with just SQL statements. *Packages* are a way of grouping together related procedures and functions, or procedures and functions that might be used frequently by an application. When a procedure or function within a package is referenced, all the functions and procedures in the package are loaded into memory. *Triggers* are assigned to tables and provide additional functionality either before or after a DML process. Triggers are useful for maintaining audit trails in the assigned tables, performing additional DML on other tables based on the just-completed DML statement, and so on.

Figure C.1

Network traffic example.

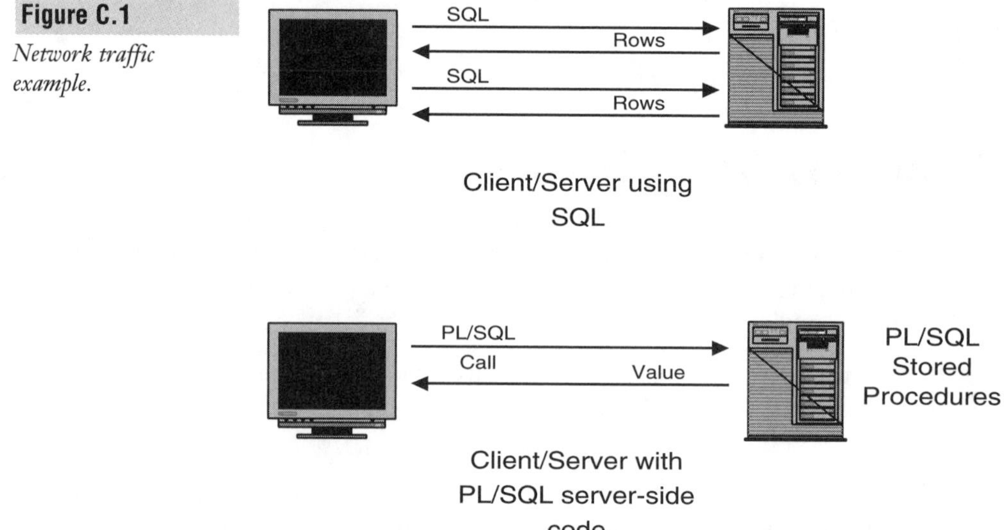

You will learn how to code these same procedures, functions, and triggers in Chapter 3, "Building the Sales Tracking Application Forms and Reports."

These procedures and functions can reside at either the client or the server (where the Oracle8i database is). However, as illustrated by Figure C.1, the server is usually a much more powerful machine for performing processing, and any time you can cut down on network traffic, the application will perform much better.

PL/SQL also can be coded directly into applications such as SQL*Plus. Figure C.2 illustrates how this would look, using PL/SQL to manipulate data from SQL*Plus variables.

Figure C.2

*PL/SQL in SQL*Plus example.*

```
Oracle SQL*Plus
File Edit Search Options Help
SQL>
SQL> VAR P_TEST CHAR(20);
SQL> l
  1  DECLARE
  2  v_test   CHAR(20);
  3  BEGIN
  4  :P_TEST := 'This is a Test';
  5* END;
SQL> /

PL/SQL procedure successfully completed.

SQL> print P_TEST

P_TEST
--------------------------------
This is a Test

SQL>
```


PL/SQL Basic Syntax

All PL/SQL has the same basic format: a `DECLARE` section where cursors and variables are defined, and a `BEGIN` and an `END` where the SQL syntax and PL/SQL code is placed. This is known as a *PL/SQL block*. *Exceptions*, or *exception handling*, are errors or flags in PL/SQL. Exceptions are a way of gracefully handling certain conditions within the PL/SQL block, such as no records returned from the SQL query or last record returned from the SQL query. Other exceptions can be syntax errors in the PL/SQL code itself.

Cursors—Oracle's way of processing SQL statements and storing the records returned from a query, enabling the PL/SQL block to easily handle individual rows from a query that returns multiple rows. A cursor is a work area in memory for PL/SQL.

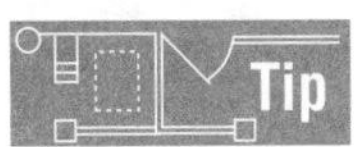

Use the `show errors` command when working with PL/SQL in SQL*Plus to show any error conditions.

This section will use the Quest SQL Navigator tool. SQL Navigator is a good tool for creating and debugging PL/SQL code. Appendix A, "Installation and Configuration of Oracle8i NT-Based Software," covers how to get the tool, provides a trial license key, and illustrates how to install the tool on your computer.

Log in to SQL Navigator as `SCOTT` with the `TIGER` password to work the exercises in this chapter.

Two types of PL/SQL blocks exist. The *anonymous* block is the basic unnamed PL/SQL block and is used in SQL*Plus, and 3GL programs such as C and COBOL. On the other hand, *named* PL/SQL blocks can be declared as procedures or functions.

In addition, these named PL/SQL blocks can reside on the server or at the PC (client side) and can be called (or executed) from other PL/SQL blocks (either anonymous or named). Both procedures and functions can accept input variables, but only functions can return values. Figure C.3 shows the basic syntax of a PL/SQL block.

Start the SQL Navigator tool from the Start menu. From the SQL Navigator menu bar, select New Editor, the Stored Program Editor. This will display the box illustrated by Figure C.3. Give the procedure a name and click OK. This will create a basic PL/SQL block for a procedure (see Figure C.4). Notice the `BEGIN`, `EXCEPTIONS`, and `END` clauses (the `END` is hidden from view, so use the vertical scroll bar on the right side of the edit window to see the remainder of the code) are automatically created.

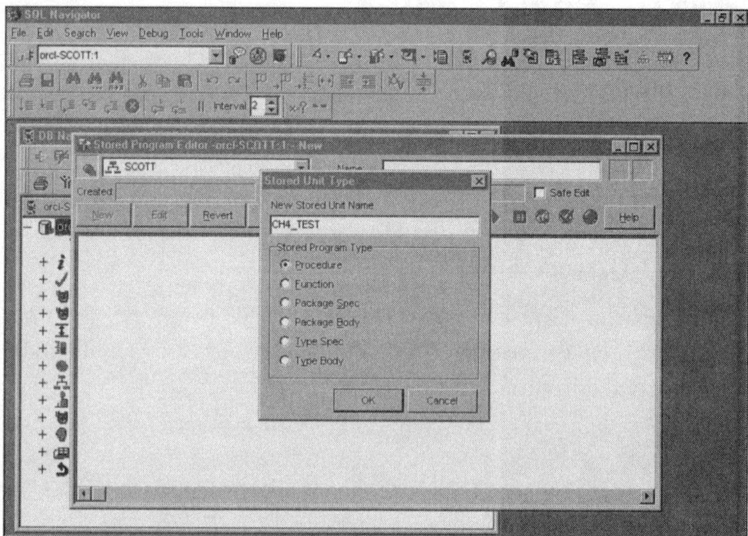

Figure C.3

Creating a procedure using SQL Navigator.

Two types of triggers that utilize PL/SQL blocks also exist. *Database* triggers are defined on a table to perform certain functions at certain times. These triggers execute when certain events occur, such as before or after a record is inserted. Figure C.5 shows the various database trigger levels supported by Oracle8i. This trigger edit window in SQL Navigator is accessed by clicking File, NEW Editor, Trigger. Notice the Timing box determines whether this database trigger will fire before or after the action determined in the Triggering Event box. The Fire For box determines whether the trigger will be executed for each row affected by the DML SQL statement or just once per DML SQL statement. *Application* triggers are also executed automatically and are used by Developer v6.0. Chapter 2, "Building the Sales Tracking Application Database," discusses their use and illustrate how to create them.

Figure C.4

Basic PL/SQL block in SQL Navigator.

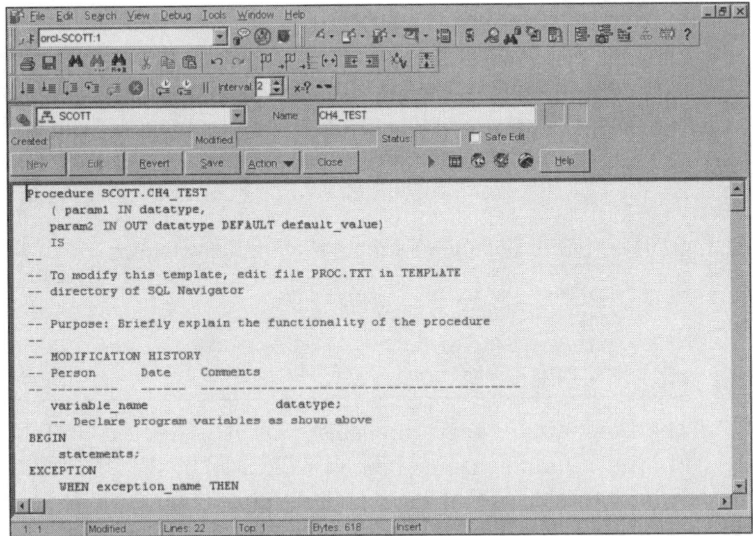

Figure C.5

Database triggers supported in Oracle8i.

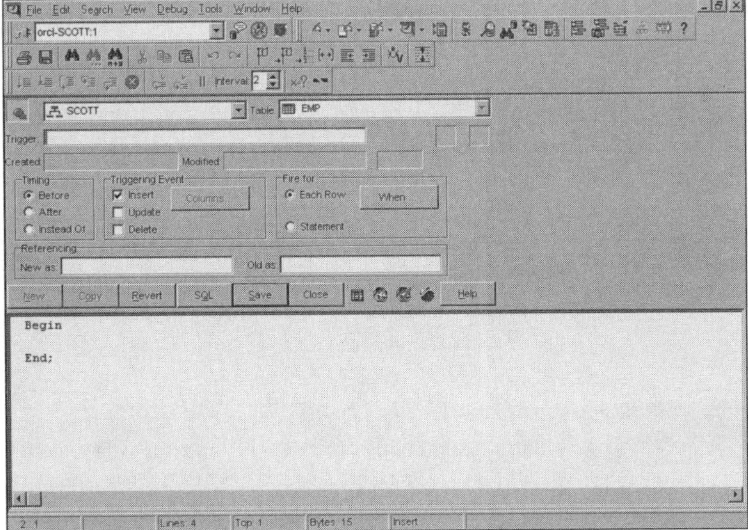

PL/SQL Variables

PL/SQL *variables* are used throughout PL/SQL to store data, store the results of a calculation, store the results of a SQL query, and manipulate the data in other variables. The syntax is rather simple: `var_name [CONSTANT] datatype [NOT NULL] [:= var/calc/expression]`. The `var name` must be unique to the PL/SQL block. In addition, the `CONSTANT` option will not allow the variable to change throughout the PL/SQL code execution. This feature would be handy in situations in which the

PL/SQL block might be subject to somewhat regular code changes. The datatype follows the SQL standards. The := is the method of assigning a value to the variable. The value can be set equal to a constant, the result of a calculation, or the result of a SQL query. Oracle developers follow some simple guidelines to ensure a unique name for variables and give other Oracle developers an idea of the nature of the variable. Listing C.1 shows some common naming conventions used by Oracle developers.

Listing C.1—PL/SQL Common Variable Naming Conventions

```
v_    Standard variable     v_empno
c_    Constant variable     c_sysdate
p_    SQL*Plus variable     p_infield
g_    SQL_Plus global var   g_field_pos
```

The same variable name can be used inside nested PL/SQL blocks (PL/SQL within PL/SQL), and the name of the variable used by the PL/SQL block will be the locally defined variable or that variable declared in that PL/SQL block.

For example, Figure C.6 shows variable `v_avar` in the outer PL/SQL block and `v_bvar` in the inner or nested PL/SQL block. Variable `v_bvar` can reference `v_avar`, but `v_avar` *cannot* reference `v_bvar`. The code in the gray box in Figure C.6 is invalid and will generate an error because the outer PL/SQL block is making reference to a variable defined in the inner PL/SQL block. To save and execute the code block, click the green, triangular box on the bottom toolbar.

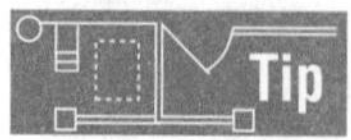

It is advisable to always use unique variable names because referencing variables with the := in inner PL/SQL blocks is a convenient way of passing results to outer PL/SQL blocks when nesting PL/SQL blocks.

If you place the mouse cursor on the error code returned (`PLS-00201` in Figure C.6) and left-click twice, you will get SQL Navigator's Oracle Error Information, as illustrated in Figure C.7.

Figure C.8 illustrates naming some variables and populating them with values. `%TYPE` and `%ROWTYPE` are special datatypes that will retrieve and use the datatype for a particular column from the database (object-oriented inheritance, which is discussed in Chapter 1, "Introduction to Oracle8i and the Auto Sales Tracking Application").

`%TYPE` is useful to guarantee that the datatype and length of the variable match that of a column in the database. Notice the `INTO` clause in the SQL statement. This is how data is passed from the tables to the PL/SQL variables.

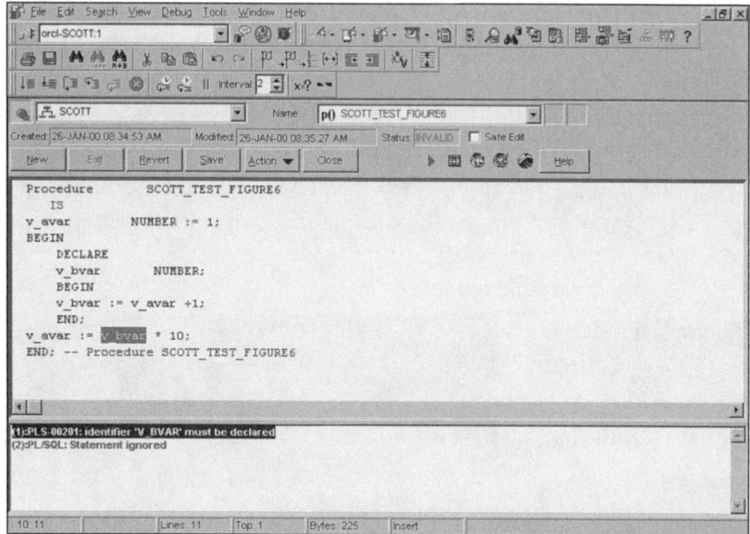

Figure C.6

Variable references in nested PL/SQL blocks.

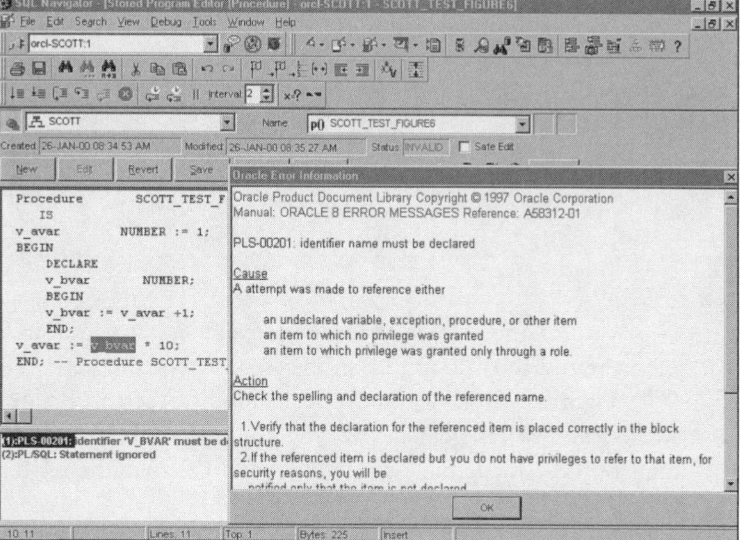

Figure C.7

SQL Navigator's help with errors.

Figure C.9 shows how to execute the newly developed procedure in DEBUG mode. This will enable you to stop the execution of the code, see the contents of variables, and change the contents of the variables. A couple ways are available to set a break point. You can left-click on the line where you want execution to stop and then press the right mouse button and select Toggle Breakpoint—this will highlight the whole line in yellow. You also can press the Toggle Breakpoint button on the toolbar next to the X=? button. The button with a down arrow (on the far left, on the same line of the toolbar) will run the procedure to the first break point. Because this is a procedure, SQL Navigator will start a Calling Code Generation Wizard. Therefore, you can just click Next and Finish, accepting the defaults. When SQL Navigator hits the break point, it will stop and display the line of code at the break point.

Figure C.8

Declaring and populating variables.

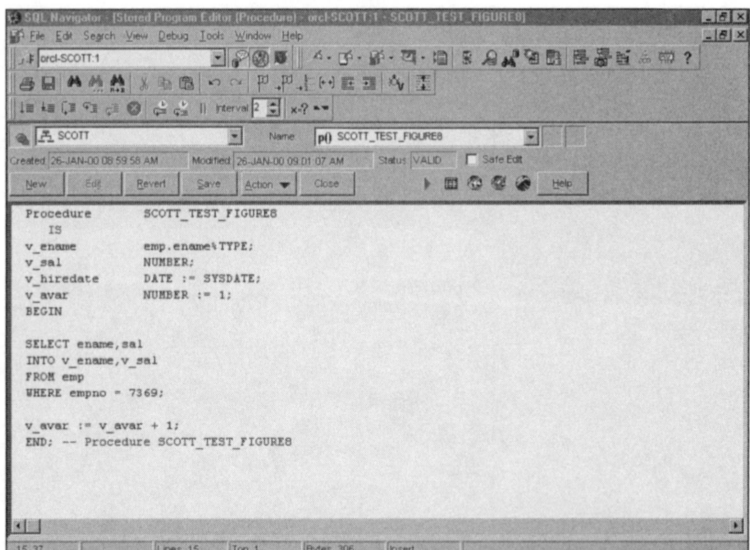

Now you can move the mouse cursor over a variable, and its contents will display momentarily and also display in the status bar at the bottom of the screen (see Figure C.9). Figure C.10 shows the Evaluate/Modify Variable dialog box (by pressing the X=? button with the cursor over the desired variable) that not only shows the contents of the variable but also enables you to change the contents.

This break point/debug mode will be very useful in visualizing returned rows later when you learn about loops and cursors.

Figure C.9

Setting break points in SQL Navigator.

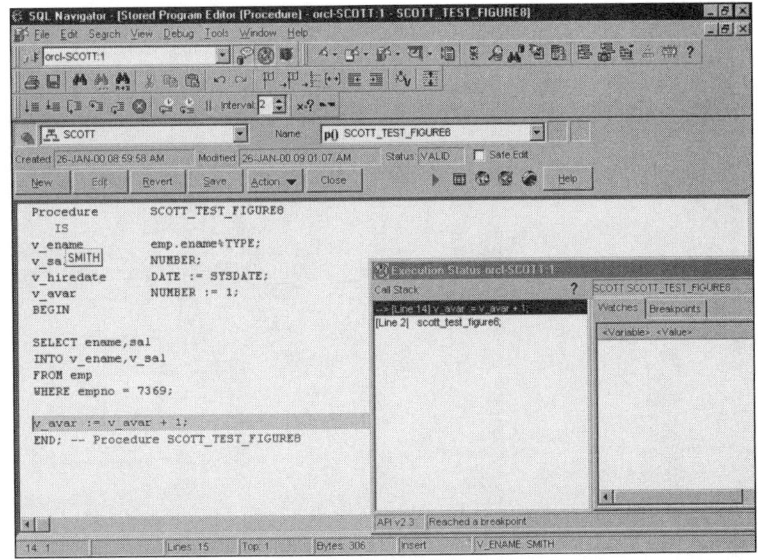

Figure C.10

Changing variable contents on the fly.

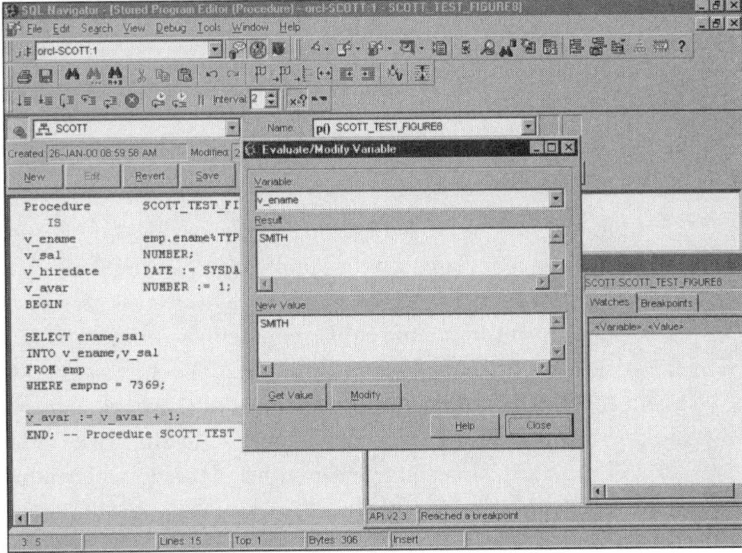

Similar to `%TYPE`, `%ROWTYPE` is convenient to use to guarantee that the same datatypes are used and that all the columns of a particular table are used. This, too, is a form of object-oriented inheritance. This feature will guarantee the number of columns and the associated datatypes always match that of a particular table. Figure C.11 illustrates a practical use for `%ROWTYPE`. Notice how `v_ename` and `v_sal` are set by qualifying the columns returned from `emp` with the `emp_record` prefix.

Boolean variables are useful for storing the results of a calculation or comparison, or simply holding a TRUE/FALSE/NULL value.

Figure C.11

Using the %ROWTYPE *datatype feature.*

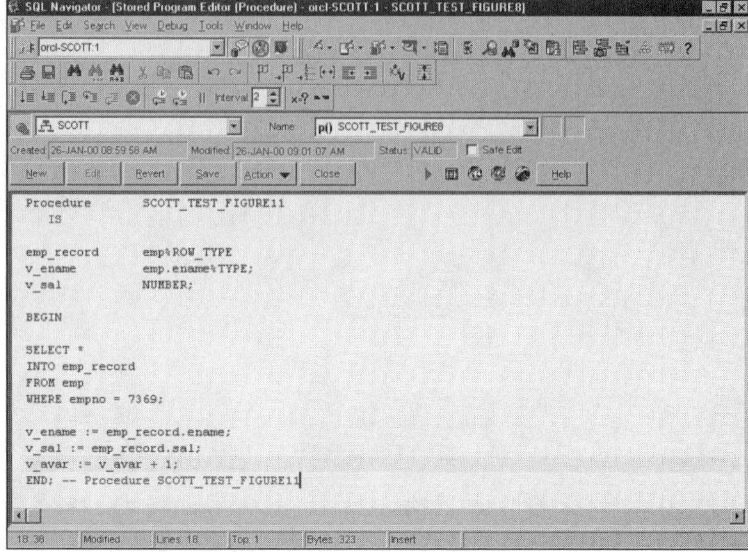

Boolean variable—Basically, a single computer bit that holds a true or false condition. Booleans are useful for holding the success or failure of a procedure, IF statement, and so on.

Variables also can be passed both to and from the SQL*Plus environment. Notice :g_dept_sal is populated by the simple query in the PL/SQL block, but that %DEPTNO is passed to the PL/SQL block. This is a classic use of BIND variables and is an efficient way of coding SQL statements within PL/SQL blocks. Figure C.12 shows this functionality from within SQL*Plus. Notice the SQL*Plus PRINT command is useful for displaying the contents of a variable. However, PL/SQL has no such feature as PRINT. Notice that Figure C.13 shows how to reference SQL*Plus variables and display results by using the SQL*Plus environment setting SET SERVEROUTPUT ON and the PL/SQL feature DBMS_OUTPUT.PUT_LINE.

PL/SQL supports all DML-type queries and SQL queries; however, PL/SQL does not support the use of DECODE or GROUP BY functions (such as AVG, MIN, MAX, and so on).

Figure C.12

*Referencing SQL*Plus variables inside PL/SQL.*

```
Oracle SQL*Plus
File Edit Search Options Help
SQL>
SQL> VARIABLE g_raise NUMBER
SQL>
SQL> DECLARE
  2  v_sal NUMBER := 1000;
  3  BEGIN
  4  :g_raise := v_sal *1.2;
  5  END;
  6  /

PL/SQL procedure successfully completed.

SQL> PRINT g_raise

  G_RAISE
---------
     1200

SQL> |
```

Figure C.13

Using PL/SQL function `DBMS_OUTPUT.PRINT_LINE`.

```
Oracle SQL*Plus
File Edit Search Options Help
SQL>
SQL>
SQL>
SQL> SET SERVEROUTPUT ON
SQL>
SQL> DECLARE
  2  v_sal NUMBER := &Plus_SAL;
  3  BEGIN
  4  DBMS_OUTPUT.PUT_LINE ('SQL*Plus variable Plus_Sal = ' || TO_CHAR(v_sal));
  5  END;
  6  /
Enter value for plus_sal: 1000
old   2: v_sal NUMBER := &Plus_SAL;
new   2: v_sal NUMBER := 1000;
SQL*Plus variable Plus_Sal = 1000

PL/SQL procedure successfully completed.

SQL> |
```

PL/SQL Cursors

Cursors are Oracle's way of processing *SQL statements*, checking their syntax (known as *parsing*), substituting any bind variables, finding the path to the data (known as the *explain plan*), and eventually executing and assigning a buffer to hold the row(s) returned.

SQL statement—Actually loaded into the Oracle8i buffer, which is known as the *library cache*. The data buffer is established in the Oracle8i buffer pool. The *explain plan* is the path that Oracle8i will use to actually get the data, including which indexes will be used.

Two kinds of cursors exist in Oracle8i: implicit cursors and explicit cursors. An *implicit* cursor is one in which a SQL statement is defined without any cursor control statements, such as the `CURSOR` statement (see Figure C.14). SQL queries in implicit cursors can only return one row. DML statements can process any number of rows. *Explicit* cursors are for those SQL queries that return more than one row. These cursors have a command structure so that the PL/SQL block can control the return of data or rows from the database.

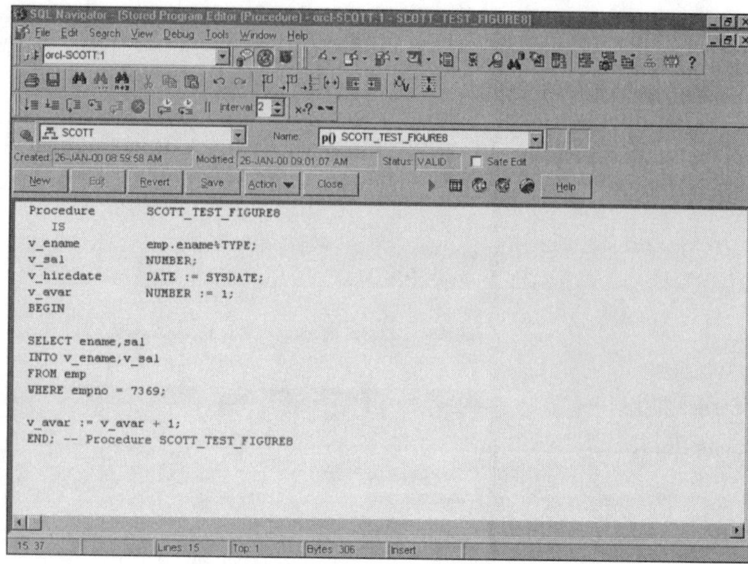

Figure C.14

Implicit PL/SQL SQL query.

SQL Navigator has a code assistant that is useful in defining the basic syntax. This code assistant can be accessed either via the menu bar (Tools, Code Assistant) or by the Code Assistant button on the top tool palette. The code assistant has code syntax layouts for just about any programming task desired. Notice Figure C.15 uses the Syntax and Web Catalog tab. Simply left-click and hold (drag and drop) on the desired code feature and then move the mouse pointer (it will pull a shadow object) to the desired part of the PL/SQL block in the editing window. This will place the PL/SQL code fragments in the editing window, where you can then change the black type items to the values desired. Figure C.16 shows the results after modifications.

Notice that the implicit cursor has the `INTO` clause in the `SELECT` statement where the explicit cursor does not (refer to Figure C.14). Also notice that the explicit cursor has a name, must be opened and closed, and places the `INTO` clause in the `FETCH` statement to populate the PL/SQL variables with data. Notice also that the columns listed in the `SELECT` clause are in the same order as listed in the `FETCH` clause.

Implicit and explicit cursors have some attributes that will contain information about the cursor function. Listing C.2 shows the cursor attributes, and Figure C.17 shows the logic flow of defining and using explicit cursors. These attributes play a major role in cursor control, as you will learn in the next section of this chapter.

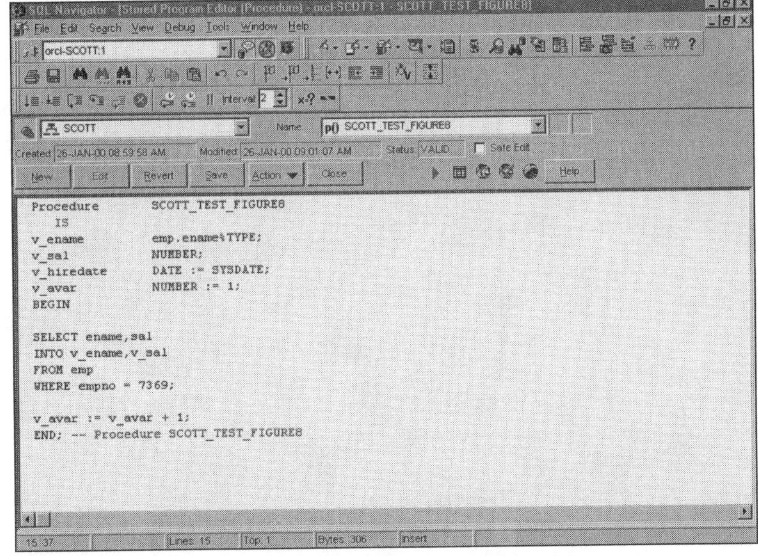

Figure C.15

Building an explicit PL/SQL SQL query with SQL Navigator.

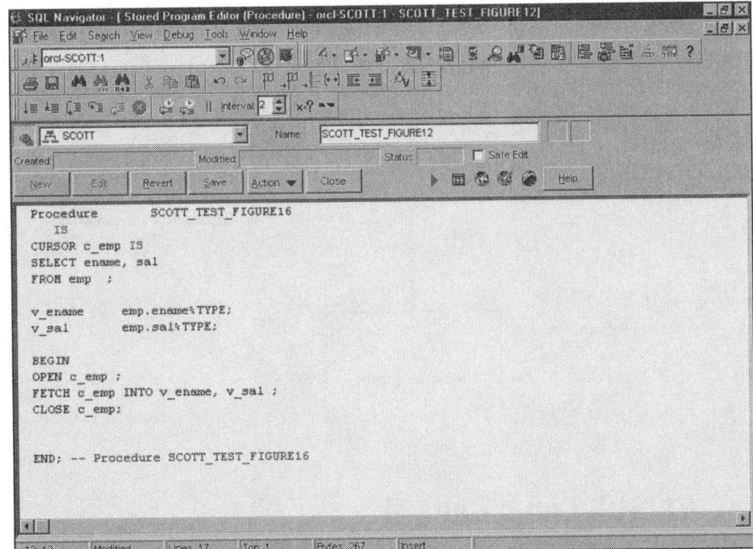

Figure C.16

Explicit PL/SQL SQL query.

Listing C.2—Cursor Attributes

```
%ISOPEN       Returns a TRUE if the cursor is open.
%NOTFOUND     Returns a TRUE if row is not returned.
%FOUND        Returns a TRUE if a row is returned.
%ROWCOUNT     Contains number of rows returned so far or number of rows
              processed by the SQL statement.
```

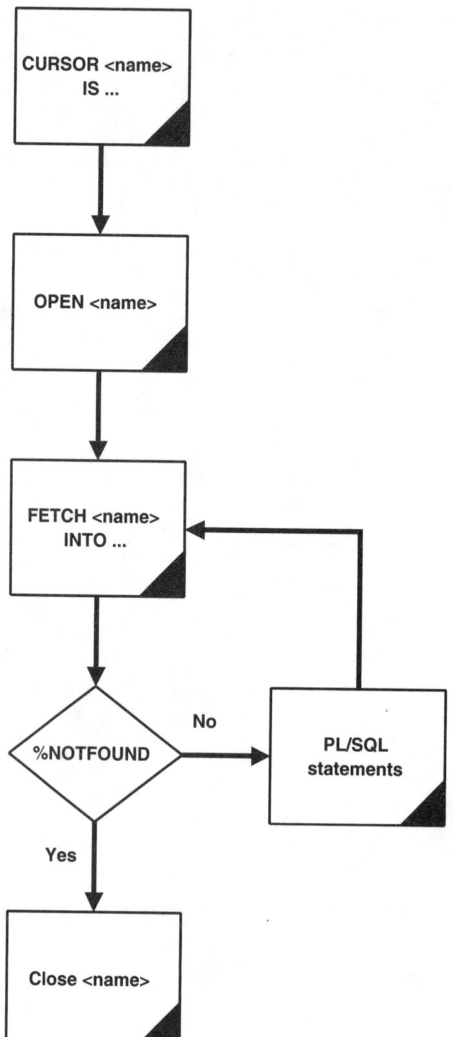

Figure C.17

Explicit cursor logic flow.

PL/SQL Logic Control

The two ways to control the flow of logic within a PL/SQL block are the `IF-THEN-ELSE` and `LOOPING` commands. These commands can be intermixed, depending on the requirements of the logic needed.

IF-THEN-ELSE

The `IF` statement allows for the checking of the contents of a variable and the performing of additional instructions based on whether the condition tested `TRUE` or `FALSE`. If the condition tested `TRUE`, the `THEN` clause is then followed. If the condition tested `FALSE`, the `ELSIF` or `ELSE` is followed.

The syntax is simple:

```
IF <condition> THEN statement[s]; [ELSIF condition THEN statement[s];]
➥[ELSE statement[s];] END IF;
```

A simple `IF` statement might not have any `ELSE` conditions at all. Figure C.18 illustrates the program logic flow of `IF-THEN-ELSE`, and Figure C.19 illustrates a more complex `IF-THEN-ELSIF-ELSE` program logic.

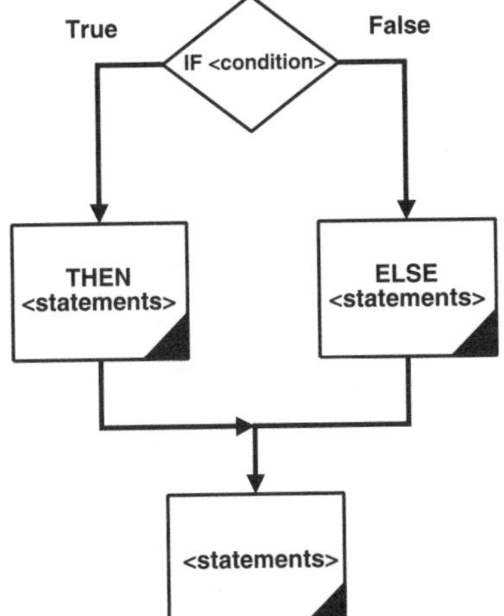
True
False
IF <condition>
THEN <statements>
ELSE <statements>
<statements>
PL/SQL statements;
IF <condition> THEN
<statements>;
ELSE
<statements>;
END IF;
PL/SQL statements;

Figure C.18

`IF-THEN-ELSE` logic illustration.

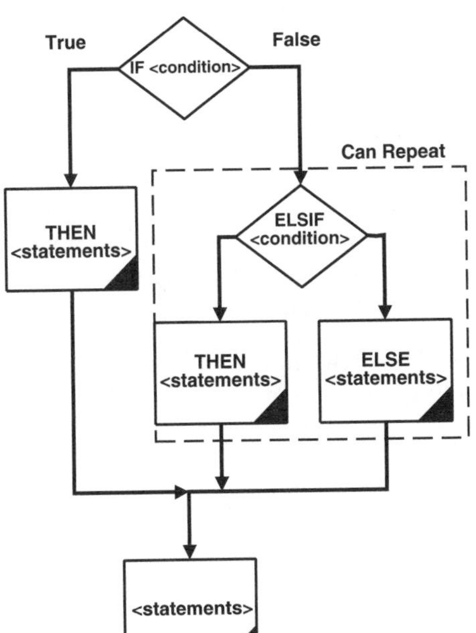
True
False
IF <condition>
Can Repeat
THEN <statements>
ELSIF <condition>
THEN <statements>
ELSE <statements>
<statements>
PL/SQL statements;
IF <condition> THEN
<statements>;
ELSIF <condition> THEN
<statements>;
[ELSIF <condition> THEN
<statements>;]
ELSE <statements>;
END IF;
PL/SQL statements;

Figure C.19

`IF-THEN-ELSIF-ELSE` logic illustration.

Listing C.3 shows a couple different `IF` statements. Notice the first `IF` statement simply checks one value. Each `IF` statement also needs an `END IF` statement. The second `IF` statement in Listing C.3 shows the use of the `ELSIF` statement. Notice that this code is easier to read and easier to code because of the lack of additional `END IF` statements.

Listing C.3—`IF` Statement Examples

```
...
IF job = 'SALESMAN' THEN
    v_raise := sal * .10;
ELSE
    IF job = 'CLERK' THEN
        v_raise := sal * .15
    END IF;
END IF;

..
IF job = 'SALESMAN' THEN
    v_raise := sal * .10;
ELSIF job = 'CLERK' THEN
    v_raise := sal * .15
ELSE
    v_raise = sal *.20
END IF;
```

LOOPING

PL/SQL provides three types of mechanisms used for repeating processes or looping: the basic loop, the `WHILE` loop, and the `FOR` loop. Each loop has some kind of an exit statement or a way to stop looping.

The basic loop syntax is as follows:

```
LOOP statement[s]; EXIT [WHEN <condition>]; END LOOP;
```

`EXIT` will check for a condition to test `TRUE` and will then leave the loop and execute the next PL/SQL statement or SQL statement that follows the `END LOOP` statement. Figure C.20 contains a basic loop example.

The `FOR` and `WHILE` loops handle when to exit in the `FOR` or `WHILE` clause. The syntax for the `FOR` loop is as follows:

```
FOR counter IN low-range..high-range LOOP statement[s]; END LOOP;
```

The `WHILE` loop loops while some condition tests `TRUE`. The syntax is as follows:

```
WHILE <condition> LOOP statement[s]; END LOOP;
```

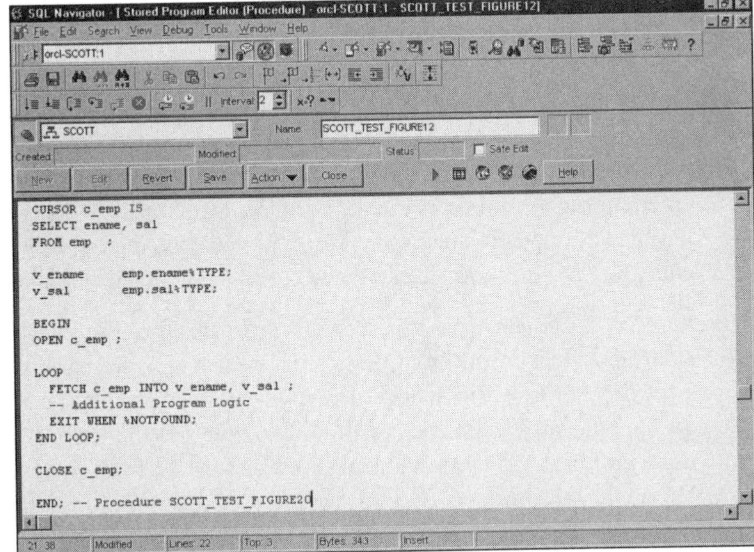

Figure C.20

Basic loop example.

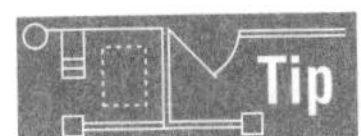

It is very good practice to *not* make adjustments to the looping counter being used in the `EXIT` condition from inside the loop.

Figure C.21 shows the `FOR` loop in use with explicit cursors. In this example, using the `FOR`, an implicit open and fetch are performed. An implicit close is performed on `END LOOP`. PL/SQL will automatically perform this loop while rows exist in the cursor.

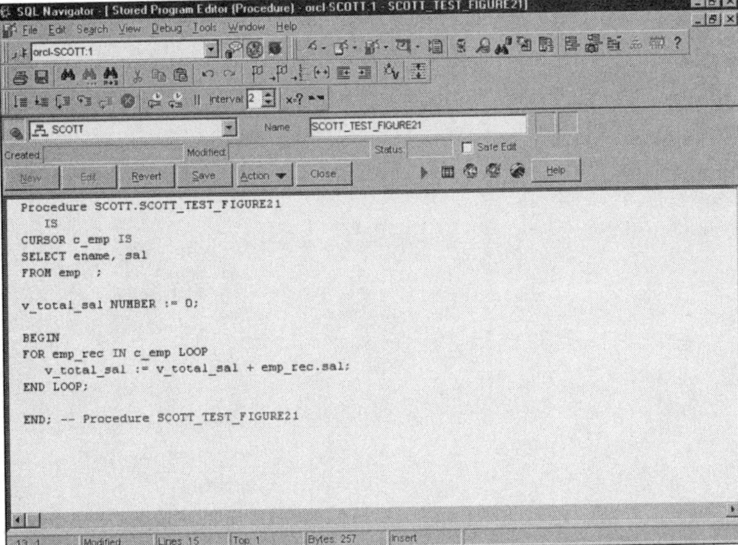

Figure C.21

Explicit cursor using the `FOR` loop.

Debugging Our PL/SQL

It is important with any programming language either to be able to follow the code line by line or to be able to stop the code at certain points to check the contents of variables to ensure that the program is functioning as intended. Being able to visually see the code executing is an important ability when debugging or trying to find errors in the code. For example, if the expected result is not returned or the program never ends (a possible runaway loop), it would be nice to be able to step through the code, line by line, and check all the contents of all the variables.

Figure C.22 uses Quest SQL Navigator to visualize the variables, including the returned values from the SQL statement with each iteration of the loop. Notice that a break point is set (by placing the mouse cursor on the line and clicking the Toggle Breakpoint button) on the last line of code inside the loop. Next, you should click the Run Debugger button and accept the defaults from the Calling Code Generation Wizard. Each time you click the Run Debugger button, the loop is processed once. Figure C.22 displays the variable `v_total_sal` (by clicking the X=? button with the cursor on the variable). This variable is getting `sal` added to it in the `FOR` loop (the Run Debugger button was clicked three times). The Run button tells SQL Navigator to proceed to the next step or break point. This particular looping example shows the use of an explicit cursor using the `WHILE` loop to process the result set of the multi-row result set SQL query (the PL/SQL in Figure C.21).

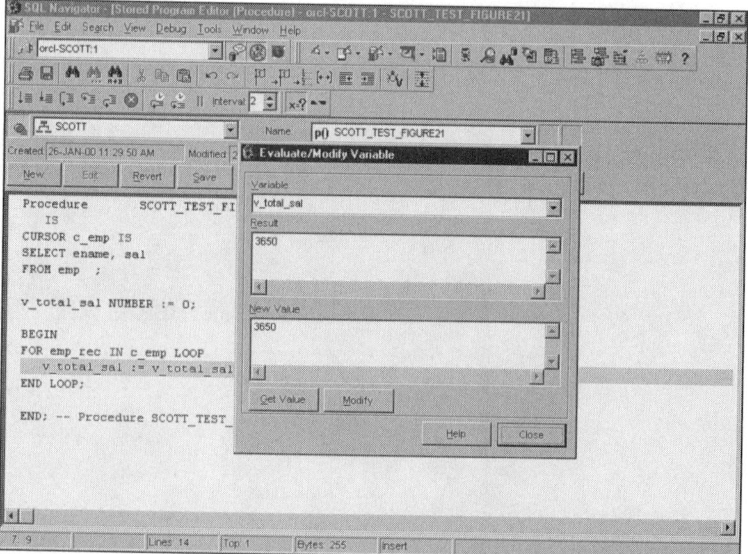

Figure C.22

Using SQL Navigator to debug a PL/SQL block.

Error Handling in PL/SQL

As defined earlier in this chapter, exceptions are errors or flags in PL/SQL. They are a way of gracefully handling certain conditions within the PL/SQL block, such as no records returned from the SQL query or last record returned from the SQL query. Other exceptions can be syntax errors in the PL/SQL code itself or errors returned from Oracle8i.

The syntax for exception handling is optional. If the exception area of the PL/SQL block is not handled, it is propagated to the calling routine. For example, the SHOW ERRORS command in SQL*Plus is used to show any errors from PL/SQL that were not handled by the PL/SQL block. The exception syntax is as follows:


```
DECLARE
variables
BEGIN
statements;
EXCEPTION
  WHEN exception [OR exception …] THEN
   Statement[s];
  [WHEN […]]
  [ WHEN OTHERS THEN
   Statement[s];]

END;
```

Notice in the previous example that only one WHEN clause needs to be defined. The WHEN OTHERS clause should be used because it ensures that the PL/SQL block handles the exception, preventing the routine that ran the PL/SQL block from having to deal with the error condition. The WHEN OTHERS, if used, must be the last clause. The RAISE_APPLICATION_ERROR procedure will return an error to the application, much like an Oracle error would be returned. This is a convenient way to handle errors specific to an application.

Figure C.23 shows many of the predefined exceptions available. SQL Navigator contains all the exceptions that are easily accessed through the code assistant (from the Tools menu or the Code Assistant button) by using the PL/Vision Professional Library Catalog. Two common exceptions that should always be defined are NO_DATA_FOUND and TOO_MANY_ROWS.

Exceptions can be implicit (Oracle raises the exception) or they can be explicitly raised by the PL/SQL block. Two PL/SQL functions are available when Oracle errors occur: SQLCODE and SQLERRM. SQLCODE returns the Oracle error number, and SQLERRM returns the Oracle error message. Notice that these are used in Listing C.4 in the WHEN OTHERS clause (lines 22–25). Their values are returned into variables, and these variables are then used by the `PUT_LINE` function. The `RAISE` command explicitly creates an exception and sets a specially defined variable. Listing C.4 shows a PL/SQL block that uses both the implicit (line 20 with `NO_DATA_FOUND`) and named (lines 3, 14, and 18) errors.

Figure C.23

Predefined exception conditions.

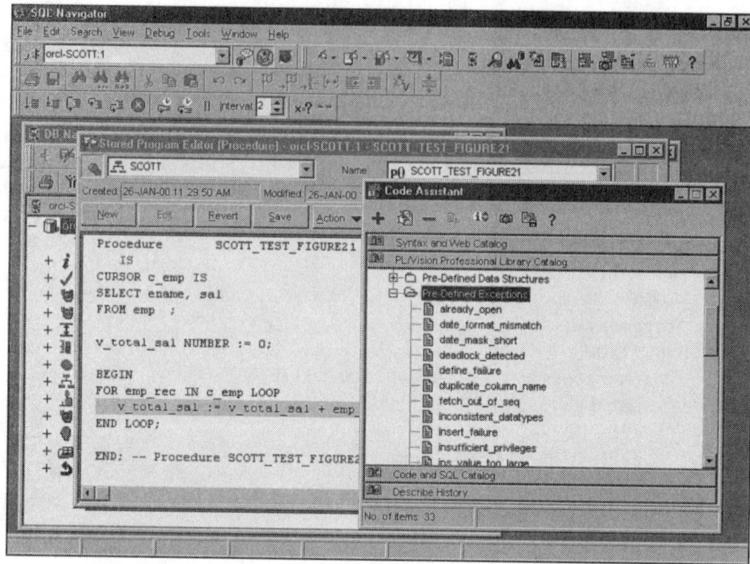

Listing C.4—Exception Coding Examples

```
1:  DECLARE
2:  ...
3:  e_end_rows          EXCEPTION;
4:  v_oraerr            NUMBER;
5:  v_oraerrm           VARCHAR2(255);
6:  v_sal               NUMBER;
7:  CURSOR dept10_emp_curson IS
8:  SELECT deptno, ename, sal
9:  FROM emp
10: ORDER BY deptno;
11: BEGIN
12: v_sal :=0
13: FOR emp_record IN dept10_emp_cursor LOOP
14:    IF emp_record.deptno > 10 THEN raise e_end_rows;
15:    v_sal := v_sal + sal;
16: END LOOP;
17: EXCEPTION
18:    WHEN e_end_rows THEN
19:        DBMS_OUTPUT.PUT_LINE('Dept 10 Salaries: ' || TO_CHAR(v_sal));
20:    WHEN NO_DATA_FOUND THEN
21:        DBMS_OUTPUT.PUT_LINE('No Employees Found');
22:    WHEN OTHERS THEN
```

```
         v_oraerr := SQLCODE;
         v_oraerrm := SQLERRM;
         DBMS_OUTPUT.PUT_LINE('OraErr: ' || v_oraerr || ' ' || v_oraerrm);
END;
IF job = 'SALESMAN' THEN
    v_raise := sal * .10;
ELSE
    IF job = 'CLERK' THEN
        v_raise := sal * .15
    END IF;
END IF;

..
IF job = 'SALESMAN' THEN
    v_raise := sal * .10;
ELSIF job = 'CLERK' THEN
    v_raise := sal * .15
ELSE
    v_raise = sal *.20
END IF;
```


Summary

This appendix gave you a good overview of the Oracle PL/SQL language. We discussed all the basics of PL/SQL, simple constructs, looping, `IF-THEN-ELSE` logic, reading and writing records from the database, and exception handling.

We use all this information in building the Sales Tracking Application, and in Chapter 10, "Building the Web Site with PL/SQL," when we build the Sales Tracking Web site.

In this appendix

- *Understanding SQL Functions*
- *Table Join Conditions*
- *SQL Subqueries*

Appendix D

Advanced SQL Queries

This appendix covers a variety of topics related to SQL queries, including functions, advanced queries (joins and subqueries), complex views, and read consistency (Oracle8i locking mechanisms).

Understanding SQL Functions

SQL functions perform a variety of tasks such as date compares; date formatting; a host of character functions such as string length, substring functions, and uppercase/lowercase; and several numerical functions such as round, truncate, and arithmetic operations.

SQL functions fall into two categories: single-row functions and multiple-row functions. *Single-row* functions operate on each row, whereas *multiple-row* functions operate on a group of rows.

Single-Row Functions

Several kinds of single-row functions exist. *Character* functions can convert character strings to number or date formats. *Number* functions manipulate the returning numeric value, and *date* functions are used to manipulate, compare, and perform calculations between dates. In addition, SQL has a couple of general single-row functions that do not fit into one of these character, number, or date categories.

Character Functions

Character functions convert or change the output of the stored `CHAR` or `VARCHAR2` fields. `UPPER`, `LOWER`, and `INITCAP` are three of the conversion character functions. Figure D.1 shows examples of `UPPER` and `INITCAP` functions.

Figure D.1

Using UPPER *and* INITCAP *functions.*

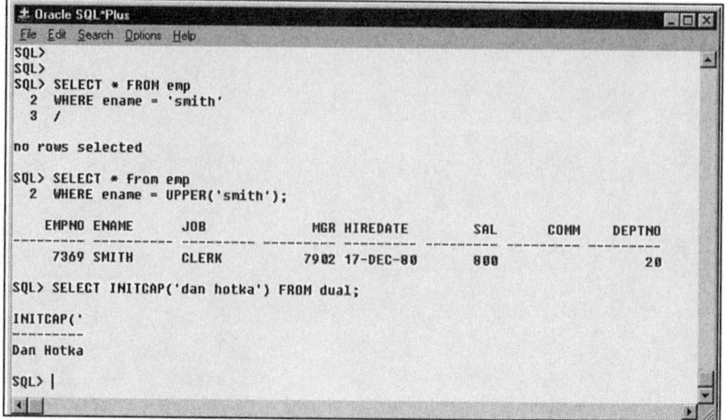

DUAL table—Contains one column and one row and is useful if you want to run a function only once. Because the DUAL table has only one role, whatever function is run in the SELECT statement will run just once.

The character manipulation functions are a powerful way to create desired output. Character manipulation functions include CONCAT, INSTR, LENGTH, LPAD, RPAD, SUBSTR, and TRIM. Figure D.2 shows some practical uses for some of these functions.

The || in Figure D.2 also causes concatenation between strings and database columns. Notice the handy DROP commands created when combining the SQL syntax for dropping a table with that of the table name from the TAB view. Using the SPOOL command (covered in the section "Oracle SQL*Plus for Reports" in Chapter 3, "Building the Sales Tracking Application Forms and Reports") creates a SQL script that could be used to clean up the accounts of employees who have left the company.

Concatenation—When two or more columns are merged together, many times merged with some text items, to form a single column of output.

TO_CHAR, TO_NUMBER, and TO_DATE are powerful functions that enable the conversion of one type of data to another and enable different types of date formats for both inserting and query purposes (see Figure D.3). TO_CHAR can be used to change a date into a date format different from the Oracle8i default of DD-MON-YY. Likewise,

TO_DATE is used to convert a valid date in almost any format into the DATE format that Oracle8i understands. TO_NUMBER enables valid numbers stored in character fields to be used in calculations, and so on.

Figure D.2

Character manipulation function examples.

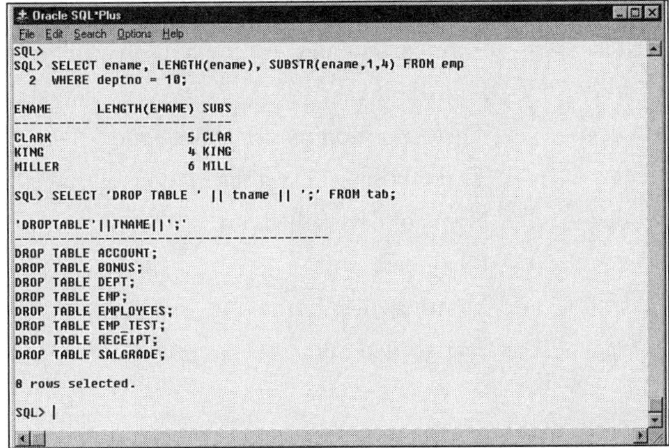

Figure D.3

TO_CHAR and TO_DATE function examples.

```
Oracle SQL*Plus
File Edit Search Options Help
SQL>
SQL> SELECT ename, TO_CHAR(hiredate,'MM/DD/YYYY')
  2  FROM emp
  3  WHERE deptno = 10;

ENAME      TO_CHAR(HI
---------- ----------
CLARK      06/09/1981
KING       11/17/1981
MILLER     01/23/1982

SQL>
SQL> SELECT ename || 'was hired on ' || TO_CHAR(hiredate,'Month Day, YYYY')
  2  FROM emp
  3  WHERE deptno = 10;

ENAME||'WASHIREDON'||TO_CHAR(HIREDATE,'MONTHDAY,
------------------------------------------------
CLARKwas hired on June      Tuesday  , 1981
KINGwas hired on November  Tuesday  , 1981
MILLERwas hired on January   Saturday , 1982

SQL> INSERT INTO emp (empno, ename, TO_DATE('01/10/2000','MM/DD/YYYY'));
```

The following are some of the valid date and time formats that can be used with both TO_CHAR and TO_DATE. Consult the *Oracle8i SQL Reference Manual* for all the combinations of date and time formats.

Partial List of Date Formats

DD	Numeric day of month
MM	Numeric month of year
YY	Two-digit year
RR	Century function (see the note that follows)
YYYY	Four-digit year
Mon	Three-position month abbreviation
DY	Three-position day abbreviation
Day	Name of day spelled out
J	Julian date
MONTH	Month spelled out
YEAR	Year spelled out

The RR command is used in place of the YY function and assists with century identification on two-position years. If the year tested is 00–49 and the current year is between 00 and 49, RR returns the current century. If the year tested is 00–49 and the current year is between 50 and 99, RR returns the previous century. If the year tested is 50–99 and the current year is between 00 and 49, RR returns the next century. If the year tested is 50–99 and the current year is between 50 and 99, RR returns the current century.

```
Current year = 1999, Date=01-SEP-96, RR= 1996, YY=1996
Current year = 1996, Date=15-JUL-45, RR= 2045, YY=1945
Current year = 2003, Date=17-MAR-56, RR=1956, YY=2056
```

Partial List of Time Formats

AM or PM	Time of day indicator
HH	Hour of day
HH24	Hour in military time
MI	Minutes
SS	Seconds
SSSS	Seconds since midnight

Date Functions

Six date functions are available that perform various calculations such as the number of months between two dates, adding months to a date, getting the next day or previous date, and rounding or truncating dates.

The `MONTHS_BETWEEN(date1,date2)` function returns the number of months between the two dates, whereas the `ADD_MONTHS(date, n)` function returns a date `n` months (both future and past) away from the date given. The `NEXT_DAY(date, 'char')`, in which `char` is a day of the week, returns a date of the day of the week in the `char` field following the date. `LAST_DAY(date)`, on the other hand, returns the date of the last day in the month of the date. `ROUND(date[,'date format']` and `TRUNC(date[,'date format'])` both perform their function to the nearest date unless a date format is given, and then these functions perform the function to the precision referenced in the `'date format'`.

Figure D.4 shows some practical examples of `DATE` functions in use.

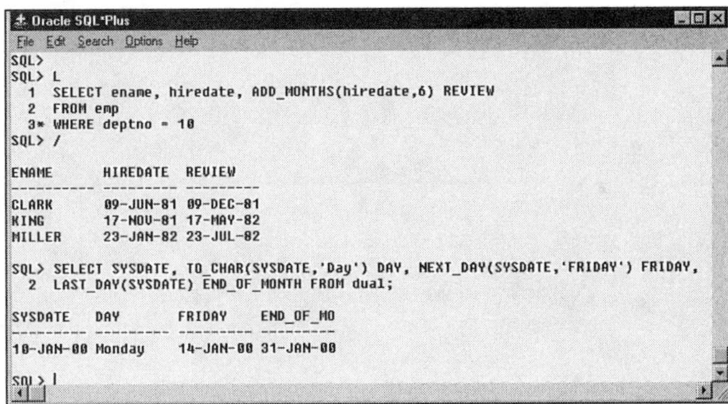

Figure D.4

`DATE` *function examples.*

Numeric Functions

Several numeric functions exist, such as `ROUND`, `TRUNC`, and `MOD`. The `ROUND(number, precision)` function rounds the value of the number to the desired precision. In contrast, the `TRUNC(number, precision)` function just drops off the parts past the desired precision. The `MOD(number,number)` function, though, calculates the remainder between two columns. Figure D.5 illustrates how these functions are used.

Other Single-Row Functions

The remaining two functions that do not fit any of the previously mentioned categories are `NVL` and `DECODE`. `NVL` stands for null value and provides the capability to assign a value to a null field. Figure D.6 shows adding the `SAL` and `COMM` fields to illustrate that when something is added to nothing, you get nothing. The `NVL` function was added to the `COMM` field—notice that the arithmetic then works correctly.

Figure D.5

ROUND, TRUNC, and MOD numeric function examples.

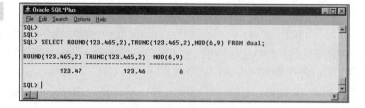

```
Oracle SQL*Plus
File Edit Search Options Help
SQL>
SQL>
SQL> SELECT ROUND(123.465,2),TRUNC(123.465,2),MOD(6,9) FROM dual;

ROUND(123.465,2) TRUNC(123.465,2)  MOD(6,9)
---------------- ---------------- ---------
          123.47           123.46         6

SQL> |
```

Figure D.6

NVL function example.

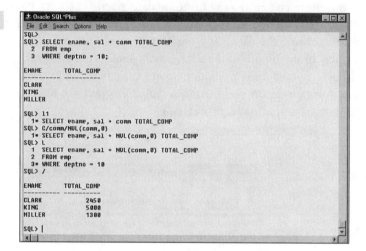

```
Oracle SQL*Plus
File Edit Search Options Help
SQL>
SQL> SELECT ename, sal + comm TOTAL_COMP
  2  FROM emp
  3  WHERE deptno = 10;

ENAME      TOTAL_COMP
---------- ----------
CLARK
KING
MILLER

SQL> l1
  1* SELECT ename, sal + comm TOTAL_COMP
SQL> C/comm/NVL(comm,0)
  1* SELECT ename, sal + NVL(comm,0) TOTAL_COMP
SQL> L
  1  SELECT ename, sal + NVL(comm,0) TOTAL_COMP
  2  FROM emp
  3* WHERE deptno = 10
SQL> /

ENAME      TOTAL_COMP
---------- ----------
CLARK            2450
KING             5000
MILLER           1300

SQL> |
```

Notice in Figure D.6 that the SQL*Plus buffer editor `Change` command, `C/comm/NVL(comm,0)`, was used to add the `NVL`.

The `DECODE` function is the `IF-THEN-ELSE` logic to SQL. The syntax looks like the following:

```
DECODE (col/variable/expression, string1, result1 [, string2, result2][, …]
[, default value]
```

`DECODE` works like this: If `string 1 =`<`condition`> then return `result1`, else if `string2 = `<`condition`> then return `result2` (and so on), else return the default value. If no default value exists, `NULL` is returned if none of the strings matched the original column, variable, or expression. Figure D.7 illustrates how to reference a field value and return a character string based on the value. `DECODE` has many applications that we discuss in Chapter 3.

Figure D.7

DECODE *function example.*

```
Oracle SQL*Plus
File Edit Search Options Help
SQL> L
  1  SELECT ename, DECODE(deptno,10,'New York',
  2                               20,'Dallas',
  3                               30,'Chicago',
  4                               40,'Boston','Des Moines') Location
  5* FROM emp
SQL> /

ENAME      LOCATION
---------- ----------
SMITH      Dallas
ALLEN      Chicago
WARD       Chicago
JONES      Dallas
MARTIN     Chicago
BLAKE      Chicago
CLARK      New York
SCOTT      Dallas
KING       New York
TURNER     Chicago
ADAMS      Dallas
JAMES      Chicago
FORD       Dallas
MILLER     New York
HOTKA      Des Moines

15 rows selected.

SQL> |
```


Multiple-Row Functions or Group Functions

SQL has several numeric functions such as MIN, MAX, SUM, AVG, STDDEV, DISTINCT, and COUNT. These functions, when used by themselves, return one row from the query—the output of the function. COUNT is very useful for counting the number of rows in a table (or result set). When these functions are used in combination with the GROUP BY clause, the query returns one row for each unique data grouping. Figure D.8 shows the numeric functions in action, Figure D.9 shows the same functions with the GROUP BY clause, and Figure D.10 shows GROUP BY with the HAVING clause. The HAVING clause allows for only those groups that meet certain criteria.

Figure D.8

COUNT, MIN, MAX, AVG, *and* SUM *numeric functions example.*

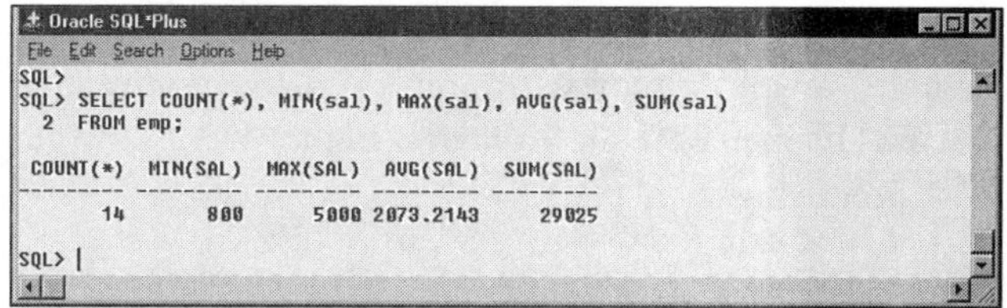

```
Oracle SQL*Plus
File Edit Search Options Help
SQL>
SQL> SELECT COUNT(*), MIN(sal), MAX(sal), AVG(sal), SUM(sal)
  2  FROM emp;

 COUNT(*)  MIN(SAL)  MAX(SAL)  AVG(SAL)  SUM(SAL)
--------- --------- --------- --------- ---------
       14       800      5000 2073.2143     29025

SQL> |
```

Figure D.9

GROUP BY *function example.*

```
Oracle SQL*Plus
File Edit Search Options Help
SQL> L
  1  SELECT job, count(*), MIN(sal), MAX(sal), AVG(sal), SUM(sal)
  2  FROM emp
  3* GROUP BY job
SQL> /

JOB        COUNT(*)  MIN(SAL)  MAX(SAL)  AVG(SAL)  SUM(SAL)
--------- --------- --------- --------- --------- ---------
ANALYST           2      3000      3000      3000      6000
CLERK             4       800      1300    1037.5      4150
MANAGER           3      2450      2975 2758.3333      8275
PRESIDENT         1      5000      5000      5000      5000
SALESMAN          4      1250      1600      1400      5600
                  1

6 rows selected.

SQL> |
```

Figure D.10

GROUP BY with a HAVING clause example.

```
SQL>
SQL> L
  1  SELECT job, count(*), MIN(sal), MAX(sal), AVG(sal), SUM(sal)
  2  FROM emp
  3  GROUP BY job
  4* HAVING count(*) > 2
SQL> /

JOB         COUNT(*)   MIN(SAL)   MAX(SAL)   AVG(SAL)   SUM(SAL)
--------- ---------- ---------- ---------- ---------- ----------
CLERK              4        800       1300     1037.5       4150
MANAGER            3       2450       2975  2758.3333       8275
SALESMAN           4       1250       1600       1400       5600

SQL> |
```

Figure D.11 illustrates how to use the DISTINCT clause in a query. Notice the first COUNT returns a count for the table but when included with the DISTINCT clause, it returns the number of unique values.

Figure D.11

DISTINCT function example.

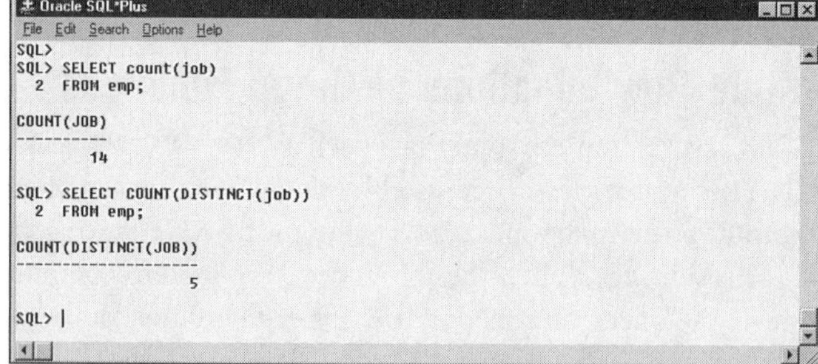

```
SQL>
SQL> SELECT count(job)
  2  FROM emp;

COUNT(JOB)
----------
        14

SQL> SELECT COUNT(DISTINCT(job))
  2  FROM emp;

COUNT(DISTINCT(JOB))
--------------------
                   5

SQL> |
```

Using Multiple Functions

Multiple functions can be nested inside one another to provide the result desired. For example, say the employees are reviewed six months after they are hired but these reviews happen only on Mondays. Figure D.12 shows a query that would be useful for producing such a list.

The ROUND function is typically placed outside most calculations to correctly size the result. Similarly, the NVL value is included on numeric columns that could contain null values. Figure D.13 shows a couple calculations using these two functions.

The final example (see Figure D.14) shows the DECODE function being used with a calculation giving those in department 10 a 10% increase, department 20 a 20% increase, department 30 a 30% increase, and department 40 a 40% increase in salary.

Figure D.12

Multiple-date functions.

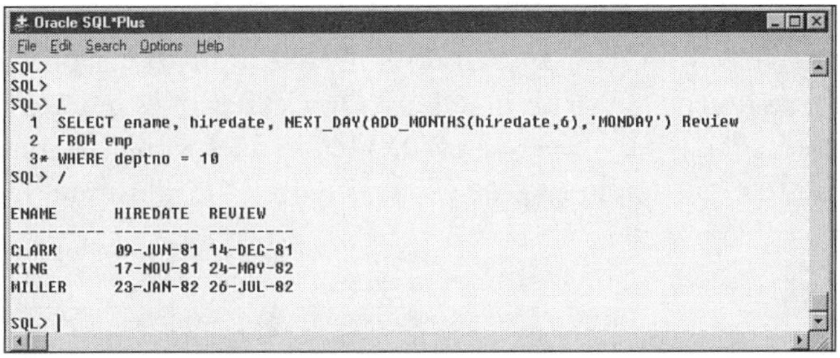

```
Oracle SQL*Plus
File Edit Search Options Help
SQL>
SQL>
SQL> L
  1  SELECT ename, hiredate, NEXT_DAY(ADD_MONTHS(hiredate,6),'MONDAY') Review
  2  FROM emp
  3* WHERE deptno = 10
SQL> /

ENAME      HIREDATE  REVIEW
---------- --------- ---------
CLARK      09-JUN-81 14-DEC-81
KING       17-NOV-81 24-MAY-82
MILLER     23-JAN-82 26-JUL-82

SQL> |
```

Figure D.13

ROUND and NVL functions example.

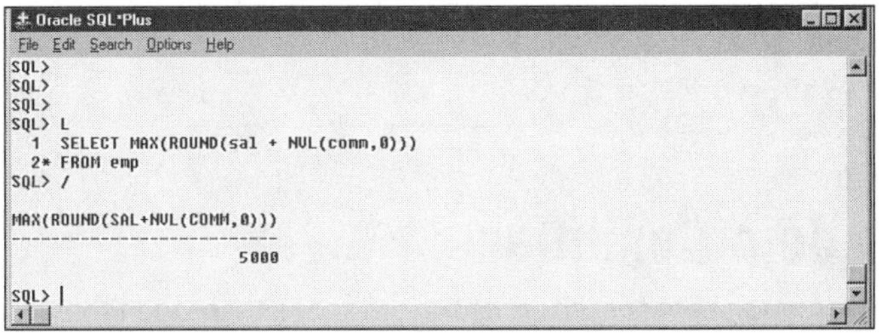

```
Oracle SQL*Plus
File Edit Search Options Help
SQL>
SQL>
SQL>
SQL> L
  1  SELECT MAX(ROUND(sal + NVL(comm,0)))
  2* FROM emp
SQL> /

MAX(ROUND(SAL+NVL(COMM,0)))
---------------------------
                       5000

SQL> |
```

Figure D.14

DECODE and ROUND function example.

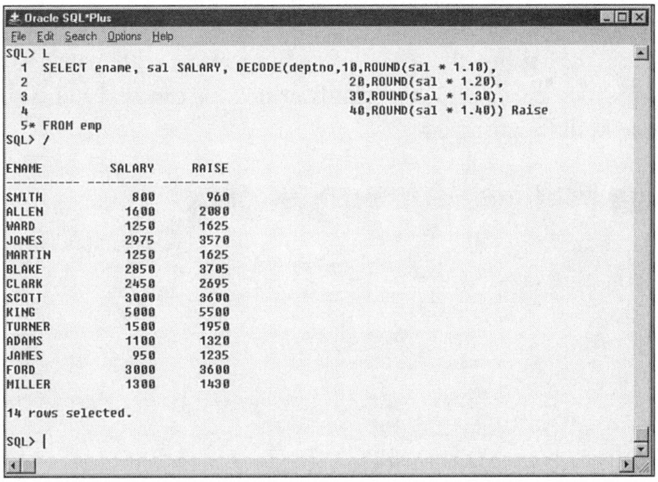

```
Oracle SQL*Plus
File Edit Search Options Help
SQL> L
  1  SELECT ename, sal SALARY, DECODE(deptno,10,ROUND(sal * 1.10),
  2                                         20,ROUND(sal * 1.20),
  3                                         30,ROUND(sal * 1.30),
  4                                         40,ROUND(sal * 1.40)) Raise
  5* FROM emp
SQL> /

ENAME         SALARY     RAISE
---------- --------- ---------
SMITH            800       960
ALLEN           1600      2080
WARD            1250      1625
JONES           2975      3570
MARTIN          1250      1625
BLAKE           2850      3705
CLARK           2450      2695
SCOTT           3000      3600
KING            5000      5500
TURNER          1500      1950
ADAMS           1100      1320
JAMES            950      1235
FORD            3000      3600
MILLER          1300      1430

14 rows selected.

SQL> |
```

Indexing on Functions

In Oracle8 and earlier versions, using a function in a `WHERE` clause (for example, `WHERE UPPER(ename) = 'SMITH'` or `WHERE empno + 10 > 1000`) on an indexed column caused Oracle RDBMS to not use the index but to read all the rows in the table to perform the function. The main reason for having an index is for quick results from tables with thousands of rows. Oracle8i solves this problem of not using indexes on columns with functions. Oracle8i enables indexes to be created and includes the typical function used. This enables a quick result when it is necessary to include a function in a `WHERE` clause. Figure D.15 illustrates how to create an index on a column with a function.

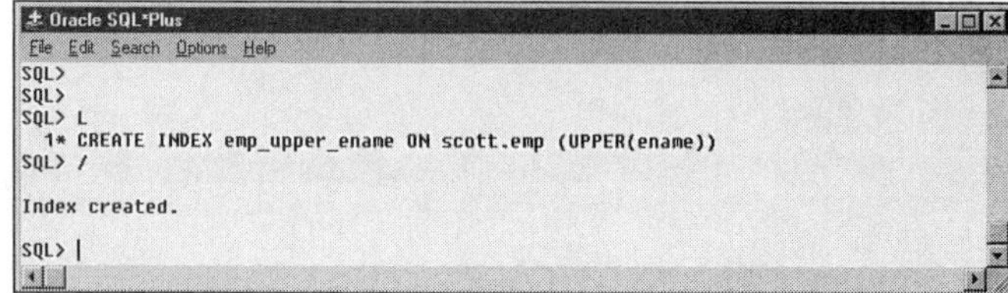

Figure D.15

Creating a function-based index.

Table Join Conditions

This section covers getting data from more than one table at a time (joins). *Joins* are used to combine columns from two or more tables. Figure D.16 shows a simple join between EMP and DEPT. Notice that the table name is specified with each duplicate name of columns between the two tables (see the `WHERE` clause in Figure D.16). Figure D.17 shows the same query but using a table name ALIAS. This alias can be used any place that further qualification is necessary, such as columns with the same name in different tables.

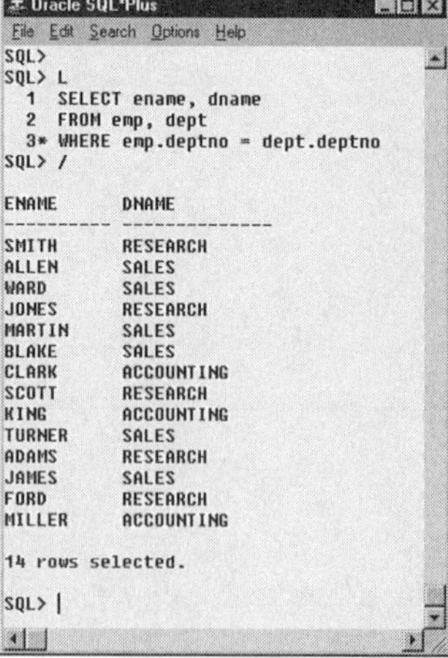

Figure D.16

Simple table join example.

Figure D.17

Simple table join with table name qualification example.

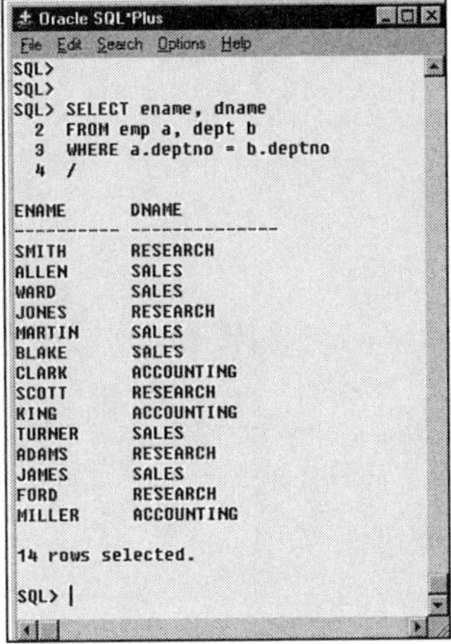

D

Figure D.18 shows what happens if you forget the `WHERE` clause joining a condition between the tables. Notice that for each row in the DEPT table, all the rows are returned from the EMP table. Oracle8i returns all the rows from one table for each row in the second table. This is known as a *Cartesian* join and is usually not the desired result.

Figure D.18

Cartesian join example.

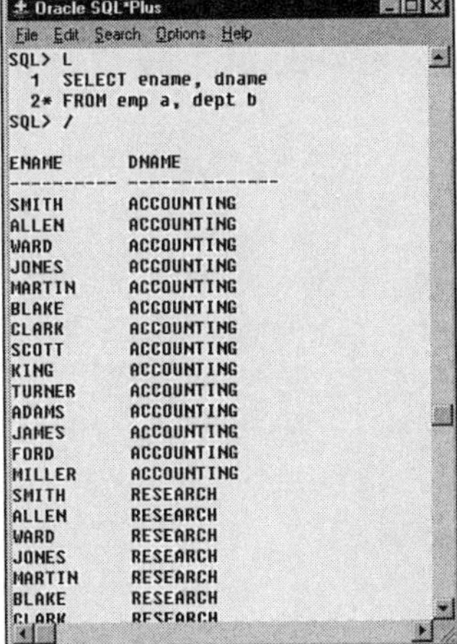

An *outer* join is useful to show all possible conditions, even when no matches exist from one of the tables. Figure D.19 shows the outer join syntax. Notice the `(+)` `syntax on` in the `WHERE` clause. This tells Oracle to return rows from the join whether a condition match exists or not.

Figure D.19

Outer join example.

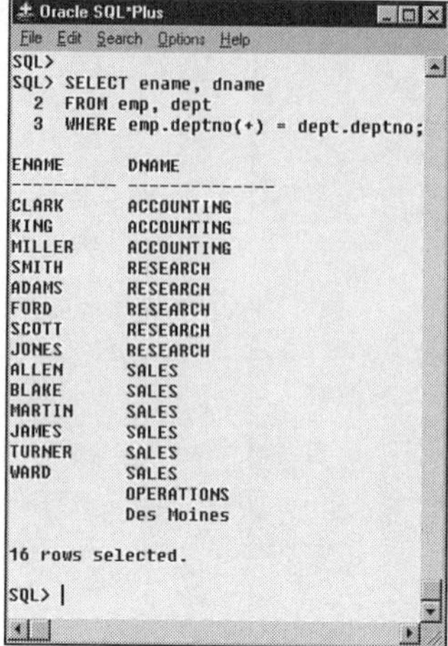

Self joins are similar to a join between two tables except the conditions are against two different columns of the *same* table. Qualifying the column names is necessary. The EMP table has an employee ID column (`empno`) and a manager column (`mgr`), which also is an `empno`. Figure D.20 shows a query that displays the employees and their associated managers. Notice the outer join condition to show that the `PRESIDENT` does not have a manager.

Figure D.20

Self join example.

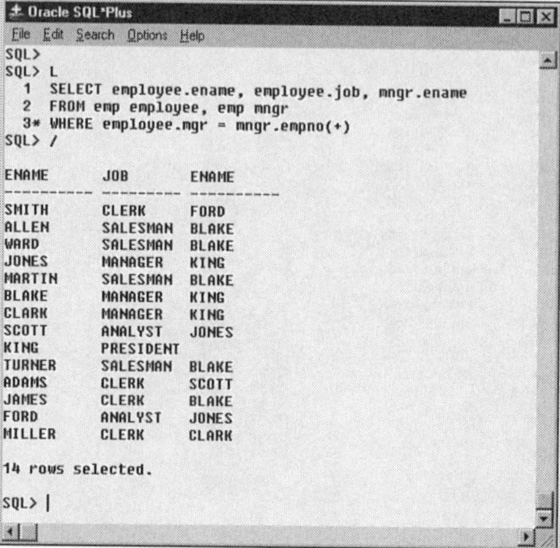

Whenever two or more tables in a join condition do not have an equal condition, it is referred to as a *non-equijoin*. Figure D.21 shows how this works. Notice that the `WHERE` clause has a condition that will return only one row from the SALGRADE table. This relationship is essential because without it you will get a Cartesian join. Oracle8i, however, will still return all the rows that match the condition from EMP for each row returned from SALGRADE.

Figure D.21

Non-equijoin example.

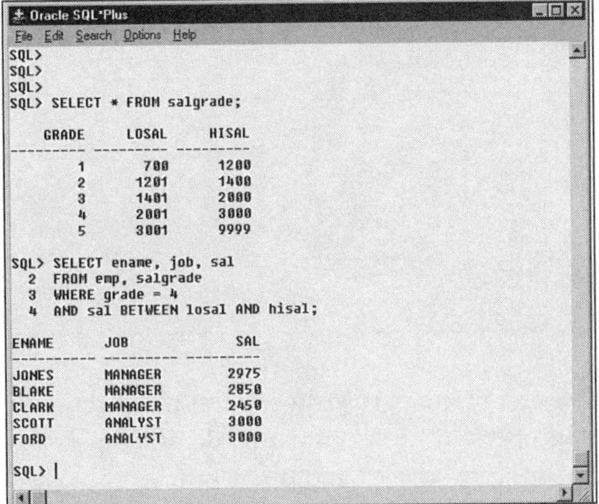

```
Oracle SQL*Plus
File Edit Search Options Help
SQL>
SQL>
SQL>
SQL> SELECT * FROM salgrade;

    GRADE      LOSAL      HISAL
--------- ---------- ----------
        1        700       1200
        2       1201       1400
        3       1401       2000
        4       2001       3000
        5       3001       9999

SQL> SELECT ename, job, sal
  2  FROM emp, salgrade
  3  WHERE grade = 4
  4  AND sal BETWEEN losal AND hisal;

ENAME      JOB              SAL
---------- --------- ----------
JONES      MANAGER         2975
BLAKE      MANAGER         2850
CLARK      MANAGER         2450
SCOTT      ANALYST         3000
FORD       ANALYST         3000

SQL> |
```


A method of combining the result sets of several queries into one result set is available. The `UNION` operator combines two or more result sets together and removes any duplicate rows. The `INTERSECT` operator, on the other hand, returns rows that two or more queries have in common, and the `MINUS` operator returns just the rows between two tables that are not in the other.

To work the examples, you will need to create three new tables (based on the EMP table), as illustrated in Figure D.22.

Figure D.22

Creating example tables.

```
Oracle SQL*Plus
File Edit Search Options Help
SQL>
SQL>
SQL> CREATE TABLE dept10 AS
  2  SELECT ename, job, sal
  3  FROM emp
  4  WHERE deptno = 10;

Table created.

SQL> CREATE TABLE dept20 AS
  2  SELECT ename, job, sal
  3  FROM emp
  4  WHERE deptno = 20;

Table created.

SQL> CREATE TABLE dept30 AS
  2  SELECT ename, job, sal
  3  FROM emp
  4  WHERE deptno = 30;

Table created.

SQL> |
```

The rule for using this technique is that each query must return the same number of columns and the same data types for each column. Figure D.23 illustrates the `UNION` command. Notice that you can include an `ORDER BY` clause and that this clause uses the position of the column in the sort order.

Figure D.23

UNION operator example.

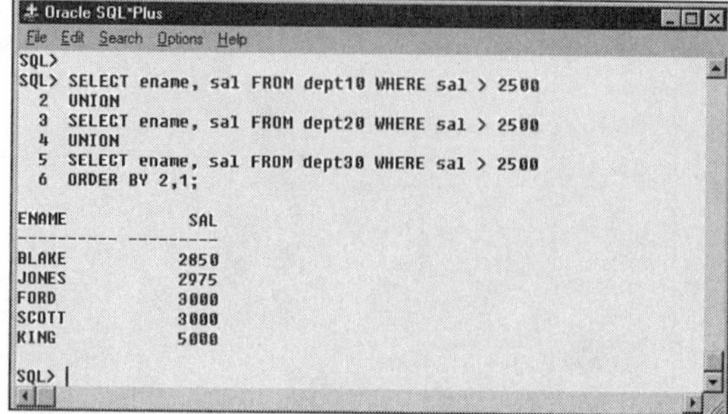

The `INTERSECT` operator shows rows in common between two or more tables, whereas the `MINUS` operator shows rows that do not appear in two or more tables. Figure D.24 shows the `INTERSECT` and `MINUS` operators in use.

Figure D.24

`INTERSECT` and `MINUS` operator example.

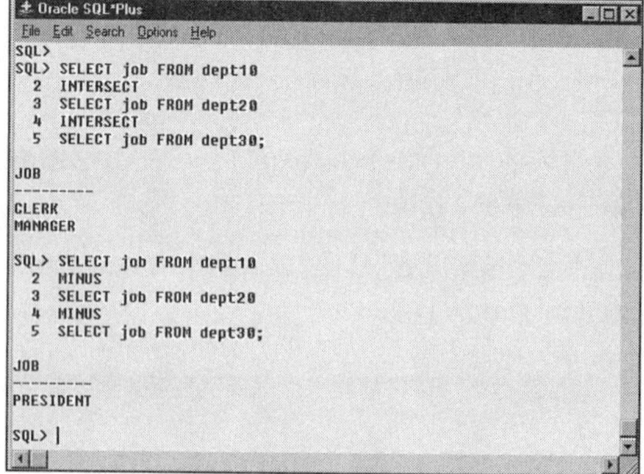

SQL Subqueries

This section covers getting data based on unknown information (subqueries). *Subqueries* are useful when the condition of one query is based on information in another table. The syntax is as follows:

```
SELECT column[s] FROM table[s] [(SELECT [column[s] FROM table[s] [WHERE…]
[GROUP BY …] WHERE column|constant|expression operator (SELECT [column[s]] FROM
table[s] [WHERE …][GROUP BY …])
```

You cannot use an `ORDER BY` in a subquery. The subquery is supplying row or column information to the outer query so no reason exists to return rows in any particular order. Notice that you can have a subquery as part of the `FROM` clause. This section illustrates an example of how this would be useful.

Subqueries can be nested, which means a subquery can contain a subquery. No technical limit to the depth of this type of query exists.

The subquery or inner query executes a single time before the main or outer query executes. The result set from the inner query is then used by the outer query.

A query can contain multiple subqueries, in that each part of a `WHERE` clause can contain a subquery. The `HAVING` clause can have a subquery as well.

The four basic types of subqueries are those that return a single row, those that return multiple rows, those that return multiple columns in a single row, and those that return multiple columns in multiple rows.

The single-row subquery has a subquery that returns only a single row. The comparison operators that test for the returned result are = (equal), > (greater than), >= (greater than or equal to), < (less than), <= (less than or equal to), and <> (not equal). The subquery always is placed on the right side of the comparison operator, and it is always enclosed in parentheses. Figure D.25 shows a query that returns all the employees and their salaries, if above the average salary.

Figure D.25

Single-row subquery example.

```
SQL>
SQL> SELECT ename, sal
  2  FROM emp
  3  WHERE sal > (SELECT AVG(sal) FROM emp);

ENAME             SAL
---------- ----------
JONES            2975
BLAKE            2850
CLARK            2450
SCOTT            3000
KING             5000
FORD             3000

6 rows selected.
```

Figure D.26 illustrates what happens when a single-row comparison operator is used on a subquery that returns more than one row.

Figure D.26

Single-row subquery error example.

```
SQL>
SQL> SELECT ename, sal
  2  FROM emp
  3  WHERE sal > (SELECT sal FROM emp WHERE deptno = 10);
WHERE sal > (SELECT sal FROM emp WHERE deptno = 10)
             *
ERROR at line 3:
ORA-01427: single-row subquery returns more than one row


SQL> |
```

Subqueries are useful when you want to list some columns and use a `GROUP BY` function. Figure D.27 shows a query that finds the last employee hired. Notice that the first query failed, but when the `WHERE` clause is fitted with a subquery, the query returns the desired results.

Figure D.27

GROUP *function subquery example.*

```
SQL>
SQL> SELECT ename, MAX(hiredate) FROM emp;
SELECT ename, MAX(hiredate) FROM emp
       *
ERROR at line 1:
ORA-00937: not a single-group group function


SQL> SELECT ename, hiredate
  2  FROM emp
  3  WHERE hiredate = (SELECT MAX(hiredate) FROM emp);

ENAME      HIREDATE
---------- ---------
ADAMS      23-MAY-87

SQL> |
```

The multiple-row subquery operators are `IN`, which is equal to any value in the result set; `ANY`, which is compared to each value returned by the subquery; and `ALL`, which is compared to every value returned by the subquery. Multiple-row subqueries can return one or many rows. They are called multiple-row subqueries because they have the capability to handle more than one row returned by the subquery. For instance, say you need to find the highest-paid employees of each department to solicit their participation in an employee satisfaction survey. Figure D.28 shows a SQL statement that you can use to accomplish this. Notice in the figure that `DEPT 20` has two individuals. This is because both of these people make the maximum salary for the department. Also notice that eliminating the job `PRESIDENT` from the output is in the subquery. Because the `PRESIDENT` is the highest-paid person in `DEPT 10`, if this were in the outer query's `WHERE` clause, we would not have gotten a row for `DEPT 10`.

Figure D.28

Multiple-row subquery example.

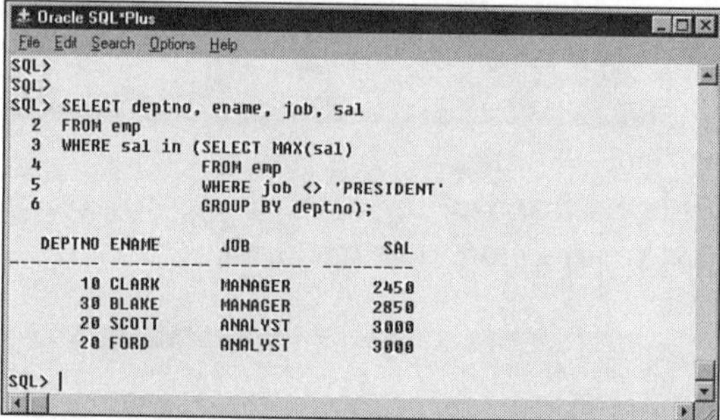

Sometimes it is necessary to compare more than one column from the results of a subquery. Multiple-column subqueries return more than one column. The rule here is that the same number of columns specified in the `WHERE` clause must be returned by the subquery. Multiple-column subqueries come in two types. This first type is *pairwise*, in which two or more columns are returned by the same subquery. In the second type, *nonpairwise*, multiple subqueries each return a single row. Figure D.29 shows both kinds of subqueries in action as well as the different result sets produced.

The big difference between pairwise and nonpairwise is that pairwise ensures that the combined columns are from the same row, whereas nonpairwise returns the rows that meet the column criteria but not necessarily where the column combination appears in the same row.

Figure D.29

Multi-column subquery examples.

```
Oracle SQL*Plus
File Edit Search Options Help

SQL> SELECT ename, job, sal
  2  FROM emp
  3  WHERE (job, sal) IN (SELECT job, sal FROM emp WHERE deptno = 20);

ENAME      JOB              SAL
---------- --------- ----------
SCOTT      ANALYST         3000
FORD       ANALYST         3000
SMITH      CLERK            800
ADAMS      CLERK           1100
JONES      MANAGER         2975

SQL> SELECT ename, job, sal
  2  FROM emp
  3  WHERE job in (SELECT job FROM emp WHERE deptno = 20)
  4  AND sal IN (SELECT sal FROM emp WHERE deptno = 20);

ENAME      JOB              SAL
---------- --------- ----------
SMITH      CLERK            800
ADAMS      CLERK           1100
JONES      MANAGER         2975
SCOTT      ANALYST         3000
FORD       ANALYST         3000

SQL>
```

Oracle8i supports a subquery in the `FROM` clause. This type of SQL statement is also known as an *Inline view*. When this type of a SQL statement is used, the result set from this subquery becomes the data source for that particular `SELECT` statement. Figure D.30 illustrates how this might work when looking for those employees who make less than the average salary. Notice how the subquery has a table alias name B.

Figure D.30

`FROM` *clause subquery example.*

```
Oracle SQL*Plus
File Edit Search Options Help
SQL> L
  1  SELECT b.deptno, a.ename, a.sal
  2  FROM emp a, (SELECT deptno, AVG(sal) AVG_SAL
  3               FROM emp
  4               GROUP BY deptno) b
  5  WHERE a.deptno = b.deptno
  6* AND a.sal < b.AVG_SAL
SQL> /

   DEPTNO ENAME             SAL
--------- ---------- ----------
       10 CLARK            2450
       10 MILLER           1300
       20 SMITH             800
       20 ADAMS            1100
       30 MARTIN           1250
       30 JAMES             950
       30 TURNER           1500
       30 WARD             1250

8 rows selected.
```

A related subquery is one in which a field in the inner query is referenced by the outer query. Figure D.31 shows a related subquery being used to return the same result set as in Figure D.30. Notice the table alias.

Figure D.31

Related subquery example.

```
SQL>
SQL> SELECT deptno, ename, sal
  2  FROM emp a
  3  WHERE sal < (SELECT AVG(sal)
  4               FROM emp b
  5               WHERE a.deptno = b.deptno);

   DEPTNO ENAME             SAL
--------- ---------- ----------
       20 SMITH             800
       30 WARD             1250
       30 MARTIN           1250
       10 CLARK            2450
       30 TURNER           1500
       20 ADAMS            1100
       30 JAMES             950
       10 MILLER           1300

8 rows selected.

SQL>
```

Top-N analysis is a convenient way to show the top five selling products, or in our case, the highest-paid employees who are not salespeople or the president (see Figure D.32). Top-N SQL queries rely on a subquery in the FROM clause and utilize the *pseudo column* ROWNUM, which also could be displayed as part of the SELECT clause.

Pseudo column—A table column that is not explicitly defined; that is, one that comes with each table. ROWNUM is associated with the result set of queries.

Figure D.32

Top-N analysis query example.

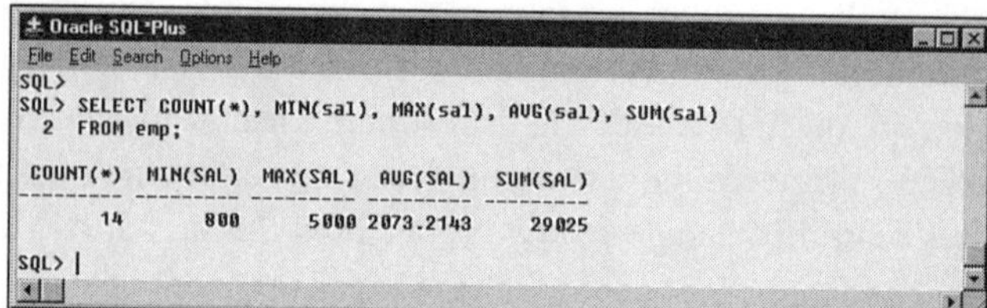

```
SQL>
SQL> SELECT COUNT(*), MIN(sal), MAX(sal), AVG(sal), SUM(sal)
  2  FROM emp;

 COUNT(*)  MIN(SAL)  MAX(SAL)  AVG(SAL)  SUM(SAL)
--------- --------- --------- --------- ---------
       14       800      5000 2073.2143     29025

SQL>
```

Complex Views

Now that you understand subqueries, GROUP BY functions, and so on, I can tell you that the SELECT clause used to create the view can contain these features as well. Figure D.33 illustrates creating and then selecting from a view that uses the GROUP BY functions.

This kind of view cannot accept DML SQL statements (such as INSERT, UPDATE, or DELETE).

Figure D.33

Complex view example.

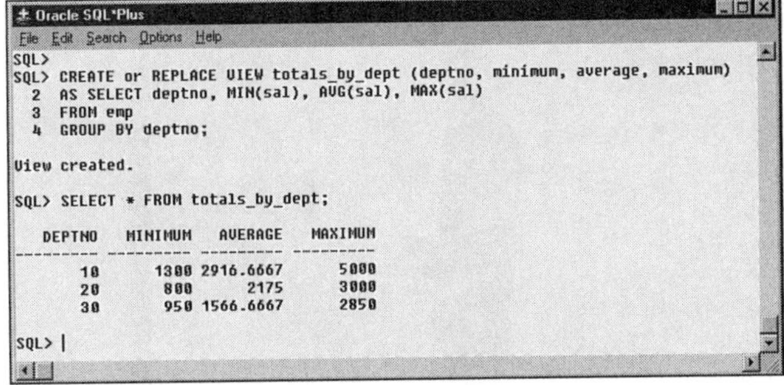

Views also can be created with the `READ ONLY` option to ensure that no DML SQL statements will be processed against them (see Figure D.34).

Figure D.34

Read-only view example.

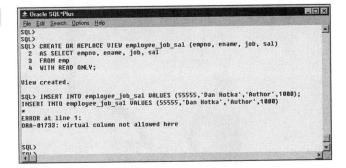

```
Oracle SQL*Plus
File Edit Search Options Help
SQL>
SQL>
SQL> CREATE OR REPLACE VIEW employee_job_sal (empno, ename, job, sal)
  2  AS SELECT empno, ename, job, sal
  3  FROM emp
  4  WITH READ ONLY;

View created.

SQL> INSERT INTO employee_job_sal VALUES (55555,'Dan Hotka','Author',1000);
INSERT INTO employee_job_sal VALUES (55555,'Dan Hotka','Author',1000)
*
ERROR at line 1:
ORA-01733: virtual column not allowed here


SQL>
```

Read Consistency

The Oracle RDBMS has always supported read consistency. *Read consistency* ensures that the data will remain consistent for the duration of a SQL query from the start of the query. What this really means is if user A starts a query at 10:00 a.m. and user B makes an insert to data at 10:05 a.m., when user A's process gets to the change of user B, the SQL statement will see the data as it existed prior to the change made by user B. Figure D.35 illustrates read consistency as depicted in this example.

In any environment with more than one user trying to use resources, a mechanism for sharing must be established. Oracle8i uses various locking mechanisms to ensure that only one resource is updating a particular row at a time. Oracle supports two kinds of locking: exclusive and share. An *exclusive* lock prevents any other user from making any changes to the object. A *share* lock allows multiple users to manipulate data in different parts of the object. Most locking is implicit—Oracle8i automatically locks rows, blocks, and tables for certain types of operations. Figure D.36 shows an explicit share lock on the rows being affected by this particular SQL statement. All locks are released with a `COMMIT` or `ROLLBACK` statement. Figure D.37 illustrates Quest Instance Monitor showing the locking situation created by Figure D.36.

Figure D.35

Read consistency example.

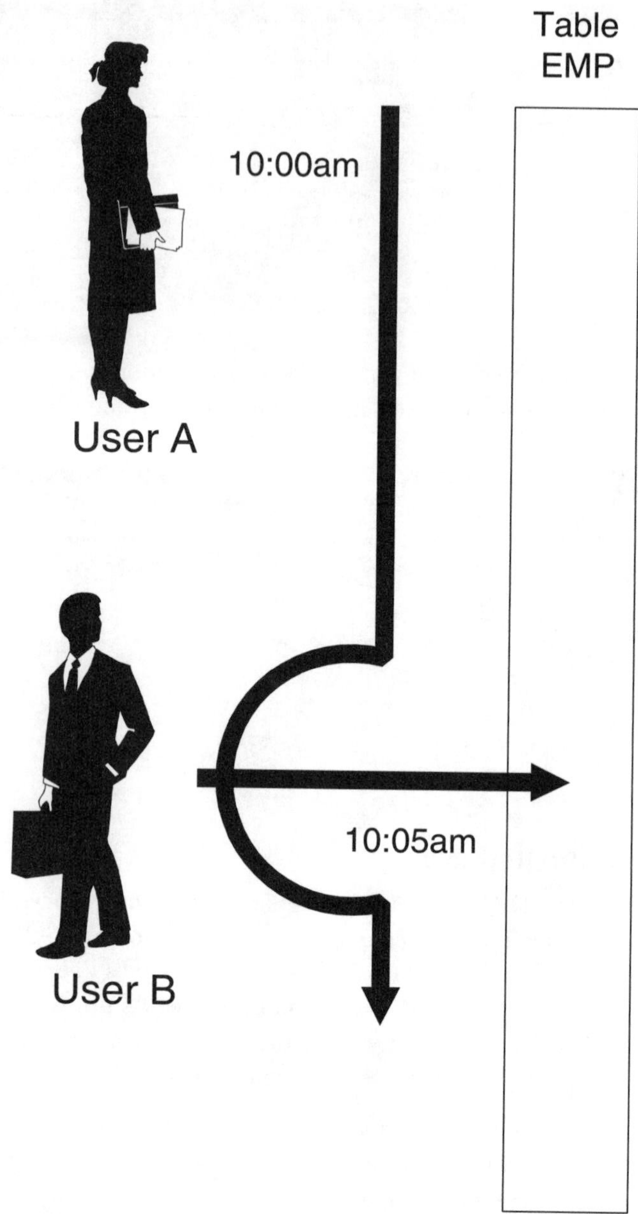

Figure D.36

Row-level locking example.

```
Oracle SQL*Plus
File Edit Search Options Help
SQL>
SQL>
SQL> SELECT *
  2  FROM EMP
  3  WHERE deptno = 10
  4  FOR UPDATE;

     EMPNO ENAME      JOB              MGR HIREDATE         SAL       COMM     DEPTNO
---------- ---------- --------- ---------- --------- ---------- ---------- ----------
      7782 CLARK      MANAGER         7839 09-JUN-81       2450                    10
      7839 KING       PRESIDENT            17-NOV-81       5000                    10
      7934 MILLER     CLERK           7782 23-JAN-82       1300                    10

SQL> |
```

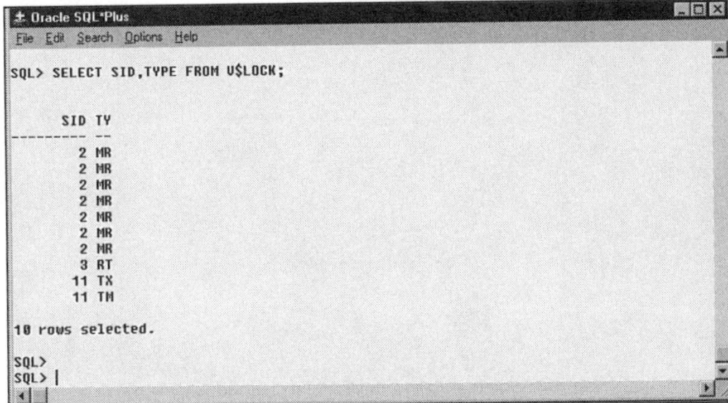

```
Oracle SQL*Plus
File Edit Search Options Help

SQL> SELECT SID,TYPE FROM V$LOCK;


       SID TY
---------- --
         2 MR
         2 MR
         2 MR
         2 MR
         2 MR
         2 MR
         2 MR
         3 RT
        11 TX
        11 TM

10 rows selected.

SQL>
SQL> |
```

Figure D.37

Quest Instance Monitor showing the row-level lock.

Index

Symbols

A

E

F

J

K - L

M

P

Q

R

S

T

U

V

W - Z

Europe
Poland
Germany
France
Spain
Italy
Turkey
Algeria
Libya
Sahara